PAYCOCKS AND OTHERS:
SEAN O'CASEY'S WORLD

ACKNOWLEDGMENTS

Grateful acknowledgment is due to Macmillan, London, St Martin's Press Inc., New York, and Macmillan Publishing Co. Inc., New York for permission to quote from the following works by Sean O'Casey: *Collected Plays* in 4 vols., *The Bishop's Bonfire, The Drums of Father Ned, Three Plays, I Knock at the Door, Pictures in the Hallway, Drums under the Window* and *Innishfallen, Fare thee Well.*

Portions of Chapter 3 have appeared in the *Southern Review*, N.S. 6 (Summer 1970) as 'The Mother-Madonna-Matriarch in Sean O'Casey', and I am grateful to editors Lewis P. Simpson and Donald E. Stanford for permission to republish. Parts of Chapter 8 and Chapter 9 appeared in the *James Joyce Quarterly* as 'A Covey of Clerics in Joyce and O'Casey' (vol. 2, Fall 1964), and 'Kelly, Burke and Shea' (vol. 8, Fall 1970), and I thank editor Thomas F. Staley for republication permission.

A special thanks goes to Professor Bob Smith with whom I spent nine years at Kent State University mostly exchanging ideas about Sean O'Casey over jars of Jameson and through states of chassis.

Bernard Benstock

PAYCOCKS AND OTHERS: SEAN O'CASEY'S WORLD

'I believe there is something in you and your strong point
is characterisation.'

Lady Gregory to Sean O'Casey

GILL AND MACMILLAN • DUBLIN
BARNES & NOBLE BOOKS • NEW YORK
a division of Harper & Row Publishers, Inc.

First published in Ireland in 1976

Gill and Macmillan Ltd
15/17 Eden Quay
Dublin 1
and in London through association with the
Macmillan Publishers Group

Published in the USA in 1976 by
Harper and Row publishers, Inc.
Barnes and Noble Import Division

© Bernard Benstock 1976

Gill and Macmillan SBN 7171 0769 8
Barnes and Noble ISBN 0-06-490363-X
LC 75-36767

Jacket design by Henry Sharpe

Printed and bound in the Republic of Ireland by
Iona Print Limited

Contents

PREFACE   vii

1. The World Scene   1

2. A Pride of Paycocks   10

3. A Veneration of Mothers   66

4. The Hero as Hero   94

5. The Heroine as Hero   145

6. Argufiers and Leprechauns   190

7. Senior Citizens   219

8. A Covey of Clerics   239

9. A Cluster of Minor Characters   259

   NOTES   294

   SELECTED BIBLIOGRAPHY   306

   INDEX   310

For Shari, her book
for reasons only she understands

Preface

ALMOST twenty years after he began his career as a
playwright, Sean O'Casey began a second writing career with
a series of autobiographies in quasi-fictional form. For
another two decades these two careers dovetailed, and in
taking his measure as a creative writer—now that his life's
work is complete—we acknowledge in O'Casey a master of
two forms: both are essentially traditional, but with strong
elements of experimentation and a definite degree of unique-
ness. The territories examined in the plays and the six
autobiographic volumes overlap to a great extent, and
aspects of those areas are at times duplicated in dramatic and
in narrated versions. Cutting across the material of the two
forms (and including the eight short stories as well) offers a
unified glance into O'Casey's domain; doing so in terms of
his 'people' is particularly rewarding, since O'Casey's primary concern throughout was with the human personality. His
approaches were diversified, but despite the essentially good-
natured humour of his view of human nature, it is nonetheless the viewing of an analytical prober. At times his scalpel
was sharp (he made enemies and acknowledged animosities),
but in these cases his motives were surgical; most often his
tool was the magnifying-glass rather than the knife, and his
point of view was delightfully unique.

When the literary critic finds himself thinking in terms of
'types', he usually is thinking in the pejorative, assuming that
individuality in life and in art is the *sine qua non* against
which type-casting sins. There is a world of difference, however, between the stereotype and the prototype, although the
conscious manipulator of melodrama as a theatrical form can
often employ stereotype for artistic advantage (and O'Casey

of course assumed the conventions of the melodrama with enthusiasm for his purpose as a playwright). Yet it is essentially the prototype that concerns us in a study of O'Casey's characterisation: those remarkable individuals who bear the stamp of their family and species, who echo their predecessors and engender successive generations of chips from the block. At his best O'Casey re-worked this material with careful concern for the individuality of his new creation, many a character beginning life as a fixed entity in a known orbit, but suddenly breaking stride and shooting off to establish a galaxy of his own. The known world always has determined proportions of its own (a family contains basic members: father, mother, children, and so forth; society has its class structure; organisations their chains of command; a love affair involves two or more people playing time-honoured roles). It is within these schematic constructions that O'Casey's characters are being examined, in an effort to determine the framework of the world he built within his literary output.

Despite the handful of fine studies of O'Casey's works (and the usual mounds of peripheral information accumulated), there remain several areas still open for investigation. David Krause's collection of O'Casey's letters will fill an important gap, and the projected biography by Ronald Ayling an even more important one. O'Casey himself has been responsible for the lack of an adequate biography, having usurped the biographer's function with his copious Autobiography written in a style that no one will be able to approximate, much less surpass. But the autobiographical pieces are in themselves a kind of literary fiction rather than gospel, O'Casey having taken vast liberties in fact and chronology. This study of O'Casey's 'world' stays within the confines of that literary twilight zone in which O'Casey's sister is named Ella (although her real name was Isabella:[1] in *Inishfallen, Fare Thee Well* O'Casey slips and calls her Bella) and the family name is Casside. Many of the characters can be traced back to their originals: Krause tells us that O'Casey roomed with a pedlar named Michael Mullen[2] (on whom O'Casey based the character of Seumas Shields in *The Shadow of a Gunman*); we know that the speech heard in the second act of *The Plough*

viii

and the Stars is that of Patrick Pearse, and that Red Jim in *The Star Turns Red* is modelled on Jim Larkin. Saros Cowasjee concerns himself in his book on O'Casey with tracing the source characters, and there is little need to duplicate his findings, except in isolated instances where a quick identification can be helpful.[3]

An important project for the future will require the efforts of a textual editor. There are discrepancies throughout the printed versions of the plays and the autobiographies, probably due to the author's poor eyesight, but also to his forgetfulness. Many of the errors in the plays occur when O'Casey does not give first names for characters in his list of 'Characters in the Play': in *The Plough and the Stars* Mrs Gogan calls herself by four different first names; in *Red Roses for Me* Mullcanny is called by three; in *Within the Gates* the older chair attendant is named Herbert and the younger one Godfrey, yet at one point the older one calls his companion Herbert; in *Inishfallen* seductive Mrs Ballynoy has two first names, while in *Pictures in the Hallway* seductive Alice has two last names. Twice in *Inishfallen* O'Casey tells the story of Liam O'Flaherty's visit to his tenement flat with Garnett, but confusing Garnett *père* with Garnett *fils*, O'Casey calls him Edward the first time and David the second. And the variety in the spelling of proper names is legion, even when the author is not making puns with them. Also, in the last act of *The Drums of Father Ned* a speech that could only be delivered by Mrs McGilligan is attributed to Mrs Binnington instead. Corrected editions of the plays and autobiographies are needed, and a cumulative index for the six autobiographies would also be of great value.

Nor has O'Casey's publisher yet brought out a complete edition of the plays. The four volumes of *Collected Plays* (New York: St Martin's Press; London: Macmillan) have been reissued, containing ten full-length plays and five one-acts, but *The Bishop's Bonfire* and *The Drums of Father Ned* exist only in separate editions, as do the last three one-act plays. The two earliest one-acts can be found in *Feathers from the Green Crow*, which also includes four of the short stories, the other four appearing in *The Green Crow*. There is also the minor problem of nomenclature (what constitutes the size of a full-length play and what is a one-act?): 'Figuro in the Night' has two scenes but can legitimately be termed a one-act play, but 'Behind the Green Curtain' has three scenes and is as long as the full-length *Shadow of a Gunman*, a two-act play.

Editions of the primary works used in this study are the following:

Collected Plays Vol. 1 (London: Macmillan, 1949): *Juno and the Paycock; The Shadow of a Gunman; The Plough and the Stars*; 'The End of the Beginning'; 'A Pound on Demand'. *Collected Plays* Vol. 2 (London: Macmillan, 1949): *The Silver Tassie; Within the Gates; The Star Turns Red*. *Collected Plays* Vol. 3 (London: Macmillan, 1951): *Purple Dust; Red Roses for Me*; 'Hall of Healing'. *Collected Plays* Vol. 4 (London: Macmillan, 1951): *Oak Leaves and Lavender; Cock-a-Doodle Dandy*; 'Bedtime Story'; 'Time to Go'. *The Bishop's Bonfire* (New York: Macmillan, 1955). *The Drums of Father Ned* (New York: St Martin's Press, 1960). *Behind the Green Curtains; Figuro in the Night; The Moon Shines on Kylenamoe; Three Plays* (London: Macmillan, 1961). *I Knock at the Door* (New York: Macmillan, 1939). *Pictures in the Hallway* (New York: Macmillan, 1942). *Drums under the Windows* (New York: Macmillan, 1945). *Inishfallen, Fare Thee Well* (New York: Macmillan, 1949). *Rose and Crown* (New York: Macmillan, 1952). *Sunset and Evening Star* (New York: Macmillan, 1954). *Feathers from the Green Crow* (ed. Robert Hogan; London: Macmillan, 1963): 'Kathleen Listens In'; 'Nannie's Night Out'; 'The Corncrake'; 'The Seamless Coat of Kathleen'; 'Gulls and Bobbin Testers'; 'Irish in the Schools'. *The Green Crow* (New York: George Braziller, 1956): 'The Star-Jazzer'; 'I Wanna Woman'; 'The Job'; 'A Fall in a Gentle Wind'.

For easy reference inclusive page numbers for all quotations from these O'Casey works can be found in the square brackets immediately following the end of the quotation. The only change made in the quotations is that the italicised portions are reset in regular type where there is no coupling of both types within a quotation.

I

The World Scene

SEAN O'CASEY was christened in the spring of 1880 in the Parish Church of St Mary in Dublin, Ireland, and died in the autumn of 1964 in his rented house in St Marychurch, Torquay, England. In the eighty-four-year interim he lived his life, as a labourer and a writer, in the limited confines of his native Ireland and adopted England, in the metropolitan areas of Dublin and London, until finally settling in the Devon coastal area where he died. Except for a trip to New York in 1934 he remained a relatively untravelled man (even an overnight journey to Cambridge is enough of an event to merit a chapter in his autobiographic *Sunset and Evening Star*). A self-imposed exile from his homeland for almost forty years, he passed that time only a short distance from the Irish Sea. As a literary artist O'Casey travelled far in time, belying the sedentary existence in space: without leaving Ireland he journeyed from the British Ireland that saw the rise and fall of Parnell, the lulled aftermath and the complex era of bloody conflicts, to an Irish Free State with changes and contrasts within a handful of years that many countries take generations to experience.

Ireland during the past century has had a distinguished history of self-exiled writers, men who carried with them a preoccupation with Ireland wherever they went, and some with a recollection so perfect as to provide a lifetime of native material for works composed on foreign soil. O'Casey's distinction from this familiar pattern is that he remained aware of the changes taking place within Ireland even while no longer there.[1] His plays written in exile not only remain essentially based in Irish locales but keep time with the social changes within the land and the world at

1

large. Bing Crosby is a topic of conversation in *Cock-a-Doodle Dandy* and the score to *Kiss Me Kate* appears on the piano in *The Drums of Father Ned*: there is no mistaking O'Casey's direction of 'Time: The Present' when he so designates his plays.

The O'Casey reputation was of course established while he lived and wrote in Dublin, and is based on such Dublin tenement dramas as *The Shadow of a Gunman* (1923), *Juno and the Paycock* (1924), and *The Plough and the Stars* (1926). For the forty-six years from birth to exile Sean O'Casey lived in the slums of the Dublin of these plays. *Gunman*, for example, sets the scene in a room in 'a tenement in Hilljoy Square, Dublin' (an obvious pseudonym for Mountjoy Square) [**Shadow, 92**], while Mr Gallogher, who lives nearby, gives his specific information as 'the house known as fifty-five, Saint Teresa Street, situate in the Parish of St Thomas, in the Borough and City of Dublin' [**Shadow, 117**], a fictional address of definitely autobiographic intention. *Juno* only tells us that the Boyle family live in 'a tenement house in Dublin' [**Juno, 3**], while *The Plough* is equally general. The basic sameness of these locations affords a centre of gravity in O'Casey's early work, where the specifics of time are more important than place, where 'May 1920' [**Shadow, 92**] immediately informed the Abbey Theatre audience what they should have already known from the title, that the 'Gunman' was a Sinn Feiner at war with the British Auxiliaries and Black and Tans. *Juno*, a play about the Civil War that followed, is set in '1922' [**Juno, 2**], and *The Plough* returns us to the Easter Rebellion: 'November 1915' [**Plough, 160**] for the first two acts and 'Easter Week, 1916' [**Plough, 160**] for the last two. That O'Casey's next play, sent from London to the Abbey Theatre, should open in a Dublin apartment that 'looks on to a quay' [**Tassie, 5**] should have surprised no one, although the transition in place and dramatic setting for Act Two marked a definite alteration in O'Casey's approach to drama. With *The Silver Tassie* the playwright retraced his steps to the 1914–1918 period of the Great War, and concerned himself with Irish soldiers in the British Army before, during, and after battle in France. The war scene in France, which irked Yeats because O'Casey had never lived through the experience on the spot, but won much praise from Shaw, showed O'Casey moving away not only from his familiar centre of gravity but from the naturalism which established his reputation.

O'Casey returned to the known Dublin in later plays, plays written while resident in London. After a London setting for *Within the Gates* he moved to a Dublin locale in *The Star Turns Red*, but not for another known historical occasion; instead he dealt with hypothetical history, history being made. Again it is the Time of the play that is vital: 'The action of the play takes place during the last few hours of a Christmas Eve. TIME.—Tomorrow, or the next day' [**Star, 240**]. Written during the closing days of the Spanish Civil War, it transcends the Dublin that O'Casey ever knew (or any that has as yet been known by anyone), for a situation which overlays European events of the late thirties, O'Casey's prophecy for the future, and a Dublin composed of O'Casey's recollections, imagination, and anticipation. Not that he was yet finished with his role as dramatic commentator of the historic events during his years in Ireland: four years later he wrote his last major Dublin play, *Red Roses for Me*, to commemorate the 1913 Dublin strikers (to whom he had dedicated *The Star Turns Red*: 'To the men and women who fought through the Great Dublin Lockout in nineteen hundred and thirteen' [**Star, 239**]). *Red Roses* divides its action between 'rather dilapidated rooms in a poor working-class locality' [**Roses, 127**] and two Dublin street scenes: 'A Dublin street, beside a bridge over the river Liffey' and 'Part of the grounds round the Protestant Church of St Burnupus' [**Roses, 126**]. Unlike *Tassie* and *The Star* (and in keeping with the first three plays), it specifically locates its Dublin scene in the programme. O'Casey's St Burnupus is obviously the Church of St Barnabas, to which the young O'Casey himself went, as he records in *Pictures in the Hallway* and *Drums under the Windows*, in which the Burnupus-Barnabas pun is already used (*Pictures* and *Red Roses* were being written at the same time, so that while in Devon O'Casey was re-experiencing this period of his life and times for both autobiographic and dramatic purposes).

Half of O'Casey's full-length plays then are anchored in

3

the Dublin he knew, as were a handful of the shorter ones: 'Hall of Healing' is set in the 'waiting-room of the Dublin Parish Dispensary for the Poor' [Hall, 234] and has its origin in an autobiographic counterpart in *I Knock at the Door*; 'Nannie's Night Out', written during the Dublin years and produced at the Abbey in the interim between *Juno* and *The Plough*, is located in a 'small dairy and provision shop in a working-class district' [Nannie, 303]. 'Bedtime Story' takes as its setting a 'bachelor-flat in Dublin' [Bedtime, 226] but a significant cut above the tenements of the other Dublin plays, 'one of the old houses of Dublin, decayed a little, but still sternly respectable, and kept presentable' [Bedtime, 227], even better than the final residence he himself lived in before leaving Dublin. (When handling the same idea for the short story 'I Wanna Woman', O'Casey changed the city to London and elevated the respectable rooming house to a rather posh apartment.) One early one-act sketch, 'A Pound on Demand', where two drunken labourers entangle themselves with bourgeois respectability, government bureaucracy, and the stiff arm of the Law, is set in a 'Sub-Post Office' in 'Pimblico' [Pound, 294] and avoids ever indicating whether this is Ireland or England, although we can assume that Pimblico is as close to the London borough of Pimlico as St Burnupus is to St Barnabas. The play can be played as English in England and Irish in Ireland.

This sort of 'universality' may seem somewhat over-extended for so insignificant a piece as 'A Pound on Demand' but is instrumental in O'Casey's most expressionistic drama, *Within the Gates*. Here the locale is obviously London's Hyde Park, as O'Casey specifically explains in various places,[2] and is intended to be seen as a microcosm of the world of the early thirties. From the battle scene of Act Two of *The Silver Tassie* to the entire framing of the action in this next play there is an apparent line of development. In the first instance the playwright interrupted the progression of naturalistic scenes (a room in a slum apartment, a hospital ward, a football clubroom) to introduce the world of war, where the mood, tempo, language and tone of the scene are physically supported by the setting itself: the 'lacerated ruin of what was once a monastery', 'heaps of rubbish mark where houses once stood', 'spiky stumps of trees', 'a green star, sometimes a white star', 'a life-size crucifix', 'A gun-wheel to which Barney is tied', 'the shape of a big howitzer gun', 'a brazier in which a fire is burning', and the signs which read, 'PRINCEPS PACIS', 'HYDE PARK CORNER', and 'NO HAWKERS OR STREET CRIES PERMITTED HERE' [Tassie, 35–6]. The violent interruption of normality is immediately felt with the rising of the curtain on this scene. But the *Within the Gates* scene strives for a different effect, the normal world of an urban park where a cross-current of human beings pass and encounter each other. The intensity of contracted and concentrated action so dominant in the war scene is absent here, where the setting passes easily as a natural one. It is only in the changes of scene through the four seasons of the year that expressionistic techniques in setting become apparent, but even these seem relatively natural ones, as the colours change and the mood of the play is thus mirrored from spring through summer and autumn to winter. The most powerful instrument of this sort of impact comes from the 'War Memorial in the form of a steel-helmeted soldier, the head bent on the breast, skeleton-like hands leaning on the butt-end of a rifle' [Gates, 117] (returning us dramatically to Act Two of *The Silver Tassie*). Inobtrusive as it is in the spring scene, it takes on larger significance thereafter: thus, in Scene II 'The Memorial, touched by the sun, now resembles a giant clad in gleaming steel' [Gates, 149]; in Scene III 'The figure of the Soldier now shows a deep black against the crimson hue of the sky' [Gates, 176]; and in Scene IV 'Light from an electric lamp behind the War Memorial shines on the head and shoulders of the figure, making them glow like burnished aluminium; and the bent head appears to be looking down at the life going on below it' [Gates, 203].

Universality of place is enlarged by omnipresence of time in *Within the Gates*, as both the setting and the action reflect the changes wrought by the seasons. The use of stage location for such emphasis expands in the 'naturalistic' Dublin scene for *The Star Turns Red*, where walls of 'vivid black' [Star, 241] immediately transcend stage reality; but it is our awareness of 'TIME.—tomorrow, or the next day'

5

[Star, 240], coupled with the programme note that the play 'takes place during the last few hours of a Christmas Eve' [Star, 240], that dislocates our sensibilities from realistic expectations. A black-walled tenement room, a green-walled union hall, and the lounge room of the Lord Mayor's house with walls of purple and gold—this is the set of contrasts that O'Casey works into the play to stress the interaction of reality and symbolic action. Such generalised settings anchored in specific place designations had already been apparent in his first performed one-act play, 'Kathleen Listens In', where we have no information except that we are viewing the 'Garden before the house of the O Houlihan Family' [Kathleen, 278] in 'TIME: The Present'. Only the Irish flag on the staff in the garden acts as any real identification of time-and-place (a technique that O'Casey went on to duplicate in *Cock-a-Doodle Dandy*). Yet the extent to which Sean O'Casey could insist that a stage setting come to life and live its own existence, affected drastically by change, is not seen until *Oak Leaves and Lavender*, his celebration of the Battle of Britain. Here one of the most conventional stage sets, the 'great room of a Manorial House of a long-past century' [Oak, 4], is expected to undergo transformations from scene to scene that can hardly be perceptible to the eye of the audience until the final version. The wall panelling suggests at the beginning 'the rods and motionless shafts of machinery'; circular panels hint at 'germs of revolving cogwheels'; chandeliers at 'the possible beginnings of gigantic gantries' [Oak, 5], and so forth throughout the room. This Prelude description is only slightly altered by Act One: 'the panelling seems a little stylised away from its normal lines and curving', but by Act Three 'the aspect of the big room has changed with the changing world outside it' [Oak, 85]:

> Its broad and pleasing panelling has become like the ties, the belts, and bars connecting various parts of machinery together, and making of them an active, unified whole. The capacious fireplace, resembling it before, has now assumed the almost similar—though something stylised—shape of a great drop-hammer. The columns flanking the doorway have become machinery shafts. The bureau has

become a lathe, though still preserving the vague outlines of what it once was. The two lesser windows have turned into wheels carrying belts to the chandeliers, now turned up on their sides, and ready to revolve, too, in unison with the rest of the machinery. [**Oak, 85.**]

O'Casey is using his stage set to make a political statement, and has presented the stage designer with a monumental and complex blueprint.

In *Purple Dust* also he had employed the conventional set for transformations into symbolic action, although on the surface the descriptions for these and several of the later plays read like parodies of *Stately Homes and Gardens of England and Ireland*—a far remove from the Dublin tenement room, pub, shop, street and Union hall. Tudor architecture dominates *Purple Dust* as eighteenth-century rococco did *Oak Leaves*, with rural Ireland of the past rather than rural England. 'A wide, deep, gloomy room that was once part of the assembly or living room of a Tudor-Elizabethan mansion' [**Dust, 3**] is in the process of undergoing a transformation that O'Casey is not as enthusiastic about as the industrialisation of the Hatherleigh Manor in England: two wealthy Englishmen have engaged workmen to make the place livable, pretending to a respect for the elegance of the past while really interested in installing their modern conveniences. O'Casey is both unsentimental about reviving the Tudor past and contemptuous of the hypocrisy and snobbery of the nouveau riche. The painted beams are 'too conspicuous and, therefore, ugly' [**Dust, 3**]; but these renovations are insignificant compared to the greater transformation that takes place much against the will of the new tenants: the visitation of the flood at the end of the last act spells total destruction for the shaky house, its inglorious past, and the futile attempts of the new rich. The 'green waters tumble into the room' [**Dust, 119**], as symbolic a change to the Tudor house as the mechanisation of the rococco one.

Rural Ireland became the world scene for O'Casey in his final phase as much as Dublin was at the beginning and the universalised scene in the central phase. He could certainly not have had as much contact with the Irish countryside as he had had with his native Dublin, even when he still lived in Ireland, but once settled in Devon he focused almost exclusively upon it. Visitors from Ireland supplemented the information offered by the mass media, but it was essentially an awareness of how Irish winds shift that kept him so well informed.[3] His fictional Irish towns and villages may not be on any Irish Ordnance map, but they are as vivid and exact as Yoknapatawpha County and Laputa. It is just a short journey from the Dublin of the 1913-to-1923 period to O'Casey's rural communities of the forties and fifties: Clune na Geera (*Purple Dust*), the unnamed farm community of 'The End of the Beginning', Nyadnanave (*Cock-a-Doodle Dandy*), 'the butt-end of an Irish town' [**Time, 261**] in 'Time to Go', Ballyoonagh (*The Bishop's Bonfire*), Doonavale (*The Drums of Father Ned*), Ballybeedhust ('Behind the Green Curtains'), and the title town of 'The Moon Shines on Kylenamoe' (in 'the valley of Kylenamoe in the County of Melloe' [**Moon, 125**]). ('Figuro in the Night' returns us to a Dublin suburb, 'a district just on the environs of Dublin; a new district, part of the city borough' [**Figuro, 89**].) There are important distinctions regarding these communities; Doonavale and Ballybeedhust, for example, are apparently rather industrialised towns of a newer Ireland, although in the first case industry is thriving and healthy, producing an aware proletariat with efficient leadership, while in Ballybeedhust the pun in the town name is diagnostic: internal strife and bigotry succeed in destroying Chatastray's factory and it is sold. In contrast to such towns is Kylenamoe, where there is the railroad station 'and thirty houses a mile away, fourteen of them empty,' whose inhabitants, 'th' lot o' them, man an' woman, if not there already, is on th' tip o' 70' [**Moon, 144**]. Nor is the 'butt-end of an Irish town' any more promising, nor the Marthraun farmlands and bog outside Nyadnanave, described by the Porter who trudged out with a parcel as a 'god-forsaken hole!' [**Cock, 166**]. The total composite of such towns, villages, rural areas, and suburbs gives O'Casey an opportunity to examine a variety of possibilities within the confines of contemporary Ireland, where he is keen to locate the worst and best elements.

But these locales are primarily reflections of the people

who live in them, and it is essentially in his presentations of his characters that the playwright makes his most basic statements, and it is in an investigation of O'Casey's people that we can best discover his attitudes and ideas.

2

A Pride of Paycocks

THE tendency to write chapters of the 'moral history' of
Ireland seems almost obsessive with many of the major Irish
writers of our times: Joyce made the specific announcement
in a letter to a prospective publisher of *Dubliners*; Shaw
hardly limited himself to Ireland, feeling called upon to
preach to the Gentiles as well, England and even Europe;
Yeats issued his pronouncements from atop Ben Bulben, his
aristocratic Olympus; and even Wilde, although tenant of
one of the most transparent of glass houses, cast stones at the
major immorality of the bourgeoisie, Philistinism. For Sean
O'Casey, a latter-day representative of the Land of Saints and
Scholars, the tradition was firmly established when he began
his frontal attack in the early 1920s, and although his tactics
were later highly diversified, he never relented in his direct
characterisation of the totem of spiritual paralysis in his age,
the paycock, despite his fond affection for many of his
individual paycocks.

Paycockism first struts across the O'Casey stage in the suc-
cinctly titled *Juno and the Paycock* in 1924.[1] It is personified
in the now famous Captain Jack Boyle, who engendered a
line of successors and variant descendants and who himself
represents a long line of the species. His entrance is anticipated by Juno's comment that he is 'struttin' about the town
like a paycock with Joxer, I suppose' [**Juno**, 4], and is rein-
forced by her description of the First Law of Paycockism:
'that's what he's waitin' for—till he thinks I'm gone to work,
an' then sail in with the boul' Joxer, to burn all the coal an'
dhrink all the tea in the place, to show them what a good
Samaritan he is!' [**Juno, 5.**] The pride of the paycock is to
ape his 'betters'—not the austere and thrifty industriousness

of his immediate 'betters', the middle class, but the ne'er-do-well bon vivants of the aristocracy. When flush he is the soul of generosity, thriving upon the esteem that he can purchase with such largesse, with no scruples concerning the legitimacy of his access to the boons he distributes. It would be a serious misreading of *Juno and the Paycock* to assume that Captain Boyle's transgressions are against the values of the bourgeoisie, although O'Casey specifically intends his audience to be guilty of such a misinterpretation in the early scenes of the play. The audience cannot fail to accept Mrs Boyle's reasons for condemnation of her husband, and O'Casey gives her a suspicious number of middle-class values to uphold: she is leery of trade unionism, in awe of the power of the employer, and incapable of seeing the efficacy of group solidarity—which she views as a betrayal of individual initiative—and cares a lot less for abstract principles than she does for concrete practicality. We are invited to react against the obvious violation of the 'proper scheme of things' when we see the family situation mocked by the husband who does not acknowledge his responsibility as breadwinner, but relies on the earning power of wife and daughter. 'You'd think he was bringin' twenty poun's a week into the house the way he's going on,' Juno complains. 'He wore out the Health Insurance long ago, he's afther wearin' out the unemployment dole, an' now, he's thryin' to wear out me! An' constantly singin', no less, when he ought always to be on his knees offerin' up a Novena for a job!' [**Juno**, 5–6.] Her religiosity further endears her to the bourgeois instincts of the Abbey audience, and by extension the paycock's lack of religious propriety further alienates him.

O'Casey's handling of Juno Boyle is an odd instance of playing both for and against the dramaturgical convention. The traits that she first exhibits are there to ingratiate her with the narrowly middle-class mentality of much of the audience, making acceptable her emergence as a truly heroic figure at the play's resolution, while those who see through her early narrowness and conventionality are witness to the transformation that produces the final Juno rising above her situation and her own limitations. But the Captain is an equally complex figure. O'Casey maintains carefully ambivalent attitudes toward his sin of Pride: the pride which 'goeth before a fall' is present in Boyle, but his fall, a definite consequence of his faults, is primarily a pratfall. He remains consistently a comic character despite the many tragic elements of the play.

Captain Boyle's crime is not against the values of the middle class, but against those of his own. If he chooses not to work and support his family, it is a choice made for both perceptive and selfish motives: he understands the exploitation that is the nature of his relationship to any employer, and like Shaw's brigands in *Man and Superman* he elects to defy the system; but he also caters to his own slothful inclinations and is willing to exploit any means of sustaining himself without work, even at the expense of others. The working-class solidarity that would be the meaningful expression of his rebellion against his employers is absent in the paycock, while his daughter Mary is present as a reminder both to us and to him of the positive alternative to his disloyalty to his class. She is the irate proletarian out on strike (but with a pretty green ribbon in her hair).

The pride of the paycock is a common malady in O'Casey's plays, but the most extreme examples are those that, like Yeats's swans in Coole Park, run in pairs. The ersatz 'captain' and his 'butty' Joxer Daly are the archetypal pair from which such duos in later plays are modelled. In his own ways Joxer is as much a paycock as his more-esteemed companion: they complement each other and square off against each other, Joxer all the while playing foil to the greater paycock. Boyle's gesture is his strut; Joxer's is his shoulder-shrugging. Again it is Juno who sets the stage for their appearance: 'There'll never be any good got out o' him so long as he goes with that shoulder-shruggin' Joxer. I killin' meself workin', an' he sthruttin' about from mornin' till night like a paycock!' [**Juno, 9.**] (Juno's explanation of Boyle's behaviour is the typical bourgeois cliché of 'evil companions', and she is no doubt given to assuming that good conduct results from proper allegiance within the bosom of the family.)

The role of the Joxer varies to a large extent in its various

12

depictions throughout O'Casey's canon, but in *Juno* it is essentially that of the sycophant and the Judas, the yes-man and the betrayer. This duality contains its logic in the basic necessity felt by Joxer to protect his precarious position from the aggrandisement of the more aggressive Captain: he is a foxy Reynard to Boyle's wolfish Isegrym. When the Captain is being munificent, Joxer Daly fawns upon him without a vestige of shame. In the opening appearance of the pair Joxer is heard swearing that Boyle is singing 'a darlin' song, a daaarlin' song!' [**Juno, 9**]; during his second session with Boyle (after having been chased out by Juno), he pronounces that the Captain's ungrammatical nautical term is 'a darlin' word, a daarlin' word' [**Juno, 26**]. In Act Two he again gets an opportunity to corroborate the Captain's aesthetic taste: Boyle's choice of 'Home to Our Mountains' is dubbed 'a darlin' song, a daarlin' song' [**Juno, 50**], and Joxer goes on to request that Boyle recite his poem, 'a darlin' poem' [**Juno, 57**]. But Boyle is not equally generous with his praise of Joxer even during their most exalted moments of friendship: at the initial breakfast he countermands Joxer's enthusiasm for a book called 'Elizabeth, or Th' Exile o' Sibayria' ('Ah, it's a darlin' story, a daarlin' story') with a rather curt 'You eat your sassige, an' never min' *Th' Exile o' Sibayria*.' [**Juno, 23.**] Boyle's advantage is that of host and provider, even before the windfall of the 'banjaxed' will. He dispenses breakfast in Act One with a grand swagger (although it is only tea and gravy that he gives Joxer, keeping the actual 'sassige' for himself). As parasite Joxer has to accept second-best with humility, always carefully skirting the thin edge of the Captain's unpredictably treacherous temperament. Joxer is made to eat not only humble pie but also crow, the Captain exulting in his advantage over his less-fortunate friend.

But as sycophantic as he is, even Joxer has his moments of rebellion against the domineering Captain. Pathetically left suspended on a narrow roof ledge outside the Boyle window, he is ear-witness not only to the announcement of the Boyle family's good fortune, but is made acutely aware that he has been totally forgotten by his friend in a moment of financial triumph. Boyle neglects him and then denies him (apparently oblivious that Joxer is still within earshot just outside the

13

window); he self-righteously assumes his new middle-class respectability with the pronouncement: 'Juno, I'm done with Joxer; he's nothin' but a prognosticator an' a . . .' [Juno, 34]. His rage overwhelming his fear of Juno, Joxer denounces his capricious betrayer; his denunciations are damaging and apparently final, since he unmasks two of Boyle's most important façades: that he never was a deep sea sailor and that the pains in his legs which kept him from honest work were deceptions. 'He'll never blow the froth off a pint o' mine agen, that's a sure thing,' Boyle states with conviction, contending, 'I'm a new man from this out . . .' [Juno, 35] as Act One ends. Yet the new Boyle welcomes back the old Joxer as Act Two opens (two days later), without any trace of recrimination on either part. Boyle's windfall is too tempting to keep Joxer's new-found integrity intact for long, and Joxer's willingness to lick his boots is too important for Boyle to stick to his resolution.

The reciprocal nature of their mutual dependence is fully exploited by the playwright both for its continually comic possibilities and for an extended cynical statement on the nature of the paycocks in Irish society. Their volte-face is the sort of theatrical trick that no comic playwright could exploit more than once during the course of a single play, yet O'Casey has the temerity to try it again—and is even more successful the second time. The second schism is caused by Joxer's assumption that he has finally gained the upper hand. His first act of rebelliousness had been a rash reaction to neglect and insult, but the next seems a calculated attack on an adversary who has lost his advantage. The Wolf has been shorn of his fangs and is particularly vulnerable because he is unaware that his disadvantage is known to anyone but himself (the legacy has fallen through and Joxer has found out that the Boyles will be getting no money at all). The Fox then taunts his defanged 'friend' into a rage and enjoys his sweet revenge. Boyle attempts to lord it over Joxer in the usual way, only to have the wormlike Joxer turn upon him and give him the lie. The Captain's usual bluster ('I always knew you were a prognosticator an' a procrastinator!' [Juno, 72]) is to no avail; Joxer's denunciation this time is fully calculated—he has nothing to lose since Boyle is now apparently stony broke and hopelessly in debt. 'The anchor's weighed, farewell, ree . . . mem . . . ber . . . me' [**Juno, 72**] he taunts (the nautical refrain again emphasising his previous ripping off of Boyle's disguise), 'Jacky Boyle, Esquire, infernal rogue, an' damned liar.' [**Juno, 72.**] And again he stalks out. But whereas he had previously returned sheepishly to renew his friendship with the prospective legatee, this time Joxer waits to be summoned. His advantage is a small one but he plays it for what it is worth, and Boyle, having lost all else and his family as well, calls to Joxer only a few minutes later to come with him: 'Joxer, Joxer, are you there? . . . I'm going down to Foley's—are you comin'?' And the parasitic yesman, his pride again pawned for a drink paid for by the Captain's last coins, comes running: 'Come with you? With that sweet call me heart is stirred; I'm only waiting for the word, an' I'll be with you like a bird!' [**Juno, 78.**] Joxer's bird is the kind that is content to peck at the leavings dropped by the paycock.

The Boyle-Daly team of primary and secondary paycocks exists as O'Casey's finest comic characterisations of the species, but it should not be assumed that the playwright worked continually to reduplicate his achievement in *Juno*. It was not in slavish imitation of his own accomplishment that he went on to exploit the theme of paycockery in Ireland, but with a sense of the infinite range of possibilities inherent in the type. A subdued version of the two Irish birds can be found in Sylvester Heegan and Simon Norton of *The Silver Tassie*, for example, where their function is artistically different from that of Jack Boyle and Joxer Daly. As comic cowards Sylvester and Simon play the familiar role, providing several fine moments of hilarity as they attempt to ward off the militantly zealous interest of a religious missionary groping for their souls, as they solve the problem of how to confront a violently outraged neighbour, as they cower before a nurse's prescription of a bath, and as they are confounded by the complications of the modern telephone. But in contrast to Boyle's arrogance and selfishness and Joxer's spinelessness and vindictiveness, the personalities of the paycocks of *The Silver Tassie* are pallid and benign. Their attempts to browbeat each other are minimal and

15

stem only from desperate self-defence, and their collective and individual acts of cowardice are pathetic, if not actually endearing. For *The Silver Tassie* solicits a very different sort of response from the audience, and the two providers of comic relief are diminished in significance in the play. Any attempt by O'Casey to give them the kind of star billing that they enjoyed in *Juno and the Paycock* would have seriously damaged the nature of the drama. *Juno* is predicated upon the emergence of mother and daughter to central positions as 'heroines' at the expense of the incorrigibility of the pay-cock and his 'butty', all other males having also relinquished any claim to the title of hero: Johnny, twice heroic in past action, has failed the third test and is executed for cowardice and betrayal, eliminating the 'natural' candidate from con-tention; Charlie Bentham (having ironically conjured up the concept of 'the greatest good for the greatest number') turns out to be a cad in the traditional role of the absconded seducer; and Jerry Devine, the good Socialist, flees from the prospect of marrying Mary. The young men readily dis-qualify themselves; the old men are far beyond the pale; only the goddesses, Juno and Mary, rise in stature and dig-nity toward heroic possibility. But this feminist triumph is absent from *The Tassie*, where the young men are left with the full brunt of the necessity of fulfilling the heroic func-tion. Just as Mrs Heegan as mother is inconsequential com-pared to Mrs Boyle, so the comic paycocks are incidental to the drama which is essentially Harry Heegan's.

Sylvester and Simon are almost too kindly to qualify as paycocks at all. Unlike the Captain, who remained ego-centrically indifferent to either his son's heroism or his son's suffering, Sylvester Heegan is vastly proud of Harry's accom-plishments on the football field and in hand-to-hand combat (with a 'Police Constable 63 C under the stars of a frosty night on the way home from Terenure' [Tassie, 8]) and is sympathetic with Harry's plight as a wounded war hero. In fact, it is as a proud father that the elder Heegan struts, rather than on his own behalf; he invents no imaginary exploits of his own: he is no self-appointed and self-adver-tised former sea-captain like Boyle, but remains throughout an employed member of the proletariat, described by

O'Casey as 'a docker all his life since first the muscles of his arms could safely grip a truck, and even at sixty-five the steel in them is only beginning to stiffen' [**Tassie**, 5].[2] Like all the other participants in the opening scene of the play, he is in awe and admiration of his football-hero son, praises his accomplishments and expresses full confidence that Harry will return in time to embark for France. Whereas the concerned mother worries that Harry will be late, the complacent father displays an unquestioning confidence in his son's perfection, refusing even to acknowledge the possibility of misjudging time and missing the boat.

But the extent of his confidence in the invulnerable Harry is not quite matched by Sylvester Heegan with a full measure of commiseration for the destroyed hero who returns from the front. The hospital scene in Act Three affords O'Casey an opportunity to show the bitter war hero surrounded by his sympathetic friends and family, but the playwright's sense of irony carries beyond such simplicity. The depiction of the war in the second act is followed by a hospital scene in which Sylvester and Simon are disclosed as patients, with an empty third bed on display for the audience. Our surprise at this sudden return to the inconsequential comic material of the first act after the horror of the expressionistic war scene is not allowed to fade, for only a few lines of comic dialogue go by before the angry hero wheels himself into the room, fully returning us to the horror of the play's tragic potential. Although the crippled soldier is a new sight for the audience, he is apparently already a familiar figure to his father and Simon, and it is neither shock nor sympathy that they display, but discomfort. Harry's presence creates a pall in the room: 'Sylvester slides down into the bed, and Simon becomes interested in a book' [**Tassie**, 58]. Having the older men as patients in the same ward with the wounded warrior is unnecessary coincidence but O'Casey insists upon it. If all of Harry's first-act admirers were gathered now in his hospital room as visitors, the central focus would fall exclusively on Harry. But O'Casey's view of human behaviour belies such a concentration of focus (*this* would have been the unnatural stage device for O'Casey, one that he refuses to accept as consistent with the reality of human existence). It is

17

instrumental in O'Casey's view of life that each of us necessarily concentrates the major emphasis of focus upon himself,
that each character normally sees himself as the centre of his
own drama. The first return of the wounded man might have
caused the kind of sensation which focused attention upon
him, but Harry is now a familiar figure on the scene. The
first shock of his condition has worn off and his presence em-
barrasses and dispirits the others. Mrs Heegan and Jessie
Taite are visitors, although the latter has shifted her interest
from Harry to Barney and refuses even to enter Harry's
room; Susie is a nurse in the hospital; Sylvester and Simon
are patients; Barney and Teddy are also wounded patients;
and Mrs Foran is there ostensibly to visit her own husband.
The proud Father, for whom Harry had been the apple of
his eye, is now absorbed by his own forthcoming minor sur-
gery, and even the horror of having to bathe supersedes his
sympathy with his son.[3]

Yet there is genuine feeling for Harry displayed by Sylvester both here and in the next act, the football club celebration, but the destruction of Harry's prowess has adversely
affected Sylvester's strut. He has been badly deflated by the
loss of his reason for pride, and displays the symptoms of the
paycock in his egocentrism. He cannot help interpreting
Harry's misfortune as a conspiracy against himself, that he—
instead of Harry, or as well as Harry—has suffered a reversal,
has been deprived of something that should rightfully be his.
Captain Boyle denounces Johnny and Mary ('Oh, a nice son,
an' a nicer daughter, I have' [Juno, 78]) at the crucial
moment when both are in need of his commiseration; Sylvester Heegan instead turns away from Harry's problem to
his own, or to any aspect of life around him that would disengage his interest from Harry. Unable to solve Harry's
dilemma he prefers to ignore it: at the club dance he notes
that 'me an' the old woman tried to persuade him that, seein'
his condition, it was better to stop at home, an' let me represent him' [Tassie, 84]. He is not insensitive to what is happening to Harry, just powerless in the face of it. His major
statement of sympathy is: 'To bring a boy so helpless as him,
whose memory of agility an' strength time hasn't flattened
down, to a place wavin' with joy an' dancin', is simply,

18

simply——' [**Tassie, 84**.] ('Devastating, I'd say,' adds Simon.)
But essentially a venial paycock, Sylvester is a universal one:
he reminds us all of the basically egocentric nature of our
own focus.

The Heegan-Norton genres of paycock are distinctly different from the Boyle-Daly prototypes, although they demonstrate the important qualities of cowardice, self-interest,
braggadocio, and a refusal or inability to accept virile responsibilities, and they too move essentially in twos. It is
interesting then to turn back to O'Casey's first produced play
for an ur-paycock who anticipates Jack Boyle in many ways,
but is seen exclusively on his own. He comes into contact
and conflict with many other people, particularly the play's
protagonist, but lacks the diminished image of himself that
Boyle can see in Daly or Heegan in Norton. In fact, very
much in stark contrast to O'Casey's poet-'hero' Donal Davoren,
antagonist Seumas Shields comes close at moments to making
the play his own. The title figure, Davoren, is only the
'shadow' of a gunman (the real gunman being a thread-and-
hairpin pedlar named Maguire), and Shields at times displays
a degree of sense that aids in diminishing the already transparent stature of the poet manqué. But Shields, as a precursor to Boyle, demonstrates many of the paycock characteristics that O'Casey delights in underscoring for the Irish
character. His initial appearance as a slugabed is further enhanced by his Boylish tendency to find fault with others for
traits that are so obviously his own: from beneath the bed-
clothes he denounces Maguire ('I suppose he was too damn
lazy to get up; he wanted the streets to be well aired first'
[**Shadow, 96**]), and has no compunction about generalising
his denunciations ('No wonder this unfortunate country is
as it is, for you can't depend upon the word of a single
individual' [**Shadow, 96**]).

There is no mistaking the strut of Seumas Shields. Mr
Mulligan, the landlord (who 'has no love for Seumas, who
denies him the deference he believes is due from a tenant to
a landlord' [**Shadow, 100**]), is quite specific in characterising
his nemesis: 'You're very high an' mighty, but take care,
you're not goin' to get a drop.' [**Shadow, 101**.] But this hardly fazes Shields. 'You're a terribly independent fellow'

[**Shadow, 102**] the landlord persists, but even his eviction notice fails to ruffle a feather of the paycock. 'Ah, go to hell!' [**Shadow, 103**] Seumas roars, ignoring the eviction papers. When Donal accuses him of gloating over the possibility that Shelley is roasting in hell, Shields pompously announces, 'I rejoice in the vindication of the Church and Truth.' [**Shadow, 97.**] But certainly his most pompous pontification comes in his battle of brave words with the shadowy Donal. 'Thanks be to God I'm a daily communicant,' [**Shadow, 133**] he says (this after we have watched him wake after noon and bemoan the fact that he missed Mass because no one woke him). 'There's a great comfort in religion; it makes a man strong in time of trouble an' brave in time of danger. No man need be afraid with a crowd of angels round him; thanks to God for His Holy religion.' [**Shadow, 133.**] The paycock preens, while the audience knows full well that trouble and danger lurk near, and that Seumas Shields is soon 'goin' to get a drop'.

Yet Shields has a good deal more justification for his feeling of self-importance than an obvious fraud like Captain Boyle. Unlike the Boyle who quotes the Irish for 'God save Ireland' when he means 'Rest in Peace', assumes from Ibsen's titles that his books are for children,[4] and pretends he understands Bentham's blather about theosophy, Shields is demonstrably well read. He starts his day by crediting Morpheus and Somnus for his sleep (and the audience is given the impression that he knows his Greek mythology better than does his poet room-mate), and succeeds in identifying every quotation that Donal flings at him. He recognises Shelley's *Prometheus Unbound*, although he damns the atheistic poet to a 'jazz dance down below' [**Shadow, 97**]; for Shakespeare he cites play, act, scene, and speaker, and goes on to apply the situation to that around him. But his most perceptive statement on literature nonetheless manages to surprise us, as he lectures the haughty poet on the purpose of his art: 'I don't know much about the pearly glint of the morning dew, or the damask sweetness of the rare wild rose, or the subtle greenness of the serpent's eye,' he begins, in a series of images that give authority to his pronouncement, and in diction that O'Casey purposely avoids tampering with for dialect spelling,

'—but I think a poet's claim to greatness depends upon his power to put passion in the common people.' [Shadow, 127.] To our astonishment O'Casey is discovered employing his particular paycock at this instance as his spokesman!

Our suspicion that O'Casey will lift the damner of Shelley to heroic heights at the conclusion of *The Shadow of a Gunman* (over so thin an opponent as Donal the poet) is proved short-lived. He emerges from his encounter with the landlord fairly well (and certainly landlords are traditional whipping boys in such instances), and he carries a few of the moments with Donal as well, but he fails a most crucial test in being unable to appreciate the possibilities in Minnie Powell. Whereas Donal, self-confessed 'poet and poltroon' [Shadow, 157] by the end of the play, is amorously able to accept Minnie ('Very pretty,' he admits, 'but very ignorant' [Shadow, 124]), Seumas lacks sufficient personal involvement with anyone to see beyond the detriment of her ignorance. Jack Boyle's major fault, assuming that his own self-protection is paramount and expecting others to concur, is also Shields's. The controversy with Donal over Minnie's merits categorises the differences in their attitudes, resulting in Donal, as much a coward and self-seeker as Seumas, realising that 'shame is your portion now till the silver cord is loosened and the golden bowl be broken' [Shadow, 156–7], while the religious Seumas ('I knew things ud go wrong when I missed Mass this mornin'' [Shadow, 145]) can only explain the night's events in terms of his superstition: 'I knew something ud come of the tappin' on the wall!' [Shadow, 157.]

Yet into the mouth of the paycock the author chooses to put occasional words of wisdom in his campaign to disclose the fallacies in his potential hero, the poet-poltroon. At the core of Donal's failure as a hero is his own paycock characteristic: his self-importance blinds him to his responsibilities toward others. Seumas's concept of poetry as existing in order 'to put passion in the common people' [Shadow, 127] meets with scorn from the would-be poet: 'Damn the people! They live in the abyss, the poet lives on the mountain-top.' [Shadow, 127.] Not only does the paycock 'get a drop', but the poet is toppled from his mountain-top by the end of the play, recovering sufficiently to become aware of his faults, while his counterpart continues unaffected with his delusion of self-importance. This 'drop' takes place despite a kind of practical intelligence that often redeems Seumas throughout *The Gunman*; 'With all due respect to the gunmen, I don't want them to die for me,' he states, pointing out the senseless horrors of the conflict between the Republicans and the British. 'It's the civilians that suffer,' he says, making one of O'Casey's most important statements: 'when there's an ambush they don't know where to run. Shot in the back to save the British Empire, an' shot in the breast to save the soul of Ireland.' [**Shadow, 132**.] But paycock that he is, there is no overlooking his personal cowardice, and at his better moments Seamus admits and explains: when Davoren confronts him with a rather devastating accusation ('I remember the time when you yourself believed in nothing but the gun'), Shields replies: 'Ay, when there wasn't a gun in the country; I've a different opinion now when there's nothin' but guns in the country.' [**Shadow, 131**.] At first this retort is both comic and illogical, but on second consideration it makes sense as a statement of political reality, and reflects Seumas's understanding of the absurdity of the conflict in Ireland.

The special qualities that distinguish the heroine Minnie Powell are seriously lacking in both the paycock-with-a-touch-of-practical-sense and the poet-who-is-too-much-the-poltroon, and would have been sufficient to redeem either man. O'Casey demands little from his 'heroic' characters, and a mere slip of a girl capable of a human and altruistic act (even if inspired by insipid romantic motivations) can be elevated to the most exalted position in the drama, especially when the males are so inconsequential by comparison. That human gesture would have been enough to ennoble either Donal or Seumas, and in their controversy over Minnie's qualifications they indicate how far apart they are. Shields's first concern is for propriety, a rather bourgeois notion for a 'pedlar' of 'spoons, forks, laces, thread' [**Shadow, 97**], and somewhat out of keeping with his refusal to pay his rent: 'The oul' ones'll be talkin','' he asserts, regarding Minnie's presence in their room, 'an' once they start you don't know how it'll end' [**Shadow, 129**]. But his next attack concerns

Minnie herself: 'Surely a man that has read Shelley couldn't be interested in an ignorant little bitch that thinks of nothin' but jazz dances, fox-trots, picture theatres an' dress.' [Shadow, 129.] Here he treads on delicate toes, for O'Casey has repeatedly defended just these aspects of the popular culture of today's young people as a healthy contrast to the puritanical and morbid piety of their elders, and Donal is quick to reassert the defence: 'Right glad I am that she thinks of dress, for she thinks of it in the right way, and makes herself a pleasant picture to the eye.' [Shadow, 129.] Seumas, it is important to note, is a much younger paycock at thirty-five than the sixty-year-old Boyle or sixty-five-year-old Heegan, and his lack of an ability to appreciate pretty Minnie for what his eyes should tell him is there is central to the O'Casey condemnation of the sex-fearing Irish male. (A later O'Casey creation is an interesting case in point, the John Jo Mulligan of 'Bedtime Story', who manages to 'seduce' his lady love, but is terror-stricken by the possibility that his landlady, an 'oul' one' named Miss Mossie, will find out.)

Donal continues his defence of Minnie Powell, rationalising her ignorance in the face of Seumas's education: 'Education has been wasted on many persons, teaching them to talk only, but leaving them with all their primitive instincts.' [Shadow, 130.] He assumes that he means Seumas in particular, but his own 'primitive' cowardice later convicts him as a 'poltroon'. 'Had poor Minnie received an education' (and now again we hear O'Casey's voice), 'she would have been an artist. She is certainly a pretty girl. I'm sure she is a good girl, and I believe she is a brave girl.' [Shadow, 130.] Of these three cardinal virtues, goodness remains negligible—O'Casey neither knows nor cares whether Minnie is good (Angela in 'Bedtime Story' is certainly no angel, but O'Casey makes her infinitely preferable to Mulligan, Miss Mossie, Daniel Halibut, or any of the others). Her prettiness is important, however, and Donal's capacity to acknowledge it raises him well above the prudish Seumas; her bravery (which should have been the man's instead) is proved before long, much to both the relief and shame of both men. But Shields derides the lover's image of the

23

beloved, revealing his pathetic snobbery: 'A Helen of Troy come to live in a tenement!' [**Shadow, 130.**] His sneering ill fits his democratic insistence only moments before about poetry and the 'common people' [**Shadow, 127**], but he is far more accurate in his jab at Davoren: 'she looks upon you as a hero—a kind o' Paris . . . she'd give the world an' all to be gaddin' about with a gunman.' [**Shadow, 130.**] He goes on to accuse Minnie of a potential infidelity, marking this aspect as the prime characteristic of her sex, that she would transfer her affections to a 'British Tommy with a Mons Star' [**Shadow, 130**] not long after her Irish gunman was executed. 'An' as for bein' brave, it's easy to be that when you've no cause for cowardice; I wouldn't care to have me life dependin' on brave little Minnie Powell—she wouldn't sacrifice a jazz dance to save it.' [**Shadow, 130.**] His prejudice against women (and what is worse, his projection of his own inadequacies upon them) destroys whatever good qualities Shields had mustered so far. He is too much a paycock to see the irony in his words, but Donal is not much better when it comes to extending his appreciation of Minnie into a course of action for himself.

The paycock is of course a comic creation throughout, and in *The Gunman* we are treated to a dumb-show demonstration of paycockism while the prototype himself stands before us. Shields has a perfect double in Adolphus Grigson, a blustering drunk who browbeats his wife, asserting his male superiority as virulently as Seumas, while thumping his Protestant chest as vociferously as Seumas swears by 'Holy Saint Anthony': 'I tie meself to no woman's apron strings, Mr Shields; I know how to keep Mrs Grigson in her place; I have the authority of the Bible for that.' [**Shadow, 139.**] It is then that O'Casey lets us see the paycock in double focus: Shields on stage cowering before the Black and Tans, snivelling and bootlicking ('Seuma . . . Oh no; Jimmie Shields, sir,' [**Shadow, 148**] he responds when commanded to identify himself, eradicating the Celtic first name; when asked, ''Ere, where's your gun?' he replies, 'I never had a gun in me hand in me life' [**Shadow, 148**]—a statement of pure truth that is nonetheless purer irony); then Mrs Grigson's description of her husband's equally cowardly performance off-stage ('they had the poor man sittin' up in bed, his hands crossed on his breast, his eyes lookin' up at the ceilin', an' he singin' a hymn' [**Shadow,** 150]); followed by Shields and Grigson, after the Tans have left, boasting to each other about how brave they had been. Grigson's comparison of his own 'cool' behaviour and his wife's terror is comic counterpart to Shields's fear that Minnie will give him away ('Holy Saint Anthony grant that she'll keep her mouth shut,' [**Shadow,** 152] he prays). 'Mrs G. lost her head completely,' Mr G. reports, '—panic-stricken. But that's only natural, all women is very nervous.' [**Shadow,** 154.] It is the supreme weakness of the paycock to underestimate the power of a woman, since his only claim to strength is at the expense of the 'weaker' sex.

The solitary paycock is a rarer bird than those who run in pairs, and without a mirror in which to reflect his glory he can, like Seumas Shields, be somewhat more substantial than the thoroughly vain egoist. With *The Plough and the Stars* O'Casey introduces one of his finest comic creations, Fluther Good, with many of the characteristics of the paycock prototype, but with distinctions that elevate him above all of the male characters of the first four 'tenement' tragicomedies. O'Casey's attachment to Fluther is a matter of perpetual record: often in his autobiographies he uses him as an important standard, a barometer of correct attitudes and balanced values. In *Sunset and Evening Star,* for example, O'Casey condemns G. K. Chesterton for his snobbish inability to identify himself with the working class. 'No, this was no man for a symbol on a workers' banner,' he says of Chesterton; 'One could ne'er imagine this man striding along between Feemy Evans and Fluther Good.' [**Sunset,** 12.] In *Rose and Crown* he stands before the gate of the Holy Cross Convent, where efforts are being made to enrol his child, and muses, 'barriers to keep out the Fluther Goods' [**Crown,** 186], later breathing sighs of relief that the child is refused because the family cannot afford to pay full tuition. In *Inishfallen, Fare Thee Well* he describes the Abbey Theatre riots during *The Plough and the Stars,* when 'Barry Fitzgerald became a genuine Fluther Good, and fought as

Fluther himself would fight, sending an enemy, who had climbed on to the stage, flying into the stalls with a flutherian punch on the jaw' [**Inish, 239**]. Fluther, in his creator's estimation, is apparently someone to be reckoned with, rather than merely a preening paycock to be dismissed as a 'stage Irishman'. During rehearsals O'Casey bemoaned the state of affairs backstage which seemed capable of preventing Barry Fitzgerald from perfecting his Fluther: 'All this made Fitzgerald more nervous than ever, for he had none of the arrogant courage, and none of the jovial determination, which, under different conditions, might have made a great man of Fluther.' [**Inish, 235–6.**]

It is O'Casey's intention then to 'make a great man of Fluther', a process that remains always a potential. 'Arrogant courage' and 'jovial determination' are the raw materials, qualities lacking in Boyle completely and in Shields to too great an extent. Obviously the playwright's identification with the character goes beyond what we see in *The Plough and the Stars*, especially when we see Fluther's independent performance in *Inishfallen*: O'Casey, attending a performance of Yeats's *At the Hawk's Well*,[5] bristles at the Merrion Square chamber theatre claque, and mischievously imagines his own Fluther among them, 'in their evening best, the men immaculate in shiny sober black, the women gay and glittering in silk sonorous, and brilliant brocade' [**Inish, 373**]. He 'wondered how they would feel, what would happen, if Fluther, furiously drunk, came tumbling into the room, looking for someone to fight him' [**Inish, 374–5**]. The comic possibilities in this scene of disparate elements absurdly brought together complies with Georges Feydeau's classic concept of comedy, bringing together on stage two persons who should never logically be allowed to meet. Feydeau's intentions are objective, however—the creation of a comic situation; O'Casey's subjective purpose soon becomes apparent as he squares off the prototype of the Dublin slums with the denizens of Merrion Square:

An ignorant, ignoble savage, shouting that he wouldn't let that poet fella make little of Fluther's religion; lost to, and separate from, these elegant ones here in Yeats's drawingroom. And yet, Fluther was of the same family; bone of their bone, flesh of their flesh; a Christian, too, never missing Mass on Sundays. What headlines his visit would make in the morrow's newspapers! Fluther runs wild in Yeats's drawingroom; Shocking scene; The poet tries to reason with him; A number of dress-suits ruined; Six constables remove Fluther Good! [Inish, 375.]

There is no doubt about which side O'Casey is on during this fray, nor the glee with which he entertains the possibility of the ignoble Fluther abusing the noble Yeats—the same Yeats who had recently stood up on O'Casey's stage to defend *The Plough and the Stars* against the Savage and the Ignoble, 'as he conjured up a vision for them of O'Casey on a cloud, with Fluther on his right hand and Rosie Redmond on his left' [Inish, 239].

There is much in this 'mythical' Fluther's attitude that O'Casey certainly does not believe in, 'Fluther's religion' for one thing. His pietistic attitudes are apparently an easy extension of Seumas Shields's (although the concept of 'never missing Mass' is closer to Seumas than to anything implied by Fluther in *The Plough and the Stars*), and early in the play Fluther Good announces his creed: 'I think we ought to have as great a regard for religion as we can, so as to keep it out of as many things as possible.' [Plough, 170.] His first quarrel is with the atheistic Covey, to whom he proposes Adam and Eve as a corrective to the Covey's contention of 'mollycewels an' atoms' [Plough, 170], refusing to 'stand silent an' simple listenin' to a thick like you makin' a maddenin' mockery o' God Almighty.' [Plough, 172.] Like Seumas's concern for what the 'oul' ones' would say, Fluther compounds his piety with prudery, shuddering at Giorgione's 'Sleeping Venus' on the Clitheroe wall: '"Georgina: The Sleepin' Vennis",' he reads, adding, 'Oh, that's a terrible picture; oh, that's a shockin' picture!' [Plough, 173]—his prudish censure only compensated for by a rather objective afterthought that indicates that he does have a discerning eye ('Oh, th' one that got that taken, she must have been a prime lassie!'). But 'Fluther's religion' also is countervailed by an element of anti-clericalism indicated in the pub scene:

27

'Fluther has a vice versa opinion of them that put ivy leaves into their prayer-books, scabbin' it on th' clergy, an' thryin' to out-do th' haloes o' th' saints be lookin' as if he was wearin' around his head a glittherin' aroree boree allis!' [**Plough, 200.**] Fluther sober is a devouter soul than Fluther soused,[6] but it is characteristic of the paycock to expound two opposing points of view at alternate instances without a touch of shame at the possible hypocrisy. Captain Boyle's denunciation of the clergy reflects his attitude before the legacy is announced, when Father Farrell arranges a job for him: 'D'ye know, Joxer, I never like to be beholden to any o' the clergy. . . . If they do anything for you, they'd want you to be livin' in the Chapel . . . the clergy always had too much power over the people in this unfortunate country.' [**Juno, 24–5.**] But when the legacy has puffed up the pay-cock, he is far more receptive to the approaches of Father Farrell: 'Father Farrell is a man o' the people, an', as far as I know the History o' me country, the priests was always in the van of the fight for Irelan's freedom.' [**Juno, 38.**]

If these few statements are diagnostic, a pattern is discernible which ranges from Boyle's hypocrisy of convenience through Shields's narrowly religious fears to the unthinking acceptance and defence of his faith which characterises Fluther's approach, although it is balanced by a degree of criticism toward the clergy. O'Casey enjoys Fluther's rough-and-ready embrace of life, and when his stage direction describes him as 'rarely surrendering to thoughts of anxiety' [**Plough, 162**], O'Casey pinpoints the important difference between Fluther and the anxiety-ridden Seumas. But the playwright harbours no illusions about Fluther, who emerges from the play as one of the 'better' Dubliners, yet not quite of the sort of heroic stuff that is astonishingly revealed in Bessie Burgess. It is not just that the bald, forty-year-old carpenter, 'square-jawed and harshly featured' [**Plough, 162**], with scar under left eye, bent nose, and 'scrubby' mustache, does not have the look of a hero anywhere about him—the much younger Davoren turned out to be a poltroon—but that Fluther falls short of an ideal that O'Casey expects from him in particular. In that hypothetical smash-up of Yeats's theatrical gathering, O'Casey takes a hard look at his Fluther:

Yet there was life in this Fluther that these elegant persons lacked; and life in them that Fluther hadn't got. What a pity, what a shame, they couldn't share their gifts between them. Fluther had his rights and he had his qualities. Fluther, on Sundays, sober; his old suit brushed, a faded bowler hat set rakishly on his head, a newly-washed shirt showing over the top of his waistcoat, coming up the poor street, would be surrounded by children, some preceding. some following him, and all crying out, Sing us a song Fluther. [**Inish,** 375.]

We never actually see all this of Fluther Good in *The Plough and the Stars*, where he is circumscribed and contained by the events of the play, but we recognise in this description O'Casey's tendency to extend the significance of the crusty carpenter beyond the framework of the play, admitting his personal identification: 'And, bar Yeats and a few others, Sean was as far away from these elegant people as the doughty Fluther. Far farther, for he was nearer to Fluther than he was to them.' [**Inish,** 376.]

Much depends upon the emergence from *The Plough* of Fluther's individuality, especially from a play that has no other claimant to the position of central character (the most heroic gesture is Bessie's; the most pathetic situation is Nora's; Clitheroe is suspect from the beginning, and his reported death is far less tragic than its effect on Nora). Only Fluther, surviving the quarrels of the first two acts, sustains himself through Acts Three and Four as the sort of 'decent' person that O'Casey is offering the audience for its acceptance. But the bickerings of the first half of the play almost subsume Fluther (as they completely overwhelm Boyle and his butty), and it is only by constantly moving Fluther out of the inner circle of conflict that O'Casey rescues him for his later role.

Fluther's initial action makes for an important first impression: he is the craftsman proud of his accomplishment: 'He has just finished the job of putting on a new lock, and, filled with satisfaction, he is opening and shutting the door, enjoying the completion of a work well done' [**Plough,** 162]. For those who have witnessed Jack Boyle fleeing from the spectre of a potential job and Seumas Shields sleeping away the shank of the day, Fluther stands in significant contrast, while for those approaching the new play without an introduction to the standard habits of the paycock, Fluther's opening conversation with Mrs Gogan serves the same function. A gossipy and ill-mannered neighbour, she avails herself of the open-door policy of Dublin tenement life to bring in a package being delivered to Nora Clitheroe. She opens the package and examines its contents, comments unfavourably on it and Nora, and goes on to gossip maliciously to Fluther about the Clitheroes. To all of which Fluther remains aloof and noncommital, a commendable refusal to join Mrs Gogan in her malice. But having failed to enlist him in a campaign of diatribe against Nora, she succeeds in convincing him that his health is seriously failing, reducing the impressionable carpenter to a state of near collapse, from which the appearance of the Covey rescues him. Behind the colloquy of Fluther and the gossip moves Uncle Peter, an excitable old man in the process of dressing himself in gorgeous finery for a parade. The Covey next engages Fluther in religious controversy, and an important change from the passive attitude with Mrs Gogan to a nearly virulent one with the atheist begins to reveal the quarrelsome figure that O'Casey postulates in the 'scene' with Yeats. Yet the real conflict with the Covey is Peter's, not Fluther's, indicating that the Covey is difficult to take and that Peter is a far more hostile customer than Fluther Good. It is the old man who is most like a paycock; O'Casey describes him as 'cocking his head in a way that suggests resentment at the presence of Fluther, who pays no attention to him, apparently, but is really furtively watching him' [**Plough**, 162]. If the 'cocked' head is not sufficient to reveal Peter's basic nature, surely his Forester's uniform is: 'green coat, gold braided; white breeches, top boots, frilled shirt. He carries the slouch hat, with the white ostrich plume, and the sword in his hands' [**Plough**, 180].⁷ (Mrs Gogan had already hinted that he was like 'something you'd pick off a Christmas Tree. When he's dhressed up in his canonicals, you'd wondher where he'd been got.' [**Plough**, 166.]) But the paycock strut in full dress is not just confined to old Peter. Mrs Gogan is quite nasty about Nora's fineries,

like the new hat in the package she brings in ('God, she's
goin' to th' divil lately for style' [**Plough, 163**]), and about
Jack Clitheroe's penchant for a Citizen Army captain's uniform: 'He was so cocksure o' being made one that he bought
a Sam Browne belt, an' was always puttin' it on an' standin'
at the door showing it off, till th' man came an' put out th'
street lamps on him. God, I think he used to bring it to bed
with him! But I'm tellin' you herself was delighted that that
cock didn't crow, for she's like a clockin' hen if he leaves
her sight for a minute.' [**Plough, 166.**] There is no overlooking O'Casey's barnyard setting, the 'cocksure' Clitheroe and
his 'clockin' hen' wife, and Nora's own denunciation of Peter
and the Covey as 'a pair o' fightin' cocks!' [**Plough, 175.**]

The basic disputants of Act One are obviously the fringe
members of the Clitheroe household, Nora's uncle Peter and
Jack's cousin, the Young Covey—the clash of opposing forces
of disrespectful Youth and cantankerous Old Age. Mrs
Gogan's potential as female guttersnipe is easily apparent,
second only to the viciousness of Bessie Burgess, whose single
appearance in the first act draws the most fire: drunk and
disorderly she pushes her way into the Clitheroe apartment,
curses Nora as a 'little over-dressed throllope' [**Plough, 178**]
(which Mrs Gogan has never dared call her to her face), and
physically attacks her—Fluther coming to Nora's rescue and
Clitheroe finally ejecting her. It is no surprise then when
the battle-lines of Act Two are drawn not only between
Peter and the Covey, but between the two harridans, residents in the same tenement, of opposing religious convictions and a matching pair of scurrilous temperaments. Jinnie
Gogan[8] and Bessie Burgess as 'fightin' cocks' outdistance the
comparatively tame men by the end of Act Two (only
Fluther and the Barman physically keeping them from
committing mayhem), establishing a species of payhen that
more than rivals the pugnaciousness of even Boyle and Joxer.
What O'Casey has succeeded in doing is pairing off Peter
and the Covey, and Mrs Burgess and Mrs Gogan, from the
complex of five potential combatants, leaving Fluther Good
isolated as an individual, a complex character on his own
without a necessary counterfoil. He has attempted to act as
peacemaker in the pub, and closes the scene by his gallantry

31

to Rosie Redmond. Where the Young Covey has displayed his prudishness by reacting in horror to the prostitute and rejecting her, Fluther has instead demonstrated his virility and chivalry, but more specifically his humane refusal to judge Rosie. As such he behaves within a tradition established by the playwright for his autobiographic hero, Johnny Casside, who in *Inishfallen* welcomes the over-eager Mrs Ballynoy[9] into his bed (under circumstances somewhat altered to reproduce the events in *The Gunman*) and in *Pictures in the Hallway* capitulates before the sexual advances of Daisy Battles.

It is in Act Three that the best elements of Fluther Good are revealed. He has spent the night searching for Nora during the holocaust of the Easter fighting, and returns 'half leading, half carrying her in' [**Plough, 219**]. This act of heroism is understated during the course of the scene. It has been anticipated by Mrs Gogan's reported dream of a dead Fluther being brought in on a stretcher 'dhressed in th' habit of Saint Francis' [**Plough, 218**]. But the entrance of the live Fluther goes unheralded, as all attention is logically focused on the grief-stricken Nora, whose distress and derangement carry the emotional burden of this scene and much of the next, until the half-unintentional sacrifice of Bessie Burgess startles the audience into a new sense of awareness. While Bessie rises meteorically to heights of greatness from the depths of her established viciousness, Fluther maintains an even level as a dependable and quietly heroic man. The progression has been a subtle one from his refusal to join Mrs Gogan in snide comments about Nora, his sheltering of Nora from Bessie's attack, his role as pacifier in the pub, and his acceptance of Rosie. There is no sudden act of self-sacrifice, but there is no wavering from a consistent policy of aid and comfort for Nora and the other unfortunates of the tenement. In contrast to the grand cockerel Peter, Fluther marches off into the fray to claim his share of the looted stuff ('to thry an' save a few things from th' burnin' buildin's' [**Plough, 226**]), and in contrast with the warrior, Capt. Brennan, he maintains his composure before the British soldiers ('Thry to keep your hands from shakin', man,' [**Plough, 248**] he advises the Irish officer). The scene with the British search party is an interesting replay of the similar situation in *The Shadow of a Gunman*, with Fluther as calm as Grigson claimed to have been. He denounces the British tommies to their faces, his exit line summarising his defiance to them: 'Jasus, you an' your guns! Leave them down, an' I'd beat th' two o' yous without sweatin'!' [**Plough, 255.**] This is the same belligerence demonstrated in the Merrion Square salon, and it certainly betrays its gutter origins. Yet there is a quality in it that we have seen O'Casey admire and second, and a touch of real pride which stems from a vital source: 'Who are you callin' a blighter to, eh?' he confronts the English sergeant, 'I'm a Dublin man, born an' bred in th' city, see?' [**Plough, 255.**]

Nor are we expected to raise much of an eyebrow at Fluther's looting during the insurrection. Although he certainly never read Proudhon or even heard of the French socialist, he would instinctively have acknowledged his concept that all private property is stolen, as much as little Johnny Casside knew enough to swipe 'a lump of bacon' and 'an egg' [**Door, 261**] knocked from a stall by a careening drunk and carry them home. Nor could the pious Mrs Casside be expected to do other than lecture him to 'never do the like again' [**Door, 264**], and then accept them into her larder without a second misgiving. Careful as he often is to respect the middle-class attitudes of his audience, O'Casey nonetheless takes several such opportunities to remind that audience that the values of the Dublin poor are inherently different from theirs—and often more logically justifiable[10].

The risk run by the playwright fascinated with the paycock creature is in creating the stereotype known as the 'stage Irishman', and O'Casey has shown himself to be aware of it and on occasion has been reminded of it. His autobiographies catalogue several such occasions. In the last volume he records the objections of an Irish Socialist who claims to know 'the Irish *lumpen-proletariat* and the Irish Working Class' [**Sunset, 319**], and in the name of both or either seems to object to O'Casey's perpetration of 'the stage Irishman' as a 'new and peculiarly unacceptable stage-Irishism' [**Sunset, 318**]. In most cases the term describes the creation of American and British playwrights, an Irish character interspersed among a cast of non-Irish, a servant or 'low fellow', often drunken, belligerant, foul-mouthed, lazy, who stands out in contrast to his non-Irish 'betters'—a contrast which serves to comment adversely on the nature of *all* Irishmen. O'Casey's paycock type, we have seen, moves freely among his fellow Irishmen: he is not singled out in every case for maximum abuse; he often has his own redeeming qualities; and he is often no worse than others, when even the best elements around him display significant flaws. Boyle is almost villainous in highlighted relief against his wife and daughter (although there is certainly no male in *Juno and the Paycock* who can afford to cast stones at him), while Juno as wife is a nag, no matter how complete her justification, and Mary's preference for Charlie Bentham over Jerry Devine betrays elements of social climbing. Bessie Burgess displays every symptom of stage-Irishism in the first half of *The Plough*, only to reveal positive characteristics so potent that the audience might well suspect that the stage Irishman is a prejudicial totem that they brought with them to the theatre rather than observed in the playwright's characterisation. Having shown that the paycock need not be exclusively masculine by ranging Bessie's claws against Mrs Gogan's fangs, O'Casey went on to inter the entire concept of any anti-Irish feelings he might be suspected of harbouring by portraying a pair of British paycocks in *Purple Dust*. And were not the British critics as incensed as the Irish critics had been? O'Casey was even accused at the time of undermining the war effort by an untimely attack on the British![11]

Yet Basil Stoke and Cyril Poges rank alongside Boyle and Joxer as the finest paycock creations in the O'Casey canon. Their haute bourgeois pomposity and chauvinistic snobbery endow them with comic possibilities that no stage Irishman could conceivably pretend to. There can be little doubt that O'Casey in *Purple Dust* is making a statement *about* the British, any more than there is that throughout his work he has been making very specific comments about the Irish— not as racial types, but as people within a certain environment, social animals with particular human problems. Long before bringing Stoke and Poges to rural Ireland, O'Casey

34

had an opportunity to present Englishmen on his stage for scrutiny, and indeed *Within the Gates* presents almost an entire cast of Britons in a London park—although he apparently was far more interested in universalising both his characters and his setting. Charlie Bentham must have appeared much too English for the Abbey Theatre audience, Boyle stating the case against him even before he appeared by referring to 'his Majesty, Bentham' [**Juno, 39**]—he clinches their suspicions by running off to England by the end of the play. The 'Visitor' in *The Silver Tassie's* war scene is a caricature of the stiff-upper-lip attitude (especially when it is demanded of others rather than of one's self) and prefigures the Stoke-Poges mentality with its panoply of easy clichés for everyday use: 'The uniform, the cause, boy, the corps,' [**Tassie, 41**] he lectures the 'crucified' Barney, on the rack for stealing a chicken; the Staff Wallah in the same scene is an easily recognised caricature of the military ('Order to take effect from 6 a.m. following morning of date received' [**Tassie, 52**]), but the Visitor represents something more pervasive than that, as seen by his attire, 'semi-civilian, semi-military' [**Tassie, 40**].

The British superiors in *The Tassie* are intended as satiric figures, but Stoke and Poges are characters in a 'wayward comedy' and are far more involved and involuted. The ways of approaching their absurd situation are numerous: city slickers mired in the wilds of the Irish countryside; stodgy middle-aged men, prematurely aged, sipping from a bitter Fountain of Youth, pretending that the taste is sweet and waiting for the miraculous effect; former conquerors returning to the scenes of their exploitation as visitors without the least sense of guilt or awareness of the incongruity. These three aspects are ever-present in the play, operating against the backdrop of Thomas Gray's 'Elegy Written in a Country Churchyard', which presumably takes place in the churchyard of St Giles in Stoke Poges, Buckinghamshire, England. The combined tagname of the two Englishmen (making an interchangeable entity of their individual personalities) suggests the Gray poem, and the series of events in *Purple Dust* corroborate our suspicion that their lives are a burlesque, 'Far from the madding crowd's ignoble strife'.

The initial appearance of the English gentry and their Irish mistresses is a frolicsome song-and-dance pæan to the countryside:

> Rural scenes are now our joy:
> Farmer's boy,
> Milkmaid coy,
> Each like a newly-painted toy,
> In the bosky countrie!—[Dust, 7]

but the beginning of Act Two affords a rude awakening for Stoke and Poges. Instead of Gray's 'breezy call of incense-breathing morn', the Englishmen find themselves cold and stiff on their mattresses on the floor: 'Bitter, bitter!' complains Basil, 'What would I not give now for a cosy flat; a cosier bed; and a blazing hot-water bottle!' [Dust, 49.] 'The cock's shrill clarion' and the 'moping owl' receive little welcome from the newly ruralised gentlemen: 'Damn that cock and cuckoo! Did you hear that cock crowing, Basil, and the cuckoo calling?'[Dust, 48.] These country sounds which 'rouse them from their lowly bed' receive an equally unenthusiastic response from Stoke: 'Deafening, aren't they! And the owls, too, all the night. Jungle noises!' [Dust, 48.] Neither mistress is true to Gray's description of farm women ('the busy housewife ply her evening care'), but they dash about enjoying their luxuries and carefree existences, mocking the ineffectual gentlemen. And a far cry from the 'lowing herd' that 'winds slowly o'er the lea' is the cow that confronts them in their living room, whom they mistake for a bull, are in terror of, and finally triumph over (Stoke shoots the harmless beast). A parody of the country folk that Gray celebrated, Poges and Stoke display neither 'useful toil' nor 'homely joys', but can be best appreciated juxtaposed against the famous quatrain from the 'Elegy':

> The boast of heraldry, the pomp of pow'r,
> And all that beauty, all that wealth e'er gave,
> Awaits alike th' inevitable hour.
> The paths of glory lead but to the grave.

If the major comic thrust of the play exists in the incongruity of urban gentry playing country squire, its basic structure exists in the Stoke-Poges character, the paycock approach to life in general. Their naive misconception about the farm is rather pathetic and fairly human (few of the tenement Dubliners we have met in O'Casey's earlier plays would have fared much better down on the farm), but selfishness, vanity, inflated egos, self-glorified ignorance, and class superiority destroy any chance that they would have had of soliciting audience sympathy.[12] In the main, Cyril Poges is intended as the more reprehensible, the more insufferable paycock of the two, but the Boyle-Joxer relationship is nonetheless apparent, and both can claim the paycock title with ease. The Joxerian Stoke, however, is a fully developed character, not merely a foxy sycophant. At thirty he is much younger than his companion (he is Donal Davoren's age, and his amorous connection with the beautiful Avril is easier to accept than that of Poges—who is sixty-five, Sylvester Heegan's age and older than Boyle—with Souhaun, the 'handsome girl' of thirty-three). O'Casey tells us little about him in those usually devastating descriptions available to the reader and as instructions to the actor,[13] except that he has a 'rather gloomy face which he thinks betokens dignity, made gloomier still by believing that he is something of a philosopher' [Dust, 6]. The 'half-bald head' and 'large horn-rimmed glasses' [Dust, 6] do not promise much. Like Joxer he is the victim of the more wolfish character, who attacks him where he is most vulnerable and succeeds in stripping him of his most important defence. What Souhaun describes as 'a little friendly discussion about a common country flower' [Dust, 27] (but is regarded by Basil as a philosophic examination of essentials) elicits Poges's denunciation of him as a 'half-educated fool!' [Dust, 26]. Laying claim to the knowledge of Hume, Spinoza, Aristotle, Locke, Bacon, Plato, Socrates, and Kant, among others' [Dust, 27], Basil is a parody of the 'intellectual' prig (even Seumas Shields seems to have more real information at his command, without claiming to be a philosopher):

If we take the primrose, however, into our synthetical consideration, as a whole, or, *a priori*, as a part, with the rest of the whole of natural objects or phenomena, then

there is, or may be, or can be a possibility of thinking of
the flower as of above the status, or substance, or quality of
a fragment; and, consequently, correlating it with the
whole, so that, to a rational thinker, or logical mind, the
simple primrose is, or may become, what we may venture
to call a universal. [**Dust, 25.**]

The entire complex is there: the jargon and inflated vocabu-
lary; an attitude of condescension; the inflation of a pedes-
trian molehill into a pedantic mountain; a complete lack of
levity; unnecessary qualifications and repetitions—Basil
stands convicted by his own performance as a pompous ass.

It should have taken very little effort on Poges's part to
demolish him, and only a greater snob would fail to realise
that Stoke has publicly made himself sound absurd. Both
Avril and Souhaun see through him easily ('Basil is only trying to share his great knowledge with us,' his mistress comments 'ironically' [**Dust, 27**]; 'We must remember that Basil
passed through Oxford,' [**Dust, 27**] her friend adds, equally
arch), but Cyril Poges rushes in with bullish furore. The
'half-educated fool' has called him an 'ignorant man' [**Dust,
27**] and he is sufficiently incensed to prove to all that he is
even worse than that: 'here I am today, a money'd man,' he
boasts in non-sequitur, 'able to say to almost any man, come,
and he cometh, and to almost any other man, go, and he
goeth—and quick too; able to shake hands with lords and
earls, and call them by their Christian names.' [**Dust, 27.**]
Poges falls back on the self-defence of the self-made man of
wealth: accused of ignorance he illogically counters with
evidence of his affluence and power. And 'without an in-
herited penny to help' [**Dust, 27**], he adds, as a direct slap at
Basil, 'And I never passed through Oxford!' [**Dust, 28.**] The
usual last recourse—he makes a virtue of what he is most
ashamed of. Basil Stoke's paycockery is based pathetically on
a single flaw in his character; Cyril Poges's is all-pervasive
and malignant.

The Poges-Stoke duo dominates the action of the play to a
greater extent than the Paycock and his butty, whose entire
conflict provided only a secondary level of plot to the serious
state of affairs involving Juno, Mary and Johnny. Cyril and

Basil are at the forefront of the *Purple Dust* comedy, to which subsidiary characters add other comic effects (Barney, Cloyne, the two workmen, Cornelius, the Canon, the post-master), with a romantic subplot involving Avril and Souhaun and their Irish lovers. O'Casey found himself with ample room in which to develop a good number of possibilities in his British variants of the familiar paycock. Basil is far more complex than Joxer, not as easily recognisable from the beginning by an exaggerated gesture or a pet phrase: he has an existence independent of Cyril Poges, while Joxer has none except in conflict with the Captain. He is younger and in apparent possession of the most attractive female; he attempts to lord it over the older and stuffier Cyril with his Oxford education; he gallops off on horseback and has his great drop; he has the heroic distinction of shooting the dangerous cow; but he dwindles into irrelevance in the final act, leaving the major comic absurdities to Poges and his lovely mistress to O'Killigain. Yet two of his courses of action (as equestrian and as big game hunter) have provided the hilarious highlights with which the first two acts conclude.

At his worst Basil Stoke manages to injure only himself; he never quite shares with Donal Davoren the distinction of accurately recognising himself as a poltroon—at his best he senses the doom awaiting them and the hopelessness of their situation. Although he mocked the danger of the Irish workmen running off with the women ('Beware the sound of a galloping horse!' [**Dust**, 109]) he soon changes his tune and announces, 'We're lost!' [**Dust**, 116.] Poges remains intrepid to the end. He can never for a moment believe that his money and authority can seriously be questioned and will not prevail against any circumstance. His outward manifestations of paycockism are obvious enough: he dances in with the others, a pig emblazoned on his smock; he next appears carrying a portrait of himself (as does Basil—they are still birds of a feather at this early instance in the play); pours forth a wealth of misinformation throughout, cocksure that he is right; assumes others are inferior to him, especially the Irish, only respecting those who agree with him and only when they *do* agree with him; and bristles with annoyance when he cannot have what suits his convenience, like a business call through to London when he wants it. All these are merely instances from the opening act; he compounds them as the play progresses. His disdain for those who serve him and work for him, and the Irish in general, testifies to his class snobbery and his chauvinism, but his attempt to humiliate even his friend and his high-handed treatment of Souhaun put him beyond the pale. He does not strut like Boyle for the applause from others; even this awareness that there are others outside of himself is missing. Instead he moves about relentlessly, always assuming that anyone in his path will quickly get out of his way. He expects others to supply a piece of information ('what was his name?' [**Dust,** 41]) and when the answer is incorrect, he is contemptuous, although he does not know either. He insists that O'Killigain is intelligent when he assumes that O'Killigain will agree with him, but is annoyed when he does not. When Boyle is guilty of fawning upon those from whom he expects to profit, we recognise the basic hypocrisy. But only Canon Chreehewel,[14] absurdly enough, commands that sort of response from Cyril Poges; all others he treats as inferiors, his overweening arrogance being far more lethal than Boyle's hypocrisy. When Basil is brought in from his fall, unsympathetic Cyril declaims without a trace of irony: 'I hope you realise the sterling trouble you give people by your damned refusal to recognise your limitations!' [**Dust,** 44.]

Having seen this much of Cyril's behaviour, we can glance back at O'Casey's initial description of him in order to realise how fully the character lives the part assigned to him by the author. This stage direction alone affords a maximum definition of the most pernicious kind of paycock, one that has the power to destroy more than just his own life and that of his family:

> He has a fussy manner, all business over little things; wants his own way at all times; and persuades himself that whatever he thinks of doing must be for the best, and expects everyone else to agree with him. He is apt to lose his temper easily, and to shout in the belief that that is the only way to make other people fall in with his opin-

ions. He has now persuaded himself that in the country peace and goodwill are to be found; and expects that everyone else should find them there too. [Dust, 6.]

O'Casey is rarely vindictive toward any of his characters, and demonstrates frequently a willingness to tolerate most elements of individual idiosyncrasy, bending over backward to disclose human traits in the most despicable, and personal justifications for all unacceptable actions. Whether Poges knows the real aesthetic value of a quattrocento bureau or not, we cannot but commiserate as he watches it being mistreated by the workmen (see Destructive Desmond at work in the Auden-Isherwood play, *The Dog Beneath the Skin*); and few of us are sufficiently detached from our twentieth-century lives not to expect all-night telephone service as an existing fact. Poges is being 'put upon' by the local Irish of that Clune na Geera community of 'peace and goodwill'. But although he expects peace and goodwill from others, he never displays any towards anyone else.

A small-scale mirror of the two grandiose British paycocks can be seen in the two Irish workmen who provide many of the minor irritations visited upon Cyril Poges. O'Casey merely labels them as first and third workmen (the second is Philib O'Dempsey, a decidedly important figure in the play and worthy of a named position in the *Dramatis Personae*). Strictly figures of Joxerian fun, they passively comply with every wish of their employers, but never manage to do anything right. Their primary purpose is to feather their own nest, and since the Englishmen seem foolishly intent upon wasting their money on a worthless wreck of an Irish country house, the workmen are willing to let some of the squandered cash come their way. They are true country bumpkins with no perceptible aesthetic sense, and thus serve as ideal complements of the pretentious British, whose aesthetics were purchased on the commercial market. (Balanced between these two pairs are O'Killigain and O'Dempsey, whose values become an established reality in *Purple Dust*, proving victorious when Avril and Souhaun are won over to them.) Since Poges and Stoke are there to be swindled, the workmen see no reason that they should not

41

profit: they serve as middle-men for entrepreneurs offering to sell hens and cows to the newly countrified squires, and although their motives are never revealed as such, there is no doubt in the reader's mind that there is nothing but unscrupulous financial self-interest involved. As servants they display no loyalty to their masters, but it takes no time at all for the reader to become aware that O'Casey associates no positive value to any such display of the loyalty of servitude. The O'Casey who exonerates Johnny Casside for stealing bacon and an egg has no intention of expecting anyone stealing from Poges and Stoke to stand trial.

In many ways the rural paycock is only a country cousin of the urban variety of the species, but certain distinctions in breed will become apparent. The shift from the Dublin tenements to the Irish countryside was officially inaugurated with the composition of *Purple Dust*, by which time O'Casey had left the urban centres of Dublin and London for the closer proximity to nature found near Totnes in Devon. Several earlier one-act plays, however, had already shifted the O'Casey scene across rivers and into trees, the very early 'Kathleen Listens In' and the later 'The End of the Beginning'. The latter in particular contains a pair of bucolic paycocks worth examining; their spoonerised names, Barry Derrill and Darry Berrill, alone are indicative of the juxtaposed paycocks whose adherence of the Tweedledum-Tweedledee principle disallows any claim they may have to individuality. Siamese twins, they struggle to break whatever bonds join them—unaware that they share vital organs that cannot be halved without destroying both; or insist upon being the sole claimant of that organ. (Like Humpty Dumpty, Seumas Shields and Fluther Good are precariously perched and vulnerable to a 'great fall', but they at least preserve a measure of singularity and self-reliance, while the paired paycocks destroy themselves and each other.) In this particular case the tangible demarcation (like the age gaps between Peter and the Covey, Poges and Stoke) is physical dimension: Barry is 'thin' and Darry is 'stocky ... with a pretty big belly' [**End**, 264]. In temperament there is a second distinction, Barry 'easy-going' [**End**, 264], Darry 'obstinate'. Darry in fact has many of the earmarks of Captain

Boyle, although Barry as foil falls far short of Joxer. Bad-tempered, hypocritical and lazy, the former in this case adds vanity to his vices, but is most easily categorised by his tendency to shift the blame to others—with his butty as the pathetic victim of his abuse. The comedy is a slight one, and the mildly Joxerian Barry, hardly a significant character at all, allows himself to be used, fighting back only feebly. He fawns on his bullying companion almost masochistically, lacking both Joxer's foxiness and his viciousness. He would gladly shift the blame on others when caught (and a very real fraction of the destruction in the Derrill household is actually the smaller man's fault), but he has no skill at dissembling, lacks the courage to brazen things out, and finds himself blamed instead for more than his share. 'The End of the Beginning', like the urban 'A Pound on Demand', is a characteristically O'Caseyan low comedy, sketch and raw material for the more complex comic elements of many of his best plays.

Among the rural Irish paycocks, Feelim O'Morrigun stands out as one of the most complex of O'Casey's characters, a worthy successor to Fluther Good. Although *Oak Leaves and Lavender* remains one of O'Casey's most obviously propagandist works, Feelim's subtleties are appreciable. In many ways this drama of World War Two is a reverse image of the ill-timed *Purple Dust*, the 1940 comedy that so offended the British, coming as it did at the darkest hours of the Battle of Britain. Not that O'Casey had any remorse about his slam at the heavy-booted British autocrats tromping through rural Ireland, but in his continued response to the political world around him the playwright set out to record the anti-Nazi sentiment he felt during the war, setting his scene in England, where he lived throughout the war period. Unlike *Within the Gates*, a previous play with an English locale, *Oak Leaves and Lavender* is a play *specifically* about Great Britain, the country, its heritage, its politics and its people. But in this otherwise exclusively British milieu O'Casey places no less than three Irishmen, in much the same way as Poges and Stoke found themselves quite volitionally in Ireland in the previous play. Feelim, the central focus of the play, has answered an advertisement for a butler's position in the Hatherleigh manor, and here he is performing this function as well as duties added on by the war effort. (His son Drishogue has come over with him, intent on joining the Royal Air Force; and a third Irishman, a minor character, a foreman who 'speaks with an Irish accent' [Oak, 89], appears in the third act to serve an important function, but his presence as an Irishman goes without comment.) In his creation of all three of these Celts among the Sassenachs, particularly Feelim, O'Casey has a very specific purpose: British landowners in Ireland are familiar figures (although O'Casey is making a larger point in timing their presence almost two decades after Irish independence), but Irish volunteers fighting in Britain's war against Nazi Germany, especially with Eire neutral, are not so well known. And O'Casey focuses significantly on the Irish airman.

It is as an extension of Fluther Good that Feelim O'Morrigun is most important, the Fluther that went on to obsess his creator even after his personal drama during the Easter Uprising ran its course in *The Plough and the Stars*. Several paycockish traits taint Feelim during the first act (inviting our careful scrutiny as he moves through the events of *Oak Leaves and Lavender*), but they are countermanded by some of those elements which served to redeem Fluther for us. O'Casey, who has so often been abundantly liberal with his thumbnail descriptions of his people in opening stage directions, is rather sparse in his depiction of the Irish butler: aside from his physical appearance, we are only allowed to know that he is 'as cunning as a fox (except when he is in a temper)' [Oak, 12]. He is quick to anger over the clumsiness of others; he puritanically clicks his tongue when Jennie sings a ballad that is a bit bawdy, and voices a rather conventional attitude in his attempt to dissuade her from her interest in Dame Hatherleigh's son. He displays an unmanly fear in his acceptance of the superstition that the manorhouse is haunted (although even the sceptics in the audience will have to attest that the ghosts here are as real as those in *Hamlet* and *Macbeth*, and that omens loom as large as in *Julius Caesar*). Like Captain Boyle he pretends to a nautical past: 'I happened across an English

44

paper advertising for a butler in a house of six servants: so, fearing there wasn't too much to be done, I replied, sayin' I was fully qualified, though all my credentials went down in a torpedoed ship.' [Oak, 18.] Feelim, however, is quick to disengage himself from his practical lie, refusing to lie either to himself or to Monica. Through the first act, then, these impressions accumulate, nagging reminders of the paycock personality, but so well toned down as to suggest the sort of balanced technique used in creating Fluther. The question that evolves from this comparison is whether Feelim transcends Fluther's limitations, whether O'Casey can find anything more in his typical, fallible Irishman at the later instance.

The same elements which were perceptibly petty in other paycocks are present in Feelim, and yet O'Casey presents them at all times at a sufficient remove from pettiness to keep Feelim fairly untouched. We have seen him find fault with the clumsiness of others (the play opens with reports of Tom's injury and Mary's, and off-stage we hear the resounding crash of still a third minor mishap). The paycock's scorn for such human frailty usually is followed by his own blunder (the pot-kettle comparison so prevalent in 'The End of the Beginning') but not so with Feelim. He works efficiently and well throughout the play, and even his manipulation of the meter-reading comes off without reflecting adversely upon him (unlike the Simon-Sylvester fiasco with the telephone in *The Tassie*). Two crucial tests in Act One establish Feelim's claim to being something better than a paycock: Mrs Watchit's tealess tea and Dame Hatherleigh outlining her project for excavating the Ark of the Covenant from the Hill of Tara. In the first we have that same change of attitude which brands the mercurial paycock as supremely hypocritical: to Feelim Mrs Watchit is 'efficient as she is considerate' [Oak, 30] for bringing him tea—he is so effusive with praise that his reversal is all the more hilarious. When all that pours from the teapot is hot water, Feelim spares no invective; his erstwhile benefactress is now 'an old fool', a 'very pest in the place', and even suspected of 'gallivantin' after soldiers' [Oak, 30]. His powers of exaggeration would do any paycock proud as he suspects a serious danger to the

45

war effort in her inefficiency, enough to cause threatening revolution 'all over the world!' [**Oak, 32**]. Yet despite the excess of his vituperation, Feelim is justifiably angered by an oversight on Mrs Watchit's part, while he himself seems to function well under an entanglement of complicated red tape. His handling of Dame Hatherleigh wins for him a real vote of confidence: his delicate treatment of the rather dotty woman is fully compassionate. We had seen his fatherly feelings toward Monica Penrhyn early in the scene: her opening line ('I wish you were my dad, instead of my own') was immediate evidence that Feelim would never descend in our estimaton to the level of a Captain Boyle who cursed both his unfortunate son and daughter. But Monica is a lovely young girl with a strong affection for him, while the dotty Dame is little more than a burden. Yet Feelim bends over backward to soothe her troubled mind, assuring her that both her son and her husband will return safely from the war, and putting up with her endless nonsense about British Israelites and the excavation of the Ark, despite the obvious irritation of being completely unsure about what is expected from him in his half of their dialogue.

The situation as O'Casey arranges it is suitable for pathos, and the playwright could have limited the exchange to just that, yet Feelim, playing the conversation by ear and only able to 'divine' the right responses to the Dame's expectations, produces a colloquy as rich for its humour as it is for pathos. A lesser man would have been nettled for being so disadvantaged: Boyle's attempt to keep up with Bentham's occultism produced a strained and forced politeness because of the anticipated legacy. Feelim, however, allows himself to look foolish rather than hurt the pathetic woman's feelings. It is only when she is out of earshot that he gives vent to his invective: 'Didja hear that rigamarole! Dig out Tara, she says, to find th' Ark of the Covenant. Think of your sthrong connection, says she, with the lost Ten Thribes. Abraham, Isaac, an' Jacob, I know, were three of them, but th' names of th' others has escaped me memory.' [**Oak, 41.**] Scant knowledge—and most of that wrong—is typical enough of the paycock; admitting to ignorance definitely recommends Feelim O'Morrigun.

46

Feelim emerges from the first act with mixed reviews, and the author's designation of him as cunning remains enigmatic. Surely Monica and Jennie exhibit far more zest for natural living (a key O'Casey attribute) than the forty-five-year-old butler, while the young Drishogue bests his father in political and intellectual sophistication. Fluther Good had no such competition: compared to Drishogue, Jack Clitheroe is vain and cloddish, while the Covey is dogmatically opinionated; compared to Monica, Nora is a frivolous clothes-horse, a Nora who deserves her doll's-house existence. While Feelim is obviously 'God-fearing' (meant here quite literally, as distinct from 'religious'), Drishogue displays a suavely non-commital attitude toward Final Things. Compare Feelim's 'Things happen when th' world turns from God' [Oak, 48] with his son's comment, 'If death be the end, then there is nothing; if it be but a passage from one place to another, then we shall mingle with a great, gay crowd!' [Oak, 29.] Like Shields and Good (and even Boyle), O'Morrigun is made to carry the uncomfortable burden of Irish Catholicism on his weak shoulders. But *Oak Leaves* was not intended as a crucible in which to stir up the religious question—*Within the Gates* was a more suitable receptacle, and *Cock-a-Doodle Dandy* would later provide O'Casey with another one; it is political propaganda that is paramount here, and the other controversy is stalemated with a deft statement by Drishogue: 'In this fight, Edgar, righteousness and war have kissed each other: Christ, Mahomet, Confucius, and Buddha are one.' [Oak, 29.] And the political clash brings Feelim head-on into conflict with his hero son. Whereas cynical Edgar is willing to allow Drishogue his Communism, traditionalistic Feelim is not, and delights in Deeda Tutting's condemnation of Communist Russia. But O'Casey manages to rescue both Feelim and the U.S.S.R. before the first act is over, awarding Drishogue complete victory over Mrs Tutting, with Feelim handing over the prize. Even though he echoed with enthusiasm everything the anti-Communist uttered, Feelim finally is forced to turn against her when her vicious irascibility lacerates her ally with her enemy: the anti-Communist is so personally obnoxious that Feelim runs afoul of her tongue, severing their

47

entente. Drishogue coolly carries the day, and Feelim finds himself on the winning side just in time.

If Feelim is too moralistic for O'Casey's taste, then Act Two introduces the British Puritan, Feelim's local counterpart, in the person of Father Penrhyn. They square off at each other immediately since Drishogue O'Morrigun is involved with Monica Penrhyn, and Feelim's reaction to Penrhyn's 'Why don't 'ee keep your son fr'm molestin' me daughter?' [Oak, 65] is simply, 'Why don't 'ee keep your daughter from molestin' me son?' [Oak, 66.] But the Englishman soon shows himself to be the surlier, the more priggish and more irritable of the two, so that Feelim comments when he sees the farmer resort to whisky, 'A lot of it, maybe, 'ill make you a little reasonable.' [Oak, 66.] Yet little else in the second act contributes to advancing the balance of positive and negative qualities in the potential paycock. He is justifiably angry at those who want to save their own necks and abandon Britain during the war for safety in America, as well as defensive about his non-combatant aspects as an Irishman whose country abstains from the war. He continues to disapprove of Drishogue's alliance with Monica, despite his affection for both of them, and remains a solid source of strength and comfort for Dame Hatherleigh, although he misses her subtly hidden announcement of the death of her husband in combat. It is clear that the playwright is saving Feelim for a decisive performance in the final act.

At several junctures in Act Three Feelim begins to show his real mettle. The scene opens with his usual kindness and consideration for Dame Hatherleigh, now quite distracted with suppressed grief. But he soon finds himself in a short exchange with his fellow Irishman, the factory foreman. The foreman bristles at Feelim's slur at 'devalerian authoritarianism', but Feelim, despite his own allegiance to the Catholic Church, launches an attack on the new Irish theocracy that has the true O'Casey accent to it: 'Turnin' th' poor people into shock brigades of confraternities an' holy sight-seein' sodalities, so that they're numb with kneelin', an' hoarse with th' dint of recitin' litany an' prayer!' [Oak, 91.] It is this sort of set speech indicative of the character coming into his own and amassing a certain degree of stature that demon-

48

strates the author's specific approval. Even a bit of gallant blarney during the feverish activity of the war effort is to Feelim's credit, as he tries to charm the Land Girls out of their animosity for the conscientious objector: 'If I told yous what I think yous are, it's not diggin' th' land yous would be, but sportin' about in the whitest o' linen an' gayest of silks, with young an' handsome gallants festooned with ordhers, an' swords danglin' from their hips, cravin' a dance in a lighted hall, or a long kiss outside, under a tree, an' the twilight fallin'!' [Oak, 92.] This piece of pleasant poetry is spoken between two fits of Feelim's justified indignation, the joust with the Irish foreman and the confrontation with Pobjoy, the 'conchie', in which the Irishman reads the Englishman a lesson in English history, citing Milton's birth-place and Nelson's deeds. As the author's spokesman Feelim is given the ticklish job of defending war against Pobjoy's pacifism, much like Drishogue having to defend the Soviet Union against Mrs Tutting's Red-baiting. Feelim handles the assignment with logic and brilliance, especially in his reply to Pobjoy's definitive statement, 'I don't believe in violence': 'Neither do I; but life is full of violence, and we're in the middle of life. Birth is noisy, and death isn't a quiet thing. (*Getting eloquent.*) There's violence in fire, wind, and water; in th' blast that brings a well to being; in the plough that cleaves th' ground; there is violence even in th' push that sends the leaves fluttering to the ground in the autumn; man alive, there's violence in th' struggle that gets me up in th' morning!' [Oak, 94.] There is no mistaking the choice English in Feelim's speech, and certainly no mistaking O'Casey's stage direction. And to Pobjoy's 'Let them who take the sword perish by it,' Feelim retorts: 'Thousands of children who never took the sword perished by it because we took it into our hands a little late.' [Oak, 96.]

There is no Drishogue in Act Three to carry the author's point of view. News of his death, and that of Edgar and Jennie as well, provide the dramatic moments of the act, and Feelim bears the full brunt throughout. His eloquent justification of the war also includes defending the Irish against the Old Woman's charges of cowardice, and Feelim is very much up to it, citing Irish participation in centuries

49

of England's wars. Unlike the loud-mouthed paycock he is a mine of correct information, and even his temper, which brought him dangerously close to disaster, is effectively channelled in his rational anger. News of his son's death stuns him momentarily (O'Casey describes his reaction as being 'as if in a stupor' [Oak, 105]), but he recovers quickly. 'Yous are askin' me silently what'll I do now,' he comments, 'an' will I go back to where I came from?' [Oak, 106.] A return to de Valera's theocracy is out of the question for Feelim, and instead he pledges to take his son's place in the conflict: 'Here on this spot, at this moment, Feelim O'Morrigun takes up th' fight where Drishogue laid it down!' [Oak, 107.] The channelled anger is heard in his cry, 'Hearts of steel, well tempered with hate, is what we are today—hearts of steel! Hearts of oak don't last; so hearts of steel we are!' [Oak, 106–7]—an important echo of the Mrs Tancred–Mrs Boyle prayer in *Juno*: 'Sacred Heart o' Jesus, take away our hearts o' stone, and give us hearts o' flesh! Take away this murdherin' hate, an' give us Thine own eternal love!'[15] [*Juno*, 87.] There is a significant change from 'murdherin' hate' to Feelim's concept of 'well tempered with hate'.

Yet the elevation of Feelim O'Morrigun as an active participant in the anti-fascist war does not make him O'Casey's ideal Irishman. Feelim's last piece of stage business lessens the positive effect and reminds us that no miracle has taken place, that Feelim is no Drishogue, that idealistic Communist with an overwhelming zest for life. Monica's 'good news' that she carries Drishogue's child shocks the incipient grandfather: 'Oh! that was wrong of him!' [Oak, 107] he contends ('his puritan nature asserting itself' [Oak, 107] O'Casey comments editorially in the stage direction). But Monica angrily counters with the piece of information that playwrights have so often dragged in at a play's end to rescue the reputation of the lovers from the puritanical ire of the audience ('we were married a month ago at a registry office' [Oak, 107]). What should make everything acceptable again and rescue the concept of the 'zest for life' from immorality has no impact, however, on the Catholic Feelim: 'Woman, woman, that isn't anythin' in th' nature of a marriage at all.' [Oak, 107.] Nonetheless, Feelim O'Morrigun is very much a redeemed paycock in the line of Seumas Shields and Fluther Good, and as much an advance from Fluther as Fluther was from Seumas. He will never win the hearts of an audience to the extent that Fluther Good does (any more than *Oak Leaves and Lavender* will ever be considered as good a play as *The Plough and the Stars*), but at the later date Sean O'Casey went as far with the type as he could towards moulding the best elements of the Irish character from the clay that so often produced the most worthless of paycocks.

Such worthlessness has often been perceptible in a disinclination to work, the first noticeable characteristic of Captain Boyle with mythical pains, Seumas Shields sleeping until noon, and the two workmen in *Purple Dust* dragging their feet, if not actually sabotaging the work on the manor-house. In contrast a man like Fluther takes pride in his craft and Feelim outdoes everyone with his industriousness. Yet hard work does not redeem Aloysius, the central character of 'Hall of Healing',[16] one of O'Casey's most vicious and petty paycocks. There is nothing redeemable about him (despite his renditions of 'The Rose of Tralee'[17] at the beginning and end): Aloysius does not even strut well, but shuffles and glides across the clinic floor. He rules his domain like a tinhorn tyrant, bullying and browbeating the already 'defeated' poor who obsequiously present themselves for his abuse, while bootlicking and kowtowing to the doctor who is his superior. He is despicable in both roles and is easily comprehensible as the coward-bully who so often is seen as overseer, strawboss, foreman[18]—the small man who has been invested with a modicum of authority and power. That most pathetic creature, the Old Woman of eighty, fails to move him to pity, and he pushes her back out into the cold, maintaining the strict letter of the law regarding clinic hours. Nonetheless he ironically fails to please the dyspeptic doctor who abuses him as much as he abused the Old Woman and other unfortunates. (The one strain of comedy in this 'Sincerious Farce' [**Hall**, 233] is derived from Aloysius's frantic inability ever to do the right thing when observed by his superior, despite the extraordinary zeal with which he undertakes his duties as dispensary watchdog.) He cites the usual authority to justify his cruelty: 'I'd like to know how we'd fare without th' regulations' [**Hall**, 244]; he bullies the weak but steers away from confrontation with anyone who stands up to him, as Red Muffler does at first; he lacks even a glimmer of insight into himself, protesting vehemently when the doctor accuses him of gossiping: 'Gossip, is it? Me gossip? An' on duty? Aw', never!'; and he is of course invincible in his ignorance, handing out diagnoses and medical advice to the patients. But most characteristic is his religious unction, which has given him the sobriquet of 'Alleluia'—one that he even applies to himself. Alleluia is at his lowest when he waylays the retreating patients, particularly the small boy who only has twopence left, for donations: 'Remember th' Holy Souls. Put one o' th' pennies on th' card for th' Holy Souls.' [**Hall**, 266.]

The 'Hall of Healing' marks one of the few instances during the last twenty years of Sean O'Casey's career in which he returned to the Dublin scene for the setting of a play, and a scene as he remembered it from the past. He had already handled the immediate experience in the first volume of the autobiographies, in a chapter coincidentally entitled 'The Hill of Healing', as well as one called 'Pain Parades Again'. In the latter we find the germinal incident of the one-act play, when Mrs Casside 'hurried to the dispensary where the porter told her that her sick boy alone in his bed 'ud have to take his chance, and hurry or no hurry, she'd have to take her turn with the rest of the people; and that neither he nor the doctor was at the hasty beck and call of those entitled to Poor Law Dispensary relief' [**Door**, 186–7]. In the last autobiographic volume the author expresses his dismay at realising that such dispensaries had hardly changed during the fifty years between this childhood event and the writing of 'The Hall', so that what was intended as another 'swift glance back' remained ironically contemporary.[19]

Except for 'The Hall' all of the plays within those last two decades were concerned with penetrating glances across the Irish sea into the countryside of the native land from which he remained a self-exile. That he chose rural Ireland may seem strange for the former Dubliner, yet after *Oak Leaves* he produced seven plays of varying lengths about the rural

52

Irish, anticipated by the workingmen of Clune na Geera. Many of these later plays examine a new breed of Gaelic paycock, the newly rich landowners and village businessmen of de Valera's Erin. Michael Marthraun and Sailor Mahan of *Cock-a-Doodle Dandy* represent the former and latter respectively, one generation and several Irish miles removed from Boyle and Daly. Their peasant and proletarian roots are discernible in O'Casey's listing of 'Characters in the Play': MICHAEL MARTHRAUN, a small farmer, now the owner of a lucrative bog'; 'SAILOR MAHAN, once a sailor, now the owner of a fleet of lorries carrying turf from bog to town' [**Cock,** 119]. Although detached from tenement Dublin and carrying the full weight of their own individualities as characters, they invite comparison with the paycocks of *Juno* to so specific a degree that one can surmise that the playwright's intention was to evoke such a recollection.

Let us assume a Jack Boyle whose legacy did *not* fall through, whose new-found allegiance to the Father Farrells of the Church had inaugurated him into the Knights of St Columbanus, and whose wealth and prestige have made him cock-of-the-walk in what the Porter describes as a 'god-for-saken hole' in the country, with his name now 'havin' Councillor at his head an' Jay Pee at his tail' [**Cock,** 166]. There are refinements, to be sure, but he is just as arrogant with just as little basis for it; the new clothes made by Needle Nugent have given way to his present costume of 'blackish tweed', set off by a 'heavy gold chain . . . across his waistcoat', a 'wide-leafed collar, under which a prim black bow is tied' [**Cock,** 122], but now he yearns for even finer adornings in a 'brand new tall-hat that Mr Marthraun bought to wear, goin' with the Mayor to greet His Brightness, th' President of Eire' [**Cock,** 144].[20] His rejection of his daughter Loreleen parallels Boyle's castigation of Mary, and by the end of *Cock-a-Doodle Dandy* both his daughter and his wife follow the example of Mary and Juno and walk out on him; Marthraun's sober statement, 'I've no one left to me but th' Son o' God' [**Cock,** 221] is an ironic change from Boyle's drunken comment on the world in 'a terrible state o' chassis' [**Juno,** 89]. And throughout the play Sailor Mahan's string

53

of nautical metaphors ties in with Captain Boyle's spurious career on the high seas.

Yet the relationship between Marthraun and his 'joxer' is significantly different from that in *Juno*, although their function in the play is essentially the same. Like Boyle and Daly they are not the people who matter, although they make a great deal of noise and attract attention to themselves, unaware of their relative insignificance. Loreleen, Lorna, Marion, and Robin Adair are affected by the events of *Cock-a-Doodle Dandy* and act upon those events, while Mahan makes a gesture towards action and immediately retreats into hiding, and Marthraun, reacting only passively, is merely abandoned. They are creatures of sound and fury, very much full of themselves, but signify nothing—in true paycock fashion. Marthraun's fury is louder than Boyle's by dint of his exalted position: he is unafraid of his wife, and is well established as lord of the manor; Father Domineer is his cohort, rather than a meddling priest who may disturb his status quo by finding him a job. Freed from the fears of the tenement rat he feels secure in his position, making his fall all the more important to the reader. The bourgeois paycock falls from a higher ledge than his lower-class counterpart, and we are given a clearer insight into his awareness of that fall (drunken Boyle is sheltered from a full understanding of what has happened to him and Seumas Shields is unaffected by the Auxies' raid). Like Poges, but to an even greater extent, Marthraun is shown a clear glimpse of the handwriting on the wall.

Both Marthraun and Mahan are sketched with less acid than the paycocks of *Juno*: it is not the innate viciousness or pettiness of their personalities that justifies their fall, but their conscious acceptance of the status quo of their society. Boyle is a victimiser because he feels himself a victim; Joxer is vindictive because he has to grovel for what he can get. Marthraun and Mahan comfortably sit back and enjoy their security and wealth, engaging in their gentleman's dispute over business, a matter of a mere two shillings that will mean very little one way or the other to either of them. They both engage in their haggling with practised ease, like Conroy in 'Time to Go', 'farmer owner of a hundred and fifty acres' [**Time, 260**], who is attempting to swindle Cousins, 'farmer owner of twenty acres'. Yet, although Marthraun is a fairly passive agent in the events of the drama, he is swept aside by the forces of change represented by the three women of his household and the mysterious messenger, Robin Adair, O'Casey's most consistent spokesman. It is unnecessary for the audience to actively dislike Mick Marthraun; it is more important that they react strongly against what he stands for. His most absurd characteristic is his superstitious fear, yet from the very raising of the curtain O'Casey parades the dancing Cock with 'the look of a cynical jester' [**Cock, 122**] before the eyes of the audience. Whereas Feelim O'Morrigun attempted with manly dignity to overcome his fears of the shadowy dancers and the smell of lavender, Mick Marthraun gives himself up quite completely to his belief in the evil omens that can destroy him— and because he does, they manage to succeed.

In grovelling terror he is quick to renounce his own daughter, 'that painted one, that godless an' laughin' little bitch' [**Cock, 123**], so that even Mahan is shocked by his unnatural attitude ('Why, man, she's your own daughter by your first young wife!' [**Cock, 123**]). Next he eagerly denounces his present wife ('there's evil in that woman!' [**Cock, 125**]) so that it soon becomes obvious that there is no one that Marthraun will not cut adrift to assure his own safety and comfort. Like the true paycock he is adept at attributing vile motivations to others that he is actually guilty of himself: Mahan has exact evidence that Lorna was unwilling to marry Mick, but the husband defends his avarice by insisting that 'she had her blue eye on th' fat little farm undher me feet; th' taut roof over me head; an' th' kind cushion I had in th' bank' [**Cock, 126**]. And before the first exchange of dialogue in the play is over, we learn that Mick has cheated Lorna's father out of a lucrative bog for a mere fifty pounds, knowing that he needed the money to send his crippled daughter Julia to Lourdes. That Marthraun can then boast that *he* financed the journey to Lourdes is the final piece of evidence against him. From there on the audience can watch with delight while the 'evil forces' torment the abysmally superstitious farmer.

55

3

Throughout *Cock-a-Doodle Dandy* Mick Marthraun is out to protect his investment and O'Casey is intent on exposing him for just that. And Marthraun's primary source of support comes from the Church: to a worker who objects to his severely reduced paycheck, he blithely replies: 'That's a social question to be solved by th' Rerum Novarum.' [**Cock,** 131.] The Church has insulated the capitalist from his workers' objections to their exploitation; in exchange Marthraun willingly echoes all ideas advanced by the clergy: 'Remember what the Missioner said last night' [**Cock,** 124]; 'we must suffer th' temptation accordin' to the cognisances of th' canon law' [**Cock,** 149]; 'Looka, Sailor Mahan, any priest'll tell you that . . .' [**Cock,** 159]; 'It's a blessin' that so many lively-livin' oul' holy spots are still in th' land to help us an' keep us wary' [**Cock,** 160]; 'It's all right, Father—he'll do what your reverence tells him' [**Cock,** 186]; 'You heard what Father Domineer said.' [**Cock,** 200.] He cites Church sanction for his stand against the rights of workers to organise and bargain collectively ('It's this materialism's doin' it—edgin' into revolt against Christian conduct' [**Cock,** 133]), and condones the Church's campaign against books, plays, films, and dancing, since he understands its rationale in his own terms: 'An' all th' time, my turf-workers an' your lorry drivers are screwin' all they can out of us so that they'll have more to spend on pictures an' in th' dance halls.' [**Cock,** 164–5.]

As in the case with the religiousness of most paycocks, Marthraun's piety is soon compromised, and in a manner which gives O'Casey double-barrelled ammunition against him. Twice during the course of the day's events Marthraun lowers his guard against the evil inherent in his women and allows himself to be lulled into moments of lecherous enthusiasm. These lapses—and in both cases it is the maid Marion who has tempted him into a kiss or a squeeze or a dance—relieve Marthraun of the puritanical onus that he carries much of the time and give us a reason for finding something human in him after all. If human he is a hypocrite; if consistent he is a prig; and although touches of such humanity emerge in Scenes One and Two, they are quickly dispelled (first by Mick's noticing 'horns' triumphant on the heads of the women, and then by the arrival of Father Domineer), and it is essentially as a pious prig that Mick Marthraun elects his doom.

It is to Sailor Mahan's credit that he attempts throughout to keep at a moderate remove from the absurdity of his friend's extreme position. Unlike Joxer he is fairly reasonable and rather likeable, and whereas there is little to choose from between Boyle and Joxer, Mahan manages for the first two scenes to be a decent alternative to the prosperous farmer, but only because O'Casey is saving him for a last-scene retribution of his own. A sceptic and a rationalist, Mahan begins by deriding Marthraun's zealous superstitiousness and attempting to remind him that the evil spirit he is denouncing is his own daughter. Even Shanaar's mumbo-jumbo leaves him unimpressed, although Marthraun declares the old man to be 'full of wisdom an' th' knowledge of deeper things' [Cock, 135]. (O'Casey specifically labels Shanaar 'a "very wise old chawthumper", really a dangerous old cod' [Cock, 119], so that Mahan is perceptive in his statement that 'That Latin-lustrous oul' cod of a prayer-blower is a positive danger goin' about th' counthry!' [Cock, 148].) But scepticism and moderation are insufficient to redeem Mahan, especially since he can no more doubt what his eyes and ears tell him than can the audience: strange things are indeed happening in *Cock-a-Doodle Dandy* that would unhorse the most positive of rationalists; the play is after all a fantasy, and it is not whether a character *sees* the Cock as much as what sort of a relationship he establishes for himself with the 'demon'. Marthraun is immediately in terror of it, as he is of anything which threatens to disturb his safe world, while Mahan at least has enough of a flair for life to refuse to be challenged by it. But the same element that temporarily humanises Mick proves to be the Sailor's undoing: his lechery is not merely the healthy sort of sexual self-expression that is commendable in Loreleen, but a guilty and secretive lust for momentary release in dark corners of 'th' Red Barn' [Cock, 196]. The indications in the first two scenes that he is capable of giving himself up to his appetite (to Marion: 'What about a kiss on your rosy mouth, darlin', to give a honied tang to th' whiskey?' [Cock,

150]; to Loreleen: 'Here's a one who always yelled ahoy to a lovely face an' charmin' figure whenever they went sailin' by—*salud!*' [**Cock**, 182]) are soon belied by his commercial proposition to Marthraun's daughter. He offers to finance her escape to England in exchange for a quick tumble in the hay of the Red Barn, a business venture no less ignominious than Mick's financing Julia's journey to Lourdes. Mahan's demise is as sordid as his mercantile concept of sexual pleasure: 'Th' people pelted him back to his home an' proper wife, Father,' comes the report, 'an' he's there now, in bed, an' sorry for what he thried to do.' [**Cock**, 215.] The image conjured up of a remorseful Sailor Mahan hiding in his bed, coupled with the later sight of Michael Marthraun left high and dry by wife, daughter, and maid, signals a moral victory for O'Casey over some of the worse elements of paycockism. Unhampered by the necessities and logic of stage realism, the playwright constructed his fantasy with the characteristics usually found in the morality play, as much so here as in the two plays that he specifically designated as moralities, *Within the Gates*[21] and 'Time to Go'.

Paycock qualities, so compactly found in the two characters in *Cock-a-Doodle Dandy*, are rather diffused through several characters in *The Bishop's Bonfire*. Councillor Michael Reiligan is a successor to Councillor Michael Marthraun, and a far more arrogant and vicious person. His pride is the hauteur of his social position in the Ballyoonagh community, wealth and power making him a closer approximation of Cyril Poges than the less influential Marthraun. During the first act he is promoted to Papal Count, which makes him all the more insufferable in his contempt for all those socially beneath him (such promotion is an important functional device in *The Bonfire*, where the Ballyoonagh counterpart to Father Domineer is the Very Reverend Timothy Canon Burren, whose advancement to Monsignor in the second act parallels that of Reiligan to Count in the first). Reiligan, however, is a relatively unrealised character, and the play is even less about him than *Cock-a-Doodle Dandy* was about Marthraun. For most of *The Bonfire* Reiligan is a thoroughly unregenerate person, vicious and nasty to almost everyone: one daughter he keeps as a kitchen slave, although he constantly reminds her that she is a lady, while the other, saved from household work by her piety, gets almost as little affection from him ('All right, all right, go, but get outa the way! It's desolation's goin' on here, that's what; so go on, you, for prayers are no use here now' [Bonfire, 35]). For Foorawn there is a prie-dieu in the Reiligan household that no one else is permitted to use, and the mason Rankin, caught in the act of praying by Reiligan, is strenuously berated: 'That pray doo is the private perquisite of Miss Foorawn, and not meant for one of your stattus.' [Bonfire, 49.] While the blessings of Saint Casabianca are being bought for Reiligan by one daughter, the other is being saved to buy him secular blessings; with the aid of the canon he frightens away the penniless man she loves and substitutes fifty-eight-year-old Farmer Mullarky (against his will as well as Keelin's): 'He doesn't care a damn about me!' Keelin cries, 'He's in debt to me Da, and him an' me Da want to join their property.' [Bonfire, 86.] Having neatly separated that which is Caesar's from that which is God's, Reiligan is intent on appropriating both.

Contemptuous of all those who are socially beneath him, mean-spirited in his treatment of his own children (his son has no less reason to complain than Foorawn and Keelin: 'A waterfall of money flowin' for a Bishop, an' him denyin' his son a tiny tenner; his own son, mind you' [Bonfire, 52]), and fawning before the powers of the Church, Reiligan is easily recognisable. Yet one characteristic stands out as somewhat unusual: for one who so meekly says 'Yis' to the canon (the opening scene is full of such deference and provides our first insight into the character), he manages to remain firm for a long time in refusing to dismiss either Manus Moanroe or Codger Sleehaun, despite Canon Burren's insistence. It seems to be neither real backbone nor any special fondness for either of those two 'bad Catholics' that motivates him, but the usual concern with the monetary value of his employees. Of the Codger he says. 'Well, Monsignor, he's the best man in all the country round to trim a rick or thatch one' [Bonfire, 97]; of Manus, 'A gifted fella, too, Father, as clever on the busi-

ness end of a farm as the Codger is at the hand-work.'
[**Bonfire, 97.**] But the octogenarian Codger is sacked nonetheless, despite the protests of Foorawn, Father Boheroe, and
the Prodical, and Reiligan is cold-bloodedly businesslike
in accepting his 'loss': 'I'm sorry at losin' the Codger, but
he must be nearin' his end anyhow.' [**Bonfire, 106.**] His
reaction to Manus's quitting is astounding: at first he is
predictably chagrined at the inconvenience ('Nonsense! You
couldn't leave me—me righthand man' [**Bonfire, 107**]),
followed by an ambiguous note of concern coupled with a
reminder of his hold on Manus ('Look at the state you're
in, an' you've no money'), but finally leading to a touch
of poetic pathos unheard of before from Reiligan: 'Your
goin' would leave the stars over Ballyoonagh lonely.'
[**Bonfire, 107.**] Manus, however, reacts without surprise at
Reiligan's sentiment: 'Bar the Codger, you are the only man
who ever told me there were stars over Ballyoonagh.'
[**Bonfire, 107–8.**] The paternal affection denied his own
three children wells up at this moment for the bitter Manus,
and with a final 'I'm sorry, very sorry, Manus.' [**Bonfire,
109**] Reiligan disappears from the play, leaving the final
tragic denouement to Father Boheroe, Foorawn, and Manus
Moanroe, as if the playwright, having introduced this varying note into his character, could find nothing else to do
with Count Reiligan.

Reiligan shares the stage with a host of characters vying
for central focus (and indeed *The Bishop's Bonfire* is the
one play in which O'Casey is least concerned with establishing a hero: one would have to scrape together Danny's 'gay
heart', Manus's justifiable anger, the Codger's gift for song,
Keelin's intense love and Foorawn's final gratuitous act,
with Father Boheroe's pervasive wisdom, to amalgamate a
single heroic figure). Among the odd collection of personages
we find a pair of lesser paycocks, the Protestant Prodical and
the Roman Rankin, the masons at work on Reiligan's wall.
Reiligan is an extension of the prosperous Councillor
Marthraun, while the two masons are descended from the
first and third workmen of *Purple Dust*. In humble work-
clothes they lack the paycockish elegance of Reiligan's papal
uniform (it should not be overlooked that the Count's

entrance in the third act is in 'full uniform of a Papal Count—short jacket, long trousers, braided cuffs and collar, elegant sword, feathered cocked hat, and all' [**Bonfire, 86**]— somewhat reminiscent of old Peter in his Foresters' regalia), but Rankin and Carranaun perform the familiar function of feuding with each other, as well as many of the others that they come in contact with, abusing Reiligan's expensive furniture as much as the workmen mistreated Poges's (Danny and the Codger share in this), and strutting about full of their own importance. Their most paycockish characteristic is their religiosity, the Protestant attempting without success to stave off his temptation for drink (like Fluther), while the Catholic fears most the evil in female pulchritude (Keelin taunts him with the same malicious mirth that motivated Lorna, Loreleen and Marion). They have a greater portion of the stage to themselves than their predecessors in *Purple Dust* and more personality, and O'Casey even manages to inject a final positive note for one of them: the Prodical, one of the Codger's defenders, finally prefers whiskey and the old man's friendship to piety and the bishop's bonfire, and is praised rather gratuitously by Father Boheroe: 'He has helped to build hospitals where the sick shelter, homes where we live, churches even where we worship; he serves God as a mason better than I do in my priesthood, or you in your chastity.' [**Bonfire, 113**.]

Although there are many superficial similarities between *The Bishop's Bonfire* and O'Casey's next full-length play, *The Drums of Father Ned* (prosperous men of influence attempting to control the lives of their grown children; two contending clerics representing opposing concepts; the feverish preparations for an important event in a small-town Irish locale), the tone of the two plays differs greatly, from the stark tragedy of Foorawn's death capping the destroyed hopes of Manus, Keelin, and Father Boheroe to the triumphant victory of the young people (who follow Father Ned) and the paralytic defeat of their entrenched enemies. The later effort, 'an idle, laughing play', as O'Casey calls it, owes much of its new tone to the diminished significance of the Councillor-paycock who figured so largely in both *Cock-a-Doodle Dandy* and *The Bishop's Bonfire*, although Alderman

Aloysius Binnington, Mayor of Doonavale, and Councillor 'Mick'²² McGilligan, Deputy Mayor, are certainly direct off-shoots of such councilmanic types as Mick Marthraun and Mick Reiligan. The entire process of *The Drums* consists of the playing out of this motif of the prosperous and powerful paycock. The Prerumble, an opening scene some twenty-five years prior to the events of the play proper, pushes the potential paycocks into prominence, suggesting that their stubborn feud will remain the central preoccupation of the events of the drama. All the possibilities are there: each thinks himself patriotic and pious; each is consumed with his own importance; each hates the other for characteristics that are so overwhelmingly dominant in both of them. Like Mrs Burgess and Mrs Gogan, Binnington and McGilligan are so much alike that there is nothing to choose between them, and one suspects early in the play that some mark of differentiation will separate them eventually (like Bessie Burgess's heroism). But O'Casey has chosen to focus on them at first only to withdraw them from the spotlight, and no such individuality ever emerges. Instead they remain thoroughly interchangeable, merge into each other, and atrophy together.

All that has happened to the squabbling paycocks in twenty-five years is that they have grown twenty-five years older. The Prerumble, set in the times of the Black-and-Tan Terror, shows us the pair in a situation like that which confronted Shields and Davoren; the British Officer establishes the theme in his astonished report: 'I understand, in spite of this animosity, you do business together.' [Ned, 8.] The matter-of-fact rejoinder by Binnington ('That's different, for business is business,' [Ned, 8]) is echoed by McGilligan: 'Yis, business is business.' As middle-aged paycocks they are still doing business together, and early in Act One Binnington compounds the astonishing circumstances by informing his wife that they are having dinner at the McGilligans', and that the present business venture includes an Orangeman from the North. Again quite ingenuously he explains, 'Ah, have sense, woman! I'm tellin' you it's only pure business we're doin', uncontaminated with any smidereen of friendliness.' [Ned, 21.] Soon after, McGilligan himself arrives in the Binnington household, and again the echoes are echoed and re-echoed: 'An' business is business,' says McGilligan; 'Yes, business is business,' [Ned, 26] adds Binnington. It is business that has elevated the two to their exalted positions in the community, for like Marthraun and Mahan they are parvenu paycocks, their wives concerned with their deportment lessons 'for the Reception our President's givin' for important persons in Dublin Castle' [Ned, 16]. The new richness of their homes mirrors that of the Reiligan manor, where 'everything in it is new, except the things that are newer,' [Bonfire, 46] while Chez Binnington is 'furnished with an attempt at Irish middle-class pomp and circumstance' [Ned, 13]. And the McGilligans are intent on not only keeping up with the Binningtons but outdistancing them as well, as their shared domestic, Bernadette Shillayley, reports: 'Th' McGilligans'll best youse at it. Theirs is a bigger piano than yours, an' yesterday they got in a palm three half as tall . . . again as that one. They're the ones thuddin' their way up in th' world!' [Ned, 17–18.] The up-and-thudding McGilligan is then seen in his full paycock regalia: he is 'wearing his municipal robe, red like Binnington's, but with a deeper cape and cuffs of green, bordered with gold braid; a richer and more pompous robe than the Mayor's' [Ned, 24]. Binnington is no less enraged than Caliban at seeing this image of himself: 'I suggest you should know—if you know anything—that it is a dereliction of good taste for a Deputy Mayor to wear a more gorgeous gown than the Mayor.' [Ned, 25.] The fate of their gorgeous attire parallels their own demise. During the last moments of the play the once-proud paycocks, challenged by their children, deserted by their wives, and in general divested of their powers, attempt to rise and win back what they have lost. Each calls for 'Me robe!' and 'Me cocked hat an' me chain!' [Ned, 100–101], 'but the robes seem to have become too big for them, the chains dangle down too far, and the cocked hats fall down to their eyes' [Ned, 101].

The drumming optimism of O'Casey's last full-length play spells defeat for such ineffectual paycocks, vainglorious Micks who have had their day (in O'Casey's Doonavale at least). The vast assortment of vices and crimes that the author had previously attached to the various paycocks are limited to only a handful here, those of the middle-class capitalist. Marthraun before him and now Binnington rail against the same bugaboo ('This appalling materialism's spreadin' everywhere,' [Ned, 23] Binnington complains, while totalling up his business figures; Marthraun's words were not much different, 'It's this materialism's doin' it,' [Cock, 133] while haggling with Mahan). What they mean by materialism is the demand of labour for better pay, while the businessman's desire for higher profits is not included in their limited definitions. The latter becomes the divine right of the bourgeoisie and enjoys Church sanction, so McGilligan is quick to assert that 'Our needs'll be well satisfied if we listen to, an' act on, what our pastor says.' [Ned, 32.] But young Michael Binnington[23] has seen through the double standard and the basic malaise of the social condition that fosters the enterprises of his father and McGilligan: 'To you the hammer knockin' nails into timber and th' sickle swishin' down corn are noble because they bring you money to widen the walls of a bank.' [Ned, 32.]

Thus the revolt against the power of the paycock spreads among the young people of Doonavale, yet not necessarily against the person of the paycock. Careful emphasis is given that this is not a personal squabble or a Freudian overthrow of the father figure by newly pubescent juveniles. Nora McGilligan dispels the notion implied by Michael Binnington when she tells him: 'Oh, not against our fathers! We're fighting what is old and stale and vicious: the hate, the meanness their policies preach; and to make a way for th' young and thrusting.' [Ned, 81–2.] The two town officials, so concerned with their suspect business deal with the Orangeman from the North that they forgot to file their applications for nomination to the election list, are ineffectual embodiments of a dying age (and the priest is no longer a Domineer but a Fillifogue). They fight their old battles unaware of the spirit of Father Ned and the Tostal growing up around them, and just how antiquated their fight is becomes apparent from the continuation of the same quibbling that consumed them a quarter of a century before. In the Prerumble each accused the other of disloyalty to the

Irish cause, and in the first act they are still fighting the Civil War of 1922–23. Binnington calls his business associate 'A Gael who betrayed the dead when he took th' treaty, gave away Ulsther, an' took an oath of allegiance to an English King,' [Ned, 25] but McGilligan's retort is: 'An' when you and your gang found yous would lose th' pay if yous didn't enther th' Dail, yous ran to th' registherin' Officer, an' all Ireland heard your mouth smackin' th' Testament takin' th' oath!' [Ned, 25.] With their heads buried in the past Binnington and McGilligan find themselves bypassed by the future. Michael and Nora are unconcerned with the political rivalry of Free Stater and Diehard; neither of them was as yet born when the issue was a live one.

O'Casey's description of the middle-aged Binnington is benign, if not actually kindly: 'Business-man, patriot, and pietist, he loves himself more than anything else living or dead, though he isn't really a bad chap.' [Ned, 15.] For few of his other paycocks would O'Casey offer that last comment, and yet this should not be construed to mean that O'Casey has mellowed towards the man who 'loves himself more than anything else living or dead'. Many of O'Casey's plays show how the selfish and petty man has cruelly marred the lives of those around him, but only in two of the longer plays, *Purple Dust* and *The Drums of Father Ned* (as in the shorter 'Figuro in the Night') is there a clear-cut victory over the household tyrant. In *Purple Dust* it is the British paycock who is ejected symbolically from his former fief. But the triumph is suspect because of the implied sexual rivalry between the old walrus buying himself the loyalty of a mistress and the virile and attractive lover wooing and winning her away. It is the flaw in Poges's character which is responsible for the attitudes against him (no matter how indicative it may be in the context of the conqueror mentality), while the defeat of the Irish paycocks by Michael and Nora (whose successful recruitment of their mothers has the same effect as the winning of the Irish mistresses from their British lords) is without rancour or personal prejudice. As people Binnington and McGilligan do not deserve to be singled out for severe abuse; as political paycocks and Micks of influence they merit the scorn and abandonment meted out by their progeny.

3

A Veneration of Mothers

IF Captain Jack Boyle is the prototype for an ever-changing series of O'Casey characters, then Juno can be seen reproduced in other women created by Sean O'Casey. She is the goddess Juno despite her husband's inability to recognise the real significance of the name he gave her, just as her pregnant daughter Mary is the Blessed Virgin—so that both pagan Roman and Roman Catholic female deities are depicted in their Dublin tenement existences. Throughout his plays O'Casey develops the three phases of woman: as maiden, as mother, and as old crone. But goddess that Juno may be, she has also demonstrated rather petty attitudes and parochially limited points of view. The goddess in the slum takes on many of the characteristics of the slum, and her death-battle with the worthless paycock finds her at times having to fight on his level. Nonetheless, Juno eventually rises above her environment and her situation, emerging as one of O'Casey's most extraordinary characters. It is a commonplace to assert that Sean O'Casey revealed a marked propensity for creating female characters who are far superior in most ways to their male counterparts, and that the mother figure in particular is treated with respect and esteem. It is no less a commonplace to cite O'Casey's love for his own mother, the Susan Casside of the autobiographies, as the source material for his Junoesque mothers.

Yet Mrs Casside is as much a product of O'Casey's creative imagination as Juno Boyle. The six volumes of third-person autobiography present characters and incidents in order for the author to make specific comments: he has selected and embellished his material for the same artistic purposes that motivated his plays. Nothing is included simply because it

66

happened to him (nowhere does he include his date of birth, merely 'sometime in the early eighties, on the last day of the month of March'[1]), but only that which can be used for a particular effect or a particular comment. As such Susan Casside is developed for meaningful analysis—as is Juno Boyle—and is as artistically contrived. The biographer may some day describe the 'real' Mrs Casey to us; the autobiographer only tells us what he wants us to know and how to utilise the knowledge he offers. Frank O'Connor, for one, has difficulty accepting the 'momism' of the autobiographies, commenting on O'Casey's devoted mother 'who spoiled him and whom he exploited shamelessly. (Since I suspect that I did more or less the same thing myself I am not inclined to take a lenient view of the case.) O'Casey was an idealist, and he was going to be nothing but an idealist, even if he had to do so at his mother's expense.'[2]

In many ways it is Mrs Breydon, the mother in *Red Roses for Me*, who serves best as a compact repository of source material for the basic type. She shares with Sheila Moorneen (one of the least promising of O'Casey's young heroines) the responsibility of shifting audience reaction into alignment with Ayamonn's ideas and actions. Whereas the hero remains consistent throughout in his attitudes—his behaviour changes from personal motivation to social motivation, from participation to active leadership—it is Mrs Breydon whose point of view changes. Many of her early attitudes parallel those of the Mrs Boyle of the first act of *Juno and the Paycock*, although there is a touch of Protestant refinement in Ayamonn's mother designed to distinguish her immediately from the common denominator of tenement ignorance, as well as petty bourgeois touches socially above the Boyle family level. Juno's mistrust of the trade union movement is mirrored in low key by Mrs Breydon's early statement ('There's this sorryful sthrike, too, about to come down on top of us' [Roses, 132]), but that safe statement is her only expression on the subject until the final scene of the play, where she voices her concern over the danger to her son: 'Stay here, my son, where safety is a green tree with a kindly growth.' [Roses, 211.]

Her basically conservative response is in direct relation to

the perilous situation Ayamonn is moving into, and it remains essentially protective rather than political until her ire
is raised by the threats of Inspector Finglas. While Sheila
attempts to plead with the Inspector, Mrs Breydon denounces him: 'Look at th' round world, man, an' all its wondhers,
God made, flaming in it, an' what are you among them,
standing here, or on a charging horse, but just a braided an'
a tasselled dot!' [Roses, 212.] This is strong language from
a woman who had earlier acknowledged the universally accepted magic of the Inspector's pomp in attracting young
girls: 'I'm tellin' you th' hearts of all proper girls glow with
the dhream of fine things; an' I'm tellin' you, too, that the
sword jinglin' on th' hip of Inspector Finglas, the red plume
hangin' from his menacin' helmet, an' th' frosty silver spark-
lin' on his uniform, are a dazzle o' light between her tan-
talised eyes an' whatever she may happen to see in you.'
[Roses, 134.] With both Tom Finglas and her Ayamonn before her for proper comparison, Mrs Breydon makes the
significant choice: 'Go on your way, my son, an' win,' [Roses,
213] she tells Ayamonn; 'We'll welcome another inch of the
world's welfare.' [Roses, 213.]
    Although there are important factors in Mrs Breydon's
character that lead her directly into this crucial blessing of
her son's political action, there are also aspects of her personality and her prejudices to be overcome. Her sensibly
realistic attitudes in Act One are in welcome contrast to
Ayamonn's initial naiveté, but they often border on the
cynical and on a consequent acceptance of the status quo.
When she asserts that 'The bigger half of Ireland would say
that a man's way with a maid must be regulated by his faith
an' hers, an' the other half by the way her father makes his
livin',' [Roses, 134] her percentages leave little room for a
dissenting opinion, should she choose to have one. Ayamonn,
who concurs with neither of the outsized halves, thus finds
no ally in his mother. Her objections to Sheila are unfortunately accurate; she finds the existing faults, but it is actual prejudice that has brought her to them. 'She's a Roman
Catholic,' she tells Ayamonn, 'steeped in it, too, the way she'd
never forgive a one for venturin' to test the Pope's pronouncement.' [Roses, 133.] Her criticism of parochial
68

Catholicism does not relieve her of her touch of Protestant provinciality: having admired the repainted Catholic statue of Our Lady of Eblana, she superstitiously retracts by saying, 'It's done now, God forgive us both, an' me for sayin' She's lovely. Touchin' a thing forbidden with a startled stir of praise!' [**Roses, 162.**] Nor is she actually free of the 'Catholic' superstitions she feels so superior to: when Ayamonn jokes about the statue's possible powers of miracle, his mother becomes anxious: 'Hush, don't say that! Jokin' or serious, Ayamonn, I wouldn't say that. We don't believe in any of their Blessed Ladies, but as it's somethin' sacred, it's best not mentioned.' [**Roses, 161.**] We are reminded of a similar inconsistency in Mrs Casside, when Johnny muses over bringing a sprig of hawthorn into the house:

> But all the people round said it was unlucky to bring hawthorn into a house, all except his mother, who said that there was no difference between one tree and another; but, all the same, Johnny felt that his mother wouldn't like to see him landing in with a spray in his hand. It was all nonsense, she'd say, an' only a lively superstition; but you never can tell, and people catching sight of hawthorn in a house felt uneasy, and were glad to get away out of it. So it was betther to humour them and leave the lovely branches where they were. [**Hallway, 57–8.**]

O'Casey's clever handling of Johnny's narration leaves little doubt that the benighted attitudes of the neighbourhood have somewhat rubbed off on Mrs Casside as well.

It is apparent then that the gentility of this mother-figure has its limitations, and it is neither her creed nor her class that contributes to her basic saintliness. Rough-and-ready Juno lacks these slight advantages, but it is more important that she has been thoroughly hardened by the total meanness of her existence, while the Breydon-Casside woman has been 'stiffened' slowly by the gradual increase in her adversities. Juno's heroic decision to damn her husband and stick by her daughter has a magnitude absent in Mrs Breydon's blessing of her son's cause. Her lifelong devotion to her geraniums, musk, and fuchsia has no analogue in

Juno, who sees Mary's concerns with blue-or-green ribbons as pretentious frippery for a girl out on strike. There is a steady line of progression for the flower-tending Mrs Breydon: her concern for her child ('You'll undhermine your health with all you're doin'' [Roses, 132]) evolves into her care for a sick neighbour ('No harm to use an idle hour to help another in need' [Roses, 138], despite Ayamonn's petulant misgivings: 'You think more of other homes than you do of your own! Every night for the past week you've been going out on one silly mission or another like an imitation sisther of charity.' [Roses, 138.] (Juno had no such established position of altruism on which to base her new concern with the plight of others; it is not until her son has been killed that she can appreciate fully the sorrow of her neighbour, Mrs Tancred.) Mrs Breydon's goodness has already created her reputation among her more unfortunate neighbours, and in the third act she is lionised by the three down-and-outs, Dympna, Eeada and Finnoola:

> Dympna. . . . an' we know his poor oul' mother's poor feet has worn out a pathway to most of our tumbling doorways, seekin' out ways o' comfort for us she sadly needs herself.
> Eeada. . . . Don't I know that well! A shabby sisther of ceaseless help she is, blind to herself for seein' so far into th' needs of others. May th' Lord be restless when He loses sight of her!
> Finnoola. For all her tired look an' wrinkled face, a pure white candle she is, blessed this minute by St Colmkille of th' gentle manner, or be Aidan, steeped in th' lore o' Heaven, or be Lausereena of th' silver voice an' snowy vestments—th' blue cloak o' Brigid be a banner over her head for ever! [Roses, 196–7.]

Mrs Breydon's gratuitous acts of charity lead directly into her next phase, the rescue of Mullcanny the atheist from his attackers. 'A gang of bowseys made for me,' Mullcanny explains, 'and I talking to a man. Barely escaped with my life. Only for some brave oul' one, they'd have laid me out completely. She saved me from worse.' [Roses, 173.] The 'brave oul' one' is soon identified by Ayamonn as his mother. She has thus made the important transition from Shabby Sister of Charity to Guardian Angel. It is not her own son that she is rescuing, but someone else's son, and one whose opinions she scorns as much as do those who attacked him. She had already warned Ayamonn against association with Mullcanny and correctly prophesied the open hostility of the populace against him: 'That's another one I wouldn't see too much of, for he has the whole neighbourhood up in arms against his reckless disregard of God, an' his mockery of everything solemn, set down as sacred.' [Rose, 136.] Until this decisive gesture by Mrs Breydon, she and Sheila were equally responsible for attempting to dissuade Ayamonn from his more radical attitudes and actions, each from her vantage point arguing for conformity and the bourgeois ideals.

But now Mrs Breydon, having acted almost instinctively to save Mullcanny, has undergone a subtle change that she herself is not really aware of: she has aligned herself with Ayamonn's concept of total tolerance. Her distinction from Sheila had hitherto been that they have been tugging at Ayamonn from opposite directions, so that it is not unlikely that the audience may miss the significance of her later denunciation of Sheila towards the end of Act Two. It is no longer just personal dislike, as it had been in Act One when she said, 'many have murmured again' a son of mine goin' with the child of a man crouchin' close to their enemy' [Roses, 134]. It is Sheila's vicious denunciation of the atheist, the man that Mrs Breydon had saved from physical violence, that now incurs her indignation: 'Shame on you, Sheila, for such a smoky flame to come from such a golden lamp.' [Roses, 179.] Having come this far in partial comprehension of the alignment of forces, it remains only for his mother to understand fully the cogency of his self-sacrifice.

Mrs Breydon and Mrs Casside are in many ways mirror images of each other. Whereas the mother in the play has the advantage of compact presentation, the biographic mother is spaced out over four volumes, brought back into focus on various occasions for particular effects. That the ageing mother whose basic world is a genteel one of the past ('Sketchin', readin', makin' songs, an' learnin' Shakespeare ... I managed to get on well enough without them' [Roses,

71

132]) can overcome these limitations to support her son's martyrdom is instrumental in *Red Roses*; Mrs Casside serves a different function: in her son's autobiography (where her son is necessarily the central character), she fulfils a purpose contiguous to but independent of him. She is essentially the central character of her own drama. Whereas Ayamonn Breydon has created an existence for himself apart from the influence generated by his conservative mother ('I am drifting away from you, Mother,' he tells her, 'a dim shape now, in a gold canoe, dipping over a far horizon' [Roses, 135]), Johnny Casside is shown to be what he is as a direct result of the kind of mother he had. O'Casey gave his first autobiography the subtitle, 'Swift Glances Back At Things That Made Me', and there is little doubt that the first four books prove that the most important formative 'thing' was his mother. His intellectual, political, and religious distances from her are as acute as those of Ayamonn drifting away from Mrs Breydon, but what the leisurely books of autobiography can expose that the tightly structured play cannot is the subtle weave of the personality, the gentleness of soul and the strength of character, that form the lifelong legacy derived from the mother. Merely by tracing the occurrences of his mother's plants (geranium, musk, fuchsia), the reader can put together the total pattern of the mother's essence. They indicate both the delicate strain in the mother and the touch of beauty surviving in the drab tenement, existing throughout both as symbol and as naturalistic detail. They recur often in the glimpses of Mrs Casside's tenement life, and take on larger aspects in the play, from the opening description of the room:

> Under this window, on a roughly made bench, stand three biscuit tins. In the first grows a geranium, in the second, musk, and in the third, a fuchsia. The disks of the geranium are extremely large and glowing; the tubular blooms of the golden musk, broad, gay, and rich; and the purple bells of the fuchsia, surrounded by their long white waxy sepals, seem to be as big as arum lilies. These crimson, gold, and purple flowers give a regal tint to the poor room. [Roses, 127–8.]

When Mrs Breydon returns from her rescue of Mullcanny, her first concern is for these flowers: the windows over them have been smashed by stones intended for the outspoken atheist, but Mullcanny now safe, she *'runs over to the blossoms at the window, tenderly examining the plants growing there—the musk, the geranium, and the fuchsia'*: 'Unharmed, th' whole of them. Th' stone passed them by, touchin' none o' them—thank God for that mercy!' [**Roses, 176.**] Ayamonn leading the strike will not be as fortunate.

The red, gold, and purple flowers, probably only coincidentally the colours of the flag of Republican Spain,[3] provide the obvious identification of Mrs Breydon with Susan Casside. They do not come into prominence as symbolic of the stoic slum mother until *Drums under the Windows* (being written concurrently with *Red Roses*), where the mother's limited environment is described: 'There was the box arrangement too, carrying the musk, the fuchsia, and the geranium, doleful now, and waiting for the spring to come.' [**Window, 309.**] The 'Dark Kaleidoscope' chapter of *Drums* contains no fewer than seven references to the magical trio of flowers, emblematic of the woman's small world. Her death is forecast here: 'She would get her last look at a patch of the sky through the crooked window, over the tops of the musk, the geranium, and the fuchsia—that would be her way to a further life.' [**Window, 310–11.**] It is in this chapter that the autobiographic Sean O'Casside envisions the necessary rupture which will separate his world from that of his mother, just as Ayamonn had detailed it to Mrs Breydon early in the first act of *Red Roses* ('I am drifting away from you, Mother'): 'But his life was away from her, and he'd have to leave her wandering in her little Garden of Eden among the musk, the fuchsia, and the crimson geranium.' [**Window, 311.**]

These blooms stand for a touch of poetry in Mrs Casside's life, and the writer adopts them as the symbol of his new career as a literary artist, noting that 'he began to set down sad thoughts in bad verses, which was his little space of geranium, fuchsia, and musk' [**Window, 312**]. His mother's flowers serve as a test of the artistic sense of beauty for anyone entering their tenement room, just as later he will

73

employ his prints and his paintings to judge those who visited him, convicting those whose souls are dead to these bursts of colour.' Of Mr Henchy, an official of the Protestant Orphan Society, O'Casey says, 'He hasn't any eye for colour. ... Here are the golden trumpets of musk sounding at his very ear; a carillon of purple fuchsia bells pealing pensively, and he can hear neither; and there was the rose window of a scarlet geranium behind them, and his eyes were too clouded with worldly things to see it.' [**Window, 322.**] And as the artist turns his Irish Kaleidoscope, the synesthesia of sound and colour fuses into the characteristics of his language, the image 'halo'd by whirling crimson gerontium disks, and encompassed about with the blowing of mosque-scented trumpets of gold, and the pealing of purple con fuchsian bells' [**Window, 325**]. The mother figure has become eclipsed by her son's poetic symbolism, but these are the artistic forces that she has engendered for him, coupled with the father's gift of books.

Another heavy cluster of musk-fuchsia-geranium appears in the chapter that deals with the mother's death in *Inishfallen*, 'Mrs Casside Takes a Holiday', where the sick woman complains, 'You never watered the poor flowers last night.' [**Inish, 19.**] 'I don't know what they'd do without me,' [**Inish, 19**] she adds, introducing a realisation of imminent death. Away from the room of the dying woman her son imagines her 'in the midst of the fuchsia, geranium, and the musk,' [**Inish, 26**] and returns to find her actually near death. They become her funeral flowers soon after: 'Sean broke off a sprig of fuchsia, another of musk, and a crimson disk from the geranium, and carefully arranged them under a fold of her shroud, near her right hand. They would be her gold, her frankincense, and myrrh; her credentials to show to the first guardian saint she'd meet. I cared for these, she'd say, and honoured them, for they were of the gifts that the good God gave me.' [**Inish, 36–7.**] Again the son realises the gulf that has opened between him and his mother, separating the living and the dead: 'his new life would go on striding ever further away from the geranium, the fuchsia, and the musk' [**Inish, 37**]. It does not take long for his prophecy to materialise. In 'Hail and Farewell', the next chapter, O'Casey describes vacating the two-room tenement flat that he had shared with his mother for so many years, a departure characterised by his final statement about his mother's beloved plants. In surveying all the trivial paraphernalia of her life, the things that had meant so much to her but which he will not carry with him (just as he never visits her grave after her interment), he notes 'the clay-grimed tins that once held so proudly the geranium, the fuchsia, and the musk. They had withered when their good guardian went away. Farewell to them all. Everything here to Sean was dead and gone; he would never set eye on them again, and he never wanted to; without the honour of his mother moving among them, they had fallen from whatever grace they once had, and were damned forever' [**Inish**, 53].

O'Casey's treatment of his mother in these autobiographic pages combines both unabashed sentimentality and a determined anti-sentimentalism, probably resulting in that pure area between that is actual sentiment. He certainly did not worship her to the extent of idolatry, recognising her existence in his writings as a rounded character worthy of fuller treatment. Her faults were important to him, for they were symptomatic of what was amiss even in the best elements of the world he lived in and was now diagnosing in his six volumes of prose commentary on the 'Things That Made Me'.

A catalogue of Mrs Casside's failings would be comparable to that of Mrs Boyle and Mrs Breydon, except for the significance that the sequence of time plays its part in diffusing the effect over forty years for Sean's mother. The exigencies of the drama demand full characterisation quickly achieved, and once established it is only a matter of days in *Red Roses* (and a few weeks in *Juno*) before the important reversals will take place. By contrast Mrs Casside undergoes no significant changes over the forty years; the facets of her character once developed present a consistent pattern throughout. Her acquiesence to the will of her spiritual pastors is certainly the most annoying characteristic as it affects the young Johnny, so that the grown Sean is shown to have developed a tenacious resistance to ecclesiastical pressure, forging his strength in an area where his saintly mother had proven ineffectual. When Mr Joyce, the eye surgeon, prepares a letter to Reverend Hunter which insists that Johnny's eyes would be endangered by his attending school, Mrs Casside refuses to take it, saying, 'Oh, I daren't give the rector that, sir. . . . He would be annoyed, and it might do harm to the boy, later on in life.' [**Door, 162.**] The docile mother thus plays into the hands of the callous clergyman, who cites her as authority when he carts the boy off to school: 'You mustn't argue with your mother . . . for she knows much better what is good for you than you do.' [**Door, 165.**] This currying favour with the clergy is not entirely out of a total subordination to those who are ordained as her pastors; it also has its materialistic aspect in her 'selfless' desire to assure preferment for her son. Johnny reports 'his mother telling him that in years to come, when he was looking for a job, he might be glad of the minister's recommendation—clergymen had such a pull everywhere these days.' [**Door, 169.**] Nor is her motivation entirely unselfish: she soon reveals the irritation of the harried widow having to care for her brat: 'The doctor hasn't to keep you,' she tells Johnny when he reminds her of the doctor's orders that he not be sent to school, 'and doesn't know that I have to keep the minister on my hands.' [**Door, 169.**]

But O'Casey takes Mrs Casside full circle during the tandem chapters of *I Knock at the Door* which deal with the problem ('Pain Parades Again' and 'A Child of God'), for after all it is her strength of character, even her *stubbornness* of character, that best personifies the mother figure. This particular exchange between Johnny and his harassed mother shows her at her worst, as the boy goads her into a petty display of temper with his presumably sincere attempts at a logic that promises to upset her firm set of strictures ('if I'd 'a said I liked going to Sunday school and church, when I didn't, it'ud been a lie, 'an God 'ud 'a known it'): 'You young scut, she said, giving him a slight shake, if you thry to make fun of your mother, I'll give you a welt that you won't be the better of for a week.' [**Door, 170.**] The remainder of the chapter serves to redevelop our

76

admiration for Mrs Casside, after Johnny worries that his misbehaviour in Sunday School might bring down her wrath upon him ('Hunter'll tell me ma about it 'n turn her against me for days, 'n I hate the hard 'n cold look comin' into her eyes when Hunter howls a complaint against me; for even when I try to make up to her she'll shake her head 'n say No, Johnny, I'm black out with you for what you done in church' [**Door, 181**]). When he arrives home drenched, it is against Hunter that she turns black: 'A church that 'ud send a delicate half-starved child home to his mother in your state is round a corner 'n well outa the sight o' God,' she angrily declares in a rare moment of insight; 'Ah then, if oul' Hunter comes here before I forget the wettin' you got, I'll give him a piece of me mind about the thrue 'n everlastin' gospel of man mind thyself, for if you don't no-one else will.' [**Door, 185.**] But time passes and she will remain meekly acquiescent to church rule, but Johnny and the reader have been treated to a moment of rebelliousness in the woman that provides the source for the indomitable spirit that Sean Casside will go on to make his trademark.

This fusion of the mother's spirit with that of the son reaches its completion before the first volume ends. Johnny's defiant whack with an ebony ruler over the skull of the pandybatting teacher, Mr Slogan, may well derive from Stephen Dedalus's demand for a redress of his grievance against Father Dolan, rather than from any actual incident in O'Casey's childhood, but it certainly is a far stronger act of rebelliousness than one would expect from a timid schoolboy. The child's action is astonishing, yet it is the mother's defence of the miscreant that is the more impressive. This time she does not back down before the firm demands of Reverend Hunter: 'The harsh hand that fell on him today shall not fall on him tomorrow,' she tells the minister, 'or the next day, and its dark shadow shall he never see again. Tell that to Slogan from the boy's mother.' [**Door, 238.**] And *I Knock at the Door* ends with Mrs Casside's resolute refusal to pass over the responsibility for the boy's upkeep to the state or the Church: his sister's suggestion that he be sent to the 'Bluecoat School' (in which his brothers concur) is refused:

Every turn he'd take would be chronicled; and if one wasn't done as they had planned, the boy'd be broken into their way of doin' it; an' Johnny's my boy, an' not theirs. If they're anxious to feed him, let them feed him here; if they're anxious to clothe him, let them clothe him here. I'm not goin' to have the life in him cowed out of him, as long as I can prevent it. There's no use of harpin' on the Blue-coat School, for me mind's made up—the boy won't go into it. [Door, 287–8.]

Neither Johnny Casside nor Mrs Casside would be much cowed thereafter.

Mrs Casside's stubbornness is equivocal. When she upholds her son in the face of clerical tyranny it is an act of greatness, but when she denies her blessing to her daughter on the morning of her marriage the author offers no opinion. She is an accurate prophet in her gloom regarding the educated girl's engagement to the Army drummer-barber-marksman. Her objections to the marriage suggest class snobbery, although she quotes her husband's weightier restriction ('you know the state your poor father'd have been in had he known you knew him—he would never sanction a soldier' [Door, 77]—which may indicate the same sort of class feeling, but also implies Irish patriotism and pacifism). She lacks the power to prevent the union (or the enlistment of two of her sons, for that matter), and impotence in action leads her to petulance in behaviour. To Ella's plea, 'Aren't you going to say something to me, before I go?' [Door, 113], the cold reply is. 'You've made your bed, an' you'll have to lie on it.' [Door, 114.] Her unbending attitude towards Ella reflects her failure as a mother with all the children other than Johnny, although O'Casey implies no recriminations towards her. She accepted the steady decline into poverty stoically, and she and Johnny were the only ones who managed to survive spiritually.

It is in this portrait of a stoic that O'Casey creates his eulogy. In *Pictures in the Hallway* the adolescent Johnny worries about losing his first job: 'She wouldn't say much, if he was sacked—that was the worst of it; if she'd burst out an' bark at him, he'd find it easier to fight; but, no; she'd

78

just sigh, an' that was hard to counter' [Hallway, 153]. There is enough of an indication here that the young boy finds a saint somewhat difficult to live with, but as he matures he loses that slight sense of irritation and acknowledges fully the superlative example that she sets. In *Drums under the Windows* he lies on the couch that served as his mother's bed, and 'marvelled how his mother could sink to sleep on it. Here was a woman,' he comments, 'enduring torments quietly that would send ecstacy to a saint' [Window, 308]. And in *Inishfallen, Fare Thee Well* he writes her eulogy— one of many:

> This woman's spiritual hardihood, her unshakeable energy, her fine intelligence had all been burned to un-usable ashes in the tedious smokiness of a hapless life. Life had wasted all her fine possessions. . . . She would die alone—unhonoured and unsung. . . . And the resolve that he, too, would become as she had been—indifferent to the phases of fortune; indifferent, if possible, to what the world regarded as praise, peace, and prosperity; to bear all things—while fighting them fiercely—pain, poverty, and wretchedness with dignity and silence. [Inish, 29–30.]

Just as her flowers had become symbolic of his art, so her life became symbolic of his political crusade. He covers her coffin with a red cloth: 'It would be her red flag, ignorant as she was of all things political, and seemingly indifferent to the truth that the great only appear great because the workers were on their knees' [Inish, 36]. (It can easily be assumed from this statement that she was no more aware than Mrs Breydon of the revolutionary fires that stirred her son, that she remained a woman of a previous generation and of the class in which she had her origins.) 'But she was, in her bravery, her irreducible and quiet endurance, her fearless and cheery battle with a hard, and often brutal, life, the soul of Socialism' [Inish, 36]. Forgotten now are the very fallible aspects of the woman, her weaknesses and occasional moments of irritation with her children, so that in this fourth volume O'Casey can write: 'She had been his comforter, his rod and his staff, his ever-present help in time

79

of trouble. She had been so understanding, too; never cross-
ing him' [Inish, 17–18].

Much of the character of the mother is contained in the
author's physical descriptions of her, and of Mrs Breydon.
The first is of Mrs Casside when Johnny is three years old
and she is forty:

> with hair still raven black, parted particularly down the
> middle of the head, gathered behind in a simple coil, and
> kept together by a couple of hairpins; a small nose spread-
> ing a little at the bottom; deeply set, softly gleaming
> brown eyes that sparkled when she laughed and hardened
> to a steady glow through any sorrow, deep and irremedi-
> able; eyes that, when steadily watched, seemed to hide in
> their deeps an intense glow of many dreams, veiled by
> the nearer vision of things that were husband and children
> and home. But it was the mouth that arrested attention
> most, for here was shown the chief characteristic of the
> woman: it quivered with fighting perseverance, firmness,
> human humour, and the gentle, lovable fullness of her
> nature. [Door, 4–5.]

The far simpler stage direction that introduces Ayamonn's
mother reiterates the essential qualities of the woman, although the age gap which separates her from her son has
been drastically reduced for the play. Mrs Breydon is 'coming up to fifty, her face brownish, dark eyes with a fine glint
in them, and she bears on her cheeks and brow the marks
of struggle and hard work' [Roses, 128]. Given the compact
format of a quick description of a character, O'Casey
chooses to include two vital elements (facial aspects that are
inimitable in the character): the touch of humour and the
sign of toil and poverty. Stoicism in those who have not been
hard-pressed is meaningless to him, and saintliness that is
joyless is anathema. Towards the end of Drums we view Mrs
Casside some forty years after the initial description: 'She
must be getting on for eighty now. She who had been
buxom, was worn away now to a wiry thinness. She was a
brave woman; something of the stoic in her. Seldom he had
seen her cry' [Window, 309]. And as she lies close to death
in Inishfallen, the son remembers 'her young, fresh, and

gleaming laughter, so strange from one who had gone through so hard, bitter, and thankless a life for nearly eighty years; fifty of them little less than terrible; years that had withheld joy, raiment, food, and even hope; for she never had a hope that she could ever be better than she was. But she was always a proud woman, hating charity as an enemy, and never welcoming it, so that all these bitter years had never mastered her, never diminished the sturdiness of her fine nature' [Inish, 18].

It is of psychological interest to note the degree to which Lady Augusta Gregory replaced the dead mother for Sean O'Casside (as it is that O'Casey did not marry until in his mid-forties, several years after his mother's death—it is of para-psychological interest that this did not occur until he had left Ireland). It is nonetheless apparent that in *Inishfallen* O'Casey indicates a transfer to Lady Gregory of the warm affection and almost unquestioning regard that he had hitherto reserved for the autobiographic mother. That she served to bridge the gap between the death of Susan Casey and the marriage to Eileen Carey for the struggling playwright is a safe assumption, considering how adroitly O'Casey employs her to balance the loss of the mother in his autobiography.

His initial depiction of her should be sufficient to establish her position: 'Her face was a rugged one, hardy as that of a peasant, curiously lit with an odd dignity, and softened with a careless touch of humour in the bright eyes and the curving wrinkles crowding around the corners of the firm little mouth' [Inish, 163]. The key designations are there: the mother's pride is mirrored in Lady Gregory's 'odd dignity,' and the signs of suffering in the 'rugged' and 'hardy' face of the aristocratic woman; and they share an identical 'touch of humour'. With this immediate introduction in the 'Blessed Bridget O'Coole' chapter it is apparent that Lady Gregory is eminently acceptable. It is not long before he announces that 'he was quite at ease with the Old Lady. They got on grand together. They had many things in common' [Inish, 171-2]: the theatre, books, paintings, that 'touch of humour', and that important emblem of Mrs Casside—flowers. The primroses and violets that grew on her lawn at Coole, the forget-me-nots in the secret corner, and above all the trees: 'It was she who first taught Sean to distinguish between the oak—the first dree dat Dod made, —beech, elm, hazel, larch, and pine' [Inish, 191]. And so his eulogy to her echoes the one to his mother: 'not Yeats, nor Martyn, nor Miss Horniman gave the Abbey Theatre its enduring life, but this woman only, with the rugged cheeks, high upper lip, twinkling eyes, pricked with a dot of steel in their centres; this woman, only, who, in the midst of venomous opposition, served as a general run-about in sensible pride and lofty humility, crushing time out of odd moments to write play after play that kept life passing to and fro on the Abbey stage' [Inish, 195].

O'Casey's account of Lady Gregory lays special stress on the death of her son, Major Robert Gregory (there are two instances in which it is emphasised in the 'Where Wild Swans Nest' chapter of *Inishfallen*), one of the Three Sorrows that he attributes to her. The theme of the mother's loss of her grown son figures prominently in the plays, beginning with *Juno and the Paycock*, where it receives double focus: Mrs Tancred's grief over the murder of her son Robbie by the Free Staters is given its first touch of irony when she says, 'An' I'm told he was the leadher of the ambush where me nex' door neighbour, Mrs Mannin', lost her Free State soldier son,' [Juno, 54] but this is minimal compared to the second irony, Mrs Boyle's duplication of her grief over the execution of her son Johnny for the betrayal of Robbie Tancred. It is as mother that Juno Boyle evolves into full awareness, not only of her sorrows (she had been bewailing these in rather trivial fashion from the opening moments of the play), but for those that she shares with others around her, with other mothers. It is her daughter's plight that moves her to action, that dislodges her from her disdain for all causes and concerns except that of her own family. The world outside forcing an entry into her small world with the loss of the legacy is only a small factor compared to Johnny's death and Mary's pregnancy. Like Mrs Tancred she bewails the loss of the son, but grief is replaced by positive and brave action in making a new life for herself and Mary—and Mary's unborn child. That Juno's humanity circumvents her conventional conformity, while the free-wheeling Captain proves implacable, is the paramount triumph of the mother. Those who are defeated by life (a category that O'Casey specifically creates with the Down-and-Out of *Within the Gates*) tend to resign completely in the face of personal tragedy: Mrs Tancred refuses a cup of tea, saying, 'Ah, I can take nothin' now, Mrs Boyle—I won't be long afther him.' [**Juno,** 54.] (In *Inishfallen* Mr Moore refuses either hat or coat as he follows his wife's coffin in the rain, the same life-weariness dominant in his attitude.) Lady Gregory and Mrs Boyle transcend their 'sorras' [**Inish, 30–33**].

There is a reasonable possibility that Lady Gregory contributes to the portrait of Dame Hatherleigh in *Oak Leaves and Lavender*, the bereaved mother whose airman son is killed in combat. Although the locus of the action has been shifted from World War One to Two, the other obvious parallels are easy to establish: the aristocratic background otherwise so foreign to O'Casey's world, and the Royal Air Force officer shot down. Certainly the British Dame is nowhere as close to O'Casey as the semi-autobiographic mother of *Red Roses* or her counterpart in *Juno*, but the focus on the woman as bereaved is sharper than in *The Silver Tassie*, the World War One play that concentrates on the wounded warriors themselves. Kept at arm's length by the author, Dame Hatherleigh fails to compete with Feelim for our affection or with Drishogue and Monica for our sympathy, but is a study in sorrow unrelieved and untranscended. Like Mr Moore and Mrs Tancred she is defeated by the loss of her son (following the loss of her husband), not so much because she is British or aristocratic but because she has never been able to identify with the cause that her son actively died for. These circumstances are familiar ones by now: Mrs Boyle and Mrs Breydon shift from conservative positions antithetical to those of their children to an acceptance of the efficacy of the new causes. Dame Hatherleigh is unable to. Although she immerses herself in war work and does so efficiently, she lacks the clear insight into the justice of the struggle that Drishogue is credited with—Edgar, her son, is also deficient in this—and is somewhat absurd in her mystic belief in 'British Israel' and digging for the Ark of the Covenant in the Hill of Tara. Despite the sophistication of her social position, her faith is one of religious medals: 'I cabled forty dollars over to Saskatoon's bishop for a symbol guaranteeing instant admission to heaven to the bearer, should he fall in the fight; and a subsidiary guarantee bringing the bearer safely home.' [Oak, 71–2.] Drishogue attempts to hide his smile, but O'Casey in his own voice openly scoffs at 'Winnipeg angels, guaranteed to bring young air-fighters back home safe and sound; or, at the worst, to furnish them with immediate entrance into heaven (on payment of forty-nine dollars first).' [Inish, 335.] The Dame's weaknesses are mirrored in the playwright's description of the character, in the fact that 'almost always a look of anxiety clouds her face' [Oak, 35] and that her eyes are 'perhaps a little brighter than they should be' [Oak, 36]—the elements of incipient hysteria that mar her perceptiveness.

Nonetheless, Dame Hatherleigh is treated with extraordinary sympathy. Although, like Thomas Mann's Kleinsgutl, Sean O'Casey is willing to tear the pages from the calendar two at a time, he admires that element of grace which he finds in such aristocrats as Lady Gregory, and he cloaks Dame Hatherleigh in a sad nostalgic aura that places her beyond opprobrium. She is seen undergoing two series of changes during the course of the play: the first is the destruction of her sense of the present caused by the news of her husband's death and by that of Edgar's, the second as she comes to accept—although in an almost trance-like state —the inevitability of change. The first renders her pathetic (like Mr Moore and Mrs Tancred); the second endows her with a touch of elegance and grandeur. Her first instinct is to resist change by ignoring its possibility; before Edgar's death, but already aware that her husband has been killed, she protests when told that a factory is being built adjacent to her house: 'Not here: this house can never change; never change.' [Oak, 88.] But towards the end of the last act she concedes, 'We must all go soon. Our end makes but a beginning.' [Oak, 110.] Already attuned to the scent of lavender and the awareness of death, she insists that 'Only the rottenness and ruin must die. Great things we did and said;

84

things graceful, and things that had a charm, live on to dance before the eyes of men admiring.' [Oak, 110.] And finally her concession takes on a concept central to O'Casey's theory of change, that 'many a sturdy oak shall strut from a dying acorn; and a maiden's lips still quiver for a kiss.' [Oak, 111.] The metamorphosis of her manor into a factory is accepted in her final statement: 'And every factory and every home will carve a niche for a graceful coloured candle.' [Oak, 111.] But this acceptance is bought at a terrible price. She, who at the beginning of the play is seen as a woman 'of forty-five or so, well figured' and still holding on to 'a good part of an earlier loveliness' [Oak, 35], is now described as close to death: 'Her face is mask-like in its lines of resignation. No colour, and little life is in her voice' [Oak, 103].

In depicting mothers with sons in uniform O'Casey has created individuals of vast dissimilarity, Dame Hatherleigh, Mrs Heegan, and Bessie Burgess. The British society woman who can say, 'Our lives no longer now are free enough to call our own. Each life is owned by all,' [Oak, 71] is a far cry from the Dublin harridan of *The Plough* who shouts, 'There's a storm of anger tossin' in me heart, thinkin' of all th' poor Tommies, an' with them me own son, dhrenched in water an' soaked in blood, gropin' their way to a shatherin' death, in a shower o' shells! Young men with th' sunny lust o' life beamin' in them, layin' down their white bodies, shredded into torn an' bloody pieces, on th' althar that God Himself has built for th' sacrifice of heroes!' [Plough, 201.] And different from both is the meek Mrs Heegan of *The Tassie*, the least heroic of the three, whose primary concern is that her son not miss the boat to France and be a deserter, thus cutting off her maintenance allowance. Mrs Heegan begins as a decidedly minor character in the opening act, and dwindles thereafter into even less, one of O'Casey's least developed mother figures. The initial impression that she makes upon the audience is hardly as powerful as Bessie's opening volley of drunken abuse, but it is not intended to endear her either. Once she has made it clear that her worries about Harry missing his boat are essentially mercenary ('with Jessie hitchin' on after him, an' no one thinkin' of me an' the maintenance money' [Tassie, 18]), she repeats this aspect of her concern again and again until Harry arrives: 'An' my governmental money grant would stop at once' [Tassie, 18]; and about Jessie: 'She's coinin' money workin' at munitions, an' doesn't need to eye the little that we get from Harry.' [Tassie, 18–19.] Only the final moment of farewell to Harry at the end of the act shows her as a mother; it is a moment that is never quite re-created again. Her entrance into the hospital room in Act Three is lost among the general hubbub, and her claim that she is worried about her son's condition is soon countermanded by her offer of cold comfort to the wounded soldier: 'Even at the worst', she announces, 'he'll never be dependin' on anyone, for he's bound to get the maximum allowance.' [Tassie, 73.] Thereafter she fades completely, as the focus narrows on Harry and his tensions with Barney and Jessie.

Bessie Burgess, on the other hand, emerges as a genuine heroine in *The Plough and the Stars,* a reversal that O'Casey handles brilliantly, and that has become the trademark of his special talent as a dramatist. It is apparent that O'Casey insists on uncovering heroism in the most unlikely places, and the foul-mouthed fruit-vendor develops through the four acts into a multi-faceted individual, while the skeletal lines of the consistency of her character remain intact. She naturally offends (both her neighbours and the audience) by her invective, a flow of abuse that runs the entire length of the play, beginning with her opening salvo against Nora's middle-class pretensions and superiority:

Puttin' a new lock on her door . . . afraid her poor neighbours ud break through an' steal . . . (*In a loud tone*) Maybe, now, they're a damn sight more honest than your ladyship . . . checkin' th' children playin' on th' stairs . . . gettin' on th' nerves of your ladyship . . . Complainin' about Bessie Burgess singin' her hymns at night, when she has a few up . . . (*She comes in half-way on the threshold, and screams*) Bessie Burgess 'll sing whenever she damn well likes! [Plough, 178.]

and concluding with her cursing of Nora, whose life she
has saved at the expense of her own:

> Merciful God, I'm shot, I'm shot, I'm shot! ... Th' life's
> pourin' out o' me! (*To Nora*) I've got this through ...
> through you ... through you, you bitch, you! ... O God,
> have mercy on me! ... (*To Nora*) You wouldn't stop quiet,
> no, you wouldn't, you wouldn't blast you! Look at what
> I'm after gettin' ... I'm bleedin' to death, an' no one's here
> to stop th' flowin' blood! [**Plough, 258.**]

But her martyrdom is a sincere one, although accidental,
and as her sight begins to dim, Bessie calls to the deranged
Nora, whom she has condemned, cursed, and saved: 'Nora,
hold me hand!' [**Plough, 259.**] And she dies singing her
hymn.

Bessie Burgess's hymn-singing, like her verbal abuse, is
a characteristic mark, from Newman's 'Lead, kindly light,
amid th' encircling gloom' [**Plough, 247**] to her final 'I do
believe, I will believe that Jesus died for me,' [**Plough, 259**]
including the more secular 'Rule, Britannia' [**Plough, 220**].
Her references to her soldier son also carry through in sustaining the character: in Act One, when Nora's husband
attempts to eject her from their apartment, she says, 'If
me son was home from th' threnches he'd see me righted'
[**Plough, 179**]; in Act Two she bewails the plight of 'all th'
poor Tommies, an' with them me own son' [**Plough, 201**];
in Act Three she prefaces her rendition of 'Rule, Britannia'
by denouncing the treason of the Easter Rising as 'Stabbin'
in th' back th' men that are dyin' in th' trenches for them!'
[**Plough, 220**]; while in Act Four she reveals that her son
has been wounded:

> Bessie Burgess is no Shinner, an' never had no thruck
> with anything spotted be th' fingers o' th' Fenians; but
> always made it her business to harness herself for Church
> whenever she knew that God Save the King was goin' to
> be sung at t'end of th' service; whose only son went to
> th' front in th' first contingent of the Dublin Fusiliers,
> an' that's on his way home carryin' a shattered arm that
> he got fightin' for his King an' counthry! [**Plough, 252.**]

87

4

Bessie, a Protesant and loyalist like Mrs Casside and Mrs Breydon, is at bitter odds with her neighbours in the tenement, lacking the genteel refinement of those other two mothers. Yet O'Casey gives her a heroic role greater than that fulfilled by the others. Like them she indicates a humane instinct in caring for the sick among her neighbours, her kindnesses to the consumptive Mollser prefiguring her kindness to the pathetic Nora whom she had previously scorned and abused.

It is by contrast with Mollser's mother, Mrs Gogan, that Bessie gets her first footing with the audience and begins to counter the unfortunate impression she had been making. The pitting of Mrs Burgess against Mrs Gogan parallels the quarrel between Uncle Peter and the Covey in *The Plough*, and is a pairing off of natural antagonists that O'Casey specialises in. There seems to be little to choose between the two shrews, unless one prefers a Catholic shrew to a Protestant one, a pro-Irish to a pro-British. Both begin by criticising Nora Clitheroe, Mrs Gogan gossiping about her behind her back to Fluther, while Bessie attacks her verbally and even physically in direct confrontation. The two 'mothers' square off at each other in the pub scene. Bessie defending participation in the Great War and Mrs Gogan defending 'poor little Catholic Belgium' [**Plough, 201**]. Bessie is accused of being fond of drink, Mrs Gogan of fathering her children out of wedlock and drinking with men; Mrs Gogan is then attacked for her drinking, while Bessie is accused of spying on her neighbours. The accusations multiply, tempers rise, and the verbal conflict becomes a physical one. At this point Mrs Gogan loses whatever advantage she may have had with the audience, passing her infant over to old Peter to rid herself of an encumbrance so that she can attack Bessie: 'Here, houl' th' kid, one of yous; houl' th' kid for a minute! There's nothin' for it but to show this lassie a lesson or two ... (*To Peter*) Here, houl' th' kid, you. (*Before Peter is aware of it, she places the infant in his arms.*)' [**Plough, 205.**] The abandonment of the child (it soon winds up on the floor and Mrs Gogan is bounced from the pub, leaving it to be shunted back and forth between Peter and Fluther) weighs heavily against Mrs

Burgess's adversary, particularly when we notice in the next scene that Bessie takes quiet care of Mrs Gogan's tubercular daughter, bringing her milk when no one is looking, and when Mollser asks her to help her into the house, 'Bessie leaves the looted things in the house, and, rapidly returning, helps Mollser in.' [**Plough, 224.**] It is as a mother that Bessie Burgess first shows the best aspects of her character, making her feverish care of Nora credible. Her entente with Mrs Gogan as looters harmoniously sharing a pram as a means of conveying their spoils is a comic one, but her sympathy with Nora, her other natural enemy, is a serious manifestation of a maternal instinct transferred from her wounded son to the dying Mollser and the disturbed Nora.

Motherhood in itself weaves no magic for O'Casey. Other mothers in his plays are no more effectual than Harry Heegan's in performing the necessary act that elevates the mere condition of motherhood to an active principle. The difference lies with those mothers who can translate their love for their own children beyond the confines of their immediate families. For Juno, within the limits of the play's situation, it is in her ability to change from the conventional role of the mother as protective and punitive to a larger one of accepting her daughter on Mary's own terms, and for Bessie it is in moving outside of her own interests, as it is in moving outside her own family. Mrs Heegan is stymied by a condition she did not create and which she cannot in any way control: even when she transcends her monetary concerns, she can offer nothing but pity for her son. And when pity proves a valueless commodity, she merely abstracts herself from the situation completely: in the hospital scene, prior to the operation, she attempts to offer some ray of hope; in the football club, after the operation has failed, she hardly has a word to say, except to continue her castigation of the Jessie Taite whom she also disliked for taking her son away from her. And Mrs Heegan has her counterparts in other O'Casey plays: in the earlier 'Kathleen Listens In' and subsequently in *The Star Turns Red*.

Neither Sheela O'Houlihan (the 'woman of the house' and mother of Kathleen) nor the Old Woman (the expressionistically nameless mother of Jack and Kian) is even as much a person as Mrs Heegan, the first assuming her specific function as a political integer in the one-act political fantasy and the second a representation of a complex number of attitudes indicative of the Mother prototype. Mrs O'Houlihan worries over the health of her daughter and is concerned about her welfare, but essentially it is her social position that involves her most, the 'Gawden Pawties'. (In the new Irish nation the woman of the house has become a social-climbing bourgeoise, and O'Casey reproduces the type in duplicate in *The Drums of Father Ned*.) The Old Woman in *The Star* is very much in the foreground during most of the first and third acts, disappearing completely thereafter during the revolutionary conflict of the fourth. In fashioning her O'Casey hoped to endow her with the dimensions that Bessie Burgess proved to have, but the Old Woman, intended to expand in scope to something more than a mere individual, tends to fragment into unresolved contradictions.

As a mother she is decimated by the battle-to-the-death between her sons, but is shown to favour her Communist son Jack in contrast with her husband's championing the Fascist son Kian. Yet when Jack denies his brother, the Old Woman insists, 'He is my son; you are my son: therefore you are his brother' [**Star, 249**]; and when Kian kills Julia's father, the mother cries, 'Oh, Kian, my son, my poor, sense-forsaken son, what have you done!' [**Star, 276**] and later rationalises the murder in conjunction with the Old Man: 'Poor Kian just had to protect himself; so he drew his gun—.' [**Star, 308.**] As wife she modulates from bickering with her irascible husband to mollifying him by parroting the last sentence of every statement he makes.[5] Essentially she seems as contemptuous of him as Juno is of Captain Boyle, but she lacks Juno's strength of character and independence, and emerges as a travesty of the dutiful wife. This role is especially awkward when, having defended Julia against Joybell's attack and her husband's condemnation, she bristles at Julia's accusation of her husband and denounces her; from her insistence that 'Julia's a fully respectable girl, without a glimmer of guile in her' [**Star, 264**] she soon changes to railing against her 'dressed-up indecency' and 'paint-patterned face' [**Star, 265**]. Yet only moments later she pleads with both the Brown Priest and Kian to intercede on Julia's behalf when the girl is about to be flogged; and when the body of Julia's father is lying in state, the Old Woman protects Julia from the condemnation of the Most Respectable Man, calling Julia 'Dear Child' [Star, 316]. There seems to be at least one volte-face too many in the Old Woman's archetypal bag of tricks.

Nor is the focus any clearer in this most political of O'Casey's plays concerning the Old Woman's political function. There is no simple development from ignorance or indifference to awareness that distinguishes Juno and Mrs Breydon. After she has been unquestioningly echoing her husband's pietistic defense of the status quo, she suddenly irritates him by commenting on his belief that the Saffron Shirts and Christian Front will preserve order: 'Ay; but what kind of order?' [Star, 248.] It is safe to assume, however, that O'Casey had some definite hopes for this worried Poor Old Woman. He endows her with a vision, as 'in a reverie' she says, 'if only that wonderful and wondering light, watching our movements, happened, now, to be the star.' [Star, 255.] She explains her star as 'The star which led the three kings to where the little child lay' and 'The star of Him who is called Wonderful, Counsellor, Everlasting Father, the Prince of Peace.' [Star, 255.] The Old Man deprecates her vision and Julia is disappointed with it as being 'a little stale' [Star, 255], but Jack remains fascinated by it, seeing it as the star which he follows, especially when she notes: 'It shines as purest silver shines, all brightened by a useful and a loving hand.' [Star, 255.] Yet soon after she will kowtow before the Lord Mayor and call for the clergy, showing herself irredeemably allied with the past that is being overthrown in *The Star Turns Red*. That O'Casey had hoped for something greater and nobler from the Old Woman can be seen from his sparse stage direction offering a description: 'The Old Woman is of average height, plump, and still shows signs of the good-looking girl she once was' [Star, 242].

There is a remarkable sameness in O'Casey's description of Elena Binnington and Meeda McGilligan, the matrons of *Father Ned*; the former is seen as 'a middle-aged woman who must have been a handsome lass in her earlier age; her face still carries many traces of good looks, but it is rather a tired one now, but still trying to keep calm and gay' [Ned, 15]; the latter 'comes in with an anxious, half-frightened look on her face. She is a middle-aged woman, who must have been a handsome lass in her younger days. Her face carries traces of good looks still, but it is a rather tired one now, trying to keep calm and gay, like her sister Mrs Binnington' [Ned, 70–71]. (To retain vestiges of a youthful beauty indicates a contact with the life force in O'Casey's scheme, while the weary and frightened look suggests a loosening of the vital grip on life—the two sisters then can conceivably move in either direction when the moment of decision comes.) Nonetheless, the two women are quite different: Mrs Binnington is first seen snobbishly insisting that her piano is too elegant for the servant girl to touch, totally treasuring her lessons in deportment, and bickering with her husband, while our first view of Mrs McGilligan is of a gentler, more conciliatory and hospitable soul. As the Mayor's wife Elena Binnington is the more pretentious and the haughtier of the two, although she scores well against her pompous husband, having recognised the futility of attempting to block the Tostal festivities: 'I never seen you in an Irish dance; an' all you know of Irish is a greetin', an' even when you use one, you've to hurry in its sayin' for fear you'd lose it. That robe an' cocked hat of yours weren't fosthered from any concept creepin' outa Tara Hill.' [Ned, 20.] Elena is a notch above the arrogant mayor, while Meeda is even more human: 'Here we all are now, undher the Green Flag with its Golden Harp; th' harp that can play an Orange tune in Belfast an' a National tune in Cork, an' yet remains a thrue Harp; an' th' green grass that fattens th' cattle of Ulsther as well as the cattle on the plains of Meath, still remainin' th' thrue grass of our Irish pastures.' [Ned, 74.]

As mothers the two women are almost complete nonentities, apparently unaware of what is happening with the younger generation, although their husbands have some intentions of preventing Michael Binnington and Nora McGilligan from continuing their relationship. They have committed themselves so completely to their own interests that they move only accidentally within the world that encompasses their grown children. Only once do we discern a maternal touch, and it is a rather unfortunate one; when the servant girl democratically asks Nora McGilligan to give her a hand in bringing in the coffee, the mother is shocked, and retorts, 'Nora'll do no such thing! Your helper, indeed! I'd have you remember that my daughter is a lady!' [**Ned, 84.**][6] Yet when the children successfully rebel against their parents and seek to wrest the election from their fathers, the mothers are given an opportunity to abandon their husbands and join the young people—and they accept. The Mayor, the Deputy Mayor, and the parish priest are all stultified in a consuming paralysis, as the youth march off to follow the drums of Father Ned; Michael Binnington invites Mrs McGilligan, and Nora invites Mrs Binnington, to join the parade. It is Meeda McGilligan who immediately accedes, and successfully gets her sister to comply as well: 'Let's go, Elena.' [**Ned, 103.**] At the moment of decision the life spirit triumphs in them, as it dies completely in the men.

Nonetheless, O'Casey's full roster of mother figures does not add up to as impressive a collection as might at first be supposed. The immense power of Juno Boyle, the sensitive treatment given the two biographical mothers, and the skilful reversal executed by Bessie Burgess from harridan to heroine are in themselves O'Casey's major triumphs with the character of the mother, and these four women dominate so much of his canvas that readers have been prone to generalise on O'Casey's excessive tendency to glorify maternal feelings. This is not quite the case: not all of his older women are gentle creatures nor are all his mothers active and positive. Countering the quartet of venerated women is a galaxy of lesser lights, women torn between holding on to the best that is in life and a destructive pettiness and self-interest that is their spiritual death. At their best they are magnificent heroines, larger than life-size; but even when imperfect, they are treated with a delicate sympathy by their creator.

4
The Hero as Hero

IT is only with the later plays that Sean O'Casey develops
a type of male character who resembles the usual hero, a
lonely figure on a stage where girls and women dominate.
The young males of the early plays were quick to display
characteristics that eventually disqualified them. Donal
Davoren, for example, recognises himself to be only 'the
shadow of a gunman' [Shadow, 124] by the end of the first
act and a 'poltroon' [Shadow, 157] by the end of the second.
But if to be a gunman is to be a hero, then let us examine
the 'real' gunman of the piece, 'Mr Maguire, soldier of the
I.R.A.' [Shadow, 92]. His identity as a gunman on the run
is unknown to Davoren and Shields until they read of his
death, for until then they know him only as an insignificant
pedlar, like Shields himself, who leaves with them a bag
they assume contains the goods of his vocation, 'spoons and
hairpins'; but its contents reflect Maguire's avocation: 'My
God, it's full of bombs,' Donal reports, 'Mills bombs!'
[Shadow, 144.] The real hero then passes rather inconspicu-
ously as a more than ordinary fellow, and even the revelation of his identity fails to impress Shields and Davoren that
he is anything but an ordinary fellow: 'How can he expect
me to have any sympathy with him now?' [Shadow, 126]
Shields asks. He interprets Maguire's death as an unnecessary error that could have been avoided had the pedlar kept
his business appointment with Shields instead of courting
death where he did not belong. Davoren is no less apathetic
about his bravery ('He can hardly expect that now that he's
dead' [Shadow, 126]) but at least has sufficient commiseration to comment: 'that was a serious affair—for poor
Maguire.' [Shadow, 126.] The unnoticed Maguire serves as

a foil for the much-noticed Davoren, the one that the entire neighbourhood assumes is a gunman in hiding, while the real man moves casually among them.[1]

The would-be hero accepts the role thrust upon him, since it not only earns him the gratuitous admiration of such locals as Tommy Owens, Mrs Henderson, and Mr Gallogher, but provides the catalyst that thrusts the lovely Minnie Powell into his arms. Yet the easy assumption that Maguire's death reflects adversely on the poseur is only a limited one; actually Maguire's real counterpart is Shields, the fellow salesman who had once been in the I.R.A.: "I don't want to boast about myself, and I suppose I could call meself as good a Gael as some of those that are knocking about now . . . but I remember the time when I taught Irish six nights a week,[2] when in the Irish Republican Brotherhood I paid me rifle levy like a man, an' when the Church refused to have anything to do with James Stephens, I tarred a prayer for the repose of his soul on the steps of the Pro-Cathedral.' [Shadow, 99.] Maguire had outdistanced these 'brave' efforts of Shields's, yet there is no sign of recognition that perhaps the dead man had sacrificed himself in lieu of the living one. Davoren at least displays the sympathy that Shields should have shown, but it is Minnie Powell who proves to be *his* braver self. Her self-sacrifice eclipses Maguire's. We assume that his motivation was the general one of Irish patriotism, but we know that Minnie, whom Shields dismisses contemptuously as 'an ignorant little bitch' [Shadow, 129] and a 'Helen of Troy come to live in a tenement' [Shadow, 130], is motivated by her love for Donal and her belief that he is so important that he must not be allowed to be captured.

News of Maguire's death is belatedly discussed after a cold newspaper report, but Minnie's death takes place just off-stage; the sounds of it are audible to the audience, and the news of it is emotionally recorded immediately after by Mrs Grigson: 'An' in the thick of it, poor Minnie went to jump off the lorry she was on, an' she was shot through the buzzom. Oh, it was horrible to see the blood pourin' out, an' Minnie moanin'.' [Shadow, 156.] Minnie's death points an accusing finger at the failed hero, the shadow-

95

gunman, whose only saving grace is his recognition of himself as he really is: 'It's terrible to think that poor little Minnie is dead, but it's still more terrible to think that Davoren and Shields are alive! Oh, Donal Davoren, shame is your portion now till the silver cord is loosened and the golden bowl be broken. Oh, Davoren, Donal Davoren, poet and poltroon, poltroon and poet!' [**Shadow**, 156–7.][3]

Juno and the Paycock is even more devoid of male heroes, although there are three young men who look as if they are grooming themselves for such a role throughout much of the action. The Maguire type of hero is brought to the foreground in young Johnny Boyle, twice wounded in action ('He was only a chiselur of a Boy Scout in Easter Week, when he got hit in the hip; and his arm was blew off in the fight in O'Connell Street' ([**Juno**, 30–31]); one is expected to assume that Johnny's bravery would go unquestioned, but we see him from the beginning living in terror, a hero surrounded by devotional candles, clutching his mother and sister out of fear. With the news of Robbie Tancred's death and information linking Johnny with the dead Diehard, it becomes apparent long before he is dragged off that he has evolved into both a coward and a traitor. The romantic lead, Charlie Bentham, looks like more of a man in comparison to the grovelling Johnny Boyle, but his social and intellectual pretensions prove difficult to take, disqualifying him even before his caddish abandonment of the pregnant Mary. By Act Three only Jerry Devine remains a contender: having failed in the first act in his role as lover, he is brought back now with a chance to redeem himself by accepting Mary despite her pregnancy. Jerry's magnanimity in forgiveness overwhelms both Mary and the audience, but only because neither realises that Jerry is willing to accept an abandoned Mary, but not a pregnant one. As he backs out shamefacedly ('I shouldn't have troubled you . . . I wouldn't if I'd known' [**Juno**, 81]), the last possible candidate retreats from O'Casey's stage, leaving only the two brave women.

Nor is there anyone in *The Plough and the Stars* to fill the role. A second young Socialist, modelled somewhat after

Jerry Devine, is seen in the Young Covey, who mouths even more dogma and gospel but is none the more a man. His chief occupation is baiting Uncle Peter, hardly a match for any young male, and he is no more successful with Rosie Redmond, with whom he engages himself enthusiastically but at cross-purposes. He sees her as a possible disciple for his views; she views him as a potential client for her bed. Even more awkward in escaping the prostitute than Jerry was in ridding himself of the fallen Mary, he disentangles himself from Rosie's perfumed clutches in holy terror, and is vicious in his denunciation: 'It'll be a long time before th' Covey takes insthructions or reprimandin' from a prostitute!' [**Plough, 209–10.**] The much older Fluther, never a candidate actually for the role of masculine hero, is both more man and more gentleman than the young Covey.

Both the Covey and Fluther engage themselves as looters during the Uprising, while the combat heroics are left to the officers of the Citizen Army, two of whom are seen as fairly important, although it is Commandant Jack Clitheroe who would have qualified as hero for almost any other dramatist but O'Casey. A lover as well as a warrior, he makes the choice Dryden would have approved of, leaving weeping wife behind when country calls. But with Jack the author does not even allow us a few minutes of illusion: before we meet him we learn from Mrs Gogan that it is the lure of the uniform that has charmed Clitheroe, a piece of malicious gossip that is soon verified by the 'hero' himself. He had chosen his duty to his wife when no assignment of command had been offered him; now that Captain Brennan comes to tell him that he had been appointed Commandant, he retrieves his Sam Browne belt, his revolver, and his hat, and marches off. There is still a possibility that this chocolate soldier will redeem himself under fire, and there are indications in the last two acts that perhaps he has. Captain Brennan's bravery is somewhat suspect because of his civilian vocation (Bessie constantly taunts him with having been a chicken-butcher: 'Choke th' chicken, choke th' chicken, choke th' chicken' [**Plough, 233**]), and he

97

proves ruthless against civilian looters: 'Why did you fire over their heads? Why didn't you fire to kill?' [**Plough, 231.**] Clitheroe's humanity is commendable by contrast: 'No, no, Bill; bad as they are they're Irish men an' women.' [**Plough, 231.**]

Jack Clitheroe's death in combat is certainly one of the tragic elements in a play that O'Casey calls a tragedy, but like Maguire's it is overshadowed by the death of non-combatants like Bessie, the pathetic death of the consumptive Mollser, and the mental breakdown of Nora Clitheroe. Clitheroe's 'reported' death is paralleled by the death of his British counterpart, a character we have never met: 'Private Taylor; got 'it roight through the chest, 'e did; an 'ole in the front of 'im as 'ow you could put your fist through, and 'arf 'is back blown awoy!' [**Plough, 254–5.**] A combatant for the wrong reason, Clitheroe's death wound is a horrible accident, while that of the civilian woman, protecting his deranged wife with her own body, has the stronger emphasis of heroism about it.

Finding the Achilles' heel of any potential Achilles and uncovering the clay feet of any projected hero has marked O'Casey's approach in the first three tenement plays,[4] but with *The Silver Tassie* he undertook to examine one of the most virile totems of our society, the athlete-lover-warrior. Yet the triumphant and fully confident Harry Heegan of the first act is reduced to a bitter cripple by the war, and the play becomes a study of the emasculated hero, the active man reduced to frustrated impotence for the long, dark stretch of his mature life. Despite Housman's admonitions, this athlete did not die young, and like Johnny Boyle no longer finds himself able to be the hero he had been. For the audience there is the problem of superimposing their impressions of the powerful and self-possessed Harry of the opening scene upon the tormented shell in a wheelchair propelling himself about through Acts Three and Four, and determining what elements of the real man must have been lacking in the superficial strength of the first. But for the reader there is O'Casey's carefully thought out comment in his stage direction as we first encounter the hero:

98

He is twenty-three years of age, tall, with the sinewy muscles of a manual worker made flexible by athletic sport. He is a typical young worker, enthusiastic, very often boisterous, sensible by instinct rather than by reason. He has gone to the trenches as unthinkingly as he would go to the polling booth. He isn't naturally stupid; it is the stupidity of persons in high places that has stupefied him. He has given all to his masters, strong heart, sound lungs, healthy stomach, lusty limbs, and the little mind that education has permitted to develop sufficiently to make all the rest a little more useful. [Tassie, 25.]

The liabilities are clearly outlined in O'Casey's subtle editorialisation about the person that is Harry Heegan, and he himself in his enthusiastically boisterous scene before returning to France corroborates his creator's analysis of him. Unthinkingly he has been triumphant on the football field; unthinkingly he accepts the accolades of his friends and admirers and the affection of Jessie Taite. It is clear to the wary audience that Harry is riding the crest of a wave of success and popularity that he could easily outlive, and that he is carelessly blind to the consequence of a fall.

Harry's mindless acceptance of all the glory soon leaves us feeling that the victory he won was somehow won over us, and perhaps not too fairly at that. Barney's loyalty is casually accepted, if not actually abused; 'You ran them off their feet till they nearly stood still,' [Tassie, 27] Barney comments worshipfully, but without a nod of acknowledgment Harry goes on to toot his own horn even louder: 'An' the last goal, the goal that put us one ahead, the winning goal, that was a-a-eh-a stunner!' [Tassie, 28.] And poor Barney quickly adds a second chorus: 'A beauty, me boy, a hot beauty.' [Tassie, 28.] When Barney attempts to be familiar with Susie, in imitation of his idol, she curtly differentiates between the dog and the flea: 'I don't mind what Harry does; I know he means no harm, not like other people. Harry's different.' [Tassie, 30.] With Jessie and Susie hanging on to him, and Barney fawning upon him, Harry Heegan is the hero of the hour, and makes the most of it. He fails to detect the warnings pregnant even in his own words. 'The song that the little Jock used to sing,' he asks Barney, 'what was it? The little Jock we left shrivellin' on the wire after the last push.' ' "Will ye no come back again!" ' [Tassie, 27] Barney guesses incorrectly. And soon after, Harry's mother cautions: 'Watch your time, Harry, watch your time.' [Tassie, 27.]

Time and the war prove unkind to Harry Heegan. In the momentary flush of victory he hopes to stop the clock and ignore the movement that leads relentlessly to his destruction. His solicitous mother is most eager that he does not miss the boat that will return him to the war: 'Your father'll carry your kit-bag, an' Jessie'll carry your rifle as far as the boat.' [Tassie, 28.] But Harry irritably replies: 'Oh, damn it, woman, give your wailin' over for a minute!' [Tassie, 28.] And later his shy farewell to her introduces the one touch of tenderness that we see in him in this scene: 'Well, goodbye, old woman.' [Tassie, 33.] As much as the boisterous enthusiasm for life sparkles in Harry, there is no mistaking his hubris, the Oepidal flaw that hardens us against this potent masculine hero.

The fall of Harry Heegan draws our attention to the new man, as we scrutinise his actions for the necessary changes that might elevate the shallow egoist. From the first instant that we see the athlete-imprisoned-in-his-wheel-chair we are aware that his only desire is to return to his field of glory, that the 'stupefied' hero lacks the equipment with which to reassess his values. Simon Norton immediately touches the sensitive spot: 'What with the rubbing every morning and the rubbing every night, and the operation to-morrow as a grand finally, you'll maybe be in the centre of the football field before many months are out.' [Tassie, 64.] But this infuriates him; 'It's a miracle I want—not an operation,' he insists, and while medically it would indeed take a miracle to restore Harry to his former virility, it might require another to bring him to the point where he can learn to cope with himself as he now is. What Susie calls 'his habit of introspection' is hardly that at all, but only unthinking self-pity, his primary motivation as he broods over the football field fading out of reach and

Jessie's defection to Barney. Even Susie, who in the throes of puritanical piety had lusted after him in the first act, now prefers the Surgeon, indifferently referring to her former idol as 'Twenty-eight' [Tassie, 75], a hospital number, a faceless integer. Although the blind Teddy Foran blurts out that 'he'll have to put Jessie out of his head, for when a man's hit in the spine ...' [Tassie, 73], Harry continues to bellow pitifully for the elusive Jessie. He describes himself as a 'shrivell'd thing' [Tassie, 76], echoing the earlier description of the 'little Jock left shrivellin' on the wire' who sang 'Will ye no come back again?', and with 'intense bitterness' rails against 'the mercy of God and the justice of man!' [Tassie, 77.] While the nuns sing their hymn, Harry offers his own kind of prayer, 'God of the miracles, give a poor devil a chance,' [Tassie, 79] as Act Three ends.

Bitterness as such need not disqualify the modern Oedipus as hero. A resigned acceptance of the destruction of his manhood hardly makes Ernst Toller's Hinkemann much of a hero, nor does sardonic irony recommend Jake Barnes. Harry Heegan's boisterous anger is a consistent complement to the boisterous enthusiasm of his earlier days and does more to advance his stature. In the third act articulate bitterness begins to replace the unthinking stupefaction, and with the fourth act this tendency is accelerated. 'Red wine first, Jessie, to the passion and the power and the pain of life, an' then a drink of white wine to the melody that is in them all!' [Tassie, 81]—his first statement in this scene is an eloquent one, suggesting also a degree of detachment from himself.

If Harry Heegan can come to separate his affliction as something that has happened *to him* from something that *happens*, he may well reach a balanced attitude that would recommend him as a man. 'For me the red wine till I drink to men puffed up with the pride of strength, for even creeping things can praise the Lord!' [Tassie, 82] he adds, disclosing the dichotomy now present in his thinking, a critical attitude towards what he once accepted without thinking as his natural right, with a feeling of self-pity still present in the second half of the sentence. This sort of dual

101

motivation runs through the final act, as Harry struggles with both the horror of his condition and a larger awareness of what it means. Barney, in full possession of the spoils, can no longer be overlooked, and Harry's vehemence against his successor reflects his attitude toward his former self: 'Get out, you trimm'd-up clod. There's medals on my breast as well as yours!' [Tassie, 82.] Yet to Barney (formerly the weak worshipper, then the chicken-thief tied to the gun, now the holder of the Victoria Cross for saving Harry's life) the spoils, and to Harry the dregs, indicating that there apparently is something more than medals, more than 'silver tassies'. If Harry can see past the trophy, he may indeed be vouchsafed an important insight.

But his preoccupation is still with Jessie and still with the Cup ('that I won three times, three times for them— that first was filled to wet the lips of Jessie and of me'); he refuses to leave until they drink from the Silver Tassie, and until then he wants the Tassie in his possession. But there is a suggestion even in this nostalgia that he is celebrating a final irony, especially since his ambivalence is measured in his confused choice of wines: 'Red wine, red like the faint remembrance of the fires in France; red wine like the poppies that spill their petals on the breasts of the dead men. No. white wine, white like the stillness of the millions that have removed their clamours from the crowd of life. No, red wine; red like the blood that was shed for you and for many for the commission of sin!' [Tassie, 92.] Harry's had been the sin of pride, but a commensurate humility now would do little to elevate him in O'Casey's estimation, since the playwright demonstrates often that a resignation to suffering is far from his ideal of active participation in life.

Nor is there any possibility that so boisterous an enthusiast of active life as Harry will meekly turn the other cheek: 'Push your sympathy away from me, for I'll have none of it,' [Tassie, 93] he insists. Yet the fury with which he propels his chair in an effort to keep pace with the dancers leaves him soon exhausted, and the litany he intones with Teddy is more hypnotic chant than religious devotional. He is capable of one last outburst of fury and self-pity when he sees Barney fondling Jessie, denounces them viciously, and casts the mangled silver cup from him. One last recollection of glory before he throws the tassie away: 'Dear God, this crippled form is still your child. Dear mother, this helpless thing is still your son. Harry Heegan, me, who, on the football field, could crash a twelve-stone flyer off his feet. For this dear Club three times I won the Cup, and grieve in reason I was just too weak this year to play again.' [Tassie, 101.] The gesture of defiance in casting the cup from him has its finality, and his exit lines indicate the degree of heroism that the author now finds him capable of: the penultimate statement ('What's in front we'll face like men!' [Tassie, 102]) is as brave as the ultimate one ('The Lord hath given and man hath taken away!' [Tassie, 102]) is bitter. The balance between virile resolution and scathing defiance is the most that O'Casey can allow for Harry Heegan. Since no miracle is forthcoming, only an inkling of understanding within could have been hoped for. Johnny Boyle cringed in terror and was destroyed; with Donal Davoren the hero of *The Tassie* shares a new self-awareness.

O'Casey, however, refers to *The Silver Tassie* as a tragicomedy (whereas the three previous dramas were tragedies, presumably because of the deaths of Minnie Powell, Johnny Boyle, and Bessie Burgess), but what is most important is the emergence of Harry Heegan as the protagonist in his own drama. O'Casey in other moods and under other circumstances went on to develop other types of male heroes in his later plays, yet only on one subsequent occasion, almost thirty years later in *The Bishop's Bonfire*, does he return to the 'maimed' hero. Manus Moanroe is a returned veteran, an Irishman who fought in the Royal Air Force during World War II, as had Drishogue O'Morrigun of *Oak Leaves and Lavender*, but has returned alive. Unlike Heegan, Manus has not been physically injured; his wound is a spiritual one, deriving less from his war experiences than from the disappointments suffered before and since returning to Ireland. Canon Burren in particular objects to him and attempts to have Councillor Reiligan dismiss him from his job as his overseer. The Canon's complaints against Manus give us a fairly good idea of the complexity of this 'wounded' hero: 'You should remember he had an eye on your Foorawn before he became a seminarist and before she entered the convent. You know the scamp he has become since he flung his vocation away, and since he served in the English air force.' [**Bonfire, 4.**] It is difficult to tell from this list which of Manus's offences most disturbs the parish priest of Ballyoonagh.

This diatribe against him at the beginning of the play is balanced towards the end when Foorawn denounces Manus as a 'gaspin' throw-away from the Church eternal' [**Bonfire, 117**], a 'rusty drunkard' [**Bonfire, 117**] and a 'spoiled priest' [**Bonfire, 119**]. Even the Prodical joins in the vilification, calling him a 'dirty leaf torn out of a book. A labourer, no more, now.' [**Bonfire, 10**] but Manus writes his own epitaph in his salutation to himself with a drink in hand: 'To Manus Moanroe, the dead priest!' [**Bonfire, 108.**][5] His bitterness parallels Heegan's and stems both from the lost love of Foorawn and an awareness of the dead world around him. Yet his 'stupefaction' cannot be blamed on those who have exploited him, since Manus has long since shaken off the bond attempting to hold him, and is in a stronger position to extricate himself than Harry Heegan. Intellectually superior to the hero of *The Tassie* he is faced with a rival—the Church—for the woman he loves, a rival far more formidable than the one Harry has in Barney Bagnal.

Manus's situation is best seen in relation to the other young men of the play. In Daniel Clooncoohy he recognises an alter image of himself, a man who works with his hands, who is in love with Foorawn's sister, and who has also travelled outside Ireland (O'Casey often indicates that having seen something of the world outside is an important aspect of the man of awareness): 'his one aching desire will be to get Keelin into his arms, and her one desire to find herself there,' Manus comments about Daniel, 'but nothing will come to them save, maybe, an accidental touching of hands.' [**Bonfire, 14.**] Manus's gloomy forecast stems from his own predicament; whereas Foorawn's pledge to the Church keeps her out of his arms, it is class prejudice that ruins Daniel's chance of ever marrying the Councillor's daughter. Daniel, however, lacks the strength of character that marks Manus;

although he pledges with Keelin to defy the Councillor and the Canon, he falls apart completely when threatened by these powers of the community. Whereas the girl continues to defy her father and the priest ('We love each other! I won't let you, won't let anyone, take Dan away from me!' [**Bonfire**, 78]) Daniel capitulates entirely ('For God's sake, girl, have sense, an' don't make things worse!' [**Bonfire**, 78]). So when Canon Burren states that 'Clooncoohy won't offend again,' [**Bonfire**, 79] he discloses an accurate estimation of his own power. Daniel disintegrates under pressure, while Manus remains firm and becomes even more bitter. Daniel was at his best when he said: 'What's it matter whether a man's born under turrets or under a thatch? It's the man with the gay heart that rides the waters an' the winds; who shakes life be the hand when life looks fair, an' shakes her be the shoulder when she shows a frown.' [**Bonfire**, 71.] Yet Daniel cannot live up to his own promise, and even before Father Boheroe, who blesses their union, he loses heart: 'Who am I to think of his daughter?' [**Bonfire**, 75.] Daniel Clooncoohy's defection isolates Manus even further and focuses full attention on him as the play's masculine hero.

Two other characters also stand in a similar relationship to Manus, the less significant of the two being Lieutenant Michael Reiligan. His appearance in the second act suggests at first that here is a young man whose *active* participation in life shows up the rather passive approach of the bitter Manus, especially since his opening gesture is defiance against his father. The elder Reiligan is tight-fisted with his money in both his allowance to his son and his payment to his valuable foreman, and whereas Manus has made no protest against this exploitation (he finally steals the money he feels should have been his), the son sounds rather firm in pressing his own demands. But the lieutenant soon dispels any expectations we may have for him by dissipating his energies in an absurd scheme to protect Ireland from Russian paratroopers through the proliferation of jeeps (O'Casey uses this satire on military preparedness as the ultimate in absurdity in *Sunset and Evening Star*, where a Mick and a Dan delight over the harebrained idea). Not only is Michael Reiligan disqualified from significant stature in the play by proposing the idea, but Dan Clooncoohy is tarred as well by his sychophantic admiration for it, while the wise Codger scoffs with O'Caseyan derision.

Father Boheroe, in contrast to Dan and Mick, is a serious contender for stature in *Bonfire*, long after Mick and Dan disintegrate. His appearances in the play are obviously intended to parallel those of Manus; like Manus he approves of the relationship of Keelin and Daniel, is sympathetic toward the Codger, and earns the opprobrium of the Canon. Yet Manus in his bitterness attempts to alienate even the kindly priest, whom he denounces as one of those who 'stifle and tangle people within a laocoon of rosary beads!' [**Bonfire, 43.**] His criticism is unfair: Father Boheroe is a very different sort of priest, one with whom Manus should be able to share a definite affinity, but Manus is still reacting against the priest he himself had almost become, and is incapable of recognising any other kind. The schism exists not in their goals but in the elements of their individual personalities affecting their approaches to those goals:

> *Father Boheroe.* I wish, not to tangle them with rosary beads, Manus, but to join them with life. . . . Come, let yourself fall in love with life, and be another man.
> *Manus (sarcastically).* At peace with all things.
> *Father Boheroe.* At war with most things.
> *Manus.* You are a kind, good man, Father. (*He pauses.*) Would you do me a great favour?
> *Father Boheroe (eagerly).* Of course I would. You've but to tell me what it is, Manus.
> *Manus (tonelessly).* Just leave me alone. [**Bonfire, 43–4.**]

Putting himself outside the reach of the priest's kindness, Manus Moanroe duplicates the fault that torments him in Foorawn—she has placed herself irrevocably outside the influence of Manus and his love for her, having set up a cold steel fence around herself.

But as much as this climactic moment toward the end of Act One reflects upon Manus and the deadened part of his personality, it also suggests what later becomes quite emphatic: that Father Boheroe in all his kindness is ineffectual. While the Canon is successful in making Daniel toe the line, in having the Codger sacked, and probably in having his fellow priest summoned before the Bishop, Father Boheroe can neither convince Foorawn to accept Manus nor convince Manus to accept the loss of Foorawn. Manus's attack upon him is mild compared to Foorawn's; the devout woman's condemnation of the priest is virulent in comparison with that of the apostate. (Each of the three acts, incidentally, draws toward its conclusion with a new failure for Boheroe: the first with Manus; the second as he comforts the rejected Keelin, when all he can say is, 'My poor child, my poor child' [**Bonfire**, 80]; and the third with Foorawn.) Foorawn is specific and cruel in her analysis of the priest's ineffectuality: 'You have tried, and failed, Father. You have failed poor Keelin. . . . You have given no help to me, Father. . . . Or to Manus either.' [**Bonfire**, 114.] And all the priest can repeat is, 'I did my best.' [**Bonfire**, 114.] Only his exit line in any way activates the defiant strength within Father Boheroe: 'Oh, to hell with the Bishop's Bonfire!' [**Bonfire**, 114.]

Boheroe abandons the stage to the dramatic violence of the final encounter between Manus and Foorawn. Manus returns to steal the money from Reiligan's desk, money intended for Church work: '*Pro Deo et ecclesia.* For God and Church. For Manus and his doxies now. She forgot to write that down. Wants me to be barren as herself.' [**Bonfire**, 116.] But Foorawn interrupts the robbery and denounces the profligate, and in attempting to call the police she is shot by Manus with Mick's service revolver. The suicide note that she scribbles while dying exonerates Manus and gives him license to escape unpunished. Her final declaration of her love for him and his final sobs over her death and sacrifice do not alter either the consequences or the conclusions to be drawn: Manus has lost what he loved most and could not win for himself; he absconds with the 'holy' money for his libertine purposes, and his only regret is over the death of Foorawn, not his murder of her. Manus Moanroe and Harry Heegan, like Richard II, remain kings of their grief.

Certainly sensitivity is a major factor in the character of the 'wounded' hero, from Manus's forlorn hope of love to the development of a bitter awareness in the Harry Heegan deprived of sensitivity by those who exploit his class. The wish for death when life no longer resembles life characterises both, as seen when each comments on his experience in the war (Harry: 'When I wanted to slip away from life, you brought me back with your whispered 'Think of the tears of Jess, think of the tears of Jess', but Jess has wiped away her tears in the ribbon of your Cross, and this poor crippled jest gives a flame of joy to the change; but when you get her, may you find in her the pressed down emptiness of a whore!' [Tassie, 99]; Manus: 'Where I flew towards death at every chance I got so that I might die from all that had happened; but God laughed, and presented me with a medal; and when in another chance, I pushed closer to death, He laughed again, and added a silver bar to ripen the ribbon' [Bonfire, 42]). By contrast the Dreamer in *Within the Gates* has both sensitivity and a wholeness of body and spirit, a more permanent lease on what Daniel momentarily laid claim to, a 'gay heart'. The Dreamer, for all his gaiety of heart, can no more than Manus hold back the inevitable and fails to save the dying Jannice, but he can go further than either of the maimed heroes in preserving heart and perspective for himself—he absolves himself from self-pity. His involvement is with Life, of which Jannice is a beautiful but ephemeral aspect. He does not confuse her with the ultimate necessity, although Jannice as a whore is no worse than Jessie, nor than the pious Foorawn.

Nonetheless, the Dreamer is not the protagonist of *Within the Gates* as Harry is of *The Tassie*, nor does he quite take possession of the action in the final moments as Manus does in *The Bonfire*. The play is essentially Jannice's, with the Dreamer one of many who move in relation to her (the Bishop, the Old Woman, the Atheist, the Salvation Army Officer, the Gardener). He does, however, consistently represent a point of view that is paramount throughout the play, as he disputes with advocates of every concept that O'Casey declares against. 'Here, you two derelict worshippers of fine raiment,' he challenges the Chair Attendants in his first appearance on stage, 'when are you going to die?' [Gates, 120.] In counterpoint to the pious mouthings of the Bishop and the two Evangelists over the Down-and-Out, the

Dreamer insists: 'Let brambles, O Lord, grow thick where they are buried deep; let the fox and the vixen guard their cubs in the midst of the brambles; and let children sing and laugh and play where these have moaned in their misery!' [Gates, 227.] To the Salvation Army Officer who attempts to re-rescue Jannice, he announces: 'The rose that once has opened can never close again.' [Gates, 200.] Where the Gardener dreams only of seduction, the Dreamer muses: 'I hear a song in what you've said' [Gates, 136]—much to the Gardener's uncomprehending surprise. And even to the Atheist, with whom he enjoys a good deal of intellectual rapport, the Dreamer serves as a corrective to limited ideas:

Dreamer. And did you bring her into touch with song?
Atheist. Song? Oh, I had no time for song!
Dreamer. You led her from one darkness into another, man.... Will none of you ever guess that man can study man, or worship God, in dance and song and story! [Gates, 124.]

This function of the Dreamer in the play does not limit him exclusively to the role of a spokesman for the author; he as much exists in character as he does in what he expostulates. His very appearance, for example, is indicative of his active existence as the male hero of *Within the Gates*: 'He is a young man, lithely built, though a little thin and pale now from a hard time; but he carries himself buoyantly. His features are rugged; his eyes bright, sometimes flashing in an imaginative mood, but usually quiet and dreamy-looking' [Gates, 120]. And in a significant afterthought, during the final winter scene, O'Casey adds that important touch of colour for a further dimension ('The Dreamer wears a vivid orange scarf thrown carelessly round his neck and shoulders' [Gates, 222]). Ironically, his function is as Chief Tempter in this Eden-desert-Hyde Park setting, but it is on the nature of the temptation itself that attention is focused. All the other tempters offer Jannice a form of death (the sterile affection of the Gardener, the self-castigation of the Salvation Army Officer, the self-incarceration of the Bishop—even the lonely abandonment of the Atheist), while the Dreamer offers Life, that ephemeral substance: 'Come, sweet lass, and let's transmute vague years of life into a glowing hour of love!' [Gates, 170.] When rejected at first in favour of the Salvationist, he offers again: 'Jannice, here is peace; peace unharmed by the fire of life. I have that will give another month of gay and crowded life; of wine and laughter; joy in our going out and our coming in; and the dear pain from the golden flame of love.' [Gates, 200–201.]

There is no mistaking the sensual essence of the Dreamer's concept of life, although his desire for Jannice is certainly finer and less thoughtlessly selfish than the Gardener's (and even the Bishop and the Salvation Army Officer pay hand service to her physical charms). His gay heart is predicated upon a lust for life (with emphasis on both nouns in that phrase), whether it is a night spent on the few shillings in his pocket or a month spent on the check he received for his writing. He lies neither to Jannice nor to himself, knowing that she can no more afford to stay with him when he has no financial support to offer than he can afford to keep her at such times. Nor is he above stealing: of the three pounds given him by the Bishop for her, he pockets one (a minimal amount), and even tries to use that to buy her love for a while. 'I cannot live, or even hope, on the sweet sound of a song,' Jannice complains, 'Have you nothing else to offer?' 'I could give you a pound,' he replies, '*reluctantly.*' [Gates, 172.] As can be noted throughout the plays, O'Casey is neither sentimental about love nor bourgeois-moralistic: there is love and death in *Within the Gates*, but the Dreamer and Jannice are no Tristan and Isolde. 'I shall follow after loveliness all the days of my life,' [Gates, 121] he tells her during his initial pursuit, and when she is dying he attempts to keep her alive with his enthusiasm for life ('Sing them silent, dance them still, and laugh them into an open shame!' [Gates, 228]—almost ritualistically intoned three times with rising ferocity). But when she is dead, it is a soldier's farewell rather than a lover's that characterises his eulogy to her: 'You fought the good fight, Jannice; and you kept the faith: Hail and farewell, sweetheart; for ever and for ever, hail and farewell!' [Gates, 231.]

The poetic lover emerges as an important male hero in O'Casey's work, from Donal Davoren—who is ultimately a failure both as poet and lover—to the Dreamer, and beyond: Kelly from the Isle of Mananaun ('Time to Go'), with his song and dance and love of the Widda Machree, and Jimmy ('Figuro in the Night'), won over by the erotic revolution of the Birdlike Lad, who sings his wooing song to Alice. The major extension of the Dreamer is the Messenger of *Cock-a-Doodle Dandy*, Robin Adair, probably as buoyant and light-hearted a character as can be found in any of the O'Casey plays. Almost supernatural—in fact, a human counterpart of the supernatural Cock—he is both Robin Goodfellow and Hermes, his puckish personality and his role as message-bringer overshadowing his love affair with maid Marion. But there is nothing effeminate about Robin Adair: he is the active male among the cowering congregation of Marth-raun, Mahan, the Sergeant, the Bellman, the Porter, and One-eyed Larry. The play, however, is dominated by the three women, while the Messenger may be overlooked as a minor character with few lines to speak. This would be a serious oversight. O'Casey fully expected the women to be the central focus, particularly in the climatic moments of the drama, but with careful economy he fashioned a multi-level masculine hero in the lad with the accordion who comes on with a telegram for Marthraun and stays around ostensibly to observe the actions of others. He does not merely de-liver a telegram the way the Porter merely delivers a tall hat: he subdues the Cock in the first scene and rescues Loreleen from the rough fellows in the last; he interferes construct-ively in the Marthraun-Mahan controversies, expounds creed and sense to everyone within earshot, makes love to Marion, comforts the dying Julia, and sanctions the final decisions of the departing women, following them out of Nyadnanave after pronouncing judgment on Marthraun.

All of which distinguishes this 'minor' figure on the naturalistic level of the play, but the Messenger is most im-portant as the focal point of its fantasy. All of the people involved are best seen as they stand in regard to the mysteri-ous Cock. Those that are in terror of it are obviously those who are least alive (Marthraun, the Sergeant, Bellman, Por-ter, Larry, Shanaar, Mahan, and Father Domineer)—to them the Cock is a menace because they have chosen to regard it as such and declared themselves against it. They are then buffeted about by mysterious winds and battered by flying objects. These brainless believers in bell, book and candle stand in contrast to the three women, Lorna, Loreleen, and Marion, who learn to accept the Cock amongst them and are thus protected from his ire. It is Robin Adair who instructs them and emerges as synonymous with the Cock. During the first manifestation of the Cock's destructiveness in the Marthraun house, the women fly out in terror, but Robin reassures them: 'Looka, lovely lady, there's no danger, an' there never was. He was lonely, an' was only goin' about in quest o' company. Instead of shyin' cups an' saucers at him, if only you'd given him your lily-white hand, he'd have led you through a wistful an' wondherful dance. But you frightened th' poor thing!' [Cock, 143.] This explanation might suffice at this early instance but it is of no help in explaining the later manifestations—lonely poultry cannot engender gales of wind. But the women believe Robin and believe in him, and thereafter for them at least there are no winds. This three-part relationship to the demonic forces can be seen, for example, during a piece of comic stage business in Act Three:

> The sound of wind now rises, swifter, shriller, and stronger, carrying in it an occasional moan, as in a gale, and with this stronger wind comes the Messenger, sauntering along outside the wall, sitting down on it when he reaches the end farthest from the house. Nothing in the garden is moved by the wind's whistling violence, except Michael, the Bellman, and One-eyed Larry (who have been suddenly hustled into the garden by the wind). These three now grip their waist-bands, and begin to make sudden movements to and fro, as if dragged by an invisible force; each of them trying to hold back as the wind pushes them forward. The Messenger is coaxing a soft tune from his accordion; while Marion and Lorna are unaffected by the wind, and stand staring at the men, amused by their antics. [Cock, 209–10.]

Robin's complicity should be apparent, and the wind that rages against his enemies but spares his friends has a marked association with the music he plays on his accordion. His poetic explanation to the affected Larry indicates his malicious mirth: 'What ails yous? I feel only th' brisk breeze carrying the smell of pinewoods, or th' softer one carryin' th' scent of th' ripenin' apples.' [Cock, 210.]

The Messenger delivers his message and it is ignored: Marthraun in his excitement pockets the telegram (the ultimatum from his workers); but this is only a surface manifestation of the messages he delivers throughout the play. In the second scene in particular, where the two paycocks are holding their important conversation, he nods in continually as the spokesman for O'Casey. He hardly shares their adulation for that important American Catholic, Bing Crosby ('I was never sthruck be Bing Crosby's croonin',' [Cock, 158] he reports, a mild echo of O'Casey's attacks on 'Mister Bing Crosby' [Crown, 197] in Rose and Crown). He sneers at the Church ('Honour be th' clergy's regulated by how much a man can give!' [Cock, 159]) and assails the Irish for ignoring their shrines of historic significance while paying lip service to religion ('An' where are th' lively holy spots still to be found? Sure, man, they're all gone west long ago, an' the whole face o' th' land is pock-marked with their ruins!' [Cock, 160]). Moreover, he castigates the religion of the Irish, 'Faith, your fathers' faith is fear, an' now fear is your only fun,' [Cock, 161] while answering the clergy's objection to modern secular culture: 'Th' devil was as often in the street, an' as intimate in th' home when there was nor film nor play nor book.' [Cock, 184.] And in contrast to all that he opposes, the Messenger is quite positive about what he advocates, and he says to the Cock that he leads from the Marthraun house, 'Go on, comrade, lift up th' head an' clap th' wings, black cock, an' crow!' [Cock, 144.]

To Robin Adair is given the responsibility of summing up the consequences of the action of Cock-a-Doodle Dandy. The banished Loreleen is joined in exile by Lorna, followed close after by Marion; but Robin stays behind for a few moments to make some sort of order out of the debris. To the dying and now hopeless Julia (whom no one else dares face after her disappointment at Lourdes), he says all that can be said, 'Be brave.' 'Nothin' else, Robin Adair?' she asks.

'Evermore be brave.' [**Cock, 220–21.**] And to Marthraun, who never before would accept any of his messages but now asks, 'What, Messenger, would you advise me to do?' his blunt answer is: 'Die. There is little else left useful for the likes of you to do.' [**Cock, 221.**] With a final love song he exits to accompany his beloved Marion. As a lover, Robin is rather casual, since O'Casey preferred to minimise the love motive as the major cause of disaffection with Nyadnanave and what it stands for. Nonetheless, Robin has his moments: 'Oh, Marion, Marion, sweet Marion, come down till I give you a kiss havin' in it all the life an' longin' of th' greater lovers of th' past.' [**Cock, 161.**] Marthraun reminds him of his past adventures: 'You'd do well to remember, lad, the month in jail you got for kissin' Marion, an' the forty-shillin' fine on Marion, for kissing you in a public place at th' cross-roads.' [**Cock, 161.**] This incident prepares the way for the climax of Scene Two, Father Domineer's attack on the Lorry Driver 'who's livin' in sin with a lost an' wretched woman' [**Cock, 186**]. Jack, Marthraun's best lorry driver, defies the priest and is killed by him. His murder and the hounding of Loreleen signal the end of any possibility of the Messenger remaining in Nyadnanave.

The four major plays between *The Silver Tassie* and *Cock-a-Doodle Dandy*, those that O'Casey wrote just before, during, and after World War Two, demonstrate a concern with the hero as a leader, yet each of the four instances poses the problem differently and each handles it differently. The menace of European fascism changed a relatively pacifistic outlook upon the Irish national struggles to a militancy which necessitated dealing with the concept of leadership and the kind of man who indicates the qualities of a leader. It is safe to say that O'Casey was never too comfortable with the leader-hero concept, preferring a much gentler Dreamer or Messenger, or the quiet determination of a strong-willed woman. He mistrusted the Commandant Clitheroes and the Captain Brennans and suspected the bully and the sadist within the uniform of the soldier and the policeman, particularly the officer. Three of these plays deal respectively with revolution, strike, and the war, and in each case the masculine hero is reported dead in the final scene, Jack

during the anti-fascist revolt in *The Star Turns Red*,
Ayamonn Breydon in the police charge on the workers in
Red Roses for Me, and airman Drishogue in the Battle of
Britain in *Oak Leaves and Lavender*, as if the dramatist
could not cope with the character of the conquering hero—
or merely preferred to allow the cause to overshadow its
leader. The Martyr is a fixed entity, while the psychology of
the Victor—even when he had hitherto shown only the most
admirable of traits—can often prove unpredictable. Yet for
each fallen hero there remains a surrogate: although Jack
dies, Red Jim survives (and Kian undergoes a change of
heart); Ayamonn's death leaves an even more determined
Reverend Clinton (with significant alterations in Mrs Breydon and Sheila); and the loss of Drishogue strengthens the
determination of Feelim (while Monica reports that she
carries the hero's child).

The strongest duplication of the leader-hero occurs in the
most militant of the plays, *The Star Turns Red*, where the
strong hand of a leader is obviously needed to combat the
combined forces of capitalist control, fascist political terror,
and Church bigotry. The first act suggests that the young
Communist, Jack, is the play's protagonist, and our opening
view of him playing the 'Internationale' on the cornet provides the dual characteristics of the militant revolutionary
and the sensitive artist. There are numerous indications in
the scene that Jack can be trusted as well as liked: his
mother's preference for Jack over his fascist brother Kian,
and the antipathy of his unpleasant father; the trust that his
comrade Michael has in him to look after his daughter
Julia; Jack's patience wth the refractory Julia when she
defies him and her father and insists on going to the dance
instead of the Union hall; Jack's celebration of his cause
with song and quiet confidence in the face of Kian's avowal
of the fascist cause by shout, whip, and gun; and the general
stature of the young man head-and-shoulders above all the
others, even the weak but well-meaning mother and the
Brown Priest. With the death of Michael, Jack is left apparently alone to combat the powerful forces against his cause.
But if the first act is Jack's, the second one is Red Jim's, and
Jack is as absent here as Jim was present only in name in

the earlier scene. The personal hero, the one we are expected to identify with personally, is replaced by the impersonal hero, about whom we know nothing except that he carries the full burden of leadership on his shoulders. Where Jack had his counterpart in Kian, Red Jim is contrasted with the murderous Leader of the Saffron Shirts, the man of the whip and the gun. Jim is certainly larger than life, and the dedication of the play to the 1913 Dublin Transport strikers is sufficient to make us aware that he is modelled on Jim Larkin, for whom O'Casey maintained an admiration equal to that demonstrated by writers of the previous generation for Parnell.

The lionisation of Red Jim as a natural leader is systematically prepared for by the characterisation of those who oppose him, even before he himself makes an appearance. We had seen the Saffron Shirts and their Leader, the Purple Priest of the Rich, and the Lord Mayor, as well as the ignorant Old Man, in the first act; now we meet the Union leaders who conspire against Jim. Even their names sound oddly unappetising: Caheer, Eglish, Brallain, and above-all Sheasker, the most important of the group and consequently the logical opposite of Jim in vying for the right to represent the Union men. Sheasker, like Jim, is not present when the scene opens, so that we can hear about both as the others malign them behind their backs. Sheasker's portrait (which he thinks emphasises his resemblance to Julius Caesar) does little to endear him to us; his sense of self-importance is immediately seen, and a parallel with the Lord Mayor can be noted in Sheasker's 'broad gold watch-chain across his belly' [Star, 281] and the Mayor's 'thick gold chain of office round his neck' [Star, 265]. That Sheasker's cohorts vilify him as well as Red Jim hardly serves to bring Sheasker and Jim any closer together, but actually differentiates between them, for Jim is feared for his effectiveness and integrity (Eglish notes that 'it was Red Jim's Union keeping the strike clear of scabs that allowed the men to win' [Star, 282]), while Sheasker is despised for 'dodging everything but the soft jobs' [Star, 282]. Caheer claims that 'Sheasker's got no principle' [Star, 283] and Eglish agrees that if Sheasker 'thought he'd curry favour he'd kiss a Bishop's backside' [Star, 283];

the crowning comment is Brallain's: 'When Red Jim's down we can deal with Sheasker.'[Star, 283.] The lack of even the minimum kind of honour among these thieves places Red Jim alone against the worst kind of enemies. When the Brown Priest learns that his fellow Union leaders are going to allow Jim to be dragged off by the Saffron Shirts, he asserts, 'Oh, I am almost persuaded that Red Jim is right when such as you go all against him!' [Star, 294.]

The arrival of Jim at that perfect psychological moment when he is being most vilified then introduces in the one man an antithesis to all this viciousness, pettiness, hatred, self-interest, and ignoble cowardice. Jim's two most impressive traits are his equanimity and efficiency: he scoffs at the pack of jackals attempting to push him out of power, and, while progressively wearing away their collective assurance, is swift and successful in throwing Joybell out, exposing the alliance of the Union leaders with Sir Jake Jester, and cleaning up his own house: the drunken Brannigan who had terrorised the others is apprehended, severely lectured, and transformed into a sober and trustworthy captain by Red Jim. Although we get to know next to nothing about him as a person, we cannot but accept Jim as a leader, as the one man who can unite others behind him and bring them to victory against the overwhelming odds that face him. A quiet colossus, he seems to contain multitudes, especially when he brings Sheasker, Caheer, Eglish, Brallain, and the Secretary to heel: 'The Union chose you, did it? The men elected you, did they? Who made the Union? Who made the men men? Who gave you the power you have? I did, you gang of daws!' [Star, 203.]

The third act brings Jack and Red Jim together under the same roof, fusing the best elements of the two into a tangible amalgam, Jack's humanity and Jim's superhuman power. Jack is admirable in standing up to the religious riff-raff who seek to hand over the body of the murdered Michael to the Purple Priest for Christian burial, and two of his statements echo resoundingly as key O'Caseyan slogans: 'go, you dead, and bury your dead: the living sleep here' [Star, 317] and 'We are the resurrection and the life; whoso worketh and believeth in the people shall never

117

die!' [**Star, 317.**] He is even able to hold out against the power of the clergy, facing the Purple Priest with calm defiance, and his statement to them again marks the poetic eloquence with which Jack serves as the author's voice: 'The young in each other's arms shall go on confirming the vigour of life.' [**Star, 319.**]

But Jack's success is only a stalemate. He was unable to prevent Michael's murder or Julia's punishment in Act One, but he does prevent the Purple Priest from claiming Michael's body in Act Three. Yet it remains for Red Jim to usurp the priest's function and give Michael a worker's burial; to the Purple Priest he states: ' 'Twere better he had received Christian handling when he was living than to receive it now when he is dead.' [**Star, 324.**] Three times he gives the order ('Take up your comrade's body and let the drums strike'), but twice the Purple Priest succeeds in preventing him. On the third command Red Jim is obeyed. It seems a small victory (to be repeated on a larger scale during the revolutionary combat of the final act), but it is crucial in establishing Red Jim's dominance. He has beaten down the corrupt Union officials in his first conflict, the full weight of clerical power in the second, and must fight the military engagement against the political enemy in the last. Jack's death is intended to reach out to the audience on the personal level, but Red Jim's victory subsumes it, as the star turns red and Kian is left to mourn his brother's death in the face of the triumph of his brother's cause.

Red Jim both lacks an important dimension to make him a rounded character and is too big for a stage to contain him, and only in a play which takes place 'tomorrow, or the next day' is he at all conceivable. It is Jack who is O'Casey's human protagonist, but the brevity of his participation in the events of *The Star* are such that he fails to fill the role. At best he is merely a study for a later hero, the Ayamonn Breydon of *Red Roses for Me*. There the scope is comfortably smaller (a workers' strike rather than a workers' insurrection), the setting more precise (a known incident from the past rather than a hypothetical one in the future), and the need for a monumental leader less urgent. In addition, O'Casey could rely upon autobiographical material (both minor and major events of the play can be seen as well in *Pictures in the Hallway* and *Drums under the Windows*), material that he not only could draw from life but which he was simultaneously testing as literary matter in assigning them to Johnny Casside. But Ayamonn dead is still more valuable to the dramatist as a hero than a 'triumphant' Ayamonn, and to this extent at least he kept faith with the early study developed in *The Star*. In Ayamonn Breydon we find the most extensive treatment of a young male hero anywhere in O'Casey's plays.

In developing Ayamonn care was taken to de-emphasise his stature during the first act (a process already seen in Chapter 2 in relation to Juno Boyle). The first purpose was apparently that the personal, human qualities underscored in the cornet-playing Jack should keep the hero within the confines of the ordinary human being, making his self-sacrifice all the more significant. A second reason has to do with O'Casey's sense of theatre: change within a character points not only to human possibilities but to a feeling of compressed time which transforms thought into action. Ayamonn at first assumes that heroism by anyone will be unnecessary ('There'll be no strike. The bosses won't fight. They'll grant the extra shilling a week demanded' [**Roses**, 132]), and he certainly minimises his own importance in the entire proceedings: 'I haven't much to do with it, anyway,' he tells his concerned mother, 'I'm with the men, spoke at a meeting in favour of the demand, and that's all.' [**Roses**, 132.] This seems to be an unlikely source for outstanding leadership, much less martyrdom, and therefore precisely the sort of material that the dramatist was most interested in advancing as heroic potential.

Ayamonn, in fact, is limited by his naïveté, and it is actually Mrs Breydon, as we have seen, who seems to be the most promising person of the drama at this point. Her intuitions are far more sound than his idealistic evaluations: he underestimates the determination of the bosses and the intolerance of his fellow beings (on Mullcanny's vociferous atheism for example, Ayamonn comments that 'the people are sensible enough to take all he says in good part; and a black flame stands out in a brightly-coloured

119

world' [**Roses**, 136]), and is almost absurd in his inability to see his beloved Sheila in an accurate perspective (he actually thinks that 'her little ear's open to all that I thry to say' [**Roses**, 134]). The Sheila he has conjured up out of dream stuff owes her existence to the poetic imagination that he puts into his songs, and not to the life that has been formed by the venal world of Dublin: 'She gives no honour to gold; neither does her warm heart pine for silks and satins from China and Japan, or the spicy isles of Eastern Asia. A sober black shawl on her shoulders, a simple petticoat, and naked feet would fail to find her craving finer things that envious women love.' [**Roses**, 134.] The Sheila that we soon meet is conventional and even crass, making a mockery of Ayamonn's naïve dream, but it is the dream and the song that nonetheless triumph in *Red Roses for Me*, as the Dreamer's dream and the song of Jannice overshadow her last-minute sign-of-the-cross death in *Within the Gates*.

Act One of *Red Roses*, however, does little to establish Ayamonn Breydon as leadership material, yet one aspect of his function should not be overlooked: he is the centre of the entire web; all the characters are drawn toward him and exist in relation to him; divergent people come to him as to an oracle, a counsellor, a sage; his friends hold diversified ideas but find in him a sympathetic ear. Ayamonn is an odd Renaissance man in a Dublin slum ('Sketchin', readin', makin' songs, an' learnin' Shakespeare,' his mother complains, 'if you had a piano, you'd be thryin' to learn music. Why don't you stick at one thing, an' leave the others alone?' [**Roses**, 132]).

Ayamonn in Act Two is not quite a repetition of the Ayamonn of Act One: he undergoes two changes, a diminution in importance as a central focus and a later augmentation in stature as a person. These are not intended to cancel each other, but serve to prepare the audience for a final awareness of Ayamonn at the end of the play, when he is of enormous significance although physically no longer present. The second act then follows directly from the first; the setting remains the same and the same neighbours and friends invade the Breydon apartment, but instead of revolving completely around Ayamonn they now move significantly without him: it is Brennan who returns the statue of Our Lady of Eblana's Poor that he has stolen and repainted; it is Mullcanny who enrages the crowd into violence, and although Ayamonn has the heroic function of dispersing the rioters, he comes back to announce that it was Mrs Breydon who 'was th' oul' one who saved you from a sudden an' unprovided death' [Roses, 176]; and the most hilarious portion of the scene involves the disputes of Brennan, Mullcanny, and Roory O'Balacaun. When Eeada, Dympna, and Finnoola come in this time, it is not to seek Ayamonn's aid, but to exult over the miraculous return of the statue, oblivious this time of Ayamonn's presence. The defection of Sheila Moorneen has affected Ayamonn and he is somewhat testier now than before (he is quick to show his annoyance to Brennan over the well-meant kidnapping of the statue).

But the hero still has his moments, especially when he lectures the Irish nationalist on the meaning of freedom: 'If we give no room to men of our time to question many things, all things, ay, life itself, then freedom's but a paper flower, a star of tinsel, a dead lass with gay ribbons at her breast an' a gold comb in her hair.' [Roses, 169.] But he rises to his greatest elevation when he denounces Sheila's suggestion that he betray his fellow strikers: 'Go to hell, girl, I have a soul to save as well as you.' [Roses, 172.] This is certainly a far less poetic burst of eloquence, and in its very terse and prosaic nature it suggests a hard and realistic aspect of Ayamonn to offset earlier indications that he is too much the dreamer to be a leader as well. From this angry curse the transformation of Ayamonn moves quickly, as the rector comes to warn Ayamonn of the danger of the strike and the railwaymen come to him to ask for his leadership. 'Tell the Committee, Bill, I'll be there,' Ayamonn responds, 'and that they honour me when they set me in front of my brothers.' [Roses, 183.]

Only with the expressionistic fantasy of the third act can O'Casey wrench the audience away from the Ayamonn who has been at stage centre for almost all of the first half of *Red Roses*, but the technique, so startling in *The Tassie*, is as effective here. When Ayamonn makes his appearance late in the scene, it is as a bearer of magic, as the vital force that transforms the dross of reality for the down-and-out of Dublin into the gold of fantasy. His speeches are wildly poetic, but contain the core of his militant unionism: 'Our sthrike is yours,' he announces. 'A step ahead for us today; another one for you tomorrow.' [Roses, 198.] While on one hand giving his command, 'Don't flinch in th' first flare of a fight,' on the other he brings a spiritul revelation: 'Take heart of grace from your city's hidden splendour.' [Roses, 198.] And it is the city that becomes the central character of the scene, its hidden splendour revealed by O'Casey's stage poetry. Ayamonn is the impressario, the singer and the dancer of the transformation, and when drab reality returns for the down-and-out, he lingers as the protagonist of the dream: 'Osheen mad to sing a song of the revelry dancin' in an' out of God's own vision.' [Roses, 203.]

The off-stage death of Ayamonn in Act Four had been presaged by the dream quality of his appearance in the twilight dance of the previous act and in his own statement in the one before: 'When a true man dies, he is buried in th' birth of a thousand worlds.' [Roses, 179.] And there was Sheila's fear that Ayamonn would be 'in front of gun muzzles, ready to sing a short and sudden death-song!' [Roses, 183.] His brief appearance in the last act (before the battle) is devoid of any great speeches; in fact, he says little. Only once does he actually say anything of significance, but it serves as his statement of belief, the cause for which he is willing to die: 'A, shilling's little to you', he says to the Inspector, the man who will lead the charge in which he will be killed: 'and less to many; to us it is our Shechinah, showing us God's light is near; showing us the way in which our feet must go; a sun-ray on our face; the first step taken in the march of a thousand miles.' [Roses, 211.] His death is reported by the wounded Finnoola (with whom he danced in the fantasy of Act Three): 'He whispered it in me ear as his life fled through a bullet-hole in his chest.... He said this day's but a day's work done, an' it'll be begun again tomorrow.... He sent a quick an' a long farewell to you.' [Roses, 211.]

The essence of Ayamonn is that which survives him, his

posthumous presence. The martyred leader is best estimated by his disciples, he himself undergoing only the change from the passive expounder of a cause to the active martyr of that cause. Reverend Clinton remains a constant: like Sheila he had come to warn Ayamonn of the danger to himself, but unlike her he refuses to insist that Ayamonn heed any such advice. During the last act, prior to Ayamonn's death, he is sorely challenged by his vestrymen, Dowzard and Foster, to disavow Ayamonn (and his church-warden, Inspector Finglas, requests the same in politer terms), but Clinton remains loyal to Ayamonn's right to dissent, and is deeply affected by his death: 'Oh Lord, open Thou mine eyes that I may see Thee, even as in a glass, darkly, in all this mischief and all this woe!' [**Roses, 222.**] Ayamonn's mother, who had previously sought to shield her son from entering into danger, gave him her blessing just before battle, indicating a change of heart: 'Go on your way, my son, an' win. We'll welcome another inch of the world's welfare.' [**Roses, 213.**] (There is a solid indication that Ayamonn's 'way' is a *via crucis*, and when the Rector hears of Ayamonn's death, he 'picks up the broken cross of flowers' [**Roses, 222**].)

It is Sheila, however, who is the best barometer of Ayamonn's effect, and although she does not quite wash his feet with her tears, she is significantly altered by his self-sacrifice. Her colloquy with the Inspector, the man singularly responsible for her lover's death, reveals the Sheila that Ayamonn naïvely idealised in the opening scene. That she can say of Ayamonn's cause, 'Maybe he saw the shilling in th' shape of a new world,' [**Roses, 255**] marks a fine start. Finglas apparently hopes to replace the man he murdered in Sheila's affection,[6] but she who had betrayed the dead man while he lived now refuses this new betrayal. Although somewhat interested in the now not-unsympathetic Tom Finglas she finally denounces him '*Suddenly—with violence*': 'Oh, you dusky-minded killer of more worthy men!' [**Roses, 226.**] No star turns red for Ayamonn, but the lights are left burning in the church where his body lies, and his song is sung by Brennan as 'a finisher-off to a last farewall'. [**Roses, 277**]

Drishogue O'Morrigun resembles Jack more than he does Ayamonn, both in his relatively small role in the play and in his avowed Communist identity. But all three share the distinction of being personalised heroes, with no one in either *Red Roses* or *Oak Leaves* having the magnitude and impersonal magnetism of a Red Jim. But, although we are invited to get close enough to him to see him as a person, Drishogue remains as wooden as Jack in his infallibility (and his Monica seems equally perfect, without Julia's petulant preference for the dance hall, or Sheila's allegiance to her Church). He is an eager warrior ('Oh, how I long to take the sky by storm!'), [Oak, 25] as well as one well versed in what he is fighting for ('And even though we should die, then, damn it all, we shall die for a fair cause' [Oak, 28]). He is kind to his father and considerate of Monica, as well as a loyal friend to Edgar. He keeps his temper no matter how great the provocation. When Feelim is sarcastic in suggesting that Drishogue's U.S.S.R. is a land of perfection he simply answers: 'Far from it; only a hard, bitter, glorious struggle towards it' [Oak, 46]; with the red-baiting Deeda he retorts 'fiercely', but with dignity: 'The people cannot stop for you to catch them up; if you can't go fast enough to keep in step, then pray for death, for you've lost a use for life!' [Oak, 52.] (An advance use of Robin Adair's message to Marthraun—'Die'), and 'You waste God's time and mine, woman' [Oak, 52] (an echo of Reverend Clinton, 'It is a small thing that you weary me, but you weary my God also' [Roses, 223]).

He has a reasonable and balanced attitude: an awareness of historical continuity ('the past has woven us into what we are' [Oak, 26]), a reverence for 'the greatness in England's mighty human soul set forth in what Shakespeare, Shelley, Keats, and Milton sang; in the mighty compass of Darwin's mind' [Oak, 29] and so forth, and a respect for the possibility of an afterlife where 'we shall mingle with a great, gay crowd!' [Oak, 29]. But essentially his enthusiasm is overwhelmingly for life, which he praises poetically to everyone; to Monica he extols 'the moving patterns of flying birds; the stroll through crowded streets ... the musical wile of waves racing towards us, or slowly bidding us farewell; the wild flowers tossing themselves on to the field and into the hedgerow; the sober ecstacy, or jewelled laugh, of children playing; the river's rowdy rush or graceful gliding into sea or lake; the sun asthride the hills, or rainfall teeming down aslant behind them; a charming girl, shy, but ready with her finest favours—oh, these are dear and lovely things to lose!' [Oak, 58-9.] And to Monica's suggestion of a finer life after death, his reply is unemotional but definite: 'Give me but these, and God can keep whatever is behind them.' [Oak, 59.] Although a revoluntionary Communist, Drishogue is depicted as a moderate and temperate man.

In contrast to his British friend Edgar, the Irish hero is given a greater opportunity to excel, even though O'Casey is careful not to denigrate Drishogue's fellow airman to any serious extent. His description of the two youths is calcula- ted to distinguish between primary and secondary heroes, while stressing their common mould: Drishogue 'is a tall lad of twenty or so; a thoughtful, tense face, which is some- what mocked at by a turned-up, freckled nose. Edgar, nearly as tall, is of the same age; his face is plump where Drishogue's is lean; careless good nature, and, perhaps, less imagination, tends to make it, maybe, a trifle too placid' [Oak, 25]. Both young men are caught up in the excitement of their love affairs and their imminent roles as combat fliers, and the distinctions made by the dramatist between the two are therefore crucial to his basic concepts.

Drishogue's ideals in both love and war are contrasted with Edgar's. The latter is somewhat cynical in both areas; he views Jennie as 'grand for the time being' [Oak, 26], but when his companion asks, 'But you don't value her enough to want to spend a lifetime with her?', he is quite blasé: 'Well, hardly; in the cool of the evening, in the deep dusk of the night, she is lovely; but I shouldn't care to have to welcome her the first thing in the morning.' [Oak, 26.] Drishogue's affair with Monica is far more intense, and we learn at the end of the play that they have undergone a civil marriage ceremony and engendered a child—at Monica's instigation. (This, incidentally, is one of the few instances in O'Casey's plays in which young people in love actually marry—or even mention marriage as in any way connected with their love affair—and if we think back to the newly-wed Clitheroes of *The Plough*, we might see something of O'Casey's indifference to the legalisation of love.) Edgar's rather casual attitude toward Jennie does not reflect her love for him, and it is with horror that we later learn of her self-immolation in the burning wreckage of his aircraft: 'She tried to reach her lover,' Monica reports, 'to hold him in her burning arms, and calmly died beside him' [Oak, 105]—a rare instance of Anglo-Saxon suttee.

Edgar's shallowness is equally revealed in his attitude towards the war he is involved in. Drishogue's belief in a fair cause only elicits an impatient response from him: 'Oh, all causes are fair to those who believe in them; I believe in none. I have no cause to die for, such as you love; no principle' [Oak, 28];[7] when Drishogue suggests England as a cause. Edgar is even more impatient: 'Which England? There are so many of them: Conservative England, Liberal England, Labour England, and your own Communist England—for which of them shall I go forth to fight, and perchance, to die? [Oak, 29.] It must be remembered that in contrast to Edgar, Drishogue is an Irishman, a citizen of neutral Eire, and has volunteered to come fight. But when Monica mistakenly suggests that her lover has come to fight for England, Drishogue is indignant ('Love of England! Good God, woman, I have no love for England!' [Oak, 61]) and he is very specific about where his loyalties lie:

I'm fighting for the people. I'm fighting against the stormy pillagers who blackened the time-old walls of Guernica, and tore them down; who loaded their cannon in th' name of Christ to kill the best men Spain could boast of; who stripped the olive groves and tore up orange trees to make deep graves for men, heaping the women on the men, and the children on the women. I was too young then to go out armed for battle, but time has lengthened an arm long enough to pull the Heinkels and the Dorniers out of the sky, and send them tumbling down to hell! [Oak, 61.]

The basic distinction in *Oak Leaves* is not between the Irish hero and the British hero (each dies as valiantly as the other), but between the idealist with working-class roots and the cynical aristocrat who has lost contact with a people and a cause.

Drishogue as an Irish airman who foresees his death is the last in a series of these three heroic young men who die for their ideals; had he lived he might have become the disillusioned Manus Moanroe who returned to Ireland to find his native land no whit the better for his efforts. The one Irish hero who survives during the plays of O'Casey's middle period is Jack O'Killigain of *Purple Dust*, but here O'Casey separates the combat situation from the conflict of the play itself. Like the protagonists of the other three 'leadership' plays, O'Killigain is the young man-in-love, but here the love affair is the central combat of the drama. His war experiences are already in the past, and the initial distinction is contained in the first workman's report prior to O'Killigain's appearance: 'A handsome, hefty young sthripling, with a big seam in his arm that he got from a bullet fired in Spain.' [**Dust,** 9.] As Drishogue had already indicated for us, that 'big seam' is O'Killigain's passport to instant stature, and indeed for O'Casey this particular character is a towering human being. Nowhere in all the plays is there a description of a character quite like the one O'Casey provides for Jack O'Killigain:

He is a tall, fair young man twenty-five or twenty-six years old. He has a rough, clearly-cut face; dogged-looking when he is roused, and handsome when he is in in a good humour, which is often enough. He is clean-shaven, showing rather thick but finely-formed lips. His hair, though cut-short, is thick and striking. When he speaks of something interesting him, his hands make graceful gestures. He has had a pretty rough life, which has given him a great confidence in himself; and wide reading has strengthened that confidence considerably. He is dressed in blue dungarees and wears a deep yellow muffler, marked with blue decoration, round his neck. He is humming a tune as he comes in. [**Dust,** 9–10.]

And O'Killigain more than lives up to his advance publicity. Coming immediately after *The Star Turns Red*, *Purple Dust* (although it has two male heroes) gives O'Killigain the function of serving as both Jack and Red Jim, the personal hero and the larger-than-life leader. The effect on the audience of such dimensions has to be immediate, and O'Killigain's first appearance must establish him permanently with the audience. Exposition (for an audience without the benefit of the author's stage directions before them) has helped considerably: the three workmen discuss their foreman O'Killigain in reverential tones, although it is apparent that only the second workman, Philib O'Dempsey, is actually a partisan. Not only do we learn about the 'big seam' but that Jack is 'ever fillin' the place with reckless talk against the composure of the Church' [**Dust, 9**] (the third workman), that 'Canon Chreehewel's mad to dhrive him outa th' place' [**Dust, 9**] (the first workman), and, from his defender, that there is 'ne'er another man to be found as thrue or as clever as him till you touch a city's centre' [**Dust, 9**].

But none of this is actually relevant to Jack's initial appearance; although a fighter and a leader, it is as a lover that he functions primarily, and his opening scene brings him into confrontation with Avril, the mistress of Basil Stoke. The saccharine blarney of Irish love talk may be suitable for a limited character like the Dunphy boy in 'The Moon Shines on Kylenamoe' ('Gra mo chree, I'd rather own you than own all Ireland, without division; I would, achisleh!' [**Moon, 135**]), but it would demean a grown man of strength and pride like O'Killigain. Yet O'Killigain has got to be impressive as a successful wooer of the Englishman's mistress, and do so with poetic language. Possessing a strong sense of ironic delight, he is capable of seeing the humour of his situation, and making the most of it. His love-play in front of the workmen is geared to set him off to best advantage, as he dances rings around the charmed Avril.

That he has his tongue in cheek is immediately apparent as he extols the old house which he had just joined the workmen in deriding (and they too join in with exaggerated praise). This means of establishing a rapport with her is obviously too easy, and after whirling her about in a reel, O'Killigain purposely puts himself at a disadvantage by giving her 'a sharp skelp on the behind' [**Dust**, 13]. Avril is compelled to be indignant before the onlookers, so that O'Killigain is faced with offering an abject apology (which would have lowered him in their estimation) or risk losing the nearly-won woman. His self-confidence and mischievous sense of humour give him his victory without either loss of face: 'Sure, I meant no harm, miss; it was simply done in the excitement of the game,' he comments ('with some mockery in his voice' [**Dust**, 13]), quickly shifting the disadvantage to Avril by inviting the others to comment as well: 'Wasn't it, now, Bill?' [**Dust**, 13.] Avril now must either lose face or lose Jack if she is either too quick or too slow in accepting his unsatisfactory apology. Her ploy then is to dismiss the others and leave herself alone with O'Killigain (which is of course what he hopes for); now she can hoist her green flag without compromising herself before bystanders: 'Never again, mind you—especially when others are here to stand and gape.' [**Dust**, 14.] The last phrase means total surrender, and with this signal. Jack launches into the most flagrant examples of romantic blarney, exalting her as 'a girl of grace, fit to find herself walkin' beside all the beauty that ever shone before the eyes o' man since Helen herself unbound her thresses to dance her wild an' willin' way through the sthreets o' Throy!' [**Dust**, 14.] Avril is clever enough to recognise a line of luring words when she hears them ('It's I that know the truth is only in the shine o' the words you shower on me' [**Dust**, 14]), but she is eager to take the bait nonetheless, while Jack with pretended guilelessness admits to a gift of gab. It takes no time at all now for them to arrange a night-time assignation.

Jack O'Killigain's success as a political leader is bound up with his amorous conquest of Avril, and this scene depicting his victory in the initial skirmish is important: rarely has the O'Casey lover been observed in the process of attaining the woman he loves. Harry Heegan has Jessie in tow right from the beginning, only to lose her; Jack and Julia are already in love with each other when the play opens, and

Drishogue and Monica are secretly married. Robin has served his jail term for kissing Marion, and the Manus-Foorawn affair is already a thing of the past. Ayamonn is confident of his claim on Sheila, and her defection casts serious doubts about his ability to succeed in any situation. The encounter of Donal and Minnie, however, takes place on stage, but it is Minnie who is the active wooer of the two, a sad commentary on the poet as a 'shadow' of a lover as well. Only the winning of Jannice by the Dreamer prepares us for the O'Killigain-Avril interplay, and even there the lover's awareness of the Young Whore's economic situation forces him to prevail with pounds and shillings in addition to song. O'Killigain now must not only entrance Avril and disenchant her with Basil (an easy matter since she already is contemptuous of that 'toddler thricking with a woman's legs; a thief without the power to thieve the thing he covets; a louse burrowing in a young lioness's belly; a perjurer in passion; a gutted soldier bee whose job is done, and still hangs on to life!' [Dust, 15–16]), but lead her out of Ormond Manor and all it stands for. From the beginning it can be seen that he is a leader of men (of those strong enough to follow his lead): Philib O'Dempsey has announced that 'if he goes, I'll go too.' [Dust, 9.]

O'Killigain's sexual magic with women is apparently universal: Souhaun and Cloyne in fact engage in a jealous spat over O'Killigain, who had put his arm around the maid's neck, much to her delight. At the mere mention of the foreman by Cloyne, Souhaun has her hackles up: 'If you think that O'Killigain has taken a fancy to you, you never made a bigger mistake, my girl.' [Dust, 31.] But the pretty servant's final comment to her is devastating. 'There's a withering old woman, not a hundred miles from where I am,' she announces to Souhaun (whom the playwright has described as 'a woman of thirty-three years of age' who 'must have been a very handsome girl and she is still very good-looking, in a more matronly way' [Dust, 6]), 'who ought to take her own advice, an' keep from thryin' her well-faded thricks of charm on poor Mr O'Killigain herself!' [Dust, 31.] But it is of course Avril who is destined to be carried off by 'poor Mr O'Killigain', while Souhaun accepts a similar offer from

Philib O'Dempsey. With one of his finest creations of a masculine hero in the forefront, O'Casey nonetheless considered it necessary to supplement his victory with a secondary line of attack. The personal magnetism of Jack O'Killigain might seem too personal a reason for success here, and the emphasis might remain exclusively with the Irish lover's sexual conquest. The triumph over the ghouls of the past has got to be complete: they are to be worn down by the wild Irish, their castle turned into their tomb, and each has to be made to feel the loss of what he treasures most, the Irish mistress who is symbolic of his position of control. O'Killigain and O'Dempsey, two different kinds of Irishmen, succeed in luring away Avril and Souhaun, two different types of women, from Stoke and Poges. Sexual conquest in *Purple Dust* is a metaphor for political annihilation, and provides a far subtler framework for O'Casey's viewpoint than strike, war and revolution.

The campaign waged against the Poges-Stoke Establishment by the Irish foreman is also a battle of intellectual attrition. Poges is ironically impressed with O'Killigain at first; he too is aware of the aura of majesty surrounding the man, and he attempts to attach O'Killigain to him in a feudal relationship of lord and favoured vassal. But the workingman who had answered Souhaun's incredulous question, 'How could a common worker be a king?' by stating, 'Easier than for a king to be a common worker,' [Dust, 18] has no intention of playing Poges's game. Poges fails to elicit any enthusiasm over the Tudor house and its glorious past ('I let the dead bury their dead' [Dust, 21] is all O'Killigain will say) or over Wordsworth, whom the Irishman sums up as 'A tired-out oul' blatherer; a tumble-down thinker; a man who made a hiding-place of his own life; a shadow parading about as the sun; a poet, sensitive to everything but man; a bladder blown that sometimes gave a note of music; a fool who thought the womb of the world was Wordsworth; a poet who jailed the striving of man in a moral lullaby; a snail to whom God gave the gleam of the glowworm; a poet singing the song of safety first!' [Dust, 21–2.] Poges realises that he mas misjudged his man; having insisted on this intellectual colloquy because 'O'Killigain's

131

an intelligent man, and is only too glad to learn a little about the finer things of life' [**Dust, 21**], he now quickly terminates the coversation and labels O'Killigain 'a shocking example of bad taste and ignorance' [**Dust, 22**].

But Poges's ego does not allow him to learn from the experience and henceforth avoid locking horns with the foreman, and in Act Two he again attempts to 'board' O'Killigain: of all available subjects he chooses to lecture the foreman on the greatness of England as a land of 'progress, civilisation, truth, justice, honour, humanity, righteousness, and peace' [**Dust, 73**] (and a successful exporter of these virtues to other lands!). 'An' God Himself is England's butler!' is O'Killigain's sarcastic retort, and Poges's angry cry of 'vile slander!' only encourages O'Killigain's statement that 'in a generation or so the English Empire will be remembered only as a half-forgotten nursery rhyme!' [**Dust, 74.**] Yet, until the final schism (O'Killigain's flaunting of his affair in Poges's face when the English master is attempting to be 'firm' with him about it), Poges continues to rely upon O'Killigain as a superior workman and competent foreman, in much the same way that Reiligan upheld Manus against the attacks of Canon Burren, and Sailor Mahan defended his 'best lorry-driver' against Father Domineer.

This breed of foreman is a refreshing addition to the O'Casey roster: a high mark of personal superiority and leadership qualities is inherent in the good worker, the master craftsman, the man who works with his hands and can lead others in their work. The pride Fluther Good took in a job well done is the first positive attribute associated with him. Ayamonn Breydon's employers think well enough of his work to attempt to win him over with a foremanship, as Sheila reports: 'if you divide yourself from the foolish men, and stick to your job, you'll soon be a foreman of some kind or other.' [**Roses, 172.**] In *Oak Leaves* O'Casey introduces an Irish foreman in the last act, a man of almost mysterious powers who transforms the eighteenth-century manor into a hub of industrial activity: 'the young foreman ... blows a whistle sharply, and the room becomes alive with movement—the belts travel, the wheels turn, and the drop-hammer rises and falls.' [**Oak, 109.**] In *The Drums of*

Father Ned and 'Behind the Green Curtains' two other factory foremen are presented, the first a secondary character and the second a masculine hero of the O'Killigain mould.

Tom Killsallighan in *The Drums* is a carpenter and the foreman of McGilligan's building concern (the carpenter as a symbolic figure needs only O'Killigain's important statement to be seen in full perspective: 'Th' king o' a world that doesn't exist was a carpenter' [**Dust,** 18]). Tom is overshadowed in the play by young Michael Binnington, but he holds his own as a man of action. His first appearance with other young people is in effect to push old Binnington and McGilligan out to make way for the Tostal rehearsals. McGilligan tries to repel the invasion ('I'm your boss, you're th' foreman of me buildin' jobs, an' I ordher you to get goin' with th' timber!' [**Ned,** 34]) but Tom insists that the 'timber can wait; the Tosthal can't,' [**Ned,** 34] and McGilligan is pushed out.

Tom as an O'Casey spokesman is apparent from his opening speech ('if a song doesn't encircle the hammer and sickle, or a song silence them, at times, when a man's longing goes gay, then they become, not the tools of men, but the tools of a slave' [**Ned,** 33]), but he is a rather timid lover at first, no Robin Adair risking jail for a kiss. When Bernadette tells him that Father Ned recommends that boys and girls 'linger close together' [**Ned,** 49] Tom's first reaction is: 'A dangerous thing to say' [**Ned,** 49]; but he soon changes his mind and lingers close to Bernadette. In the third act, when the issue of the Communist timber imported into Ireland becomes crucial, it is Tom who is firm in insisting that it be accepted: early in the scene he had stated, 'When I work timber, avic, I don't ask th' wood if it's Christian or Communist,' [**Ned,** 79] and during the controversy he reasserts his contention: 'There's other things need burnin' more than th' timber on th' wharf. Th' things of th' earth that God helps us to grow can't be bad, let them come from Catholic Italy, Protestant Sweden, or Communist Russia. I say take what God gives us by the labourin' hands of other men.' [**Ned,** 97.]

The Drums of Father Ned, like many another Sean

O'Casey play, does not focus greatly upon a central character, and several characters, male and female, collaborate to advance the central thesis in their actions and their ideas. Tom Killsallighan plays a lesser role to Michael Binnington, although a strongly supporting one, as can be seen from the author's description of his two young heroes; like Drishogue and Edgar they enter simultaneously. Michael is a few years older, taller, and thinner (although Tom is 'of a more muscular build' [Ned, 30]). Yet Michael is no more the hero of the play than Tom, in fact somewhat less so during the first two acts, the Tom-Bernadette romance being more prominent than that of Michael and Nora. But Michael is Binnington's son (and heir), and his rebellion against his father and his father's domain is decidedly stronger than Tom ignoring his boss's command. To the astonishment of the Mayor and Deputy Mayor, comes the news that Michael and Nora are opposing them as candidates for the Dail—the rebellion against father on political grounds is more significant than Michael Reiligan's effete blustering against his father's stinginess or Communist Jack merely ignoring the Old Man. And on occasion Michael Binnington voices the O'Casey yea, as when he declares that 'our hearts beat best to th' music of a dirge; our marching feet too often point the way to a grave. But with Father Ned, th' young will let th' dead bury their dead, an' give their thought an' energy to th' revelry of life!' [Ned, 87.] (Christ's command in Matthew 8:22, 'Follow me; and let the dead bury the dead,' is repeated often by O'Casey's heroes: Jack in *The Star Turns Red*, O'Killigain in *Purple Dust*, and now Michael Binnington.)

Before the final act is over, Michael reveals himself to us as a stand-in for Sean O'Casey, as the battle between Protestant and Catholic in *Rose and Crown* is re-enacted, with Michael reading O'Casey's lines,[8] arriving at the Joycean conclusion that God may be but 'a shout in th' street.' [Ned, 92].[9] Michael's unique bombshell, however, is even more potent than his unorthodox description of the Deity: it regards the sexual revolution that has been brewing throughout the O'Casey plays. In contrast to Monica's news that she bears Drishogue's child legitimised by their registry marriage, we have Michael's announcement to both sets of parents that their planned efforts to separate the young lovers are somewhat late; that they had 'lived in the same flat'—Nora adds, 'An' slept in th' same bed o' Sundays.' [Ned, 99.]

O'Casey was more concerned with presenting human characters than heroes. He often preferred women as the more heroic personages, and often concentrated on the small foibles that give human size to even the most important figure. The one notable exception was Red Jim, a lionisation of a real hero and a character with a superhuman task in leading a revolution against vast odds some time in the future. The title character of *The Drums of Father Ned* is an extension of that valiant leader, with many elements of the glorious Cock of *Cock-a-Doodle Dandy* as well. By abstracting Father Ned from the visual action of the play, the dramatist chose a technique which kept his abstract figure off the stage entirely. His superhuman qualities were needed for the miraculous transformation of Doonavale, and his supernatural aspects kept him well within the world of fantasy. Father Ned is ubiquitous in Doonavale but never on stage; his heroic stature need not be confined within the human form of any actor, but should be allowed to expand within the imagination of the audience. By fusing the leadership qualities of Jim with the mirthful mischief of the Cock, O'Casey arrived at his most felicitous solution to the conflict between ideology and dramaturgy in the play, a solution obviously suggested by the wild spurts of inventive fantasy that he incorporated into the late volumes of his autobiographies. In 'Figuro in the Night' he again utilised this technique, although it owes its origins more to *Cock-a-Doodle Dandy*; the Birdlike Lad, when he finally does appear before the viewers, shows himself to be essentially descended from the Demon Cock.

In 'Behind the Green Curtains' we meet the last of O'Casey's foremen-heroes, Martin Boeman. At first he is rather inauspicious: he sits about mocking the two superstitious biddies, engaging the pious Dan Basawn in religious controversy (mocking him as well), and egging on the terrified Catholic intellectuals into going into the Protestant

135

church for the funeral service of a patron of the arts. But in the second and third scenes he systematically begins to take over the limelight, primarily because the would-be hero, Senator Dennis Chatastray, proves too weak to assume his role. Boeman could have been spotted immediately from O'Casey's familiar description: 'A taller man [than Basaun], nearing 30, dressed in dungarees, but with a vivid handkerchief round his neck, and a bowler hat on his head, worn at a rakish angle.' [Curtains, 11.] We soon learn that he is Chatastray's 'foreman factory engineer' [Curtains, 18] and from his employer's respectful tone to him, even when he is mocking everyone, it is apparent that he is a valued employee. When all the others turn timidly away from the Protestant service but Reena, Boeman joins, commenting, 'I'm goin' after you, me gallus lass.' [Curtains, 24.]

Boeman's appearance in the second scene is in an official capacity, a factory dispute concerning religious intermarriage: the same Christy Kornavaun who had prevented the Catholic intelligentsia from entering the Protestant church has now been stirring up the workers at Chatastray's factory against the marriage. Boeman reports that Kornavaun 'blathered to th' girrls about bein' firm, an' that a Catholic girrl marryin' a Protestant wasn't a marriage at all; upset them all, an' held up th' work. I hooked him, and bid him a rough goodbye at th' factory gate.' [Curtains, 40.] To Reena he politely announces that 'I happen to be a Red,' adding, 'for years, pretty lady, for years,' [Curtains, 47] and as he did in his mocking conversation with Basaun, he soon gets the upper hand: when Reena cries out that he has 'no right to such opinions in this holy land of ours', he reminds her of the motto that she intends to march under: 'Free Thought in a Free World' [Curtains, 47].

An altogether familiar O'Casey hero, Martin Boeman is different only in his reluctance to accept a leading role. He defers to Chatastray throughout, apparently hoping that he can lend to his employer that modicum of courage necessary for him to stand up against hypocrisy and bigotry. Both Reena and Noneen, Chatastray's maid, have been beaten by pious Catholic bullies—as is Chatastray soon after—and Reena hopes that through her love for Dennis Chatastray

136

she can redeem him. Martin, meanwhile, stands by at the sidelines: he rescues Noneen and is going to take her away to England, to 'stop with me married sister an' me till she settles into a job' [Curtains, 76]. But when Chatastray turns tail, abandons Reena, and runs after the others to join the parade, Martin Boeman steps forward. Awkward at first as a lover ('I think I love you, Reena,' he says to her, 'very simply' [Curtain, 82]), he pulls away with embarrassment when she kisses him, but soon reveals his O'Killigain heritage, and 'roughly and warmly clasps her in his arms, and kisses her' [Curtains, 83]. He picks her up and carries her out, rescuing her from Ireland. His political convictions and his virility as a lover mark him as the final hero in a long succession of O'Casey heroes.

Unsocial Socialists

In Bernard Malamud's 'Idiots First' the dying Mendel is turned away from Mr Fishbein's door, the rich man insisting. 'I never give to unorganised charity.' To several of O'Casey's most outspoken humanitarians the personal and human needs of individuals around them are classified as 'unorganised charity' and although they are intent on saving the world, they often turn a cold shoulder to many of the individual demands made upon them. Loving mankind in the mass but furious when a fellowman treads on his toes, the anti-social Socialist often fails to see the discrepancy between what he preaches from soapboxes and what he practises in his own kitchen. And with more than usual glee Sean O'Casey undertakes to dissect this inhumane humanitarian, often championing what he believes in while satirising the kind of human being he has become. Often these socialists are O'Casey's spokesmen, but are nonetheless treated to a scathing dissection by him.

O'Casey's own identity as a Socialist, rather than any antipathy toward Socialism, is basically responsible for his hard look at the Socialist *manqué*. By the 1920s, the flame that was Jim Larkin burned only as hard and gemlike, and seemed removed from the fiery all-embracing determination prevalent in 1913, while Jim Connolly's martyrdom had been for the nationalist cause rather than that of the workers. The Bill O'Brien who sat behind the desk in Union headquarters was at least three removes from the Larkin ideal, and O'Casey had physically removed himself from active participation. Not yet a self-exile from Ireland, Sean O'Casey was already self-exiled from the workers' Ireland he had once envisioned. Detachment and irony became fixed aspects of the playwright's equipment (while passionate sympathy for particular individuals maintained a balance which prevented a cynical reaction from setting in). By the end of the thirties O'Casey tackled the problem of differentiating in dramatic form between the real labour leader and the mediocrities and opportunists who attempt to displace him. Red Jim in *The Star Turns Red* is confronted by such types as Brallain, Caheer, Sheasker, Eglish and the Secretary: his triumph over them takes place 'Tomorrow, or the next day' and is intended as a desired reversal of the historical trend in the Irish labour movement that O'Casey had known.

The confrontation between good and bad Union leaders in *The Star* is certainly an idealisation, not because O'Casey did not worship Larkin and despise Bill O'Brien with cheerful disgust, but because the hand-to-hand combat in the second act never took place in Irish Union history, the O'Briens sliding in instead to fill a vacuum left by the Larkins and Connollys. In *Inishfallen* O'Casey portrays an Old Bill O'Brien that rivals his cameos of corrupt leadership in the play: 'Bill had no look of a Labour leader about him, but rather that of a most respectable clerk at home in a sure job.' [**Inish, 6.**] O'Casey concludes that this self-proclaimed leader of the working class is not only a bourgeois, but that he is not even a 'complete' human being:

A frozen sense of self-importance animated the man; and the clever, sharp, shrewd mind at white heat behind the cold, pale mask, was ever boring a silent way through all opposition to the regulation and control of the Irish Labour movement. So this curious, silent shape, always neatly dressed, wearing in the lapel of his coat an invisible last shred of the tattered red flag, once held high by Larkin and Connolly, could be seen only at meetings,

138

or on a bicycle on his way to one; or in his newly-furnished office, if one had a passport for admission; but never, as far as Sean knew, at a picture gallery, at a play, at a music hall; or in a pub with a pint before him, or a half of malt waiting at his elbow; never even to be seen rambling a country lane with a lassie on his arm; too high-minded, too busy, too full of all sweet, good things in himself to be troubled with these things of the earth, earthy. [**Inish, 7.**]

A Union man does not live by trade unionism alone, according to O'Casey, and even his brand of trade unionism makes O'Brien suspect. Basic to O'Casey's table of values in estimating any man is the degree of his passionate involvement in life, and this boss of the labour movement emerges as a frigid virgin; the same table of values was operative when O'Casey undertook the creation of individual characters in his plays. As early as 'Kathleen Listens In' the dramatist was sticking pins in such people as Jimmy the worker to test for blood, bile, water or hot air. Every character in this political fantasy was developed for scrutiny and satire, and Jimmy is only one weak link in a vast chain of effete Irish attitudes. He is no worse than the business man or the farmer, the politicos of various shades or the Nationalists of varying degrees of convictions, but he is set apart from the beginning, and one suspects that more was expected from him than from the others.

As a representative of the Irish working class Jimmy is already separated from the others in the semi-rural and quasi-bourgeois ambiance of 'Kathleen Listens In': his claim as a suitor to Kathleen herself is not nearly as definite as those of the others, nor does he press it with any degree of assurance. Instead he complains about his lot, threatens either to go on strike or emigrate to Soviet Russia, and is at his best when he demands that the O'Houlihan house be painted red. His gripe is about overwork and lack of adequate pay, but beneath these surface complaints lurks the deeper concern with his lack of status in the new Ireland: "What's the good o' lovin' Kathleen, when she won't take any notice o' you? Others can hold her hand for hours, an' bring her for walks, but whenever she sees me, she passes me by with her nose in the air—just because I can't play the bloody piano!' [**Kathleen, 290.**] (Many years later, Bernadette Shillayley will blithely violate class barriers by brazenly playing the Binnington piano in *The Drums of Father Ned*: as a domestic in the household she does not whine with self-pity like Jimmy, but *takes* for herself what she believes should be hers.) Jimmy is frustrated in his efforts to assert his rights and can only stalk about belligerently, threatening to 'knock th' stuffin' ' out of the Business Man and shouting his slogan: 'Socialism's the only hope o' th' workers.' [**Kathleen, 296.**] But Jimmy himself seems far from hopeful.

There is quite a difference between a prototypal figure in a political fantasy and a character like Jerry Devine in *Juno*, but the latter shares the irresolute and pathetic aspects of Jimmy the workman. He is already a discarded suitor when he appears in the opening scene of the play, Mary Boyle having replaced him with the bourgeois Charlie Bentham. He has begun on the left foot with Captain Boyle by bringing news of a job and soon finds himself on no footing at all with nose-in-the-air Mary. His best ploy is his news that he is slated for the Secretaryship of the Union and would be in a position to marry Mary Boyle on an annual income of 350 pounds. Mary is set to go out on strike for her trade-union principles, but her eyes are fixed on a better financial prospect than he can offer; Jerry makes no attempt to appeal to her on the basis of his working-class situation but on the advanced status his Secretaryship would give him. (It is more than just unkind speculation to see Jerry Devine some fifteen years later as the Secretary in *The Star Turns Red*.)

From the behaviour of Jerry Devine in the last act of the play it is apparent that Sean O'Casey expected more of him than he was able to be, that the playwright himself is as disappointed as the audience with Jerry. Mary Boyle had no illusions: she finds it incredible that her former beau could be magnanimous enough to offer to marry her now that she is pregnant with Bentham's child—and her incredulity of course proves justified. They had been talking at cross-purposes: Jerry had risen to the full height of his capacity for forgiveness by proposing marriage to the woman who had previously jilted him for another and was now abandoned, but the news of her more complicated condition sends him into apologetic withdrawal. It was not just as a man that he proposed his eternal love for the discarded Mary, but in the name of his ideals: 'Mary, Mary, I am pleading for your love. With Labour, Mary, humanity is above everything; we are the Leaders in the fight for a new life.' [Juno, 80.] But Jerry's concept of a New Life is still governed by the old middle-class morality, and the Leader beats a hasty retreat when he finds that morality has been compromised; 'it's only as I expected,' the worldlier Mary comments, 'your humanity is just as narrow as the humanity of the others.' [Juno, 81.] Mary Boyle had never met a Jack O'Killigain or Ayamonn Breydon—and such men as they did not exist in the early O'Casey plays.

By the time O'Casey began to write plays in earnest he had already made the important choice between nationalistic and socialistic ideals, divorcing himself from the Citizen Army when it seemed likely that it would postpone the struggle for a workers' Ireland. It was a painful decision for O'Casey to make, and as David Krause has indicated, O'Casey lived with the dichotomy within himself between the Class War and the Irish Insurrection.[10] Once the Irish nation became a reality (and an expectedly disappointing one for him), O'Casey the self-exile in England could devote himself to Communism primarily in the thirties and forties, but in the mid-twenties the dichotomy was a very real one, as seen in *Juno and the Paycock* and *The Plough and the Stars*. There is no direct confrontation in the former. Johnny Boyle sells out the I.R.A. and is rubbed out in turn; Jerry Devine opts for the Secretaryship in his Union and is snubbed by the social-climbing Mary. The Nationalist and the Socialist exist independent of each other, two separate sub-plots in the general dilemma of the Boyle family.

In *The Plough*, however, the Covey and Uncle Peter bang heads repeatedly, acting out the differences between Nationalism and Labour on a parodically microcosmic level.

The Covey has no real role in the action of the play except as a mouther of Socialist ideas and an irritant to the foolish old uncle, and in creating him for participation in the slice of Irish life during the Rising, O'Casey had been gratuitous. His actual case against the Covey is contained in his description of the character: 'He is about twenty-five, tall, with lines on his face that form a perpetual protest against life as he conceives it to be.' [Plough, 169.] O'Casey's quarrel is not with the Covey's conception of life but with his protest against it: the author is differentiating between the justice of the protest and the personality of the protestor. There is a basic limitation in the Covey as a person which defeats his value as a Socialist; whether he is arguing with Fluther that a man is 'a question of the accidental gatherin' together of mollycewels an' atoms' [Plough, 170] or with Uncle Peter over the dirty dungarees flung on top of Peter's clean white shirt, it is the same querulous voice and the same self-important tone.

First-act encounters with Fluther and Peter show off the Covey poorly enough, but his exchange with Rosie Redmond in the second act makes him look ludicrous as well: he fails to realise that her echoing of his ideas is merely part of her come-on, and he warms up to the prospect of lecturing her on the need for the workers' 'conthrol o' th' means o' production, rates of exchange, an' th' means of disthribution' [Plough, 197]. But when she begins to demonstrate her stock-in-trade, the Covey in terror withdraws his. He flees from her as he fled from the sword-waving Peter, calling in 'Cuckoo-oo' from his safety outside—as he had done to the old man. Unable to convert Rosie without taking dangerous risks, he teams up with the pro-British Bessie Burgess (but she is soon ejected from the pub for fighting with Mrs Gogan); he again confronts Fluther, this time on Fluther's contribution to the Labour Movement, and is also ejected, leaving Fluther to gallantly take possession of Rosie. Once the Easter Rising is under way, the Covey spends his time looting and playing cards, saying little about Socialism until he meets his opposite number, Corporal Stoddard of the British Army:

Corporal Stoddard. Ow, I know. I'm a Sowcialist moiself, but I 'as to do my dooty.

The Covey (*ironically*). Dooty! Th' only dooty of a Socialist is th' emancipation of th' workers. [**Plough, 249.**]

And when the Covey attempts to engage the British Socialist further in the usual conversation, the Tommy puts an immediate end to the argument with a succinct 'Ow, cheese it, Paddy, cheese it!' [**Plough, 250.**]

O'Casey himself might never have entertained the notion of joining the unlovely Socialists, considering his experiences with them. He felt definite tugs from both directions, from the Connolly forces and from the Griffith nationalists, and records in 'At the Sign of the Pick and Shovel' (*Drums under the Windows*) how drab the fact of Irish Socialism appeared to him in the person of a 'gaunt young man' [**Window, 15**] named Tom Egan, peddling pamphlets which bore such homely names as *Socialism Made Easy* and *Can a Catholic be a Socialist?* His gaunt face, melancholy mouth, and tone of 'pitiful tolerance' [**Window, 16**] are enough to sour young Sean's interest in the movement. 'Aw, God, th' ignorance here's devastatin'! said Egan' (when Sean wants to know just what James Connolly is Secretary of); 'Secretary of the Irish Socialist Republican Party, an' if you knew all you should know, you wouldn't have t'ask.' [**Window, 16.**] To Egan there is only the sad condition of 'the woe of th' world' [**Window, 16**] but Sean has already found something more, something that adds the social quality of involvement with life to the specific cause advanced by the Party: 'There's joy and a song or two,' he tells Egan, anticipating the Dreamer's words to the Atheist, 'the people sang as they went their way to tear the Bastille down.' [**Window, 17.**]

To O'Casey being a Socialist was not enough; a man is a man for all that. The Irish champion of the cause of the workers sees through the folly of a nationalistic insurrection, while his British counterpart concedes that the call of country supersedes even Socialist principles; Fluther brings the demented Nora home from the battle area and Bessie loses her life caring for her. It is the humanity of Fluther and Bessie that is central to the author's sympathies in *The Plough*. Jerry Devine is damned because he cannot bring himself to accept the 'fallen' Mary, and sells out his humanitarian principles in his act of cowardice; the Covey gives vocal lip service to his ideas, but in no way translates them actively in the course of his interaction with other people. And even one of O'Casey's most sympathetic characters is revealed to have a dead spot in an otherwise generous heart: Ned the Atheist in *Within the Gates* has cared for the illegitimate daughter of the woman he loved, but saw his duty to her primarily in teaching her his ideas; the Dreamer soon discoveres the dead spot, asking, 'And did you bring her into touch with song?' [**Gates, 124**.] The humanitarian who insists that he 'had no time for song' [**Gates, 124**] is insufficient as a human being, despite the basic soundness of his learned ideas. It is the Dreamer, actively in love with life for whatever it turns out to be, who is the hero of *The Gates*, and the dancing whore Jannice who is the heroine.

5
The Heroine as Hero

SOPHOCLES'S Antigone bewailed not only the misery of her circumstances, but that such miseries should happen to so young a girl. Accepting the reality of her death, she comments: 'soon I shall stand on Acheron's shore, I who have no portion in the song they sing for brides, nor the evening song before the bridal chamber; but the Lord of the Dark Lane will be my bridegroom.' When we acknowledge the tragic fall of the masculine hero, we reiterate an inherent assumption that separates the stronger from the weaker sex (half-consciously we differentiate between Oedipus the King and Antigone the Young Girl). Misfortune consuming an Antigone effects a greater pull towards pity than towards terror, and seems more appropriate for melodrama than for high tragedy, yet Sophocles was not the only tragedian to make of the Antigones the stuff of tragedy. The Greeks also had their Iphigenias and Electras, as well as the maturer women, Phaedras, Medeas, and Andromaches, all of whom have been perpetuated by dramatists during the centuries that followed.

The twentieth-century dramatist then is not alone in considering women fit subject matter for tragic drama, although his frequent suspicion, that tragedy on any scale grander than the personal one looks somewhat absurd in the modern world, may have led him to prefer the young female from whom greatness and strength are not often expected and certainly never taken for granted. O'Neill's Anna Christie rises above the men who surround her, but what puny men they are! And O'Neill went on in later plays to add physical giganticism to his heroines' proportions in counterpoint over the Jamey Tyrones. Having played out his Ronnie-Hamlet, Arnold Wesker turned his attention in *Roots* to the Beatie-Ophelia—no longer does the young girl succumb with fragility to the senseless power of the masculine world: she fights back. And if this be melodrama, O'Casey makes the most of it. He had every intention of elevating melodramic devices to reputable positions in serious drama, and his women often carried the burden.

Minnie Powell first walked across O'Casey's stage in 1923, heralding a parade of young women of unusual strength, many of whom, like Minnie, eclipsed the men who were their counterparts. Not that it takes much to eclipse Shields and Davoren. As we have seen, they do more to efface themselves than Minnie would have intended: in their situations she serves as catalyst. It is only the absence of any intention on her part to play the heroine that results in her ascendance. The role that she assumes is Davoren's inspires her for a 'lesser' attempt in order to emulate the gunman-on-the-run. When the hero proves to be a non-entity, Minnie's heroism becomes the only heroic criterion in the play.

As such she is O'Casey's first important portrayal of the concept of heroism found in the most unlikely places. He would soon go on to develop the motif in his older women, in such diverse characters as Juno Boyle and Bessie Burgess, but first he gave full romantic play to the plight of the young heroine. Here, as in later incarnations, O'Casey abjured a simple diamond-in-the-rough stereotype, insisting that the heroic quality exist as innate in the character. There is no mistaking from the very beginning of *The Plough* that Bessie has guts, but bravery for self-protection or self-aggrandisement is quite different from self-sacrifice for Nora. Minnie has nothing of the gutsy about her, but immediately reveals the romantic awe of the hero that will take possession of her when quick decisions are required. The dual facets of timidity and audacity are demanded from her in O'Casey's description of her entrance into the Shields-Davoren tenement room: 'Minnie Powell enters with an easy confidence one would not expect her to possess from her gentle way of knocking.' [**Shadow**, 105.] O'Casey's responsibility then becomes a matter of demonstrating that these contradictory aspects can logically co-exist. His explanation of her personality is by now a familiar one (she shares it with the masculine heroes: survival as a self-supporting orphan has made her one of the fittest), and she wears the distinctive splash of colour that is the sign of vibrant life (her brown costume and accessories 'are crowned by a silk tam-o'-shanter of a rich blue tint') [Shadow, 105].

From their opening encounter it is apparent that Minnie Powell could easily survive because she was a female, that she had every intention of accepting a secondary role as timid admirer of the romantic gunman-poet had Davoren been able to rise to the occasion and play his assigned part. She hardly required a *real* gunman for a lover and would have settled for a poet-manqué who quoted Omar Khayyám to her from time to time. And Donal proved himself adequate with braggadocio and blarney, from 'I'll admit one does be a little nervous at first' [Shadow. 110] to 'go on, Minnie, call me Donal, let me hear you say Donal.' [Shadow, 110.] But he comes a cropper at a significant moment, when he worries that 'the people of the house would be sure to start talking,' [Shadow, 110] hardly the proper attitude for a would-be gunman of whom the entire tenement is in awe. It is Minnie instead who takes command of the situation: 'An' do you think Minnie Powell cares whether they'll talk or no?' [Shadow, 110–11] she retorts. She assumes the role of defiance when the male animal is unequal to the task; from there on she constantly accepts the heroic position that Donal abandons to her. A heroine by default, she is nonetheless unquestioning in her self-confidence, from her contempt for what the neighbours will say to the risk she takes in hiding the bombs in her room. She interprets her own bravery as minor compared to the greater one that she believes is Donal's, and dismisses her courage as a logical rather than an extraordinary act: 'I'll take them to my room; maybe they won't search it; if they do aself, they won't harm a girl.' [Shadow, 146.]

But Minnie's final act of heroism remains unexplained. In one sense it was mere accident, if she was caught in the crossfire between the ambushing Republicans and the Tans in the lorry from which she jumped—or she was senselessly killed by the Tans as she attempted to escape during the melee. But the decision to jump and run was her own, the decisive act of one who had demonstrated that she could think quickly and act upon her decision. While the men in the tenement cowered in their beds, Minnie Powell took the initiative. She died to save Davoren, and she died in Davoren's place, but she also died in her own right, an acting out of her own strength of character, a concomitant to her entering a tenement room 'with an easy confidence'.

When O'Casey reworked elements of *The Shadow of a Gunman* into his autobiography, he took for himself the part of Donal Davoren; a 'lissome young lassie' named Daisy Battles replaced Minnie Powell. Johnny Casside was no gunman-on-the-run, but a spectator at the Boer War riots running from the Dublin mounted police. Shy and bold in turns, Johnny is brought into close contact with the lissome Daisy by the crush of the crowd, and together they attempt to escape the sabre-wielding constabulary. He makes no pretence to bravery, preferring safety to confrontation, but finds himself having to defend himself with a Boer flag, successfully unhorsing a policeman and having his leg injured by the falling horse. Johnny is heroic despite himself, and even his fit of vomiting does not lessen Daisy's esteem: his reward is a night spent in the arms of the experienced Daisy Battles, despite her initial concern that he'll 'give the neghbours another chance for a fancy-born story' [**Hallway, 318**]. Daisy has none of Minnie's shyness, but is all 'easy confidence'; her security comes not as much from being a self-made woman as it does from financial sponsorship by an 'uncle'—she is one of several 'kept women' that O'Casey portrays as vibrantly alive and confidently brash. Her costume fits her character: shades of green and black, but 'flecked with scarlet' [**Hallway, 307**], and once indoors she replaces it with a dark-green shawl over her near-nakedness, a tangible shawl that suggests the imaginary one that Ayamonn Breydon sang of but Sheila never wore.

But the autobiographical Johnny is more hero than the fictional Donal, and Daisy far less a heroine than Minnie: there is no attempt to make tragedy out of the incident in the 'I Strike a Blow for You, Dear Land' chapter of *Pictures in the Hallway.* O'Casey uses the designation 'tragedy' only for the first three of his plays; he seems to have become uncomfortable with the portentous term thereafter, and despite the deaths of important characters in later plays— Ayamonn in *Red Roses,* for example—he never uses it again. The tragedy of *The Gunman* exists in the death of Minnie, while the deaths of Johnny Boyle and Bessie Burgess account for the tragic nature of *Juno* and *The Plough.* It is not until *Within the Gates,* classified as a 'morality', that O'Casey returns to the tragic circumstances of a young heroine's death. Yet Jannice performs no heroic act which leads to death; she makes no sudden decision that requires self-sacrifice or courage. Artistotle would hardly approve of the incurable illness that claims her and takes her life-or-death consideration out of her hands. Her bravery is not in the circumstances of her dying but in the manner in which she confronts death and in which she has consistently confronted life.

Jannice is immediately distinguishable as an O'Casey heroine by her beauty and the appropriateness of her mode of dress, and in this case, given the expressionistic technique of the play, the costume actually assumes the proportions of emblematic significance: 'She is dressed in a black tailored suit, topped by a scarlet hat. On the hat is an ornament, in black, of a crescent; and the hip of her dress is decorated with a scarlet one.' [Gates, 121.] This scarlet woman, who carries her black death with her, is not only good-looking but 'has an intelligent look' [Gates, 121]. Like many another O'Casey hero she is not responsible for her own faults, but is the victim of the world around her, 'the selfishness and meanness of the few clients that have patronised her' [Gates, 121]. Unlike Minnie and Daisy, Jannice is 'deficient in self-assurance' but like Harry Heegan she has not had sufficient education nor adequate social opportunities to equip her to handle the dilemmas that will confront her. Specifically, O'Casey notes, 'She has read a little, but not enough; she has thought a little, but not enough.' [Gates, 121.]

O'Casey has a particular fascination with the Doomed, those earmarked for an early death because of incurable

149

illness: the consumptive Mollser in *The Plough*, the wasted Julia in *Cock-a-Doodle Dandy*, and the consumptive Jenny Sullivan of 'Hall of Healing'. In most of these cases the author remains resigned to hopelessness: Mollser dies, Julia returns uncured from Lourdes, and Jenny is packed off to the Consumption Dispensary; in each instance these are minor tragedies, only incidental to the focus of the play. In *Within the Gates*, O'Casey takes his hardest look at the Doomed, and although Jannice is fated to die of a bad heart, she is dissociated throughout from the Down-and-Out who have morbidly accepted their doom. Julia makes the trek to Lourdes as a last religious possibility of a cure, but as early as in *Within the Gates* the only hope offered by religion is a morbid despair. The Down-and-Out lacerate themselves with the knowledge of their hopeless condition, and although spared the false illusions of the Lourdes-bound Julia, they drink a bitter opiate that offers neither hope nor forgetfulness. They have given up on life and are the walking dead, but the sound of their drum does not entice the dying Jannice: 'Let me not mingle my last moments with this marching misery,' [**Gates, 228**] she implores, and when the Bishop condemns her to follow them, she refuses, insisting that she will die dancing instead.

Jannice is the loneliest of all of O'Casey's heroines and has to remain strongest since she stands most alone. The opportunities that come to her and quickly fade are essentially temptations; her own active attempts to relieve her situation are rarely successful. She can ill afford to resist the temptations when they present themselves; after the Atheist, her foster father, refuses to take her back to live with him, the Gardener refuses to marry her, and the Bishop refuses to help her. As long as she can, Jannice follows her own bent, turning down the Dreamer's offer of a song, the Salvation Army officer's path to peace, and the Bishop's suggestion that she lodge in a Hostel run by pious Sisters. Throughout much of the action she is blocked wherever she turns and remains defiant to all schemes not dictated by her own heart. As death draws near, the circle closes round her: the Salvation Army Officer reiterates the proposition of a nebulous peace that she had once accepted and abandoned; the Dreamer repeats his proposal of love and song, but these are only of value to the living and Jannice regretfully cannot accept them again now that she is close to death; the Bishop, guilty in his recognition that she is his natural daughter, is the one she seeks—and Jannice dies making the sign of the cross. Until the very last she continues to dance and denies the lure of the Down-and-Out, and her final gesture does not betray her avowal of life: the Dreamer eulogises her for having 'fought the good fight' and having 'kept the faith'. There is little consolation for the Bishop in his insistence that 'She died making the sign of the cross!' [Gates, 231]—he is racked by the turbulence of guilt and doubt that Jannice engendered in him. Never having had the Atheist's easy confidence that the Hereafter is a myth, Jannice could opt for life until the very end, her fear of the unknown returning to her when she actually faced death. Whatever the extent of her final compromise, she displayed unusual courage when confronted by overwhelming adversity. That she is a failed heroine is more than offset by the substantial degree of heroism she has maintained.

Only two others of O'Casey's young women are killed and neither one is as significant a character as Jannice, although Foorawn Reiligan in *The Bishop's Bonfire* is the primary female character in the play and her death of major significance. Young Jennie, one of the Land Girls of *Oak Leaves and Lavender*, is only of secondary importance to Monica Penrhyn. Her death is in contrast to the determination with which Monica chooses to go on living after the death of Drishogue. O'Casey pairs off the two sets of lovers: Monica and Drishogue share a mutual love and respect for each other and concomitant attitudes toward the war against fascism and the value of life; Jennie and Edgar are mismatched, since his cynicism taints everything he touches. Jennie's zest for life and her robust sexuality do not preclude her intense love for Edgar, and she proves her love when Edgar crashes to his death—as the Foreman reports on the dead bodies found: 'The third one, they say, was some fool of a Land Girl who plunged into th' flames to thry to tear one of them free.' [Oak, 90.] Partly

151

6

self-immolation and partly an act of rash heroism like Minnie's, Jennie's death early in the last act is eclipsed by later events. The four deaths that are reported in rapid succession (Dame Hatherleigh's husband, Edgar, Jennie, Drishogue) are preambles to Monica's final determination: 'There's more to come; a living spark from himself that will soon be a buoyant symbol of our Drishogue who is gone!' [Oak, 107.] There is no intention on Monica's part to demean Jennie's heroism. In fact, her interpretation of the death is significantly different from the Foreman's report: 'She tried to reach her lover, to hold him in her burning arms, and calmly died beside him!' [Oak, 105.] But whereas the death of Jannice mirrors the despair of the early 1930s, it is the making of new life in the face of death that characterises O'Casey's attitudes during the war years.

The O'Casey technique of setting up a pair of similar-but-significantly-different young women in his plays can be observed in many of the later dramas: *Purple Dust, Oak Leaves and Lavender, The Bishop's Bonfire, The Drums of Father Ned*, and 'Behind the Green Curtains'. As we have seen before, it takes only an initial stage direction to make a distinction, despite O'Casey's predilection for both. Monica is immediately seen as total heroine:

> Monica is a young lass, sweet and twenty; pretty face, well-made body, bright eyes, a little pensive at times. A girl who would be able to concentrate on what was actually before her to do. She is dressed in a neat brown skirt and a bodice of a warmer brown. All are partially concealed by a rough unbleached apron. A gaily-coloured scarf covers her brown hair, and round her arm is a white band with a tiny red cross in its centre. [Oak, 12.]

And as soon as she has put in her brief initial appearance, she is replaced on stage by the Land Girls, Jennie and Joy; if Jennie is intended to be a lesser heroine than Monica Penrhyn, she is nonetheless given her own stature and contrasts favourably with the relatively incidental Joy:

> Jennie is a sturdy lass, inclined to be slightly florid, and though she is fairly well educated as things go, having had

a secondary schooling, she is at times somewhat rough and strident in her manner. She is enticingly shaped, even a little voluptuous-looking. She has a head of thick, dark, honey-yellow hair which she often tosses aside when she feels it clustering on her forehead. She is twenty-four, full of confidence, and likes to be thought a little Rabelaisian. Her companion is plainer, not so confident, ready to follow Jennie and look up to her. Her brown hair is straighter, but is at present in the grip of a permanent wave. She is slimmer, and, though she enjoys any coarse sally from Jennie, she tries, at times, to appear to be very refined. She has had to be satisfied with an ordinary Council School upbringing, but she is a country lass, and no fool. Both wear brown breeches, high rubber boots, brown smocks, with coloured kerchiefs, fixed peasant-wise, around their heads. [Oak, 14.]

The common denominator is invariably the attractiveness, the touch of colour, the acceptance of life—a single compound, subject to variations. There is nothing inherent in these descriptions of Monica and Jennie which would indicate why the more voluptuous of the two would choose to join in flaming death the man who loves her much too casually, or why the more pensive one can celebrate the triumph of new life in the wake of her husband's death. The alternatives as such pre-exist O'Casey's creation of the two women: he found it necessary to enact both possibilities and indicate his preference for Monica's without undervaluing Jennie's.

Several years later, when the Reiligan sisters were the centre of his interest in *The Bishop's Bonfire*, O'Casey reversed the precedence in favour of concentration on the more tragic of the two heroines. In this case, however, neither girl can achieve the triumph that was Monica's: Foorawn's situation proves more tragic than Keelin's only because of her death. It is a senseless death, and might well be considered artistically unjustifiable, except that its context supports an aberrative violence in a vicious and meaningless world. Nowhere is O'Casey as bitter and despairing as he is in *The Bishop's Bonfire*: Keelin attempts to rebel

153

but is badly beaten down, while Foorawn has morbidly accepted her situation and is nonetheless destroyed by Manus's rebellion. Her final gesture, exonerating Manus of her murder, is the strongest piece of heroism that can come from Foorawn. Keelin proves stronger in her resistance to pernicious social pressures than does her lover Daniel, but in the end she too is made to kneel before authority. The world of *The Bonfire* is a fiercely masculine one, one in which even Father Boheroe is severely singed and the independent old Codger is humiliated, and only Manus (saved by Foorawn's magnanimous *geste* of reprieve) can escape—not triumph, but only escape. The women are defenceless in such an environment and are merely helpless pawns in the power struggle.

Foorawn's doom is as preordained as was Jannice's, her cold heart as fatal as the young whore's ailing heart. No splash of colour relieves the drab black-and-blue outfit that Foorawn wears as an outer manifestation of her religious vow of chastity, 'the vow of perpetual chastity with which she has burdened herself' [**Bonfire, 35**]. O'Casey's editorialising here in the introduction to the character reminds us how carefully the dramatist composes these stage directions as statements of basic situations: Foorawn is a study in sexual repression engendered and encouraged by a sterile and hypocritical society. She herself comments on the significance of her colourless attire in relation to her rejection of Manus: 'Look at me all in black an' blue. I am no longer a lure to your seeking eyes.' [**Bonfire, 41.**] But Keelin suspects a contradiction in Foorawn, an element of the suppressed femininity that still lurks beneath the austere façade: 'If I know anything, there's silk knickers an' nylon stockin's under the skirt that feels so sober an' looks so black.' [**Bonfire, 35–6.**] The younger sister's suspicions are never confirmed, but some element of backsliding is apparent in the formidable Foorawn. O'Casey cautions that even her 'solemn and sober' costume cannot completely hide 'the slim, trim figure beneath' and that Foorawn does not succeed in entirely blotting out the temptations of the world, 'for her years are few and her heart is young and yearning' [**Bonfire, 35**]. (Foorawn, incidentally, at twenty-seven, is the oldest of

O'Casey's young heroines—at least of those for whom he provides a specific age.)[1]

The repressed aspects of the real Foorawn are best displayed in her kind affection for the old Codger, with whom she laughs and cavorts while she attempts to convert him to the straight and narrow path, but is herself almost transformed by his infectious gusto. The beautiful and amoral Codger comes much closer to awakening the dormant Foorawn than her lover Manus ever does, until his bullet brings her immediately to her senses: she then makes the decision that saves Manus, as she openly declares her unequivocal love for him. An earlier encounter with Father Boheroe epitomises the conflict that rages within Foorawn: she begins with warmth and affection for the priest, but hardens into scorn for the weak and human creature. The kind of strength that she personifies is one of mindless perversity dictated by the vow she made, and only the imminence of death can reverse the direction of her attitude towards life and Manus.

The sexually repressed female is important in the O'Casey canon. Not only is the manifestation a matter of personal debilitation, but also an aspect of a larger pattern: a constrictive world destined for atrophy. The sexually timid male is less important, figuring either as a comic absurdity (John Jo Mulligan in 'Bedtime Story'), a vicious prude (Richard Rankin in *The Bishop's Bonfire*), or a pathetically limited human being (the Covey in *The Plough and the Stars*). O'Casey even assumes that a certain touch of shyness in a male tempted by one of the 'gay lassies' is natural and proper, as witness Johnny Casside's tremulousness before the self-assured Daisy Battles. But except for a modicum of demure hesitation, young women are expected to openly embrace the natural urge at the opportune moment, and if they are appreciably lustier than their masculine counterparts, they seem all the healthier for it. Foorawn destroys herself by giving herself to God instead of Manus, a condition that is both presumptuous and *contra naturum*.

On two previous occasions O'Casey took a long look at similar females who were religiously inhibited, women for whom he showed far less sympathy than the unhappily misdirected Foorawn. In the case of Susie Monican in *The Silver Tassie*, the pendulation that had brought her so far from a natural sexual response catapults her eventually to the other extreme of sexual abandonment. And in the case of the Sunday School teacher in *I Knock at the Door*, Miss Valentine, it is a clear-cut matter of social hypocrisy: she is unctuous before Johnny's mother but openly contemptuous of the poverty-stricken and sickly child himself, preferring the well-heeled bullies and bestowing her kisses on them while humiliating the pathetic child. In Sunday School she prattles on about the sanctity of the Sabbath, but true to her charactonym she secretly desecrates its holiness in good animal fashion. And Johnny manages to find her out, so that at an early age he is able to piece together the pattern of her hypocrisy:

> lying on the grass in the Phoenix Park, me an' me ma came on her, with a fella in a green corner, kissin' 'n kissin' her, while me ma was whippin' me by as fast as she could, tellin' me not to drag me feet, for Miss Valentine's legs were outstandin' again' the green of the grass 'n the black dress driven up be the gaiety of the commotion of his hand comin' closer 'n closer to closin' the school. [**Door, 177.**]

This brief glimpse into the reality of Miss Valentine's life is never commented on by either Johnny or his mother, but it certainly colours the future playwright's concept of pious young women.

Neither Foorawn nor Susie shares the personal dishonesty that characterises Miss Valentine's treatment of Johnny. Foorawn's Catholic piety is sincere though misguided, while Susie's evangelism is held up by O'Casey to ridicule, although she herself is apparently unaware that it is wrongly motivated. In appearance the Protestant fanatic strongly resembles her Roman counterpart: both are physically very attractive (Susie has 'well-shaped limbs' and 'challenging breasts' [**Tassie, 6**]), but wear sombre clothes and drab hair styles befitting their vocations. Foorawn's disguise is the more successful; no colourful accessories mar the absolute of her surrender to piety, so that her eleventh-hour conversion to Manus is relatively unanticipated. Susie, on the other hand, wears a telltale badge of luxury, a crimson scarf, belying the role she has cast herself in at the beginning of the play. She sings hymns while polishing Harry's rifle, and trumpets the Last Judgment to the discomfort of Simon and of Sylvester. When Harry, Barney and Jessie return, Susie serves as religious spokesman for the war ('the men that go with the guns are going with God' [Tassie, 29]), but it is her ambiguous sexual existence that becomes primary. A glimpse of Jessie's legs as she is being carried in after the football victory presumably shocks Susie, and Barney's attempt at familiarity with her earns him a blast of righteous indignation: 'Manhandle the lassies of France, if you like, but put on your gloves when you touch a woman that seeketh not the things of the flesh.' [Tassie, 30.] Harry's arm around her, however, meets with no such resistance, as she declares that 'Harry's different' [Tassie, 30], and it is only Jessie's insistence that disengages the prudish Susie from her physical embrace of the hero. We know that Harry will return a changed man from the trenches of France, and Susie's tour of the front as a nurse may very well result in a concomitant change.

Act Three, in essence, presents the transformation in Harry and in Susie (and even the shift of Jessie from Harry to Barney is less important here than Susie's reversal). 'Susie Monican fashion'd like a Queen of Sheba' [Tassie, 58] is Sylvester Heegan's descriptive comment on the change ('Oh, Susannah, Susannah, how are the mighty fallen,' [Tassie, 58] he adds), and the author's description of her is of a well-dressed, self-assertive and self-willed flirt. There is no suggestion in O'Casey's commentary of any prejudice against the new Susie Monican. Her flirtation with Surgeon Maxwell is coy and self-satisfying, and she is in complete command in the hospital ward where she cares for Harry, his father, and Simon Norton. The sensual Susie is as dignified here as the religious one had been ludicrous earlier, and although she fades in significance in Act Four to allow the Harry-Jessie clash the centre of the stage, she does make the major statement of the finale of the play: 'we, who have come through the fire unharmed, must go on living.' [Tassie, 103.] Having

157

given up God for Surgeon Maxwell, Susie waltzes off in his arms.

Susie Monican undergoes the most radical change in life-style of any of O'Casey's young heroines, although hers takes place in the sub-plot of *The Silver Tassie* and is dwarfed by Harry's fall and Jessie's treachery in choosing the healthy Barney in preference to the crippled Harry Heegan. But secondary as it is, Susie's transformation is the basic pattern for many similar changes in O'Casey heroines; none is as drastic, but only because no female other than Foorawn begins with so great a liability. But what is more important is that so few of the young girls actually fail as human beings: out of almost two dozen such heroines in the plays, only four can be found to be disappointing. Jessie Taite, as we have just seen, is certainly one of the most shallow of the women; from the beginning O'Casey eyes her with suspicion, explaining that she is 'responsive to all the animal impulses of life' [Tassie, 26]. This in itself is not necessarily a detri-ment, and O'Casey follows through with approval: 'She would be happy climbing with a boy among the heather on Howth Hill, and could play ball with young men on the swards of the Phoenix Park' [Tassie, 26]; but the delimiting factor is apparent immediately after: 'She gives her favour to the prominent and popular.' [Tassie, 26.] She may well be as amoral as Molly Bloom, but she is also as self-seeking and impersonal as Circe.

No O'Casey description accompanies Jessie's entrance: we never learn whether there is a touch of crimson or scarlet or even bright blue to give us a sign (in the last act, all we learn about her dress is that it is 'a very pretty, rather tight-fitting dance frock, with the sleeves falling widely to the elbow, and cut fairly low on her breast' [Tassie, 81]). When Harry is hero she is not even magnanimous enough to allow pathetic Susie to put her arm around him, and it is Jessie that Susie lectures at the end of the play that life must go on—Jessie has no comment to make on the subject. Jessie is incapable throughout of feeling anything for anyone but herself, and is unable to hide her discomfort in the presence of the cripple who had been her lover. Nor is she as much the natural animal that she at first seems: having chosen the virile Barney as Harry's successor, she is apathetic to Barney's sexual advances and even annoyed by them, preferring dancing before an audience to love-making in private.

In developing the character of Nora Clitheroe in *The Plough and the Stars* O'Casey succeeded in delineating the most complex of his young females, about whom he remains far more objective than he does about her more heroic sisters. Part of the complexity has to do with the fact that Nora is a young wife rather than a young woman, a distinction that figures often in literature, particularly in the drama, where our experiences with a character are often limited to a handful of instances. It is in the apartment of the young married couple that the play begins and it is about young Mrs Clitheroe that gossipy Mrs Gogan sneers. Nora's appearance confirms the suspicion that at twenty-two she is not operating as a girl as much as a *hausfrau*, and a petit-bourgeois one at that. O'Casey classifies her as 'alert, swift, full of nervous energy, and a little anxious to get on in the world' [**Plough, 175**]. Her clothes are remarkably different from those of the other heroines and certainly from those of the other dwellers of her tenement: 'She is dressed in a tailor-made costume, and wears around her neck a silver fox fur.' [**Plough, 175.**] The contradiction or conflict that is inherent within her does not manifest itself in the clash between the contour of her body and the choice of her clothes, but exists within the outline of her face, where the 'firm lines ... are considerably opposed by a soft, amorous mouth and gentle eyes. When her firmness fails her, she persuades with her feminine charm.' [**Plough, 175.**] A physical suggestion of strength of character is often a requisite for the O'Casey heroine, but here there appears to be the possibility that Nora's strength is stubbornness instead, and that facets of her gentler nature may be weakness.

Nor is Nora's dilemma ever resolved in the events of the play. There is no last-minute epiphany like Foorawn's, nor a change in lifestyle like Susie's, nor even Jannice's compromise with fear while maintaining the general measure of her stoic defiance. The world of Easter 1916 moves much too fast for Nora Clitheroe: she falls victim to its relentless turbulence and senseless brutality. For a young woman to whom 'getting on in the world' was an ideal, not only has the ladder collapsed, but so has her world. Both were shaky to begin with: Nora's first action of the play is to quiet the fight between Uncle Peter and the Covey, and no sooner has peace been declared than Nora is under siege herself, attacked by drunken Bessie Burgess. That it takes the intervention of Jack Clitheroe to settle Nora's world back into stasis suggests the extent to which she depends on her husband for the basic stability of her life, and the dramatic focus of the coming events will obviously indicate how unhinged her life becomes with his departure for the Uprising and his death soon after. Nora too is a weak woman caught up in the turmoil of a masculine world, as she attempts to use her feminine charms to redress the unequal balance. Not only does she fail to move forward towards her goal, but she is eventually destroyed while fighting a holding action to retain her status quo. Audience reaction to Mrs Nora Clitheroe is intended to be unfavourable, but she manages to elicit our sympathy by the sheer pathos of her situation.

The two Noras perceptible in the first act, the lady of the silver fox fur who falls foul of the tenement harridans, and the 'little red-lipped Nora' who coaxes her husband away from political rallies and burns the letter naming him Commandant in the Citizen Army, dissolve into a single pathetic creature by the third act. Jack is off at the barricades and Nora desperately attempts to find him, earning the wrath of the patriotic women who see her as a demoralising influence on the warriors. Brought back home by Fluther, she decries the insurrection, voicing one of O'Casey's first statements in the play about the hypocrisy of the Easter Rising: 'An' there's no woman gives a son or a husband to be killed—if they say it, they're lyin', lyin', against God, Nature, an' against themselves!' [**Plough, 220.**] She had already seen into Jack's vanity in wearing his uniform, and now she dissects his motivation: 'An' he stands wherever he is because he's brave? (*Vehemently*) No, but because he's a coward, a coward, a coward!' [**Plough, 221.**] The appearance of her husband and Captain Brennan corroborates Nora's evaluation; whereas Bessie recognises the sadist in the Captain, Nora notices his fear:

Look, Jack, look at th' anger in his face; look at th' fear glintin' in his eyes. . . . He himself's afraid, afraid, afraid! . . . He wants you to go th' way he'll have th' chance of death sthrikin' you an' missin' him! . . . Turn round an' look at him, Jack, look at him, look at him! . . . His very soul is cold . . . shiverin' with th' thought of what may happen to him. . . . It is his fear that is thryin' to frighten you from recognisin' th' same fear that is in your own heart! [**Plough, 235–6.**]

But Jack Clitheroe is as much a captive of the masculine world as Nora is its victim, and viciously breaking her hold on him, he abandons her lying on the street.

The Nora of Act Four is a helpless lunatic. Bessie comments, 'I think she'll never be much betther than she is. Her eyes have a hauntin' way of lookin' in instead of lookin' out, as if her mind had been lost alive in madly minglin' memories of th' past.' [**Plough, 242.**] And although there is no arguing with the contention that her situation is a melodramatic one, it is nonetheless apparent that O'Casey is at his most skilful in tightening the noose around the helpless Nora: madness has been brought on by the loss of the child she was carrying, as well as the defection of her husband from her; were she to emerge from her hallucinatory state, what comfort could she find in reality? The foetus has been buried in the coffin with Mollser, and news of Jack's death has been brought by Captain Brennan. Mindless vegetation might well be preferable at this time to the horror of having to assess the totality of her losses. And yet even this horror seems in the offing. The death of Bessie Burgess may have shattered part of the veil protecting Nora: no longer does she babble about the country and Jack, but seems to recognise her immediate surroundings and the corpse of Bessie lying in the middle of the room: 'Hide it, hide it; don't let me see it! Take me away, take me away, Mrs Gogan!' [**Plough, 260.**] The Nora that is led away by Mrs Gogan can be forgiven her vanity and pretences, her petulance and selfishness, and can only be pitied as a multiply destroyed human being.

It may have been selfishness, as she herself confessed, that led Nora to realise the sham of masculine heroism and the cant of political shibboleths, but the accuracy of her appraisal in Act Three is substantiated when Captain Brennan reports the circumstances of Jack Clitheroe's death:

> He took it like a man. His last whisper was to 'Tell Nora to be brave; that I'm ready to meet my God, an' that I'm proud to die for Ireland.' An' when our General heard it he said that 'Commandant Clitheroe's end was a gleam of glory.' Mrs Clitheroe's grief will be a joy when she realises that she has had a hero for a husband. [**Plough**, 244.]

It is apparent that Brennan has learned nothing from his experience (and for all this fine speech, his hands shake as he holds his cards, pretending to be a civilian when the British soldiers come into the room); and if he reports Jack's words accurately, neither has Jack Clitheroe. The 'gleam of glory' had already been unmasked by Nora, and no realisation will ever bring her joy.

Nora at the end of *The Plough and the Stars* suffers from the Kathleen O'Houlihan syndrome: so frail and weak that the ordinary demands of living are too much for her. In his early 'political phantasy', 'Kathleen Listens In', O'Casey created the prototype for the debilitated young woman who has lost the battle with life, in this case the Kathleen who represents Ireland. Though her suitors clamour for her (the Republican, the Free Stater, the Businessman, the Farmer, and even Jimmy the Workman), Mrs O'Houlihan warns them that Kathleen is in no condition to be wooed, much less to make a choice: 'she's so low, that talk above a whisper sets her out of her mind' [**Kathleen**, 291]. As anticipated, the selfish demands upon her so unnerve the young girl that she begins to faint, and the doctor has her put to bed: 'She's very weak, but she'll pull round after a bit, if she gets perfect quietness: A whisper may prove fatal—she'll need perfect peace and quietness for the rest of her National life.' [**Kathleen**, 295.] O'Casey's feeble Kathleen O'Houlihan is of course allegorical and comic, but soon after he was at work on the portrait of Nora Clitheroe, a realistic representation of the same malaise.

Three decades separate Kathleen and Nora from Foorawn and Keelin, but it was only during these two periods in his creative life, in the mid-twenties and the mid-fifties, that Sean O'Casey concentrated on the failed heroine. Foorawn like Kathleen seems doomed from the start, while Keelin's failure resembles Nora's: each begins from a position of personal strength and strives to attain a goal which is brutally withheld. Keelin's potential is far greater from the very beginning, if only in her good looks and slim figure ('though her breasts be buxom' [**Bonfire, 12**]); O'Casey is careful to give her no more advance notice than that. Her costume is neither sombre nor redolent with a splash of colour, but merely a neutral balance, with no commentary on her personality to indicate her strengths or weaknesses. But if she has to carry it all herself, reveal to the audience the essence that is Keelin, the young heroine is quick to establish her superiority: she flaunts her sexual attractiveness before the puritanical Rankin, taunting and tempting the vicious prude into an act of aggression. She displays her legs to Rankin, talks back to her father, and acknowledges finally that she is in love with Danny, although she is level-headed enough to warn him, 'Oh, don't try to be too brave, too sudden, Dan. It won't be easy, it won't be easy.' [**Bonfire, 73.**]

There is hope by the middle of the play that Keelin and Danny have a chance of winning out against the Councillor and the Canon, with the support of Manus and Father Boheroe, but Danny capitulates in abject surrender before Reiligan and the parish priest, and Keelin is left broken and frightened: 'What am I to do, Father; oh, what am I to do! Dan hadn't the courage to stand up to them. Dan has forsaken me, forsaken me! I will never marry. I will die as I am; I love him, an' he's lost to me now!' [**Bonfire, 80.**] Even at this point Keelin refuses to admit defeat and offers to run away with Danny, but he is completely intimidated by her father's threats and ignores her. Keelin, however, remains defiant: she refuses to marry the old farmer that her father and Canon Burren have chosen for her, and later joins in the kitchen rebellion ('Let the Bishop pluck his own plover!' [**Bonfire, 103**]). She storms out and slams the door, and is not a party to the submission of the rebels by the coaxing and cajoling Canon. Thereafter, Keelin does not appear on stage again: the Codger and Manus depart, Father Boheroe

163

sighs in defeat, Foorawn is dead, and Danny a permanent slave to the powers that be. And the audience is left to speculate on how long Keelin Reiligan can hold out in the wake of the total rout by those powers.

Keelin is made of the stuff that characterises O'Casey's strongest heroines, but the circumstances of *The Bishop's Bonfire* militate heavily against her. Even weaker females in the O'Casey canon fare better than the defiant Keelin, but in some cases they have better protection and in other cases they at least have a fighting chance. Mary Boyle in *Juno* is saved not by her own strength of character but by that of her mother. In many ways she is akin to Nora, or at least she begins with similar liabilities: 'Two forces are working in her mind—one, through the circumstances of her life, pulling her back; the other, through the influence of books she has read, pushing her forward. The opposing forces are apparent in her speech and her manners, both of which are degraded by her environment, and improved by her acquaintance—slight though it be—with literature.' [*Juno*, 3–4.] At this juncture in his career O'Casey was still neatly dividing the conflict between the inherent value of the person and the destructive effect of society. But there is no way to determine what influenced Mary's choice of Charlie Bentham: her desire for a pretty ribbon in her hair is hardly as detrimental as Nora's fur piece, yet Mary is as overwhelmed by the news of the legacy ('A fortune, father, a fortune!' [*Juno*, 33]) as is the Paycock. Confronted by the promise of wealth, she is willing to forget the working-class principles she had upheld so vocally, and given the choice between Jerry Devine and the 'thin, lanky strip of a Micky Dazzler, with a walkin'-stick an' gloves' [*Juno*, 19], she chooses Charlie Bentham the Dazzler. At the reversal of the Boyle family fortune, however, when the men crack (the Dazzler defects, Jerry slithers out, and the Paycock goes off on his guzzling of forgetfulness), it is Juno who stands firm. Mary is close to despair ('Oh, it's thrue, it's thrue what Jerry Devine says—there isn't a God, there isn't a God; if there was He wouldn't let these things happen!' [*Juno*, 86]) but Juno takes command and provides the strength she needs.

The character of Mary Boyle owes much to the older

sister Ella that O'Casey portrays in the early autobiographies. It is obvious that O'Casey harboured mixed feelings about his sister, and the expanse of the first three volumes gives him ample room to develop the vagaries of her personality and the lifetime of events until her death. The opening vignette in *I Knock at the Door* shows her at her worst: while the mother is detailing the problem with little Johnny's eyes and the need for medical attention, the older siblings are absorbed with the procession of the Vice-Regal Ball. Except for a single ambiguous gesture as surrogate mother ('Come here, in front of me, said Ella, pulling Johnny beside her, and stay quiet and stand still and don't stir, till we see all the lovely lords and ladies tripping and trotting into the Castle' [**Door, 21**]), she is too preoccupied to concern herself with the child. The sight of ragged urchins elicits no sympathy from her ('Shame for their mothers to let them look on at a sight like this' [**Door, 22**]) as she oohs and ahs over the pomp of the rich. Vanity, conceit, hauteur, disdain—it is by these signs that we come to know Ella Casside.

The story of Ella Casside as it unfolds in *I Knock at the Door, Pictures in the Hallway,* and *Drums under the Windows* is by far the grimmest that O'Casey tells, even surpassing the destruction of Nora. The petty qualities that irked the sensitive young Johnny were more than offset by the girl's potentiality. Certainly the best educated of the Casside children, Ella became a school-teacher, and at one instance even undertook Johnny's education when ordinary classroom attendance was out of the question, introducing him to poetry (the triumph with which the first volume concludes). But immediately after the father's death Ella became enamoured of a soldier named Benson and married him, despite her mother's icy objection. The lure of Benson's red coat proved irresistible to two of Johnny's older brothers, and they too enlisted: from this point on, with three of the family breadwinners gone, poverty sets in for the Cassides. When Ella fears that Johnny's lack of formal education will result in his being a common labourer, Mrs Casside thinks, 'Your own husband won't be much more . . . but she held her tongue' [**Door, 287**]; the demobilised Benson fares even

165

worse than that: he becomes violently insane and is eventually institutionalised. Ella brings her washing home to mother, and soon brings her entire family of five children as well. And in abject poverty the mother of five suddenly dies. Sean Casside vents his spleen against Ella's folly: 'a venemous dislike of Ella charged his heart when he realised that for the romance of a crimson coat, a mean strip of gold braid, and corded tassels of blue, yellow, and green, she had brought him, herself, and all of them down to this repulsive and confused condition' [**Window, 115**]. But soon after, in a summing-up in *Inishfallen, Fare Thee Well*, O'Casey adds, 'Ella, graceful and retentive, with her white hands at home on the keys of a piano, reading music easily at first sight, full of Scott's poetry, familiar with Shakespeare and Milton, might have become a gleam from the beauty of Beethoven and Bach.' [**Inish, 20.**] Obsessed by the recollection of Ella, O'Casey was sensitively aware in creating his young heroines of the frailty of women and the vanity of human wishes.

Two of O'Casey's young girls in particular attempt to prevent their lives from becoming too involved with serious consequences but, finding escape impossible, manage to accept reality. Neither begins with Jannice's ebullience, but neither contains the element of tragedy within herself. Julia in *The Star Turns Red* and Sheila Moorneen in *Red Roses for Me* respond strongly to the deaths of the men they love, despite the opportunity to return to an evasive existence. Both are young and pretty (the immediate requisites), but Julia is little more than a stick figure in an expressionistic drama, while Sheila assumes the complexities of the more significant of O'Casey's heroines. All that we know in advance is that Julia 'is a pretty and vigorous girl of nineteen. She is dressed in petticoat, bodice, shoes, and stockings, and carries a green and black pierrette costume over her arm.' [**Star, 252.**] Sheila, on the other hand,

> is a girl of about twenty-three, fairly tall, a fine figure, carrying herself with a sturdiness never ceasing to be graceful. She has large, sympathetic brown eyes that dim, now and again, with a cloud of timidity. Her mouth is rather large but sweetly made; her hair is brown and long,

though now it is gathered up into a thick coil that rests on the nape of her neck. She is dressed in a tailor-made suit of rich brown tweed, golden-brown blouse, and a bright-blue hat.... She comes in shyly, evidently conscious of Mrs Breydon's presence; but fighting her timidity with a breezy and jovial demeanour. [Roses, 138–9.]

Mrs Breydon and Ayamonn have already had a long discussion about Sheila before she arrives, but Julia is thrust upon the stage unannounced and has to establish her own identity. Her first statements are strongly political; she is sparked with enthusiasm for the Communist cause ('But we'll face them and fight them and make them flee before us!' [Star, 253]) and yet becomes petulantly childish when Jack insists that work for the cause must take precedence and that they will not be going to the dance. He leaves without her, while she keeps repeating, 'I'm as good a Communist as he is.' [Star, 257.] Yet all this is soon out of mind as she turns around and begins to tease Joybell, the Catholic prude, in much the same manner that Keelin taunted Rankin, except that in this case the temptress goes much too far, passionately embracing the prig. Joybell reacts with sadistic lust, terrifying Julia into near-hysteria. And in a few minutes Julia has managed to antagonise Jack's parents as well, even though they defended her against Joybell.

The Julia of Act One is indeed a contrary young girl, and neither her youth nor O'Casey's expressionistic technique can quite account for the multitude of volte-faces. Before the first act is over she is back again in her pierrette costume, flinging herself on Jack, having changed her mind about going to the dance instead of the Hall: 'Misery came over me while I was dressing, and I fought against going to joy when there was work to be done.' [Star, 270.] Her newly rekindled political enthusiasm results in her slapping the Leader of the Saffron Shirts, and she is dragged out to be punished. The murder of her father permanently fixes Julia's determination, and the flighty and vacillating girl is unwavering thereafter in her loyalty to the Cause, consigning her father's body to the revolutionists rather than the priests. In the last act a tearful Julia arrives with the dead body of her lover Jack.

She remains silent throughout the confrontation of Red Jim and the Purple Priest, and while Kian turns his back on the Saffron Shirts and joins his dead brother's cause. Red Jim rouses her from her silent weeping, and 'Julia stands up with her right fist clenched' [Star, 353] (her father's dying gesture), as the 'Internationale' is played and the Red Star glows. Julia has obviously evolved from Silly Girl to Mature Woman, but is by no means the playwright's best delineation of a Real Person.

It is not only in comparison with Julia that Sheila Moorneen seems a well-rounded character; she is three-dimensional in her own right. In fact, before ever appearing on stage, she exists as an interesting enigma in Ayamonn's idealised version and his mother's prejudiced account, so that when she does arrive, it is to establish herself as she actually is. She scores her first point by offering to do Mrs Breydon's errand, but demeans herself by her concern about what the neighbours in the Breydon house will think of her being there, and what her parents' reaction will be when they hear of it. It is soon apparent that she is made of flesh-and-blood and not of the gossamer Ayamonn used in his fabrication: 'Oh, Ayamonn, I do want you to be serious for one night' [Roses, 141] becomes her refrain; and her obligation to her Church and her parents presents itself as being almost as definite as Mrs Breydon maintained. Only her whispered 'God forgive me, I'd rather come to see you' [Roses, 142] reveals a touch of the Sheila that Ayamonn has conjured up for himself. And we certainly are made to feel sympathetic to her desperate aim in having Ayamonn alone for a few minutes in order to discuss seriously their precarious situation.

Certainly the Sheila of the first act fails to live up to our expectation of the self-reliant heroine, even though we share her exasperation with Ayamonn's unreal image of her and his divided attention. She is quite touching when she returns in Act Two, contrite and concerned about their future, but it is soon obvious that her proposed solution to the problem is for Ayamonn to desert his fellow workers during the strike. And she is seen at her worst in her ugly denunciation of the wounded atheist Mullcanny: 'Hung as high as Gilderoy he ought to be, an' he deep in the evil of his rich illusions, spouting insults at war with th' mysteries an' facts of our holy faith!' [**Roses**, 175.] And she becomes so vehement ('Ay, you, that shouldn't find a smile or an unclenched hand in a decent man's house!' [**Roses**, 178]) that Mrs Breydon gently remonstrates with her: 'Shame on you, Sheila, for such a smoky flame to come from such a golden lamp!' [**Roses**, 179.] Her sincerity in her attempt to shelter Ayamonn and keep him for herself is unquestionable, but it is also obvious that Sheila has been conditioned by class, family and religion into a seriously limited human being.

When the strike breaks and violence is imminent, Sheila softens her tone but remains adamant in her desire that Ayamonn detach himself from the struggle and 'sit safe by his own fireside' [**Roses**, 210]. Her plea is even couched in the poetic terms that Ayamonn has always attributed to her but she had never before demonstrated: 'Stay here where time goes by in sandals soft, where days fall gently as petals from a flower, where dark hair, growing grey, is never noticed.' [**Roses**, 211.] More and more we begin to glimpse the basic material from which her lover had fashioned his dream conception of Sheila, as when she attempts to intercede on the strikers' behalf, gently confronting the Inspector of Police: 'Oh, cancel from your mind the harder things you want to say, an' do your best to save us from another sorrow!' [**Roses**, 212.] But the violence is destined to come and Ayamonn is destined to be its victim. Sheila is torn between her grief and her levelheaded sense of survival. Yet she can now for the first time see the justification of Ayamonn's beliefs ('Maybe he saw the shilling in th' shape of a new world' [**Roses**, 225]), and although at first tempted by Inspector Finglas's attempts to woo her,[2] she angrily turns upon him and denounces him: 'Oh, you dusky-minded killer of more worthy men!' [**Roses**, 226.] It is not a mere matter here of the older woman guiding the young girl, as it was with Mrs Boyle and Mary, but of each coming to a full realisation almost independently of the other. Mrs Breydon had given Ayamonn her blessing before the attack, and Sheila now remains faithful to his memory and his ideals.

Mary, Nora and Sheila are probably O'Casey's finest depictions of the young heroine, but they are surely not his

169

most 'positive' women: the females of the later dramas in most cases are the boldest and strongest representatives of their sex, monolithic creations both in their singleness of purpose and rocklike determination. And in most cases, following the examples of Keelin and Julia, they are the most sensual. When they appear in a 'wayward comedy' like *Purple Dust*, they are particularly well situated, and Avril and Souhaun romp through the Tudor mansion with Elizabethan gusto, appropriate counterfoils to Stoke and Poges and worthy companions of O'Killigain and O'Dempsey.

Actually O'Casey offers three young women in *Purple Dust*, beginning with Avril ('a pretty girl of twenty-one or so, inclined, at times, to be a little romantic, and is very much aware of her good looks' [**Dust**, 11]) and Souhaun ('a woman of thirty-three years of age. She must have been a very handsome girl and she is still very good-looking, in a more matronly way. She has the fine figure of her young friend Avril, but her arms and her legs have grown a little plumper. She is still attractive enough to find attention from a good many men, when her young friend is out of the way' [**Dust**, 6]), but also including the servant-girl Cloyne 'a stoutly-built, fine-looking girl of twenty-six or so' [**Dust**, 6–7]. The situation in the Tudor mansion becomes too perilous by the end of the play, and not all three beauties can rise above it sufficiently. Cloyne, despite her fascination with O'Killigain, proves too strongly moored to her subservient condition: she has played sycophant before her masters while sneering at them behind their backs, and when the flood comes she is marooned with the manservant Barney and the Postmaster on the roof of the mansion. Avril and Souhaun, however, have fled with Jack O'Killigain and Philib O'Dempsey.

Not all the pretty maidens then can seize the day and make good their escape. Cloyne seems doomed by her timidity, just as Avril at twenty-one has the best chance of making the important break. Souhaun, however, hovers in the middle between the cowed Cloyne and the audacious Avril: at thirty-three she is very much concerned with her security, and although she risks kissing O'Killigain, she reveals her real fears when Poges almost kills himself with the huge roller: 'The blasted fool! He has rocked the house and killed himself and hasn't made his will!' [**Dust, 78.**] But Souhaun has reached a plateau of financial security when Poges arranges for an annual income for her of 500 pounds a year, and she is capable of lashing out at him when he attempts to run roughshod over her: 'What d'ye think you're doing, you old dim-eyed, old half-dead old fool! I'll disconnect you as well as the telephone if you don't learn to behave yourself! You settled on coming here, and you'll put up with the annoyances! . . . Another snarly sound out of you, and I'm off to live alone.' [**Dust, 40.**] Yet Souhaun is very much aware that at thirty-three she cannot make the same sort of rash flight for freedom that the younger Avril might, and she needs O'Killigain's assurance that she is as pretty as Avril. O'Killigain is lavish with his praise ('You are one o' th' fine sights of this world' [**Dust, 75**]) and she kisses him and runs out, but Souhaun must be aware that she cannot compete with Avril for the handsome foreman, anymore than Cloyne could.

It takes some of the wind out of Souhaun's sails for her to play up to Philib O'Dempsey, a common workman, and she is self-protective in her mocking conversation with him, scornful of the idea of a 'daughter of the Ormond with a workman!' [**Dust, 94.**] But O'Dempsey had already opened a breach in her protective snobbery ('You're a handsome woman yourself; you're Irish too; an' y'ought to be sensible' [**Dust, 93**]). In her next encounter it is Souhaun who takes the initiative when O'Dempsey seems on the verge of abandoning the house to the storm and going off by himself. 'The house'll be lonesome without you,' [**Dust, 105**] she says, and he invites her to join him and share his simple and rustic life. Souhaun can still 'speak mockingly, but developing a slight catch in her voice; for she has been moved by the 2nd Workman's words' [**Dust, 106**]. Avril attempts to rescue her from O'Dempsey's tempting refrain, for she herself has as yet received no such invitation from O'Killigain. Souhaun actually anticipates Avril's escape from the world of Basil Stoke by ignoring her and allowing herself to further fall under the Irish workman's spell. O'Killigain immediately begins his temptation of Avril, so that Souhaun finally decides to 'do whatever Avril advises' [**Dust, 108**]. When the river rises it is O'Dempsey who is the first to arrive for his woman, and Souhaun goes off with him. Avril announces the departure to Poges and Stoke: 'Gone with the wind; gone with the waters; gone with the one man who alone saw something in her!' [Dust, 117]—and follows with O'Killigain immediately after.

There are indications in O'Casey's introduction of Avril that the playwright may have intended a greater degree of complexity for Avril than has actually been realised in the play itself. Some of the negative factors that have proven diagnostic in the failed heroines are presumably present in Avril herself: vanity, hardness, snobbery, and an arrested attempt at self-education. 'She is far from being unintelligent, but does little and cares less about developing her natural talents. Her eyes are large and expressive, but sometimes sink into a hardened lustre. She is inclined to think that every good-looking young fellow, rich or poor, should fall for her pretty face and figure, and is a little worried if one of them doesn't. She adopts a free-and-easy and very unnatural attitude when she is talking to workmen.' [Dust, 11–12.] Yet all it takes is her initial encounter with O'Killigain for the worst in Avril to quickly dissipate. He handles her so skilfully in his naturally free-and-easy attitude that Avril no longer has any recourse to her protective snobbery; having accepted O'Killigain as an equal (and as a prospective lover), Avril attains a superiority over Basil that never falters.

In effect, Avril has lost the bout with the naturally superior man, but accepts him as such and her own role in relation to him, freeing herself from any further obligation to the greatly inferior Basil Stoke. 'Basil is only trying to share his great knowledge with us,' [Dust, 27] she can say ironically when the two paycocks are arguing; she then wheedles a cheque out of him by comforting him at Cyril's expense, only to ride off with O'Killigain when Basil's horse throws him. Yet for all her newly solidified self-confidence in manipulating Basil Stoke, Avril is still apprehensive when Souhaun and Philib O'Dempsey have gone off but O'Killigain has not yet come for her: 'An' well it would be if I was with her.' [Dust, 117.] But fortunately O'Killigain comes for her and

Avril is exultant in her escape from Stoke, contemptuous of his accusation that she is stealing the jewels he gave her:

> I gave more than I got, you gilded monkey. It's winnowed of every touch of life I'd be if I stayed with th' waste of your mind much longer. . . . Th' thrinkets I wormed out of you are all here, an' here they stay, for th' wages were low for what was done for you. [**Dust**, 118.]

Two of the three girls in *Purple Dust* are successful in making the necessary break, and even with the one failure, the percentage of success is high. Yet when O'Casey reworked the same trio in *Cock-a-Doodle Dandy*, he gave greater attention to the servant girl, so much so that she too evolved into a strong and defiant young woman, and all three win out over the atrophied males. By contrast with Cloyne, a 'maid-servant', Marion is listed in the Dramatis Personae as 'helper in Lorna's house' [**Cock**, 119] and it is apparent that she lacks Cloyne's menial attitudes. Whereas little is said of Cloyne other than that she is 'a stoutly-built, fine-looking girl of twenty-six or so, and wears the servant's dress under her smock, and has a smart servant's cap on her head' [**Dust**, 6–7], Marion is given full treatment upon entrance:

> She is a young girl of twenty or so, and very good-looking. Her skirts come just to her knees, for they are nice legs, and she likes to show them—and why shouldn't she? And when she does so, she can add the spice of a saucy look to her bright blue eyes. Instead of the usual maid's cap, she wears a scarf-bandeau round her head, ornamented with silver strips, joined in the centre above her forehead, with an enamelled stone, each strip extending along the bandeau as far as either ear. She wears a dark-green uniform, flashed with a brighter green on the sleeves and neck, and the buttons of the bodice are of the same colour. Her stockings and shoes are black. A small, neat, white apron, piped with green, protects her uniform. [**Cock**, 138.]

This may seem a great deal of attention to expend on a mere servant girl, but it is apparent that Marion is no walk-on character carrying an occasional tray.

Loreleen, the young heroine, has already appeared and the mere sight of her has sent two workmen agog over her beauty; Lorna, the 'young second wife', has been discussed by her husband and his butty, and her loveliness and youth have been indicated as a source of dismay to the older husband. In introducing Marion then, O'Casey undertakes a major task of elevating still a third girl to status in the play: she runs on in terror of the Cock that is running rampant in the house (Cloyne had been equally terrorised by the cow she thought was a bull), but when she accidentally rushes into the arms of the Messenger, he 'clasps Marion tight in his arms, and kisses her' [Cock, 140]. It is she, rather than either of the other two women, who is the romantic lead, and it is she whom the Messenger follows out of Nyadnanave.

Once Marion has recovered from her fear of the Cock, she proves to be something of a hell-cat. Her 'master' attempts to intimidate her into playing the part of a servant, but Marion delightedly mocks him for his cowardice ('An' yous all quakin', an' even Sailor Mahan there, shakin' in his shoes, sure it was somethin' sinisther!' [Cock, 145]), and it is only when she has had a good laugh at all three cowardly men that 'she runs merrily in' [Cock, 146]. Later she flirts outrageously with Mahan and Marthraun, and they are both about to kiss her when they notice that she too, like Loreleen and Lorna before her, has sprouted horns out of her hair adornment. Robin Adair, however, has no fear of the devil in Marion, for whom he has already served a month in jail, having kissed her in public in Nyadnanave. When Marion decides to leave the town and follow Lorna and Loreleen, Robin tries to stop her, declaring his love for her. But she is adamant: 'But not here, Robin Adair, oh, not here; for a whisper of love in this place bites away some of th' soul! . . . Come, if you want to, Robin Adair; stay, if you will.' [Cock, 219.] It is not the masculine hero who rescues the maiden and carries her off, as in Purple Dust—the girls depart on their own, and the man follows the brave girl that he loves.

In most ways all three females are of equal standing in Cock-a-Doodle Dandy, unlike the primary-secondary-tertiary roles played by Avril, Souhaun, and Cloyne. Lorna, a counterpart of Souhaun, has none of her insecurities and does not have to be reassured of her loveliness in order to have the courage to act out her defiance, although 'the bright and graceful contours of her face are somewhat troubled by a vague aspect of worry and inward timidity' [Cock, 143]. She had been sold into marriage with the older Marthraun, much as Councillor Reiligan and Canon Burren were attempting to convince Keelin to marry an old farmer, and although she has not yet complained about her situation, Marthraun is convinced that she too is in league with the devil: 'An' me own wife, Lorna Marthraun, is mixin' herself with th' disordher, fondlin' herself with all sorts o' dismayin' decorations. Th' other day, I caught her gapin' into a lookin'-glass, an' when I looked meself, I seen gay-coloured horns branchin' from her head!' [Cock, 124.]

Like Marion, Lorna was frightened by the Cock, but once Robin tamed him and led him out, she too became impervious to him and his frightening influence, and she toasts him with gusto: 'Th' Cock-a-doodle Dandy!' [Cock, 181.] When Marthraun decides to have the spirit exorcised from the house, Lorna comments, 'It's all damn nonsense, though Michael has me nerves in such a way that I'm near ready to believe in anything.' [Cock, 193.] Her courage fails her on occasion, and she allows Father Domineer to send her into the house when Loreleen is being castigated; yet when Loreleen is driven from Nyadnanave, Lorna is the first to insist upon accompanying her: 'I go with you, love. I've got a sthrong pair of shoes in the sack you can put on when we're free from th' Priest an' his rabble. Lift up your heart, lass: we go not towards an evil, but leave an evil behind us!' [Cock, 217.]

Loreleen has already been to London, a fact that is established early in the play, and has come home to Nyadnanave. Her father assumes that the first elements of something amiss in the house are due to Loreleen's presence: 'I'm talkin' about whispers ebbin' an' flowin' about th' house, with an edge of evil on them, since that painted one, that godless an' laughin' little bitch left London to come here for a long an' leering holiday.' [Cock, 123.] O'Casey had himself chosen London when he exiled himself from Ireland, and continues to use it as a concept of refuge for those escaping parochial

175

Ireland, and a concept of all the godless sins of the world for those who advocate Ireland's unsullied parochialism. Not that Loreleen and her London taint could single-handedly infect Nyadnanave, although Marthraun may be right in assuming that his daughter influenced Lorna in going to fancy-dress dances: a second vital source of such infection comes from Robin Adair, an authentic Irish element, and the one that influences Marion and masters the Cock, making it a symbol of himself.

Loreleen, however, is credited with triggering the revolution that takes place in the Marthraun household and environs, and it remains an essentially feminine revolution. The two Rough Fellows who are so smitten by her in the first scene are soon reduced to terrified devouts when they see Loreleen change into a 'fancy-bred fowl': 'It's an omen, a warnin', a reminder of what th' Missioner said last night that young men should think of good-lookin' things in skirts only in th' presence of, an' undher th' guidance of, old and pious people.' [Cock, 132.] In Scene Three the Roughs drag her in, having caught her with Sailor Mahan and stolen her money (the Sailor having hurried home and taken refuge in his bed). When all of the men of the town prove to be either bullies or cowards, the forces of a fanatical puritanism or its timid followers, only the women and the Messenger remain in rebellion, leaving the town to the dead hand of Father Domineer. Although the instigator of the revolution, Loreleen is more the victim of its repression, while Lorna and Marion consciously choose to join her in exile.

The Lorna-Souhaun 'older' female is perpetuated in the one-act play 'Time to Go', where a Widda Machree unmasks the venality and hypocrisy of an Irish country town. She is described as 'a young woman of thirty. Her face is pale, well chiselled, and pure-looking. She wears a coloured scarf over her head, peasant-wise.' [Time, 268–9.] On the naturalistic level of the plot she is merely a woman who has sold a cow for more than she deems it worth, and her conscience bothers her; but she proves to be more than a real person: she shows herself capable of disappearing at will, having slipped out of handcuffs, and it is apparent that she has come to warn the greedy that they are risking damnation for their covetousness and dishonesty. She 'has a semi-plaintive air' (characteristic of her existence on the naturalistic level), 'though this is occasionally changed into a humourous, half-cynical manner' [**Time, 269**] (her supernatural self essentially, as she breaks into song and dance, accepts rebuff with equanimity, always remains unruffled). Her plaintiveness leaves her entirely when she is reunited with her 'other self', the man she presumably cheated: he in turn feels guilty about having paid too little for the cow, and they recognise in each other the completion of a total personality, first as brother-sister, but later as lovers. The Widda Machree and Kelly from the Isle of Mananaun prove too dangerous as far as the local merchants are concerned, and they are indicted for 'breaches of th' peace' [**Time, 288**], but they perform their miracles and disappear. 'Time to Go', following soon after *Cock-a-Doodle Dandy*, is very much an echo of it.

But when the young heroines next break loose from the restrictions of Irish rural provincialism, it is in *The Drums of Father Ned*, a play more like the 'wayward comedy', *Purple Dust*, than like the more sombre *Cock-a-Doodle Dandy*, although it too plays heavily with comic fantasy. 'This comedy's but an idle, laughing play/About the things encumbering Ireland's way' [**Ned, x**] advertises O'Casey, and despite the pretentious pride of its pair of paycocks, the bigotry of its Irish patriots of North and South, and the pettifogging of its puritanical Father Fillifogue, it remains sheer ebullience, in which the young people walk off with absolute mastery of the situation. The two heroines, Nora McGilligan and Bernadette Shillayley, share the spotlight with the two young men, Michael Binnington and Tom Killsallighan. Both girls are young and pretty (although lacking any of the overtly sensual beauty of most of their predecessors, but are essentially simple and wholesome). Like all the young people of Doonavale they are engrossed in the preparations for the Tostal, taking time out only occasionally to overturn the entire established world of their parents, and fall in love as well; and no distinction seems particularly discernible between the Councillor's daughter and his maidservant (the Colonel's lady and Rosie O'Grady have been completely democratised by O'Casey's magic). Bernadette plays the Mayor's piano, and refuses to be cowed by the objections of his wife, sounding an ominous warning against the power of the Binningtons and McGilligans: 'This Tosthal will make some I know dance in more ways than one!' [Ned, 19.] Nora and her cohorts carry the insurrection a step further as they take over the Binnington and McGilligan parlors for their rehearsals, Nora commenting to the astounded parents: 'Our Blessed Lord often held the hammer an' He knew well the use of the sickle.' [Ned, 32.] Both girls are somewhat quicker in accepting the Father Ned philosophy of open and unashamed love between boy and girl than are Michael and Tom, but it takes only a slight initiative of the female side to begin the mutual affection. Bernadette, however, adds to her make-up one other quality that O'Casey delights in: simple as she is, she is capable of hilarious flirtation with the Orangeman Skerighan, teasing him into an attempted seduction and then pretending to be taken seriously ill by his attack—and then letting him bribe her to keep quiet. After Bernadette has staggered out, Father Fillifogue reports seeing her scampering down the street, very much to Skerighan's astonishment.

In one of his last plays, 'Behind the Green Curtains', O'Casey returns to the more troubled view of the clash between the entrenched bigots and the rebellious heroines, like that portrayed in *The Bishop's Bonfire* and *Cock-a-Doodle Dandy*. This short play presents two O'Casey females, Reena Kilternan and Noneen Melbayle; although the scope of the play is somewhat smaller, many of the familiar characteristics are re-created in new form and in a new situation. Noneen is a decidedly secondary character to the heroine Reena, and both are limited in significance when compared to the masculine hero, Martin Boeman. But whereas Boeman is a rather single-faceted hero, the girls emerge as a good deal more complex, if not necessarily any the more convincing. Each of the two girls becomes the central focus of an altercation of almost scandal proportions: Noneen because she is the housemaid of a bachelor, and Reena because she enters a Protestant church to attend the funeral service of a patron of the arts. Reena emerges relatively unscathed; as

Bunny reports: 'Nothin' happened for a few weeks, an' proud she was she'd gone; but afther a month, th' paper she sent occasional articles to suddenly found they needed her no more. Now they hardly speak to her at Legion of Mary meetin's.' [Curtains, 41.] Noneen, on the other hand, is dragged off by masked men in a car: 'Do you know what they done to her? . . . Brought her to a house where two women stripped her. . . . Then these kind ladies put a night-dress on her. The men, with one o' th' women, tied her to a telegraph pole, and there she stayed till th' morning post-man set her free.' [Curtains, 57.]

The severity of the maid's punishment results in her clear-cut decision to leave Ballybeedhust for England, Martin Boeman acting as her rescuer. But Reena's position as a nurse and a member of the Legion of Mary protects her from the overpowering need to escape, and she in turn attempts to find a niche for herself in the existing society. Her think-ing is undergoing continual change, however: the courage that it took to enter the Protestant church when all the others demurred becomes a permanent facet of her make-up, and although she is sufficiently repentant to bring the sashes and rosettes for the others to wear at the anti-Communist march ('For being naughty, I've lost me honorary job as an organiser, and [gayly] have to do the donkey work now' [Curtains, 46]), she is obdurate when the vigilantes come for Noneen. Her attempts to aid Noneen are futile, and Reena moves further along in her questioning of the traditional beliefs that she had been advocating against the atheistic and communistic Boeman.

Yet she still envisions a life for herself in Ballybeedhust and Ireland, hoping to enlist Chatastray as her companion. No longer is she just the 'Legion of Mary lass' that Chatas-tray calls her, announcing that 'Some of us do a little think-ing, sir. I've thought long about it these many days, an' other things too. We are a huddled nation frightened undher th' hood of fear.' [Curtains, 59.] She is now capable of casti-gating Chatastray as a coward where once she venerated him as one of 'th' leaders of Ireland's thought' [Curtains, 45]. Finding herself falling in love with him now. she is still naïve enough to believe that she could brave the conditions

179

in the Irish town and that Dennis Chatastray would be able
to share her bravery: 'After hospital duties, I can cook a
simple meal for both of us; and, on my free day, we can
have a good time together.' [Curtains, 79.] But for all of
his attraction to her, Chatastray is terrified at the thought
of defying convention and risking another beating, and
while Reena's back is turned, he slithers off to the march.
When Boeman declares his love for her shyly and simply,
Reena agrees to leave for England with him. She is delighted
to find that her daring in kissing him is met by a new
audacity in the shy lover, as he carries her out of the green-
curtained room and out of Ireland.

Reena Kilternan is O'Casey's study in political education,
a process that we witness unfolding during the course of the
three scenes. Few of O'Casey's heroines ever seem to be as
politically aware as their men are militant. For all of Monica
Penrhyn's determination to believe in what Drishogue believes, she does not fully understand his motivation, even assuming at one point that he is fighting for England. It is not
the soldier who fought in Spain that Avril follows out of the
flooded mansion, but the rugged Irish lover. And it takes
the death of Ayamonn for Sheila ever to realise the significance of the shilling he died for. Each of these heroines is too
involved in having to fight against difficult odds for just
their own individual dignity to engage in the world struggle
that involves their lovers. Julia alone, despite her early
hesitance, is politically conscious and a militant counterpart
of the man she loves, while Reena undergoes the development of awareness that is so rare in these young women.
Essentially it is their enthusiasm for life and their courage
in living their own lives that make them significant to
O'Casey, who saw in them as he created them what he sees
in Synge's characters, 'the call of a brave heart for the full-
ness of life'.[3]

A Flourish of Strumpets

Occasionally O'Casey celebrates young love with all its
concomitant purity and innocence. In 'The Moon Shines on
Kylenamoe', for example, Mave Linanawn is the young girl

in love with the Dunphy boy: they babble to each other in amorous Irish, oblivious of the world around them. That world, however, is again the rural Ireland so limited and puritan, hostile to anything that suggests liberty and license. When it attempts to interfere in their romance (an Irish variant of: It's 11 p.m.; do you know where your children are?), Mave is indignant: 'Thor leat, aw Fawdhrig. Let them go, let them tarry, let them sink or let them swim.' [**Moon, 136.**] Alice in 'Figuro in the Night' yearns for the return of her lover from the fair ('Dear me, what can the matter be?' [**Figuro, 90**]) unmindful of the future image of faded love personified by the Old Man and the Old Woman; at the end of the play Johnny does return to her ('Sweet Alice, I've brought you th' blue ribbons' [**Figuro, 120**]). Such love and innocence pre-existed the seduction of Sean Casside by Daisy Battles, and hearkens back to the Johnny Casside who stole his first kiss from Jennie Clitheroe and considered it an initiation into manhood. Curly-headed Jennie[4] persists as young Johnny's dream through much of his childhood and pubescence, but is displaced when class differences interfere: 'she closed her eyes, and gave a little disdainful toss to her head. A lady-girl cashier in Sir John Arnott's select drapery house, he was too poor for a nod from her.' [**Hallway, 247.**] By then the ideal of puppy love had been displaced in quite a different way, by a young girl named Alice,[5] who offered more than mere kisses, more than merely a tentative initiation:

> ——If you thought a lot of a kiss, you'd take it, and be done with it; an', if you're genuine and want to, you can meet me tonight where you said, an' when we come to some grassy nook, you can tell me more about your Shakespeare; but you musn't try to pull me asunder when you feel you'd like a little kiss. There, she said, coming back into the room, and looking brightly into his darkened face, I know you didn't mean to be so rough, an' we'll make it all up in th' quietness of th' night when we reach th' lanes o' Whitehall. [**Hallway, 177.**]

These autobiographic 'facts' explain several basic O'Casey attitudes towards young women: most are sexually more

181

aggressive than men (and quite fortunately so); some are more involved in social climbing than in a wholehearted response to the magic of love. The Jennie Clitheroe that Johnny kissed evolves into the disdainful lady-cashier, a prototype for the Nora Clitheroe in the silver fox fur. O'Casey is rather economical in naming his characters, using the same name several times over (although he is also at times a spendthrift when giving the same character multiple names); the use of Clitheroe in these two instances appears to be intentional. And there is also a second Nora whom the mature Sean Casside loves and leaves when he leaves Inishfallen: Nora Creena is the best-developed female character in the autobiographies and serves as a prototype also for several of the heroines of the plays.

Now a practising playwright Sean is in love with his 'own ungodly goddess, buxom and confidently aggressive in her womanly wisdom, her popular loveliness queenly cloaked in the richly yellow-bordered black shawl' [Inish, 298]. The black shawl should immediately indicate the direction of the characterisation of this Nora: soon the rub presents itself in the attitude of the Catholic girl's father: 'Nora Creena's father and mother were immediately against her having anything to do with Sean. And, indeed, as Sean discovered afterwards, Nora was scantily equipped with the courage to defy, or resist, the bitter respectability of these superb people.' [Inish, 300–301.] And the parallel with Sheila Moorneen becomes even more apparent: Nora is a grand listener as Sean reads Milton and Keats to her and quotes Shaw; she is a romantic companion on moonlight strolls; but she is the product of her limited environment and lacks the individual courage and initiative to break the deathlike grip it maintains on her: 'in the core of his heart, Sean knew that Nora Creena hadn't it in her to stand out safely against opposition. She wilted under the family resentment and the priest's advice.' [Inish, 305.] So, like Sheila, she is forced by her fears into periods of estrangement from him.[6] At her best she is 'a red, red rose, a westlin' wind bearin' home the laden bees' [Inish, 306], but Sean 'realised that all they had read together, all she had listened to, hadn't added jot or tittle to her courage' [Inish, 307]. Sean cuts the silver cord that binds him to Ireland, that Poor Old Woman, as well as Nora, the pathetic young girl, assuming a preference thereafter for a Daisy Battles, brazen and lusty, to a Nora Creena, icy and pure. The evidence from *Rose and Crown*, however, indicates that in finding and marrying Eileen, O'Casey spared himself the necessity of making the choice for his life, and could confine it to his plays. Encounters with priest-frightened goddesses were left for *Red Roses for Me* and *The Bishop's Bonfire*.

A propensity for the life force alive in the ample bosom of a lusty wench remains throughout the writing of the plays and the stories, in which O'Casey reveals a fondness for the woman who is no better than she needs to be. Excesses in the name of vitality are more than condoned: the only sin is a meanness of spirit, something no Daisy Battles could ever be accused of. Not only does Daisy offer Sean her body and her bed, but feeds him and protects him and sews his torn trousers. That she is the sexually more aggressive of the two is necessitated by Sean's reluctance: like the Alice Boyd/ Norris before her, she has to spell out her willingness and assert her demand for stronger passion. When Sean obeys her request for a kiss, she comments, 'Well, you take care not to hurt yourself when you're kind to a girl.' [**Hallway, 321.**] There is little doubt that Daisy is a kept woman, endowed by a 'kind old uncle', but she maintains an independence of choice and an insistence that life offer her something more than petty routine. She has her counterpart in 'Bedtime Story' where an equally energetic Angela Nightingale seduces a far more frightened escort than Sean Casside proved to be.

An angel, yet a woman of the night, Angela Nightingale is a bird-like creature, although a natural and earthy woman. She has apparently seduced the 'constitutionally frightened' [**Bedtime, 228**] John Jo Mulligan, and during the small hours of the morning is seen leading him a merry chase, as he tries to hurry her out of his flat so that the landlady will not find out. O'Casey wastes little sympathy on John Jo the lover (the 'Jo' is ironic), whom he writes off as 'never able to take the gayer needs of life in his stride—though he would be glad to do it, if he could; but he can never become convalescent from a futile sense of sin' [**Bedtime, 228**]. Angela, on the other hand, is 'not without dignity' and 'something of a pagan' and needless to add, she is 'trimly-formed' [**Bedtime, 230**]. O'Casey's verdict is a conclusive one from the beginning: 'Far and away too good a companion of an hour, a year, or a life, for a fellow like Mulligan.' [**Bedtime, 230.**] Although obviously a scamp, she is redeemed by her sense of humour, her vivaciousness, and her love of life, in contrast to the timid, selfish male.

Angela proves to be a good judge of character: she is able to con Mulligan out of his hidden hoard by realising the extent to which he will go in order to hush up the incident and survive without punishment. His estimate of the situation is presented 'almost tearfully': 'We're in the midst of a violent sin, and you should be ashamed and sorry, instead of feeling sinfully gay about it. It's necessary to feel sorry for a sin of this kind.' [**Bedtime, 231.**] But Angela has no intention of succumbing to regret, otherwise she would never have entered into the sin in the first place. Her commentary is a singing of her theme song, 'I don't care what the people say,/Here, there, and everywhere.' [**Bedtime, 235.**] Her malicious ingenuity leads her to re-enact Bernadette's phony fainting spell just to terrorise the guilty Mulligan, and she sails out into the night with his coat, umbrella, ring, wallet, money and a cheque. O'Casey had condoned petty larceny in previous instances, but in this case he is happily turning a blind eye to Angela's grandiose larceny.

A third treatment of a similar situation was used by O'Casey in the short story 'I Wanna Woman', written during his first years in London. This earliest version of the male-female encounter is the most mordant of the three, Jack Avreen being even more unpleasant than John Jo Mulligan. The London setting and Avreen's leisurely and comfortable bachelor existence remove the material from the familiar O'Casey world; the tone is far more brittle and the environment gaudier. The temptress in this case, a tart named Alice with an expensive flat of her own and a maid as well, has none of Angela's vivacity and is redeemed only by her taste in literature (Hardy, France, Dostoevsky, Balzac)—but this is sufficient in contrast to the crass Avreen

(' "Dostoevsky's one of the Russian fellows," he said; "don't know how anyone could be interested in such a writer, though I haven't read him myself" ' [Woman, 270]).

Like John Jo, Jack Avreen is caught between the immediate demands of his lust and his innate revulsion towards sex (although no religious scruples or bourgeois worries about the neighbours bother him), and he is caught between unsuccessful attempts at seducing a Catholic girl who 'went too far altogether without going far enough' [Woman, 254] and the tart he pursues from Piccadilly to Maida Vale only to learn that pursuit in her case is superfluous. Alice is precisely what he had been hunting all evening: 'He wanted just a little elegance of manner and a saucy reticence that surrendered with a sad, sham charm what it was paid for and had to give.' [Woman, 262.] And having attained exactly what he wanted, Jack Avreen finds himself unsatisfied, revolted and cheated. He has found the particular 'bird' he hunted, one of those 'only out occasionally to add a little week-end tail to their wages' [Woman, 263], and although he lacks the self-perception to realise it, it is with himself that he is actually disgusted. And he too pays dear for his pleasure and his limitation, leaving behind not only five pounds, ten shillings, but a twenty-guinea watch by mistake. Alice too may be overly cute and all too businesslike, but she is a paragon compared to the self-centred male who uses her.

There is apparently little prejudice on O'Casey's part against the professional whore, although there is the indication that Jannice's lack of success in the profession attests to her personal superiority to it; she is 'too generous and sensitive to be a clever whore, and her heart is not in the business'. Conversely, a woman like Jessie Taite in *The Silver Tassie* is far less likeable than Jannice, although she does not engage herself professionally in the sale of her body, but barters her favours for alliance with the triumphant and successful. The young women of *The Tassie* are O'Casey's most contemptible examples of the species, only Susie redeeming herself by abandoning hypocritical religion for sexual enjoyment. In Jessie the dramatist portrays the fickle girl and in Mrs Foran the unfaithful wife. Not that O'Casey is particularly disturbed by Mrs Foran's infidelities; he sums her up as 'one of the many gay, careworn women of the working-class' [**Tassie**, 10] and displays Teddy Foran as a rough-and-ready hooligan. Mrs Foran undergoes her own change in the post-war scenes, however, emerging as the dutiful wife caring for the blind Teddy. But there are strange vestiges of the former self that appear in the last act: the once lusty woman has turned somewhat prudish (a counterbalance to parallel the change in Susie): 'Astonishin' the way girls are advertisin' their immodesty,' she comments on Jessie's dress. 'Whenever one of them sits down, in my heart I pity the poor man havin' to view the disedifyin' sight of the full length of one leg couched over another.' [**Tassie**, 90.] And when her blind husband reminisces over the pleasure of just such a sight, Mrs Foran whips the wine-glass out of his hand: 'Damn the drop more, now, you'll get for the rest of the evenin'.' [**Tassie**, 90.] Her husband's pathetic situation has changed her greatly, but in odd instances she has adopted his violent anger as well.

Certainly the most violent female in the O'Casey canon is Irish Nannie, the heroine of the early one-act play, 'Nannie's Night Out', discarded after an initial Abbey production in 1924, but mined repeatedly thereafter for later material. Irish Nannie herself is a 'young spunker' [**Nannie**, 303] ('a drinker of methylated spirit') who dances herself into drunken frenzies, during which she breaks windows, battles the police, and is invariably hauled off for stretches in Mountjoy Jail. O'Casey's brief for her is a short one and almost non-committal: 'She is about thirty years of age, well made, strong, and possibly was handsome before she began to drink. Her eyes flash with the light of semi-madness. . . . Her manner, meant to be recklessly merry, is very near to hysterical tears.' [**Nannie**, 307.] As she romps through the streets of Dublin, she is almost a parody of O'Casey's energetic heroine with a zest for sheer living, advocating a 'short life an' a merry wan' [**Nannie**, 308]. Like Jannice her heart is bad (and one version of the play has her die during the wild frenzy of her drunken bout, while another has her returned to jail). Nannie was superseded by the better-balanced and dramatically more sympathetic Jannice (her

186

cry of 'I'll die game, I'll die game!' [**Nannie, 309**] is repeated by the heroine of *Within the Gates*) and later by the more fully developed character of Mild Millie in *Drums under the Windows*, and O'Casey seems to have had no further use for her or the one-acter. Another bit of Irish Nannie emerges in Bessie Burgess, who echoes her taunt, 'Th' poor Tommies was men!' [**Nannie, 314.**][7]

There are two significant differences between the Nannie of the 1924 play and the Mild Millie in the 1945 autobiography: set at the turn of the century, the Millie incident precedes the establishment of the Free State, and unlike the Nannie who damns both Republicans and Free Staters and praises the Tommies, Millie is vocally anti-British and pro-Home Rule; also Millie is described as a younger and more sensual female. Sean Casside finds himself very much attracted to the young Millie: 'the line from her chin to her throat was fine, and went curving grandly into a bosom that was rich and firm and white. She had hips, too, that would have made a Hebe happier. . . . A handsome lass, thought Sean, and well-dressed would make many a fine man long to dance attendance on her.' [**Window, 96.**] The weary Sean, guarding his sister's evicted belongings on the street, accepts the still-sober Millie's offer to nest his head on her fine bosom, but once drunk on spunk (here called 'red biddy' and 'red poteen') she thrusts him from her: 'Go an' sit on your own steps, you! It's a wet nurse you want, so go where you'll be more likely to find one!' [**Window, 108.**]

Both Millie and Nannie are sexually indifferent, their independent personalities refusing to either sell or give themselves to men, much less in any way become dependent upon 'weaker' males. (In 'Nannie's Night Out' Mrs Polly Pender, a still-attractive widow of fifty eventually rejects all three superannuated suitors who compete for her, sensing her innate superiority over them: 'Addin' two an' two together, I think th' best thing Polly Pender can do, is to remain a bird alone.' [**Nannie, 330.**]) Millie is completely scornful about the subject of marriage: 'An' where's th' man in Dublin would be tantamount to Millie? . . . there's ne'er a man in Dublin would warrant me openin' a single button to let him come a little closer.' [**Window, 104.**] In fact, she has conformist ideas on sex, even to the extent of having misgivings about Parnell and his affair with Kitty O'Shea ('I'm a decent woman that way,' [**Window, 106**] she announces). And to Sean the drunken and violent Millie, having collapsed on the street after her wild dance, is a symbol of Ireland: 'In a way, she is Cathleen ni Houlihan—a Cathleen with the flame out of her eyes turned downwards. The feet of this Cathleen, the daughter of Houlihan, are quiet now, but none have bent low and low to kiss them.' [**Window, 112–13.**]

Except for Jannice and the Alice of 'I Wanna Woman', the only practising prostitute of any significance in O'Casey's works is Rosie Redmond in *The Plough and the Stars*, a particularly delightful minor character. O'Casey presents her with almost complete objectivity: Rosie is what she is, a professional plying her trade with guile and cunning. Her situation is rather precarious on the night of the meeting ('There isn't much notice taken of a pretty petticoat on a night like this' [**Plough, 192–3**]), and she must pay her rent, so Rosie tries every trick she can to coax some enthusiasm from the only customer in the pub, the 'anti-social' Covey. He is immediately cagey, aware that Rosie is out to cadge a free drink at his expense, but trips himself up when he is encouraged to spout his ideas to her, offering to lend her 'Jenersky's *Thesis on the Origin, Development, an' Consolidation of the Evolutionary Idea of the Proletariat*' [**Plough, 197**]. But the Covey's Marxism will not pay Rosie's rent, and her advances become too uncomfortable for the uneasy Covey: he quickly escapes from the pub, one step ahead of her clutches, leaving Rosie to denounce him and his kind: 'Jasus, it's in a monasthery some of us ought to be, spendin' our holidays kneelin' on our adorers, tellin' our beads, an' knockin' hell out of our buzzums!' [**Plough, 198.**]

Unable to get another drink on credit, Rosie finds herself treated by the expansive Fluther, and she soon sizes up the animosity between him and the Covey; she capitalises on the conflict, placing herself solidly in Fluther's camp, shoring him up and egging him on, and taking full command of him when the belligerent Covey is ejected, leaving Fluther the victor by default—and Rosie his manager. Having got him pleasantly drunk she leads him home with her. O'Casey offers no apology for her: she is young and pretty, keeps herself by practising the world's oldest profession, has no scruples about changing sides and ideas in order to please a prospective customer, and has no other existence except selling herself in order to get by.

Necessity reduces Rosie Redmond to a monochrome, despite which she maintains her hope and adds occasional touches of colour to her life whenever possible. Sex for her is merely a means toward economic stability, cancelling out its significance for her as anything personal. She wastes no time enticing men for her own pleasure, as apparently Mrs Alice Lanigan does in 'The End of the Beginning', where despite her middle-age she is the source of gossip, Darry Berrill accused by his wife of lusting after her: 'The Alice Lanigan that's on the margin of fifty, 'n assembles herself together as if she was a girl in her teens, jutting out her bust when she's coming in, 'n jutting out her behind when she's going out, like the Lady of Shalott, to catch the men— that's the Alice Lanigan I mean.' [End, 268.] Compared to the gratuitously sensual Mrs Lanigan, Rosie the whore is antiseptically clinical in selling her wares, her profession precluding any real involvement. The Alice of 'I Wanna Woman' takes refuge in reading books ('They pass in a pleasant way many a dull hour' [Woman, 269]), while Jannice attempts to find in the Dreamer both a lover and a protector, and Daisy Battles maintains both a permanent uncle and the temporary Sean. But Rosie is a good deal more limited, and makes the best of a bad situation, putting a good face on it whenever she can. Whether he is singing his songs of innocence or experience, O'Casey attempts to discover the essentially human and personal about his young women.

6

Argufiers and Leprechauns

I

As much as the world admires a hero (and a heroine), it is more vocal in its love for a clown, from Shakespeare's Falstaff to O'Casey's Paycock. Like Shakespeare's paycock figure, O'Casey's has a primary characteristic of vainglorious pomposity, and a secondary aspect no more endearing and equally universal, a tendency toward argumentation. If argumentativeness were outlawed, O'Casey's stage would be as bare as the well-known cupboard, populated only with Sammy the shy singer and Mrs Gogan's baby left lying on the pub floor. On O'Casey's stage, however, it is silence that is the crime. In 'Behind the Curtained World' he campaigns against 'the curious heresy that nowhere is silence more golden than when it appears on the stage. For now there is a monastic awe for silence on the stage so that actors and actresses are losing the power of speech, and mutter and mumble their way about behind the footlights and the curtain, keeping all their secrets to themselves.'[1] From Seumas Shields to Alec Skerighan there is rarely any such mute in an O'Casey play. There is nothing that an O'Casey Irishman likes better than to hold forth on a subject of controversy about which he knows something or nothing: two's an argument, three's a bruhaha, and four's the merrier, a verbal donnybrook. And with no risk of incurring outlawry, they have named themselves argufiers: 'I don't come here to raise no argument,' says the landlord in *The Gunman*: 'a person ud have small gains argufyin' with you.' [**Shadow, 101.**]

The topic slated for argument is never limiting, but should it be religion, the opportunities prove multiple. The forces align themselves in various combinations, with the conflict between Catholic and Protestant a dominant one. Joybell (in *The Star Turns Red*) hardly needs an adversary; he is a one-man non-stop argument all by himself. O'Casey denotes him as a 'Catholic flag-waver' [**Star,** 257] and pushes him on-stage in his Confraternity robe, offset on top by his plump head crowned with bushy hair and below by 'big, heavy, clumsy boots' [**Star,** 257]. He constantly spews unctuousness, unaware of the inappropriateness of his bubbling enthusiasms, sings the praises of the Christmas season, and is generally out of place in the tumultuous events of political confrontation taking place in the play. Between his contretemps with Julia in the first act and his petty squabble with the Old Man in the last, Joybell has his best moment at Union headquarters when he barges in during the head-on collision between Red Jim and the opposition leadership:

God rest you merry, gentlemen, let nothing you dismay. Hallo, Jim! How's the mother and the missus? Well? Yes, of course—well. How's everybody? All fit, well, and smiling, eh? But fading flowers, fading flowers waiting for our little day to end. *Lapsus annus est,* you know— the hour is gone. The Lord Mayor's waiting for Mr Sheasker to get ready for the part of Father Christmas, and give out our little gifts of tea and sugar to the deserving poor. I'll be serving, and the Lord Mayor'll be serving himself: Him who is greatest among you, let him be your servant—you know. Good deeds against the day of wrath—*Dies Irae*—of wrath, see, understand? What's all the silence for? [**Star, 300–301.**]

He never finds out: Jim ejects him from the room without further delay. Unheeded and unneeded the Joybells argue in a vacuum without audience or adversary. Susie Monican, in her first manifestation as a babbling evangelist in *The Silver Tassie,* is another of O'Casey's long-winded argufiers whose words fall on deaf ears.

When it takes two to argue, two can usually be found without difficulty. In *The Drums of Father Ned* an Orangeman like Alec Skerighan soon finds that there is always an Irish Catholic on hand to pick up the gauntlet: all he need do is play 'Lillibulero' on McGilligan's piano. 'An' a Protestant tune's no fit thing to be played on a Catholic piano' [Ned, 69] McGilligan asserts, but Skerighan insists that he is 'just thryin' tae bring a wee but of ceevilization intil Doonavale' [Ned, 69]. Oscar McGunty, a worker in McGilligan's factory, seconds his boss's objection to the intrusion of 'Lillibulero' into the Catholic confines of Doonavale, but McGilligan is furious at his intrusion into their conversation, so a pair of arguments proceed simultaneously, the Catholics against the Protestant, and labour against management. The arrival of Mrs McGilligan seriously deflates the argument: she innocently requests an explanation of the words of the song, but neither the Orangeman (who maintains that it is 'a plain an' outspoken Protestant song, mo'om, meanin' only what it says' [Ned, 72]) nor the wearers of the green (who insist that 'every note o' th' tune's stitched tight to hathred of everythin' we hold dear' [Ned, 72-3]) can explicate the lyrics.[2]

Mrs McGilligan brings the quarrel to an impasse and re-establishes order in the household—temporarily. In the next scene Skerighan is as hot-headed as ever, and the fight goes on. This time it is Binnington who bears the brunt of the invasion of the Northerner's bigoted fortress, and for those critics who have accused O'Casey of anti-Catholic bias, Skerighan should be sufficient indication that a Protestant can out-bigot a Catholic in O'Casey's world. For all his pomposity, Mayor Binnington tries to handle the issues gently (he is primarily concerned with the business deal with the Northerner), but Skerighan remains adamant in his prejudices. Even at his most conciliatory, having conceded that 'Ceevility is deep dune in a' our hearts, on' North on' South' [Ned, 85], he nonetheless insists that 'Ulsther's th' one sunsible on' foreseein' pruvence left in Ireland' [Ned, 85] and considers the South hopeless 'so lang as ye suffer th' inseedious dumination of your Church, on' th' waefu' intherfurence of your clergy in what ye thry tae do' [Ned, 87]. Binnington is the soul of caution in dealing with the volatile Orangeman, and the wives apply balm after balm, but McGilligan is quick to take up the battle: 'It's all settled already!' he shouts; 'St Pether, an' afther him St Pathrick, is our man, th' Rock on which our Church stands. What's yours piled up on? On a disgraceful, indecent attachment of a despicable English king for a loose woman!' [**Ned, 89.**] And so that argument rages, reverberating from the O'Casey autobiography through *The Drums of Father Ned*: the *Rose and Crown* volume had set the quarrel in 'New Amsterdam', where the playwright was earwitness to a pair of Irish-Americans pre-creating McGilligan and Skerighan for him. The New York host, just a half-step removed from Ulster, compulsively introduces the subject, 'The Irish wud be a grund people but for the inseedious releegion of the romun catholic church ruining thum,' [**Crown, 290**] while a Judge Lynch argues for the defence: 'Will you deny that St Patrick did penance for the Irish on the cold, windy top of Croagh Pathrick and that he got his holy mission from Rome?' [**Crown, 291.**] And Sean thinks to himself: 'Oh, God . . . Connemara's Croagh Pathrick and Belfast's Cave Hill are at it again, and, of all places, in New Amsterdam!' [**Crown, 291.**]

The Protestants of *Red Roses for Me* are Dubliners rather than Ulstermen, but although their accents are better, their song is the same. A couple of members of the Select Vestry of the Church of St Burnupus, Messrs Foster and Dowzard, make nuisances of themselves in their objections to the cross of daffodils that Ayamonn makes for the Easter service: Foster is quoted by the verger as shouting, 'Are you goin' to be a party to th' plastherin' of Popish emblems over a Protestan' church?' [**Roses, 208.**] The outbreak of violence during the strike is classified by the Select Vestrymen as 'St Bartholomew's Day's dawnin' again' and 'a hoppy Romish auto-dey-fey' [**Roses, 217–18**]. They denounce their own rector as Ichabod and shout for Breydon's head, Foster venomously insisting, 'I'll no' stick it. Look-see, th' rage kindlin' godly Luther is kindlin' me!. . . Th' bible on' th' crown! The twa on' a half, th' orange on' blue; on' th' Dagon of Popery undher our Protestant feet!' [**Roses, 219–20**]. In *Pictures in the Hallway*, where Johnny Casside like Ayamonn Breydon finds himself involved in the Protestant Church of St Burnupus, the pair of Select Vestrymen become a trinity of the same, Donaldson, Doosard and Glazier, and Johnny implicates them in his comic fantasy

193

of 'The Buttle of the Boyne', his own nationalistic sympathies in conflict with their loyalist allegiances to the Crown. Dowzard and Foster are of course caricatures in action, while the trio in the autobiography afford O'Casey an opportunity to caricature in description as well:

> The Orangemen were headed by the people's church-warden, Frank Donaldson, secretary to the Grand Loyal Orange Lodge of Dublin, a man to whom any speck of colour on a church wall or in a window meant popery and *auto-da-fés* of burning protestants every morning in Rutland Square, and twice a day on Sundays. His pale, pitiless face for ever stared in front of him, seeing nothing but the evil and the danger of a fringe on a church cloth, and a devil's conjuring trick in the sign of the cross; Edward Doosard, Inspector of the Quay Police (doddering old men, in their third childhood, watching the warehouses of the Port and Docks Board, showing gold and brass where the real police showed silver, the dockers cursing them, and the carters cutting at them with their whips whenever they got in the way), his ruby face, jowled like Dutch cheeses, his bull neck forming a circle above a white collar, like a thick rubber hose, a rusty-fleshed fat hand almost always stroking a bristly moustache, and his piggy eyes trying to tell everyone that he was a pillar of protestantism; and John Glazier, foreman in the Great Western Railway Goods Store; a true blue, if ever there was one; a man who would be ready to die for his faith, his rugged face carved like a stone creviced by centuries of frost and rain; his jagged teeth showing grimly when he mentioned some taint of ritualism in some protestant church; his hands twitching as if they were edging towards a pope's throat. [Hallway, 353.]

In the play O'Casey demotes Donaldson and Glazier to railroad foremen to involve them in the strike, and promotes Doosard to Inspector Finglas of the real police.

Protestant Brennan Moore, the landlord of *Red Roses*, also gets a chance to prate against the Roman Church ('Inflamin' yourselves with idols that have eyes an' see not;

194

ears, an' hear not; an' have hands that handle not; like th' chosen people settin' moon-images an' sun-images, cuttin' away the thrue and homely connection between the Christian an' his God!' [**Roses, 154**]), but, despite his vociferousness, he is a gentle man who has taken the Catholic 'idol' in order to have it repainted for his tenants. But he soon gets himself embroiled in an argument with Catholic Roory involving the edicts of the Council of Trent and St Patrick, Brennan contending that the saint was a Protestant—'th' evangelical founder of our thrue Church' [**Roses, 167**]— much to Roory's amazement ('Protestant St Pathrick? Is me hearin' sound, or what? What name did you mention?' [**Roses, 167**]).

There is one sure way of uniting Catholic and Protestant in O'Casey's Ireland: the introduction of a common enemy, the atheist. Roory O'Balacaun[3] and Brennan Moore are stunned when Mullcanny claims that the Pope supported the victory of King Billy over the Catholic forces of King James, both shouting 'You're a liar,' [**Roses, 167**] but immediately returning to their original dispute. But Mullcanny is as contentious as they, commenting on their quarrel: 'You see how they live in bittherness, the one with the other. Envy, strife, and malice crawl from the coloured slime of the fairy-tales that go to make what is called religion.' [**Roses, 167.**] This plague-on-both-your-houses approach is not ignored for long; Mullcanny horrifies both religious men by his reference to 'the true and scientific history of man as he was before Adam' [**Roses, 168**]. 'Th' Lord between us an' all harm!' [**Roses, 168**] intones the Catholic at the idea of eternal death; 'Lord, I believe, help Thou mine unbelief' [**Roses, 168**] echoes the Protestant, and they recommend jail for the iconoclast and burning for his books. Ned, the Atheist of *Within the Gates*, fares no better in confrontation with the orthodox, encountering in London the same sort of furore that Mullcanny experiences in Dublin. 'You shut your rotten mouth, will you! Warnt to 'ear yourself torkin', torkin', do you?' [**Gates, 131**] asserts the older park attendant aggressively, but it should be remembered that Ned is a professional atheist who regularly mounts his platform at Hyde Park Corner to argue his ideas. Even during off-duty hours, however, he can be heard in the park holding forth to any who will listen. He mocks the idea 'that Gord watches even over the fall of the sparrer' [Gates, 131], insists that 'the more a man uses 'is mind, the less 'ee uses Gord' [Gates, 150], confronts the Bishop on the ten commandments as a 'competent rule of life en' conduct' [Gates, 151], and argues first cause with the Man wearing a Trilby Hat. Ned is hardly as assertive as Mullcanny and rarely indulges in the personal invective that Mullcanny is pressured into: his is an older and cooler head.

A second atheist in *Within the Gates* serves O'Casey as the absurd argufier, taking on all comers in a pugnacious manner and with a thick Cockney accent. As the Man with a Stick he appears in the first three scenes (later modulated into the Man with an Umbrella in the last); he echoes Ned throughout, but hardly appears as knowledgeable, as he ventures off into explaining time-space theories he certainly cannot handle accurately. For a minor character he turns up often—in each of the scenes of the play; with the Chair Attendants he tries to discuss the nature of matter, to the Gardener he explains the pagan origins of the Maypole, for the benefit of the Man wearing the Trilby he challenges the authenticity of the stories of the Bible, until he reaches the exalted subject of 'spice-time'. Although essentially a comic extension of the Atheist, he shares with Ned a basic understanding of the human situation in regard to Jannice: when it is apparent to him that the Gardener has no intention of marrying her, the Man with a Stick comments, 'You've lost something, friend, you've lost a lot. If I was young as you, I'd ha' carried 'er 'ome!' [Gates, 147.] But the Gardener is as obtuse in his dealings with Jannice as he is regarding the Maypole; for all those who fail to see his drift (who fail to agree with him), the Man with a Stick has one summation: 'No brrine!' [Gates, 126.]

The quarrel between the religions comes directly from the mainstream of Irish life, but O'Casey's intrusion of the atheist as prime antagonist is a special aspect of particular interest to the author himself, a belated entrance of Darwinism into Ireland. O'Casey's sympathies are with Ned and Mullcanny and the Man with a Stick, and they often serve as his spokesmen (or at least are supported by protagonists close to the playwright himself, the Dreamer and Ayamonn), but he delights in making them look a bit too self-serious and preoccupied with their evangelical missions to 'bounce the idea of a Gord from men's minds' [**Gates, 125**].

If *Red Roses* is a major repository of Protestant bigotry, 'Behind the Green Curtains' serves as its Catholic counterpart. Dan Basawn, for example, seems to exist only as a foil to Martin Boeman's ironic scepticism, as he attempts to relate to the Communist the story of the Weeping Statue of Syracuse, believing as he does in 'a faith that has th' Christian world sizzlin' with miracles!' [**Curtains, 14.**] Boeman has no difficulty in making fun of him and a tangle of his story, and when the writers and artists attempt to enter the Protestant Church of St Ashlingoch, Basawn denounces them with fury: 'It's your bounden duty to keep from settin' a foot inside a heretical church; and it's your duty, too, to march in any demonsthration agen Atheistic Communism! (*To Boeman—fiercely*) An' you keep outa this; this is our Catholic business!' [**Curtains, 22.**] Another piece of Catholic business is represented by a deputation of three shopgirls from Chatastray's factory objecting to the marriage of a Protestant boy and Catholic girl working in the factory; as one of the trio presents it, the gist of their argument is: 'Looka, if she doesn't break from him, or he doesn't break from her, we go out, and stay out till either him or her give over th' idea of living together—for what they'll call a marriage won't be one; or till both of them flit from th' factory.' [**Curtains, 49.**]

And the supreme bigot of them all is Christy Kornavaun: he brings word from the Archbishop's palace that the mourners may not enter the Protestant church; he represents *The Catholic Buzzer*, a journal that sends out the questionnaire on the Cardinal Mindszenty Protest Meeting; he abuses Noneen for working for Chatastray and makes a pass at her; in general he terrorises the group of intellectuals, whipping them into obedient conformity, and threatens Chatastray with retribution if he does not comply: 'Be God, you'll suffer for all this, Chatastray! You'll lose your Irish ordhers as well as your American ones, an' your factory'll fall on your disobedient head.' [**Curtains, 74.**] And he picks up where Dan Basawn left off in a futile campaign against Boeman: 'You heard what he said, didn't youse? We're all Christians, aren't we? Let's dhrive th' heretic outa th' house!' [**Curtains, 72.**]

If religion is a major controversy in the O'Casey world, politics is probably more absorbing: few of the plays are without a political discussion and few of those taking part in such discussions are anything less than argumentative. 'Kathleen Listens In', in particular, serves as a listing of the combatants and their shades of political opinion, from the Anglicised Irishman who still calls Miceawl 'Mick' to the Man in the Kilts who insists that Miceawl speak only Irish, from the Free Stater to the Republican fighting the Civil War, from the Business Man to Jimmy the Workman fighting the class war, and from Joey and Johnny who form the National Party to the Man with the Big Drum who sings his Orangeman's Song. All of the characters in and around the O'Houlihan house are combative, and their offshoots people many another O'Casey piece.

Early in the first volume of the autobiography, during the scene in which the crowd gawks before the entrance to the Dublin Castle Ball, two disembodied voices rise to the surface. One belongs to 'a genteel-looking man, with a watery mouth and a drooping moustache' who says, 'We might as well have a decko at the grandeur that's keeping the country going, before Mister Parnell and his poverty-stricken dupes reduce us all again to a state of nature.' [**Door, 20.**] The second is a tram conductor (the first appearance of a figure that will be seen often throughout the Dublin volumes) who replies: 'The day isn't far distant . . . when that gent that's just gone out'll doff his hat to another tune, or hang as high as Gilderoy.' [**Door, 21.**] The gent is vulgarly echoed by the likes of Bessie Burgess in many of her tirades ('An' as for law an' ordher, puttin' aside th' harp an' shamrock, Bessie Burgess'll have as much respect as she wants for th' lion an' unicorn!' [**Plough, 228**]), while aspects of the conductor are found in Roory O'Balacaun, whom his creator designates 'a zealous Irish Irelander' [**Roses, 126**]. Roory is not only Catholic to the core but

198

Irish to the bone as well, which gives him a position for argumentation at almost any instance. He shares the tram conductor's point of view to a similarly fanatic extent, but lacks the unique quality of personal magnetism, the mysterious touch of whimsy, that magnifies the Ayamonn O'Farrel of the autobiographies. Roory is utilised by O'Casey exclusively for his single facet as revolutionary nationalist, brandisher of the Sword of Light.

Ayamonn O'Farrel remains an unnamed character (the conductor) until close to the end of the second volume (in the chapter titled 'The Sword of Light'), but throughout the first volume he is a pivotal figure. *I Knock at the Door* opens with a chapter describing Mrs Casside's attempt to save the life of her baby (an earlier Johnny) by rushing him to a hospital, but the cab is delayed in a procession honouring Charles Stewart Parnell. In the second chapter the tram in which Johnny and his mother are riding is halted by the traffic to the festivities at the Castle, and Johnny overhears the exchange between the pro-British gentleman and the Fenian conductor. The penultimate chapter takes place during a regal celebration in the city of Dublin, and Johnny and his mother mount a tram to see the festivities (this chapter, 'The Red Above the Green', balances the second chapter, 'First the Green Blade'), and the same conductor and same gent are present. 'Don't be so sure that the personalities thravellin' are set on givin' a delicate or delirious show of loyalty to anyone or anything thryin' to devastate the efforts of our brave Irish Party fightin' for us on the floor of the House of Commons!' [**Door, 269**] comments the gent ('having a wide watery mouth with a moustache hanging over it like a weeping willow' [**Door, 269**])—he is revealed to be the father of Johnny's friend, Georgie Middleton, who now has come full circle from his castigation of Parnell. But the conductor is an outspoken Fenian who denounces Mr Middleton and the other passengers as summer soldiers and sunshine patriots: 'It's waitin' a long time I'll be to see yous busy bandagin' your eyes to keep at a distance the signs an' shows of revelry when the thram penethrates into the sthreets, alive with the flags of all nations, save our own.' [**Door, 270.**] And Johnny's mother commends the conductor as 'a very sensible man, and shrewd', and lauds the Fenians as 'honest, outspoken men' [**Door, 270**].

Pictures in the Hallway repeats the balanced structure of *I Knock at the Door*, and again the tram conductor plays his part in the mystique of Johnny Casside's awakening world. The first chapter, 'A Coffin Comes to Ireland', concerns the death of Parnell, and although the conductor is not present in the recording of the event for Johnny, he appears soon after as Johnny is being taken by his Uncle Tom for a visit to Kilmainham jail ('is the young fella's father one o' the boys?' [**Hallway, 40**] asks the conductor, assuming that they are visiting a jailed Fenian). And towards the end of the book Ayamonn O'Farrel, now a friend to the mature Sean Casside, has a 'Sword of Light' chapter of his own, wherein he duplicates the role played by Roory in *Red Roses* (both encounter the protagonist reading Ruskin and deprecate any literature that does not actively serve the propaganda function for the Irish cause; but O'Farrel is a softer version of O'Balacaun, more personally sympathetic toward the protagonist, and even lending his first name for the autobiographic hero in the play). In the next chapter, 'I Strike a Blow for You, Dear Land', Ayamonn is Johnny's companion during the street riots over the Boer War, a Virgil guiding young Dante through the Inferno of Irish political imbroglios until he passes on his charge to Daisy Battles, who as Beatrice takes Johnny up the stairs to her version of paradise. And in the crowd of argufiers once again the strident voice of the archetypal Bessie Burgess can be heard holding her own against the nationalists:

> —I don't care who hears me, she shouted, for we're full of life today, an'—puff—we're gone tomorra. To every man an' woman their own opinion, square or round or crooked or cornered, which is only right an' proper, an' a fair division. Sayin' nothin' calculated to hurt a soul, I'll say yous are a lot o' starin' fools, watchin' and waitin' for somethin' yous'll never be spared to see. I wondher, she went on, raising her voice to a screaming pitch, I wondher what all of yous, what any of yous'ud do, if England went undher! [**Hallway, 308.**]

The war is a different one, but the voice is very much the same.

But the bawling Bessies are not always bellowing in the service of the British cause in Ireland, or for any other, for that matter. There is always the occasional figure in the crowd (and often a woman) just exercising her lungs, as in the turmoil surrounding the Abbey Theatre riots over *The Playboy of the Western World*. In 'Song of a Shift' (*Drums under the Windows*) Sean is overwhelmed by a boisterous crowd and attempts to learn from a Poor Old Woman what is actually happening: she does not know but admits having been participating in the running and the shouting. 'An' if I am aself, what signifies?' she asks; 'D'ye want me to be th' one odd outa th' many? It's a bit o' fun anyhow. She caught her poor thin skirt up in her poor thin hands, and caracoled along, shouting, The dirty-minded minsthrels! Belchin' out in th' sthricken faces of our year in an' year out innocence things no decent-minded individual would whisper even into his own ear! Why don't they tell us of the beautiful things we all love so well, th' dirty, dirty dastards!' [**Window, 173.**] At the Gaelic League Sean encounters the tram conductor again, also in a state of high dudgeon over the shift-business; at his most narrow-minded the nationalist exclaims: 'Some blasted little theatre or other has put on a play by a fellow named Singe or Sinje or something, a terrible play, helped by another boyo named Yeats or Bates or something, said to be a kind of poet or something, of things no-one can understand, an' he was to blame for it all, assisted by some oul' one or another named Beggory or something, who was behind the scene eggin' them on in their foul infamity. A terrible play, terrible!' [**Window, 175.**] Under cross-examination the conductor admits that he has neither seen the play nor does he know much about it, but stands ready to condemn it on principle: 'I don't know what he said in th' play, an' I don't care; but anyone'll tell you he made a go at every decent consignment left living in th' counthry.' [**Window, 176.**] The argument goes on with many argufying voices heard on the issue in the crowded League headquarters, and although the tram conductor has been highly vocal in his condemnation, it is to his credit that he follows Sean and O'Murachadha out of the meeting to join

201

forces with them: 'What yous two think, I think, he said, in the main; not altogether, mind you, but in th' main. The clergy were always in th' sthream of things goin' against Ireland. They fought men of Forty-eight, the Fenians, and then Parnell. I'm with yous right enough.' [Window, 186.]

It is axiomatic that Sean O'Casey is at his best when he is at his least didactic, when his own attitude towards complex political issues is agile and complex and he is able to see the limitations of all viewpoints and the inconsistencies of the characters who espouse them. But on occasion, even when he is obviously intent on crucifying an enemy with a mordant character sketch or caricature, when he holds up a Kornavaun or Foster or Dowzard for merciless scrutiny, he is masterful in his vindictive portraiture. Such is the case with Mrs Deeda Tutting in *Oak Leaves and Lavender* and her counterpart in the 'Dree Dames' in *Sunset and Evening Star*; these vituperative professional anti-Communists are his special *bêtes noires*, and he spares nothing in their dissection. Even a casually non-political Feelim O'Morrigun eventually sees through Mrs Tutting's outraged façade to the hate-monger lurking beneath, for instead of accepting his alliance against the Communist Drishogue, she insults 'the mystery of the Irish mind' [Oak, 52] and calls Feelim an 'old fool' [Oak, 53]. At this point O'Casey is also at his least subtle: there is not a single redeeming quality to the refugee from the O.G.P.U., and even gallant Drishogue is not above hitting her foully: when she wails about her arrested husband ('Arrested without a word, without a sign, my poor husband's dead by now for certain'), he calmly replies, 'Well, if the behaviour you're showing now is usual with you, I don't wonder your husband disappeared—it was the wisest thing he could do.' [Oak, 49.] Written just after the Second World War, and set in the early stages of the war, *Oak Leaves* is unabashedly propagandistic primarily for the war cause itself; when Mrs Tutting suggests an alliance with Nazi Germany against Soviet Russia she goes beyond the pale, and even allowing for the severe limitation of O'Casey's unde-Stalinised attitude, there is something quite recognisable in his Mrs Tutting caricature.

The replay of the scene in the last volume of the auto-

biography changes the alignment of characters: no comic
Feelim intrudes to confuse the O.G.P.U. with the Gestapo
and to pontificate that 'things happen when th' world turns
from God' [Oak, 48]; no Joy to listen with awed attention;
no Mrs Watchit to comment inanely, 'Us guessed it all
along' [Oak, 51]; and no Michael to attempt to interrupt
with his own immediate problem. Instead Sean has to face
not only the harridan herself, here called Creda Stern, but
her two attendant hags as well, Donah Warrington and Mrs
Jen Jayes. The three witches descend upon him unannounced and Sean manfully undertakes to ward them off single-
handedly. True to form Creda Stern makes all the blunders
possible, insulting the Irish mind, self-righteously maintaining that she has hold of the Truth, ranting and raving un-
pleasantly, and combining a miserable disposition with a
very unlovely physique. 'I tell you, Irishman, the Nazis are
far superior,' she snarls, 'and more to be preferred, than
your savage comrades in Moscow!' [Sunset, 129.] Sean remains implacable before such an assault, refusing to accept
anecdotal evidence and from so unreliable a source, and in
both cases—in the play and in the autobiography—he uses
the advantage of hindsight to defeat the shrew's argument:
both Mrs Tutting and Mrs Stern predict the quick destruction of the 'rotten' U.S.S.R. before the force of the Nazi
armies, and O'Casey may well have chuckled to himself as
he etched his caricatures after the war.

At his narrowest O'Casey created straw men to be knocked
down, argufiers so mean-spirited as to be unredeemable and
unforgivable, and in the case of Ernest Pobjoy the offence
may now appear far from heinous. In the midst of the
struggle against the onslaught of Nazism, Pobjoy maintained
his defiant attitude as a conscientious objector, a position
tenable in many other instances but obviously unpopular
during the united effort against the Nazis. Pobjoy is the
villain of Act Three as Deeda Tutting had been in Act One
(Abraham Penrhyn is the non-political villain of the middle
act); a modicum of sympathy is apparent in O'Casey's description of the character ('intelligent in a curious aloof
way. He can do a lot of things with his hands, is clever at
vegetable culture, and has read a little' [Oak, 86]), but in

introducing him O'Casey reveals the vital flaw: 'He can be alert when he likes, but usually goes about with his head down, and moves as if he were offering an apology for being alive.' [**Oak, 86.**] This devitalised spirit untouched by the Life Force condemns Ernest Pobjoy to a less-than-human category, a cipher for whom an excess of pity would be a waste.

The Mollsers and crippled Julias are pathetic because they are physically being prevented from living their lives, but Pobjoy like the Down-and-Out will not actively engage in life although there is no physical deterrent in his case. At first he is sullen and silent, and all of the others at the Hatherleigh estate snub him or just have no time for him, but he is goaded into arguing his case when the field hands refuse to work with him. O'Casey takes no apparent side in the dispute, when Joy and Felicity insist that Feelim 'take Pobjoy out of the fields, or we down tools; for we won't work with a damned Conchie' [**Oak, 92**] (the three Catholic shopgirls in 'Green Curtains' were no less unreasonable in denouncing the Catholic-Protestant intermarriage). Feelim attempts to find an easy way out for Pobjoy but the objector insists on invoking his conscience. At his most reasonable in attempting to teach Pobjoy the moral lessons of the war effort, Feelim sounds very much like the patriotic speechmaker who was omnipresent in the climactic scenes of World War Two movies: 'Surely, if they were bein' attacked, you'd defend your old churches; the graves in which your great men and women lie; the places where they lived; your folksong and your music?' [**Oak, 94**]; but all such sweet reasonableness makes Pobjoy all the more adamant and mean in his refusals. Beginning as a silent pathetic, perhaps even more sinned against than sinning, he is moved to articulating the worst aspects of himself in the face of Feelim's very gentle attempts at persuasion, and he reveals the same prejudice that unmasks Mrs Tutting: 'They're riskin' their lives, too, for you and your crowd in Ireland, though you and they stay snug at home, safe and cheerful. Those brave men are blown to bits while your Irish eyes are smiling.' [**Oak, 96.**] From O'Casey's viewpoint, beneath the façade of the anti-Communist lurks a proto-fascist, and beneath that of the conscientious objector he discloses the lifeless and heartless disposition of a sour bigot.

Show me a Puritan, quipped H. L. Mencken, and I'll show you a son-of-a-bitch; O'Casey is less definitive in his investigation of the puritan argufier, but he at least unearths the sexual sadist beneath the puritanical exterior. In *The Bishop's Bonfire* the Catholic puritan, Richard Rankin, is taunted by Keelin into a revelation of his violent lust, much like that of fellow-Catholics Joybell and Kornavaun and such Protestants as Alec Skerighan. But there are actually two puritan argufiers in the play, the Catholic Rankin and the Protestant Prodical, Dick Carranaun, almost as indistinguishable from each other as Lewis Carroll's pair of Tweedles. The Catholic 'neither drinks nor smokes, and his one interest in women is to keep as far away from them as possible' [**Bonfire, 2**.] (Keelin proves that his resolve is a shaky one); the Protestant is as self-righteous and pious as his cohort, but his temptation is drink ('He is always deciding to give up drink altogether' [**Bonfire, 2**]—the Codger's keg soon destroys his most recent pledge). O'Casey differentiates between them by describing the former's face as 'woeful and sour' [**Bonfire, 2**] and the latter's as 'sour and pugnacious', while Manus is quite democratic in giving each his equal due: 'I don't know which of you's the bigger bum —him who thinks he's given to heaven, or you who know you're given to drink.' [**Bonfire, 15**.]

Yet Rankin and Carranaun are quite able to tell themselves apart from each other, as they quarrel over everything (even a brick), revealing the religious war that places them on separate sides:

Prodical. . . . I'll bring back your catholic conscience, you holy hoodlum, muckin' me about like you were on a prairie outa sight of God an' scholarship!

Rankin. . . . Call me what you like, but say nothin' against me religion! . . . 'Gainst me religion, see!

. . . .

Prodical (vehemently). True religion isn't puffed up, you bastard; it's long-sufferin' an' kind, an' never vaunts itself like you do: true religion doesn't envy a man a brick, you rarefied bummer! [**Bonfire, 9–10**.]

205

But against the common enemy they close ranks immediately, the Mrs Grundys of one Church in Ireland echoing their counterparts in the other. The occasion of the bonfire excites them, both revelling in the thought that bad books and bad pictures will be burned in it. Carranaun sums up the philosophy of their united cause, despite his own hypocrisy in warning others against the one sin he is in the process of committing: 'Dan, me son, take me epicpiscopal advice, an' keep your young innocent puss outa the whiskey-tumbler, out of a bad book, an' keep far from the girls, for a young bitch's enfiladin' blessin' is the devil's choicest curse!' [**Bonfire, 82.**] And when it comes to explaining the basics of such a person as the Prodical, the author points to one definite specific: just as he is suspicious of the unfeminine female (the 'dree dames' are horrors of angularity and gauntness), so is he suspicious of unmasculine males, Carranaun having the 'high, falsetto voice of a man unmade' [**Bonfire, 2**].

One of O'Casey's sternest Calvinists is Abraham Penrhyn, very much a copy of O'Neill's Ephraim Cabot transplanted back to a farm in England, with grizzled hair and grizzled beard and a 'look of silent and bitter anger' [**Oak, 63**]. He rails against Monica's attachment to Drishogue, not only because a physical relationship between a man and a woman is 'in opposition t' God's commandments' [**Oak, 63**] but because the man involved is a 'man o' blood' [**Oak, 63**], a warrior. He conjures up the image of Monica's dead mother 'wrigglin' in agony in her abode of bliss', [**Oak, 63**], and the zeal of work underscoring the Puritan ethic: 'Us fattened bullocks for she an' 'ee, didn' I? An' reared sheep, an' ploughed land, an' sowed corn, an' watched sun, rain, an' worked, waitin', watchin' crops agrowin'.' [**Oak, 64.**] And like the Prodical he both acknowledges drink as the 'enemy of man' [**Oak, 66**] and gives himself up to it, threatening to work himself up into a drunken rage.

But the ravages of war are greater than Abe's fury, and his house is destroyed in an airraid. He is as vehement with his personal God as he is with his daughter ('Ah, God, You're too hard on them as loves You more, an' serves You better'n far 'an others!' [**Oak, 100**]), assuming that he is

206

being punished for Monica's trespasses: 'Us's a wicked daughter, ma'am, and she's brought a double woe on us.' [**Oak, 103.**] Dame Hatherleigh, barely able to cope with her own bereavements, nonetheless leads the violent man out like a docile child. Like Pobjoy he assumes himself to be a man of peace, respecting the rights of God's creatures to live and refusing to break the first commandment, but in actuality he is a man of violence worshipping a violent God. He gives himself away when he claims, 'Never took life— not even rabbit's. Us always got th' men about farm teh kill th' rabbits.' [**Oak, 100.**]

Controversial issues such as politics and religion are not the only goads for O'Casey's argumentative clan, many of whom will quarrel with anyone at the drop of a hat over the density of a chair ('if it was myde of cork it would be lighter,' insists the Man with a Stick; 'but if it was myde of lead it would be 'eavier—see?' [**Gates, 126**]). Penrhyn's bitter anger is almost bottomless and all-pervasive, while a character like Jentree ('Hall of Healing') seems to have no particular basis for his argumentativeness but his own ego-oriented eccentricities. A former wine porter, he has had his case diagnosed by the doctor as due to too much wine; quantities of water have been prescribed for him but Mr Jentree is loquacious on the subject, launching into diatribes against water: 'Me left leg's lost its motion. Not in a year, mind you, but in a day! I'd like to see him thryin' it himself.... I'll have to be carried home, if this goes on! What manner o' mortal man could swally a tank of wather in a single day? [**Hall, 259.**] His disquisition on water and self-diagnosis of his ailment are accompanied by his tottering feebly about, presumably on his last legs, but he has enough strength to pound vigorously on the doctor's door nonetheless. Jentree is obviously a self-centred blatherer, like many another in O'Casey's cast of characters, beginning as far back as in the days of Adolphus Grigson—in the troubled days of *The Shadow of a Gunman.*

Grigson is full of drunken bravado when he boasts to Davoren and Shields about his fearlessness, but is quickly sobered when the Black and Tans are heard in the neighbourhood, and he launches into sober descriptions of their nasty behaviour—even to such Loyalists as himself. He does manage to extricate himself with some vestige of dignity ('I think we had better be gettin' to bed, Debby; it's not right to be keepin' Mr Davoren an' Mr Shields awake' [Shadow, 143]), yet when Mrs Grigson reports back about the invasion of her flat, she describes her husband as cringing in abjectness before the visiting Auxiliaries: 'when they were puttin' me out, there they had the poor man sittin' up in bed, his hands crossed on his breast, his eyes lookin' up at the ceilin', and' he singin' a hymn—'We shall meet in the Sweet Bye an' Bye'—an' all the time, Mr Shields, there they were drinkin' his whisky; there's torture for you, an' they all laughin' at poor Dolphie's terrible sufferins.' [Shadow, 150.] Comic irony dictates that poor Dolphie, unaware of his wife's report, will reappear after the raid to describe his bravery under duress; he summarily dismisses his browbeaten wife and launches into his version: 'Two of them come down—"Put them up", revolvers under your nose—you know, the usual way. "What's all the bother about?" says I, quite calm. "No bother at all," says one of them, "only this gun might go off an' hit somebody—have you me?" says he. "What if it does," says I, "a man can only die once, an' you'll find Grigson won't squeal." "God, you're a cool one," says the other, "there's no blottin' it out."' [Shadow, 154.] Even if Davoren and Shields had not been privy to Mrs Grigson's earlier account, they might have detected Grigson's stock phrases (There's no blottin' it out; Have you me?) in the mouth of the British Auxiliary. And not to be outdone by a fellow blatherer, Seumas Shields launches into a fabricated account in his part of the house during the raid.

In one of his final one-act plays, 'The Moon Shines on Kylenamoe', O'Casey builds on entire comic situation on a multiplicity of argufiers attempting to solve the problem of a passenger who insists on getting off at a railway station where no one has ever before thought of getting off: late at night, Lord Leslieson, an Englishman, descends from a first-class carriage and asks the way to 'the Town'. This is enough to launch Sean Tomasheen, the porter, and Michael Mulehawn, the train guard, into a series of discussions, during which they abuse the Englishman and each other and are distracted by the wandering through of a pair of young lovers. The exasperated Englishman tries to cope with provincial Irishmen who have nothing better to do and nothing that they like better than argue—a familiar enough situation, but one that O'Casey can handle masterfully. British-Irish sensitivities, rivalry between the guard (a silver band around his cap) and the porter (only a red one around his), and a propensity to allow any new distraction to interfere, provide enough of a basis for the longwinded characters, but the scene soon attracts others as well: the lovers stay on to participate, the neighbours are awakened by the engine's whistles, and then the engine-driver joins in.

Now the porter-guard quarrel is enhanced by Andy O'Hurrie into a three-man contest with the English Lord in the middle and numerous outsiders interrupting. 'What th' hell!', he demands, 'Are we puttin' up here for th' night, or wha'? Are yous organisin' an oul'-age kindergarten, or wha'? D'ye know, Michael Mulehawn, that th' thrain has gone inta a doze waitin' for yeh? What am I to say in me report when I get to me journey's end half an hour late, an' maybe an hour?' [Moon, 141.] New disputants enter the fray, a Woman Passenger representing public opinion: 'So this is th' way yous waste our public money! We'll soon lay this kinda conduct low! Th' one first-class passenger left in th' thrain's busy at a Report of this terrible wait in th' threat in the core of th' dead an' silent night.' [Moon, 149.] It would be difficult to say which of all the contestants for the honour splits the most hairs in 'The Moon Shines on Kylenamoe,' but Lord Leslieson is allowed a definite summation of the night's events and the state of chassis in O'Casey's Ireland: 'A country of desolation, of aimless chatter, dirt, and disease.' [Moon, 154.] In such comedies as these the playwright uses as diagnostic of the entire state that spate of endless chatter.

II

Shakespeare may not have believed in ghosts, but he was able to utilise them effectively in his plays; an Irish writer intent on creating fantasy would hardly want to avoid the quality of the native leprechaun in his work—Sean O'Casey employed them liberally and imaginatively. Although there is no literal leprechaun as such, even in the rural comedies, there is a type who to varying degrees owes his basic nature and function to the determinants of these 'little men'. Some are in fact supernatural beings, completely so when it comes to the Birdlike Lad of 'Figuro in the Night': O'Casey describes him as 'a slim form of a young lad with more than a touch of a bird in his look' [**Figuro, 117**]. He heralds the exploits of the Figuro (the Mannequin Pis suddenly transplanted to O'Connell Street, the mere sight of which has been driving the women of Dublin into erotic frenzies) and is obviously identified with it, its lifelike manifestation. He announces to the 'shrinking little world that the world outside is changing' [**Figuro, 119**], persuading the hesitant Young Man (Jimmy) to fly into the arms of his Alice. The Birdlike Lad, like the symbolic Figuro, is a spirit figure representative of sexual freedom and exuberance. (In contrast the spiritual presences in *Oak Leaves and Lavender*, the Young Son of Time and the Girl who sells lavender, are closely associated with death, the former chanting to the Dancers of a time long past: 'Go; the clock will never strike again for you. Go, and leave the fair deeds you did to stir faint thoughts of grandeur in fond memory's mind.' [**Oak, 8.**])

The Birdlike Lad stands in the same relationship to the Figuro in the Night as Robin Adair does to the Cock, Robin being a presumably all-human figure. His function as Messenger connects him with the Young Son of Time tolling an end to the deeds of the past, and long after he has delivered his literal telegram of warning to Marthraun, he lingers on to observe the events taking place at the Marthraun farm, to participate in them, and eventually to direct them. The song he sings is redolent of the theme and mood of the Young Son of Time's song,

> Cling close to youth with your arms enthrancin',
> For youth is restless, an' loth to stay;
> So take your share of th' kisses goin',
> Ere sly youth, tirin', can slink away! [**Cock, 218.**]

—and the message that he brings is varied: to Father Domineer, a lecture on his priestly function ('thry to mingle undherstandin' with your pride, so as to ease th' tangle God has suffered to be flung around us all' [**Cock, 215**]); to the hopelessly invalided Julia, 'Be brave' [**Cock, 220**]; and to the hopelessly narrow-minded and mean-spirited Marthraun, 'Die.' [**Cock, 221.**] But to Marion and Lorna and Loreleen, Robin Adair sings his song of hope and escape, of 'Life becomes but a pleasant endeavour.' [**Cock, 222.**] Robin and the Birdlike Lad are the two most spritelike and ebullient members of the species, heralds of new dawns and emissaries-extraordinary of the Life Force itself.

Other O'Caseyan leprechauns are somewhat more earthy and sombre, although Philib O'Dempsey mirrors in function if not in spirit the roles of these airier types. On one hand he is down-to-earth and very much a working man, one of a trio that is engaged in rectifying the Tudor manor under O'Killigain's direction (O'Casey places him as one among other workers by designating him as the '2nd Workman' rather than as the first). He participates in the controversy on how to get the desk through the narrow doorway, and is in no way distinguishable from his peers on that occasion. His basic existence is summarised in his account of himself to Poges: 'A sound mind, armed with a firm education for seven long years in a steady school, an' now well fit to stand his ground in any argument, barrin' th' highest philosophies of the greatest minds mendin' th' world!' [**Dust, 35.**] His politics are very basic also: he is an outspoken nationalist with a strong contempt for the British: 'Our poets of old have said it often,' he announces, 'time'll see th' Irish again with wine an' ale on th' table before them; an' th' English, barefoot, beggin' a crust in a lonely sthreet, an' the weather frosty.' [**Dust, 5.**] He denounces his bosses, the English pretenders, to their faces, praising the greatness of the Irish in their past glory, their far older culture and their greater chances for the future—and although his discourse is often virulent, these speeches are nonetheless political and even commonplace. Yet this solid man has a touch of the poet about him: when O'Casey first introduces him, he comments that Philib is 'strongly built' and 'has a dreamy look'

[**Dust, 4**]; and when our forgetful author re-introduces him in Act Two, he is consistent in his description of a 'powerful man . . . with gleaming eyes' [**Dust, 67**]. (O'Dempsey is not unlike the ubiquitous tram conductor of the early auto-biographies, the Ayamonn O'Farrel of the O'Farrels of Longford, for whom 'Th' Sword of Light is flamin' still!' [**Hallway, 303.**])

There is no doubt that there is something strange about Philib O'Dempsey. 'I have me share o' wondhers, new an' old,' [**Dust, 68**] he admits with pride, confounding Poges by his claim: 'I hear sthrange things be day, an' see sthrange things be night when I'm touched be the feel of the touch of the long-handed Lugh.' [**Dust, 69.**] Essentially he assumes that such supernatural phenomena are very much a part of nature, a part of the world that really exists, and that it is not that he sees things and hears things which are not there but that others just cannot. Narrow, materialistic and com-mercially-minded people are blind and deaf to the wonders of the world. 'Barrin' a few an' O'Killigain there,' he main-tains, 'they see these things only as a little cloud o' purple dust blown before the wind.' [**Dust, 71.**]

Charlie Bentham of *Juno* claims to be a theosophist, but he is obviously bourgeois and mercantile to the core (Frank O'Connor assumes him to be O'Casey's satiric commentary on George Russell),[4] while O'Dempsey successfully balances his occultic world with the very tangible one in which he lives. There is no denying him his gift of prophecy; when he hears that Avril has galloped off with O'Killigain after Basil was thrown by his horse, he murmurs pensively, 'Th' spirit of th' Grey o' Macha's in our Irish horses yet!' [**Dust, 44.**] And early in the play he predicts the doom that will be-fall the house and those occupants that fail to heed the writ-ing on the wall: 'Settlin' here, are you? Wait till God sends the heavy rain, and the floods come!' [**Dust, 36.**] O'Dempsey is an earthly manifestation of the mysterious presence that emerges towards the end of the play to startle the occupants and predict disaster: known only as The Figure, he 'seems to look like the spirit of the turbulent waters of the rising rivers' [**Dust, 115**] and his deep-voiced jeremiad ends with: 'Those who have lifted their eyes unto the hills are firm of foot, for in the hills is safety; but a trembling perch in the highest place on the highest house shall be the portion of those who dwell in the valleys below!' [Dust, 115.]

There are several strange ones in *Purple Dust*, from the ominous Figure to the wispy Postmaster of Clune na Geera, who appears quite suddenly towards the end of the play just as the room has become darker. Sporting a 'huge fiery-red beard' [Dust, 110], he announces that he bears a message (from the Postmaster, himself); he demands that Poges stop making phone calls in the middle of the night, thus disturbing the Postmaster's sleep. Just as everything seems about to fall apart and the river is rising, the Postmaster arrives to threaten Poges in a tiny voice but with a hefty blackthorn about night phone calls, and is marooned with the Englishmen and the servants in the highest room of the old house. And in addition there is Cornelius, the 'Yellowbearded Man', who is never mentioned in the play until his sudden appearance through a hole in the ceiling from which he thrusts his head to hear news of Avril and O'Killigain running off on horseback. Cornelius is an electrician placing a light in the ceiling and has no existence at all (and almost no body), but appears to learn the news at the end of the first act and reappears twice toward the end of the second to find out about the 'earthquake' (the roller crashing through the house) and announce the 'murder' (the shooting of his cow). This leprechaun-in-the-ceiling is almost a disembodied emanation, an instance of O'Casey's comic use of the mysterious stranger.

There are other such comic leprechauns flitting through the O'Casey plays, figures that come on for one or two appearances, create confusion or comment semi-coherently on an already existing confusion, and just as quickly flit away. In fact, there seems to be a host of such bearded types: to the red-bearded Postmaster and the yellow-bearded Cornelius can be added Hughie Higgins, the Railway Porter of *The Bishop's Bonfire* and the porter (of a general store) in *Cock-a-Doodle Dandy*. The former is 'a middle-aged man with whiskers under his chin, a wide mouth, and spectacles helping a pair of weak eyes' [Bonfire, 59], while the latter is 'a middle-aged man with an obstinate face, the chin hidden by

213

a grizzled beard' [**Cock, 166**]. The Railway Porter appears at the bow-window of the Reiligan house out of breath and in a frightened state: he was supposed to have transported a statue of a saint-with-a-horn, but has arrived empty-handed instead, since the statue has been blasting its horn at him, reminding him of his sins, although no one has yet heard the sounds that have pursued him. His agitated state does not help him explain the phenomenon to the others, but he babbles on about the 'bookaneeno' and his own sins. When he reappears with the desk for the bishop, he sees the statue (brought by Rankin) and refuses to enter into the house, giving the blasting bookaneeno a wide berth. The other porter also has his burden, delivering a tall silk hat for Councillor Marthraun, although it bears a bullet hole from the shots fired by the Civil Guard at the escaped Cock (the red band around the porter's cap having been mistaken for the Cock's red crest). The damaged hat left behind soon becomes an instrument of terror for all concerned when the Sergeant of the Civil Guard arrives to explain that when he shot the Cock, it turned into 'a silken glossified tall-hat!' [**Cock, 171**.]

Occasionally the leprechaunish figure is a rather sinister one, as in the case of One-eyed Larry, the potential sacristan of *Cock-a-Doodle Dandy* who carries bell, book, and candle for the exorcism of the Cock. The author makes no secret of his dislike for the character ('His face is one alternately showing stupidity or cunning, according to whomsoever may be speaking to him' [**Cock, 192**]), and Loreleen even mocks his one-eyed condition. Sailor Mahan, who also dislikes the would-be sacristan, explains how Larry lost his eye: 'when he was a kid, he was hammerin' a bottle, an' a flyin' piece cut it out of his head', [**Cock, 197**] but Larry vehemently denies the story, his own version corresponding imaginatively with the peculiar events now taking place in the Marthraun household:

You're a liar, that wasn't th' way! It was th' Demon Cock who done it to me. Only certain eyes can see him, an' I had one that could. He caught me once when I was spyin' on him, put a claw over me left eye, askin' if I could see him then; an' on me sayin' no, put th' claw over th' other

214

one, an' when I said I could see him clear now, says he, that eye sees too well, an' on that, he pushed an' pushed till it was crushed into me head. [**Cock, 197.**]

Except for this fanciful declaration of special vision, Larry might have passed for a very prosaic character, cowardly and sycophantic, and of no more special interest than the one-eyed cart driver in *Pictures in the Hallway* who comes to transport Ella's evicted belongings, but tarries to leer at Millie's lascivious dance. (Compare, for example, the very ordinary circumstance by which the cart-driver lost his eye: 'lost in a stand-up fight, he said, with a fella twice me size, who when he found he was gettin' bet, an' had me on the ground, under him, poked a bit o' pointed stick into me eye, and turned it round, so that the doctor had to take it out; but, all the same, when he done it, I nearly did for him for I ruptured him with a friendly kick in the balls.' [**Hallway, 221.**])

Another variety of the leprechaunite species is the timid Mr Gallogher of *The Shadow of a Gunman*, whose only real claim to association with the clan is that he is almost not there at all, wispy and self-effacing. Dragged forward by the egregious Mrs Henderson, 'Gallicker' is immediately recognisable as a distant cousin of the other bearded sprites (he is 'a spare little man with a spare little grey beard and a thin, nervous voice' [**Shadow, 114**]); Mrs Henderson does most of the talking for him with only interjected corroborations on his part when called upon. He reads his letter of complaint to the 'Gentlemen of the Irish Republican Army' [**Shadow, 117**] (allowing himself to be liberally interrupted by his protectress) and even delivers a small speech of thanks after its reception. And then James Gallogher retreats from the room as if he had never been there. Taciturn figures are uncommon in the O'Casey canon, Mr Gallogher joining Sammy the shy singer of *Red Roses* as a rare bird, both dragged unwillingly before an audience to 'perform'—and both apologetic for their very existence, much less their intrusion.

But the usual leprechaun in the O'Casey mould is as much an argufier as such stolid men as Dan Basawn and Sean Tomasheen. Landlord Brennan Moore is concerned with the safety of his savings in the Bank of Ireland and the position of his Church in the community, yet he not only sets Ayamonn's lyrics to music, but spends much of his time as a roving minstrel through the slums of Dublin, an ironic corollary to Dympna selling violets and Eeada selling cakes and apples. It is O'Caseyan irony which has him nicknamed Brennan o' the Moor by his slum tenants: he may very well be a highwayman quite literally in their eyes; his alternate role as a street-singer associates him with folksong, but the septuagenarian as a romantic hero of song and tales is ludicrous transposition. Yet old Brennan has this 'other self' (the two selves joined by his tendency towards miserliness, but even this 'basic' aspect of the character is belied by his gesture of having the statue of the Madonna repainted). Even when he is at his most ordinary, the landlord concerned with the solvency of the institution in which his capital is accumulating, Brennan is also at his wildest, buttonholing anyone who will respond—even Sheila—about his view of the security of the Bank of Ireland, and actually demanding only reassurance: 'Bank of Ireland'll still stand, eh? Ay. Ravenous to break in, some of them are, eh? Ay, ay. Iron doors, iron doors are hard to open, eh?' [Roses, 214.]

A parallel to Mr Moore is the strange personage who is organist for the Church of Our Lady Help of Christians in Doonavale, the Mr Murray of *The Drums of Father Ned*. O'Casey has him tagged as 'a man of middle height, plump, and easily agitated. He carries his head a little thrust forward from his shoulders, as if he were about to rush at whomsoever he happened to be speaking to; a clipped grey moustache covers his upper lip. He speaks with a kind of lisp.' [Ned, 36-7.] By comparison with the bearded gents the moustachioed Murray does not appear quite as bizarre, but his behaviour qualifies him as an argumentative leprechaun (or a leprechaunish argufier): his primary function is as a wild thorn in the side of the parish priest who insists quite literally on the singing of hymns, while the organist maintains that Mozart is closer to God than hymns: 'Listen, you! When we worship Mozart, we worship God; yes, God, Fader Fillifogue! Mozart's moosic can be as dee murmur of a river's first flow among dee forget-me-nots an' dee meadowsweet; as gay as a dance of boys an' girls at a fair, an' no priest present!' [Ned, 43–4.] For all his forbidding presence and volatile state of agitation, it is apparent that Murray is the dramatist's spokesman on these matters and that it is O'Casey who has set him on the priest. The extra fillip that sends Mr Murray over the dividing line between the ordinary eccentric and those touched by the little folk is his brief for Angus: having managed to enrage Father Fillifogue with his insistence upon Mozart, he further infuriates him by adding Bach to the list, but the priest's anger turns to amazement when Murray also includes Angus. 'Angus, too? Angus who?' reacts Fillifogue, *stiffening in puzzlement* [Ned, 45]; if he did not know before, the priest should know now that his organist is not just unorthodox but weird as well.

The most lovable of the strange creatures in O'Casey's world is an eighty-four-year-old peasant named Sleehaun, known as the Codger. O'Casey describes him as a man who 'carries his age about with him in a jaunty and defiant way. He is tall, thin, and wiry, his face deeply seamed with many wrinkles from weathers and old age, and is strongly tanned, and as tough as leather. His head is covered with a crisp, thick mop of white hair, his upper-lip hidden by a white moustache, and his chin by a shovel-shaped white beard; his dark eyes are alert and sparkling.' [Bonfire, 16.] The Codger celebrates himself as the last of his strain in one of his earliest appearances in *The Bishop's Bonfire*, unaware that he will soon be banished by the Canon and the Councillor from Ballyoonagh: 'I'm the sole Sleehawn left standin' here in Ballyoonagh. Wife dead (rest her soul), two daughters an' three sons away, away in America, leavin' me the one lone, mohican Sleehawn[5] left standin' in Ballyoonagh. Fly away, Peter, fly away, Paul, fly away, Susan, fly away all—a fly-away country, this of ours, Father; this country of ours.' [Bonfire, 26–7.]

Like Robin Adair and the Young Son of Time, the Codger is a singer of sad songs which at once celebrate the beauty of life and love and also mourn the passing of youth, the dying out of grandeur. He sees in Ballyoonagh the dead hand of Church and state bringing blight to everything it touches: Reiligan's hay is coarse and dry, his cows wan and lean, the house new and antiseptic, cold and dead like the life in it, and he is all for adding the town to the flames being lit to honour the bishop. One of his songs in particular has familiar echoes:

> The rose that is fresh in the vase today
> Will be flung away, fadin', tomorrow;
> An' ev'ry song sung be a singer gay
> Has in it the seed of a sorra. [Bonfire, 96.]

Just as Monica had wished that Feelim were her father instead of Abraham Penrhyn, Keelin cries, 'Oh, Codger, dear Codger, I wish to God that you were me Da!' [Bonfire, 85.] Like most of O'Casey's admirable people, Michael Sleehaun is an iconoclast taunting priest and boss, and an ever-youthful celebrant of the mysteries of life, and like many of the leprechaunish figures he has his sixth and even seventh senses, as Father Boheroe maintains: 'We have authority, Canon, for believing that old men may sometimes see visions; and what the Codger sees has been seen by others.' [Bonfire, 39.] Sleehaun is in the company of the handful who are banished (Mary Boyle, Loreleen Marthraun), while Manus goes off in self-exile, the fate of many of O'Casey's best people.

7

Senior Citizens

A Gaggle of Old Geezers

A counterpart of the old Codger—and an antithesis—is old Shanaar of *Cock-a-Doodle Dandy*, whom O'Casey describes with undisguised prejudice as 'a "very wise old crawthumper", really a dangerous old cod' [Cock, 119]. Not all the denizens of Nyadnanave concur with their creator in his evaluation of the elderly religionist, Shanaar himself maintaining that he is 'a wise oul' man, a very wise oul' one, too,' [Cock, 219] and Michael Marthraun recognising him as an 'old, old man, full of wisdom an' th' knowledge of deeper things' [Cock, 134–5] (to which Shanaar offers a hearty amen: 'Ever so old, thousands of years, thousands of years if all were told' [Cock, 135]). Such antique wisdom, one would assume, is based on a very solid foundation, and indeed Shanaar self-advertises as an authority on questions of morality and matters of the occult: he gives his blessings on arrival to all in the house, but draws the line when it comes to dogs and cats. He tells various tales of witchcraft and sorcery, implicating beasts and birds as emissaries of the evil world, explaining his talent for exorcism: 'The one thing to do, if yous have the knowledge, is to parley with th' hens in a Latin dissertation. If among th' fowl there's an illusion of a hen from Gehenna, it won't endure th' Latin' [Cock, 138] (and Shanaar's hen-Latin is an odd admixture of ungrammatical and nonsensical Latinate words with English and Gaelic thrown in). His horror of women exceeds his fear of furred and feathered creatures, as he denounces the female as 'more flexible towards th' ungodly than us men, an' well th' old saints knew it', and he cautions Marthraun to deal firmly with Marion the maid: 'I'd recommend you to compel her, for a start, to lift her bodice higher up, an' pull her skirt lower down; for the circumnambulatory nature of a woman's form often has a detonatin' effect on a man's idle thoughts.' [Cock, 146.] Whereas other puritans have revealed themselves as repressing sadistic tendencies towards lust, Shanaar is too old to be accused of lascivious intent: his approach to women is unadulterated sadism, as he leads the 'Rough Fellows' in having Loreleen dragged along by the arms to confront Father Domineer. He stands back, 'gloating over the woeful condition of Loreleen' [Cock, 213], as she is being 'sentenced' by the priest.

Old Shanaar is supect by his very appearance which, although having certain elements in common with the Codger, contains several outward manifestations of his unpleasant fanaticism: 'He is a very, very old man, wrinkled like a walnut, bent at the shoulders, with longish white hair, and a white beard—a bit dirty—reaching to his belly,' and he wears 'a sackcloth waistcoat, on which hangs a brass cross, suspended round his neck by twine.' [Cock, 134.] As a religious pilgrim of sorts, welcomed and honoured by Marthraun and the others for his piety and wisdom, he rails against materialism, immodesty, feminine adornment and dancehalls, claiming occult powers and almost monastic self-restraint. Whereas many of O'Casey's leprechaunish figures are credited with inner sight, that sight is usually allied with the natural world in which they live; it is a sense of vision that expands from the beauty of the material world to include more things than exist to the prosaic eye. Shanaar sounds most like a fraudulent crawthumper when he denies things of the world and the flesh for exclusive preoccupation with those of the spirit. When offered a pound by Marthraun, he refuses it, claiming, 'If I took it, I couldn't fuse th' inner with th' outher vision; I'd lose th' power of spiritual scansion. If you've a shillin' for a meal in th' town till I get to the counthry, where I'm always welcome, I'll take it, an' thank you.' [Cock, 148.] Shanaar's spirituality of fusion and scansion, his 'partial' refusal of money and his admission of a parasitic existence, are allied to the complete bankruptcy of his claim to arcane powers.

At the end of the play, when Shanaar has succeeded in

having Loreleen banished from Nyadnanave, he is confronted with the return of Julia from Lourdes (an expedition that he sponsored and assured success for); he is unable to face her: 'What's this I see comin'? If it isn't Julia, back from Lourdes, an' she on her stretcher still! I'd best be off, for I've no inclination to thry a chatter with a one who's come back as bad as she was when she went.' [**Cock**, **219.**] Robin Adair stays long enough to comfort Julia, but Shanaar retreats in haste. It is Robin of course who is the true messenger, who countermands Shanaar's view that Marthraun is better off without the women of his household by prophesying a pitiful loneliness for the man who heeded the old crawthumper's judgment.

Other old men in the O'Casey plays are presented as cantankerous frauds, as far back as Uncle Peter Flynn of *The Plough and the Stars,* who claimed to have been involved in the Labour movement but is exposed by the querulous Covey as being ignorant of any aspect of it. Peter shares Shanaar's dirty-beardedness ('He is a little thin bit of a man, with a face shaped like a lozenge; on his cheeks and under his chin is a straggling wiry beard of a dirty-white and lemon hue. His face invariably wears a look of animated anguish, mixed with irritated defiance, as if everybody was at war with him, and he at war with everybody' [**Plough,** **162**]) and Shanaar's limited concept of Christianity: 'I'll leave you to th' day', he says to the tormenting Covey, 'when th' all-pitiful, all-merciful, all-lovin' God'll be handin' you to th' angels to be rievin' an' roastin' you, tearin' an' tormentin' you, burnin' an' blastin' you!' [**Plough, 174.**] Old Peter is without doubt a pathetic figure, the patience that he constantly implores God for never being granted him; he is hardly equipped to cope with the quicker and younger Covey, and is even left holding Mrs Gogan's baby when she is ejected from the pub. An old man's sour personality irritates most of those around him and fails to result in any satisfaction for himself.

The patent uselessness of an exraneous old creature (as differentiated from the lively and exuberant Codger) is underscored in Peter Flynn's case, and in many another from such plays as 'Kathleen Listens In' and 'Nannie's Night Out' through *The Star Turns Red* and such late plays as 'Figuro in the Night' (written when the author himself was an octogenarian). A study of political geriatrics is apparent in 'Kathleen', where the Man in the Kilts is regarded by the occupants of the O'Houlihan house as an old fuddy-duddy to be tolerated when he is present but ridiculed when his back is turned. Change has taken place in the household (although there is very little evidence that it is necessarily for the better), and the old man, representative of Gaelic League sentiments, grumbles much of the time and tries to force the Irish language on everyone—now that the house is in exclusively Irish hands. Now a lodger in the house, the old man (who 'was always in the house—he was born in it, an' I suppose he'll die in it' [**Kathleen, 284**]) has outlived whatever usefulness he might once have had. 'I'll never give yous a bit o' peace', he is quoted as saying, 'till yous all talk Irish.' [**Kathleen, 284.**] O'Casey himself had been a teacher of the language at the Gaelic League, but by 1923 had decided that the Language Question was of much less importance than economic and political ones in Ireland, rendering the Man in the Kilts an antiquated obsolescence. (Mrs Pender in 'Nannie's Night Out' expresses the author's concern when she comments on Nannie's pathetic son: 'It's a wondher they wouldn't do something for the poor little kiddies like him, instead o' thryin' to teach them Irish.' [**Nannie, 321.**])

By the 1950s and '60s O'Casey had decided that many of the political disputes of the Ireland of his youth had grown stale, and 'Figuro in the Night' serves the function of saying goodbye to all that. Whereas *The Drums of Father Ned* depicted diehard nationalists of the Troubles who had grown fat and complacent under two or more decades of the Irish Free State, 'Figuro' shows a pair of old antagonists from the old days reliving the old battles in superannuated form and incapable of facing the new ones. The middle-ageing Binnington and McGilligan are replaced here by the senile Michael Murphy and Mr Tynan, listed as '1st Old Man' and '2nd Old Man'. The former represents narrow-minded Irish nationalism (his totem is the Celtic cross), while the latter is loyal to the British crown (his totem the Obelisk); both have escaped from the erotic turmoil on O'Connell Street where the women of Dublin were aroused to lasciviousness by the statue of the urinating boy: 'It's the end, Mr Tynan; it's the end. Worse'n th' Black an' Tans'; 'A bod end, Michael Murphy; a bod end. Warse thon Wipers or th' run from Mons.' [**Figuro,** 105.] Murphy and Tynan are the last manifestations of that quarrel between the Green and the Orange, a quarrel grown old and senile but still developing, much like a fungus. And the sexual revolution taking place in 'Figuro' (the revolution in full that has been hinted at from *Purple Dust* on) has Michael prophesying the end of the world.

A portrait of a non-political old man can be found in *The Star Turns Red*, that most political of all political plays, and he too is a rather unpleasant old man (having one son who is a Fascist and another who is a Communist may contribute to either his non-political position or his unpleasantness—or both). Actually his politics are fixed and narrow, despite his own protest that he remains impartial to the blandishments of both extremists in his family ('I never held with either of them' [**Star,** 248]): he is anti-Union and even against the pope when the pope is advocating such socially advanced ideas as those in *Rerum Novarum*. His life has been spent as a worker loyal to his employers, and his political ideology is based on the superiority of such allegiance over strike tactics. He sounds the usual notes for 'law and order', invoking the military, the police, and the fascist political organisation to protect him from the danger of Red Revolution. When the Lord Mayor comes to his tenement flat, he is the soul of obsequiousness, but suddenly reverses himself when he is reminded of his duty as a member of his Confraternity to rescue his son from Communism and for the Church: 'Let the Purple Priest do it himself then! What are we paying him his dues for? Or, for a change (*Indicating the Mayor*), let his eminence, there, have a shot at it!' [**Star,** 268–9.] At first glance—and in the fixed position of most critics—the Old Man seems to be an inconsistent character that O'Casey never quite decided about, but closer examination should reveal that he is a study in inconsistency, an old man who has been knuckling under for many years, except when browbeating his wife, but who has a quick temper and occasional flashes of indignation and rebellion. The dichotomy of his personality is graphically depicted in the description: 'The Old Man is short, but still rosy with life; he has a shock of grey hair and a fierce moustache.' [Star, 242.]

Not that O'Casey holds out much hope for the old man still rosy with life. When he accuses his wife of nervously 'combing the glow' out of the fire by poking at it, he is establishing the metaphor that O'Casey intends for him: the glow is being combed out of the Old Man's rosiness by the drab life around him and his own inability to structure his life. 'I have made up my mind,' he insists; 'of course I've made up my mind; and, once I've made up my mind, I've made it up, haven't I?' [Star, 310.] Whether by cowardice or inadvertence he leaves the Old Woman with the task of facing the clergy or the Communists (whoever comes first for Michael's body), himself rushing off to serve tea at the Lord Mayor's Christmas party. And when the open conflict erupts, the Old Man demonstrates what has become his predictable tendency to run and hide, to equivocate and let others take the responsibility. The rosy spark of rebellion and personal courage has its moments of glow during odd and safe hours, but the Old Man is a portrait in futility: it is too late and he is too far gone for any new sign of integrity or strength.

There are two aspects to old age that O'Casey recognises, the physical distance from youth and the spiritual distance from life (and although condemned to the first, someone like the Codger is impervious to the second, whereas many of the other old people are self-condemned by their state of atrophy —the Old Man is chronologically thirty years younger than the Codger). To be able to follow the rebellious mood of change exhibited by the young is no easy matter for the aged (even such physically trim middle-aged gentlemen as Binnington and McGilligan are left behind in a paralytic state); to be able to respond to the physical and emotional demands of love is equally hard for those over the hill although Fluther Good at forty is quick to accept Rosie Redmond when the much younger Covey rejects her. In 'Nannie's Night Out' O'Casey pokes fun at a trio of oldsters intent on romance, the suitors desirous of marrying Mrs Polly Pender, a widow with a dairy store. They range from Oul Johnny (almost sixty) to Oul Joe (about sixty) to Oul Jimmy (well over sixty), and their physical capabilities are catalogued by the Ballad Singer in his diatribe against Johnny: 'More than me's been havin' a good laugh at yous; you that ud hardly be able to walk twiced round Nelson's Pillar without sittin' down for a rest. Oul' Jimmy that's so blind with age, that he wouldn't know a live bird in a cage from a dead wan, unless he heard it singin'. An' Oul' Joe so bent that he could pick a penny off th' ground without stoopin'.' [**Nannie, 312.**] What the old men demonstrate is their ability to squabble with each other over Polly's favours, but little else. And Polly Pender decides to give up on all three and 'remain a bird alone' [**Nannie, 330**]—or, as she says in the alternate ending: 'Yez are a nice gang of guardian angels for any poor woman to have hangin' round her. So th' whole of yous ud betther buzz off ou' o' this.' [**Nannie, 333.**]

The Old Man in Love is a comic figure that playwrights have often enjoyed dealing with, from Aristophanes to Molière, from the Commedia dell'arte to Jean Giraudoux: Oul Johnny White, Oul Jimmy Devanny, and Oul Joe have a long ancestry. In 'Figuro' O'Casey presents a colloquy between an Old Man and an Old Woman who have met on their separate ways to Dublin to investigate the cause of the commotion; each has dwindled away into lonely old age because their parents prevented them from marrying when young. The Old Woman is often nostalgic when Alice's song about Johnny so long at the fair evokes quasi-erotic emotions, but the Old Man is hardened into certainty that his father was wise in protecting him from marriage. He had once given his Nora (he is no longer sure that that is her name) blue ribbons for her brown hair, and the Old Woman had once received such ribbons from her 'Jimmy' (the same name that the Young Man has who does return to his Alice from the fair)—but their conditions of religious fear and atrophied passion are now permanent ones. 'Nora' even refuses the man's suggestion that they accompany each other on the road to Dublin: 'At this time o' night? No, John, no. Seen together under the darkened stars, what would they say about us only that there was no good in our minds? . . . I have to keep my reputation well in hand, so go your way while I go mine.' [**Figuro, 103.**][1]

In 'The Moon Shines on Kylenamoe' O'Casey presents another old 'couple', Cornelius Conroy and his wife, Martha. In some ways they are comic variants on the Old Man and Old Woman of *The Star* (Martha serves as echo to statements made by her husband, but he, unlike his predecessor, shows no irritation at this, apparently having long since learned to live with it and her). Corny Conroy is a railway labourer of about seventy ('greyish-bearded'), still actively engaged in manual labour after fifty years. His function in the play is patently comic, a crusty and stubborn old man who feels somewhat left out of things when his donkey and cart are offered without his permission to transport Lord Leslieson. Feeling slighted he refuses to allow his Jinnie to be disturbed for a night trip and remains adamant in his refusal, but once the station has been emptied of its host of disputants and the Englishman is left alone, stranded, Corny quietly reverses his position: 'Th' missus's laid down a matthress before th' fire, an' I've piled it with sods so's it'll last th' night.' [**Moon, 155.**] In addition, Irish hospitality extends to a 'breakfast of fresh eggs, home-made bread, an' lashin's o' tea' [**Moon, 156**]—for which the Conroys will definitely not accept money. The donkey and cart will then be used to bring Lord Leslieson to his destination, for which Corny will charge the market price of ten shillings (but will not accept a penny more, Leslieson offering a pound). Corny proves to be one of the nicer old men in the O'Caseyan world (hardly a Codger Sleehaun, but a 'decent skin' nonetheless), a world in which the aged rarely show that they have profited from long life to the extent of very much wisdom and seem rarely deserving of veneration.

A Gehenna of Old Harpies

Martha Conroy herself is nothing much of a character, existing primarily as an echo of her husband, but apparently wielding enough power behind her closed door to make Corny feel that he would be in trouble with her if he did not invite the stranded ambassador to spend the night. The

Old Woman of 'Figuro', however, is somewhat more important: since the major effect of the Birdlike Lad's power is over the female (driving her to seduce the men), even the Old Woman shows occasional signs of his influence. When not affected by the wave of eroticism, her normal approach to her spinsterhood is a rationalisation that she has done well to preserve her virginity and that she is grateful to her mother for preventing her marriage. When moved by the spirit she seems tempted to affirm sexual freedom and the beauty of sexual desire, but quickly relapses into her old self: 'My God, what was I sayin' a minute ago! Dhreamin' I was—a bad, bad dhream! Thro' me fault, thro' me most grievous fault!' [**Figuro**, 103.] In what might be described as a 'sexual phantasy' (to balance the 'political phantasy' of three-and-a-half decades earlier), the Old Woman exists on several levels: on the most literal she is an old spinster who meets an old bachelor on the road; on the slightly less literal level she is actually meeting the 'Jimmy' of her youth, but neither recognises the other; on the figurative level she is a foreshadowing of Alice, should her Jimmy not come back to marry her.

Two other anonymous old women are presented in *Oak Leaves and Lavender* and in 'Hall of Healing', the former a seventy-year-old harridan who, although merely an incidental figure, serves as one more crabbed and bigoted character. She excoriates Feelim and the Irish, insisting that only the Ulster Irish participating actively in the war are within the Pale and that 'we English are th' supreme examples of unity an' orderliness!' [**Oak**, 97.] The arrival of the distraught Penrhyn with news of his destroyed farm moves her to pity, and his bottle of liquor moves her to companionship ('When a person feels low, a drop of stimulant has a tremendous way o' workin' good to soul an' body' [**Oak**, 101]), but his violent temper soon has her running for her life. Her counterpart in 'Hall of Healing' is a timid patient at the dispensary who allows herself to be pushed out by Alleluia when she enters before the official opening time, is persuaded by Red Muffler despite her fear to re-enter, and is unceremoniously shunted out again: 'Out you go, an' don't put your nose in again, till th' docthor arrives.' [**Hall**, 244.] Her

227

role essentially is as comic foil to Alleluia, like whom she is profoundly and narrowly religious, seeing God's will in everything and accepting death as preferable to life. She is an anti-life figure, having given up living a long time before and now, close to eighty by her own admission, a coward in life and a beggar at life's feast, settling for crumbs. True to the type she is also a blatherer who dispenses erroneous advice and weak consolation, but when she realises that Jenny Sullivan has been hit hard by the news of a consumptive condition, her ability to console becomes quite real: 'Sit still for a few minutes, an' then we'll go home together. You'll have a lot more to go through before you'll be done for. There, sit still, child. I wouldn't say that he wasn't mistaken —th' fellow doesn't know black from white this mornin'. An' anyway, daughter, death's th' last thing th' poor should dhread.' [Hall, 265.] The Old Woman is another instance of O'Casey's last-minute redemption of an otherwise worthless human being, the finding of a spark of genuine worth when help is needed.

Such sparks are the exception rather than the rule, and tenement life in particular seems to expunge them quickly and turn middle-aged women into old hags before their time. The three early tenement plays that are the backbone of O'Casey's reputation are redolent with such housewife types, but it is not until the third play that they begin to assume prominence as something more than incidental comic characters. In *The Shadow of a Gunman* O'Casey offers two women of the house, one in each act, as comic counterpoints to the developing seriousness of the events of the play: Mrs Henderson, along with Shields, Maguire, the landlord, Tommy Owens and Mr Gallogher, continually introduces disruptive elements into the focus of the first act —the blossoming of interest between Donal and Minnie; while Mrs Grigson, along with Shields and Adolphus Grigson, provides the comic relief from the focus of the second act—the raid by the British Auxiliaries.

The pushy self-assurance of Julia Henderson is contrasted with the meek self-effacement of Mrs Grigson, O'Casey presenting opposite facets of the same coin. Although she hardly lets the mousy Gallogher say his piece, constantly interrupt-

228

ing and speaking for him, Mrs Henderson is basically a kind and jovial soul, the opening description of her insisting that 'Mrs Henderson is a massive woman in every way; massive head, arms, and body; massive voice, and a massive amount of self-confidence. She is a mountain of good nature, and during the interview she behaves towards Davoren with deferential self-assurance. She dominates the room, and seems to occupy the whole of it.' [Shadow, 114.] The scene itself does not offer enough to justify the author's commendation of her (the manipulation of the pitiful male overshadowing the good humour with which she executes it), but O'Casey is saving his substantiation for much later.

Mrs Grigson, on the other hand, seems deserving of our sympathy—and even pity; she is a fidgety worrier, concerned over her drunken husband's nocturnal whereabouts during the curfew, and is browbeaten by him when he returns from his carousal. O'Casey sizes her up as 'one of the cave-dwellers of Dublin, living as she does in a tenement kitchen, to which only an occasional sickly beam of sunlight filters through a grating in the yard; the consequent general dimness of her abode has given her a habit of peering through half-closed eyes' [Shadow, 135]. By all rights Mrs Grigson should be one of the meek that are destined to inherit the earth, but O'Casey doubts that she will and doubts that she should.

It is an unusual contrast between the two women that takes place toward the end of the play: although each is dominant as the hausfrau type in a scene of her own, the two women actually overlap when in Act One it is the voice of Mrs Grigson that calls in the news of the killing of Maguire, and in Act Two we learn of Mrs Henderson's intercession with the Auxiliary over Minnie Powell. The timid and presumably kind Mrs Grigson has nothing but scorn for the apprehended girl: 'the little hussey, to be so deceitful; she might as well have had the house blew up. . . . I hope they'll give that Minnie Powell a coolin'.' [Shadow, 153.] And, having vented her spleen, ostensibly over the danger to the residents occasioned by Minnie's having bombs in her room, she soon reveals the real source of her venom: 'With her fancy stockins, an' her pompoms, an' her crêpe de chine blouses! I knew she'd come to no good!' [Shadow, 153.]

229

The egregious Julia Henderson, however, actually has the courage of her pushiness. During the hustling off of Minnie into the lorry, it is Mrs Henderson who is suddenly heard from; as Mrs Grigson reports: 'An' big Mrs Henderson is fightin' with the soldiers—she's after nearly knockin' one of them down, an' they're puttin' her into the lorry too.' [Shadow, 153.] It is interesting that Mrs Grigson's objections to Minnie correspond to those of Bessie Burgess towards Nora Clitheroe at the beginning of *The Plough*, while Mrs Henderson approximates the role enacted by Bessie in aiding Nora at the end of the tragedy.

Juno and the Paycock has three tenement housewives in Mrs Boyle, Mrs Tancred, and Mrs Maisie Madigan. Here O'Casey has shifted the emphasis from the young couple to the older woman, with Juno Boyle emerging as a heroine of unusual strength, and the pathetic Mrs Tancred thoroughly broken by the tragic event in her family. (The essence of O'Casey's ability to elevate melodrama to the heights of tragedy is seen in the juxtaposition of the two women, Mrs Tancred's 'tragedy' played against the jubilation of the Boyle family celebration, only to be duplicated as Mrs Boyle's tragedy when her Johnny is killed.) The function of Mrs Madigan, by contrast, is quite peripheral: she and 'Needle' Nugent are only characters in the comic part of the tragi-comedy; their roots apparently are in the music hall and the broad comedies of the nineteenth century. Yet Maisie receives careful introductory treatment from the playwright because she is so much a tenement type that fascinated O'Casey. His description of her should be viewed in terms of his presentations of Julia Henderson and Mrs Grigson, so that the overall pattern of the woman of the tenement that O'Casey knew and understood begins to be seen (and is later augmented by the creation of Mrs Gogan, Mrs Burgess, Mrs Heegan, Mrs Breydon, and Mrs Casside):

Mrs Madigan is a strong dapper little woman of about forty-five; her face is almost always a widespread smile of complacency. She is a woman who, in manner at least, can mourn with them that mourn, and rejoice with them that do rejoice. When she is feeling comfortable, she is inclined to be reminiscent; when others say anything, or following a statement made by herself, she has a habit of putting her head a little to one side, and nodding rapidly several times in succession, like a bird pecking at a hard berry. Indeed, she has a good deal of the bird in her, but the bird instinct is by no means a melodious one. She is ignorant, vulgar and forward, but her heart is generous withal. For instance, she would help a neighbour's sick child; she would probably kill the child, but her intention would be to cure it; she would be more at home helping a drayman to lift a fallen horse. [Juno, 47.]

This much description plus editorialisation attests to something more than aids to an actress in playing the part: O'Casey's attitudes are directed towards a basic type composed of various prototypes and of individuals who are complex in themselves.

Maisie's behaviour is consistent with the description, but is secondary in relation to it. She performs her function as a celebrant at the feast when the legacy is in the offing (judiciously preferring whiskey to tea or stout) and is quick to walk off with the Boyle gramophone in lieu of the money she lent the Captain—now that the legacy begins to look like a mirage. Boyle's protest that the gramophone has not yet been paid for does little to dissuade the tough widow: 'So much th' betther,' she retorts. 'It'll be an ayse to me conscience, for I'm takin' what doesn't belong to you. You're not goin' to be swankin' it like a paycock with Maisie Madigan's money— I'll pull some o' th' gorgeous feathers out o' your tail!' [Juno, 71.] And when Johnny Boyle is found dead by the police, it is Maisie Madigan who comes to break the news gently to Mrs Boyle that she is wanted for the identification ('Oh, Mrs Boyle, God an' His Blessed Mother be with you this night' [Juno, 85]).

The two 'husbandless' tenement women of *The Plough and the Stars* are in direct line from the Madigan widow of *Juno* (their widowhoods are somewhat in doubt, Bessie hinting broadly that 'there's some she knows, decoratin' their finger with a well-polished weddin' ring, would be hard put to it if they were assed to show their weddin' lines!'—while

231

Mrs Gogan insists: 'me weddin' ring's been well earned be twenty years be th' side o' me husband, now takin' his rest in heaven' [**Plough, 204**]). There is very little to choose between the Catholic charwoman and the Protestant fruit-vendor for most of the play; Mrs Gogan is designated by the author as 'a doleful-looking woman of forty, insinuating manner and sallow complexion. She is fidgety and nervous, terribly talkative, has a habit of taking up things that may be near her and fiddling with them while she is speaking. Her heart is aflame with curiosity, and a fly could not come into nor go out of the house without her knowing.' [**Plough, 163**.] There is enough in such a description to prejudice the case against her, as there is in her initial behaviour: she unwraps Nora's parcel in her absence, tries on the hat, condemns Nora for 'upperosity', and gossips nastily about the married life of the Clitheroes, Jack Clitheroe's vanity, and Nora's treatment of Peter and the Covey.

 The introduction of Bessie, then, must be significantly different: her drunken attack on Nora shows her to be violently aggressive in contrast to Mrs Gogan's verbal maliciousness. But O'Casey's description of Bessie Burgess is a veiled one; he offers very little ('She is a woman of forty, vigorously built. Her face is a dogged one, hardened by toil, and a little coarsened by drink' [**Plough, 178**]), thus leaving the door open for surprising variations in her personality and for meaningful changes dependent upon the events. It is typical of his treatment of his people that O'Casey has both women reveal the same sort of puritanical attitudes: Mrs Gogan says of Nora, 'I'm always sayin' that her skirts are a little too short for a married woman. An' to see her, sometimes of an evenin', in her glad-neck gown would make a body's blood run cold. I do be ashamed of me life before her husband.' [**Plough, 164**]; Mrs Burgess's complaint is that a 'woman on her own, dhrinkin' with a bevy o' men, is hardly an example to her sex', and when she has pilfered a dress from a looted store during the Uprising, she intends to stitch 'a sthray bit 'o silk to lift th' bodices up a little bit higher, so as to shake th' shame out o' them, an' make them fit for women that hasn't lost themselves in th' nakedness o' th' times.' [**Plough, 231.**] That both the Catholic and the

Protestant share this prudish streak is another instance of O'Casey's ecumenical condemnation of Irish narrow-mindedness.

That Julia Henderson could approximate the courage of Minnie Powell (while Mrs Grigson turned instead to vindictiveness) and that Mrs Boyle could be even braver than Mary Boyle, meant for O'Casey an acknowledgment of the older woman's occasional touch of power, something that he already associated often with the personality of his mother. With Bessie Burgess and Maggie-Cissie-Jinnie-Jennie Gogan the author begins from very far back, showing us these two harridans running neck-and-neck in the wrong directions— until the third act, when Bessie's touches of kindness to Mollser Gogan begin to indicate a facet of her character not easily noticeable until now. The crucial distinction between the two women is made at the very end of Act Three, when it is imperative that a doctor be found for Nora: Fluther is too drunk and the only remaining possibilities are the charwoman and the fruit-vendor. Mrs Gogan disqualifies herself, admitting her lack of courage ('I'd be afraid to go') and rationalising ineptly thereafter: 'Besides, Mollser's terrible bad. I don't think you'll get a docthor to come. It's hardly any use goin'.' [Plough, 238.] Bessie, on the other hand, shoulders the responsibility alone, despite her apprehensions. The two women had been opposite sides of the same coin in their disputes with each other and had been almost identical when they went off looting together, despite their differences, sharing the 'borrowed' pram as a receptacle. Now the important differentiation is made, but not because one is necessarily a better person than the other as much as because one of them is the stronger, more determined, more resolute. 'I'll risk it,' [Plough, 238] says Bessie, which leads to a permanent commitment to care for the shattered Nora, and to the heroism of her own death.

These women in their forties are followed by a pair in the fifties: the Bishop's sister (*Within the Gates*) personifies the unbending spirit of the self-righteous bigot, while Mrs Watchit (*Oak Leaves and Lavender*) is delightfully absurd in her stolid ignorance. The latter is a minor but persistent figure whose comic proportions consist of serving tea without having remembered to put tea in the pot, discussing with serious intent the reading of the electricity meter[2] while forgetting that the kettle is on the fire, and constantly quoting the inane comments of her husband as if they were profundities. She is venial enough until she proudly introduces Mrs Deeda Tutting to Feelim and Drishogue, and stands by sagely adding her unqualified assent to everything the 'victim of Communism' maintains. Her creator comes close at times to finding her unredeemable, as when she champions Mrs Tutting and her cause in the first act, and Peter Constant and his in the second (he considers himself a special case and wants to leave war-torn England for the sanctuary of America, claiming that his wife's pregnancy and his Liberal politics preclude them from the war-effort). Having introduced Constant to Dame Hatherleigh (as she had Mrs Tutting to the O'Morriguns), Mrs Watchit is set to second anything he says, but Constant shares Deeda Tutting's tactless lack of appreciation for such loyalty, and turns upon Mrs Watchit cruelly when she thinks a passing car sounds like an air raid. His abuse of the woman results in a comment in her defence by the Home Guard: 'If all does as she done, ashiverin', bombs fallin' near 'n far, amakin 'tea for us as needed it, us'll do well enough.' [Oak, 77.] O'Casey is able to turn a comic situation once again into a relevant commentary on the human condition: all the nonsense about making tealess tea and reading the meter, and all of her constant reiterations of 'Us'll ask 'usband—'ee's sure t' know,' [Oak, 41] are surface froth temporarily concealing a vital scrap of bravery in her as she diligently fulfils her functions. This may be little enough to ask of anyone, but in a world of Peter Constants, Deeda Tuttings, Ernest Pobjoys, and others who defect under stress, Mrs Watchit is redeemable.

The Bishop's sister is not—even if the Bishop himself might eventually prove himself to be. 'His Sister is a few years younger, grey-haired, stiff, and formal,' reads the stage direction. 'She has more common sense than her brother, but, while there is a suggestion of good-nature about the Bishop, there is no suggestion whatever of softness about the form or manner of his Sister. Her dress is of grey stuff, stiff like steel.' [Gates, 128.] The common sense indicated is the kind that would have prevented her brother from ever having a sexual affair in his youth and would now prevent him from taking any interest in Jannice's unhappy situation. Her humourlessness is of course diagnostic, suggesting an incurable condition: she is consumed by a disdain for 'the sour touch of common humanity' [Gates, 133] in general, and for Jannice and her mother (the Bishop's illegitimate daughter and his former paramour) in particular. Her common sense dictates that the Bishop should be 'in th' midst of the incense, in the sanctuary' [Gates, 133], protected from contact with ordinary people. And she seeks to protect him from his own awakening conscience, a conscience disturbed from its incense-slumber by Jannice's dying condition. 'I tell you this fancy solicitude of yours is just a sentimental fear of something done years ago in a foolish moment,' she argues. 'I tell you, such a soul is a trivial thing to be a torment to you.' [Gates, 205.] Whereas the man of the cloth has definite qualms about condemning any soul to damnation, his secular sister takes full responsibility for choosing between the saved and the damned, and feels no twinge of pity for the latter. When the Down-and-Out drag themselves by, she is exultant that 'soon they will encompass you round about; and there will be no way of escape, even for the lady of the good looks!' [Gates, 226.]

Within the Gates is the first O'Casey play to treat a cross-section of rather despicable characters. Until this first play of the 1930s O'Casey dealt with the callow (Charlie Bentham and Jessie Taite), the weak (Donal Davoren and Jerry Devine), and petty (Uncle Peter and the Covey), and the vain (Nora and Jack Clitheroe), but the Bishop's sister, the Old Woman, the Gardener, the Chair Attendants, and the Policewoman postulate an aspect of humanity decidedly less venial. The Old Woman, for example, is certainly the least venerated mother in the entire O'Casey canon, a drunken shrew who torments her sick daughter. But before we meet her in Scene Two, we hear her story from the Atheist who had once lived with her and served as step-father to Jannice, the story of the pregnant housemaid abandoned by the theology student, of the widow of the dragoon, and later the Atheist's mistress, who brought her child out of the orphanage: 'when the maid came close to womanhood, the mother turned religious, an' begun to 'ate the kid, sayin' that while the kid was there, 'er sin was ever in front of 'er fice. Then she took to drink an' violence.' [Gates, 125.] The Old Woman who accosts Jannice for money is a hardened result of the bitter creature that the Atheist describes. O'Casey's description of her attempts to reiterate the entire series of events which brought her to this final form, but there is no doubt that she is now irrevocably beyond sympathy although pitiable: 'She is pale and haggard, and vicious lines harden the look of her mouth. Her hair is white, but her black eyes are still undimmed by age. Her thin body is still upright, showing that in her youth she was slim and vigorous, and her face still shelters traces of what were once very good looks. . . . Constant, quiet drinking has made her a little incoherent in her thoughts. . . . She had heard the voice of the Young Woman, and comes down to where the girl is speaking, gripping her roughly by the arm.' [Gates, 164.] By the end of the play the Old Woman is 'greatly bent' and homeless, and ready to exult over the imminence of her daughter's death.

Yet the Old Woman seems preferable to the Bishop's sister, as the altercations between them during the final scene would clearly indicate. The antagonism is immediate between the virtuous woman who has never been tempted and the old sinner for whom the past still holds pleasant memories; the Bishop's sister calls Jannice's mother a 'tumble-down, wicked woman', and is called 'a stony monument to good conduct and virtue' [Gates, 216] in return. It is at the second confrontation that the stony monument shows her full venom in condemning both mother and daughter: 'The pair of you ought to be stretched out naked on the ground so that decent women could trample the life out of you!' [Gates, 225.] As the Bishop's sister becomes more and more furious in her vicious rage, the Old Woman assumes a measure of dignity in her retorts, finally summarising the virtuous woman's condition: 'How savage women can be when God has been unkind and made us plain, so that no man can find a vision in our face.' [Gates, 225.] She has moved a good distance away from the religious conversion that had set her against her love-child and caused her to resort to drink in order to forget her sin: now she stands up to the Bishop, denouncing both his Church and its politics to his face, and deriding the hollow virtue that his sister represents. And it remains only for the Bishop himself to turn upon his sister in disgust and send her home that he might salvage something still from his abscessed soul.

When the Sister viciously suggests that women like Jannice and her mother should be trampled under foot, the Old Woman confidently insists that 'gallant men would lift us up on to our feet again' [Gates, 225]; but there are some women whom even the most gallant would not lift up. Two such are the 'poor old women' of 'Behind the Green Curtains', Lizzie Latterly and Angela Carrigeen: 'Both are just in their middle age, and both have the appearance of one-time hawkers, now, possibly, content to live on their meagre pensions and whatever charitable gifts they can wheedle or scrounge out of others and from charitable societies.' [Curtains, 3–4.] Almost peripheral to the situation which develops in the play, they form a comic prologue to it and are most easily recognisable as female counterparts of the Paycock and Joxer, their drunken collapse at the end of the first scene paralleling the 'terrible state o' chassis' at the end of *Juno*. Their comic business centres on their inability to recognise a portrait of Parnell, mistaking it for either St Peter or St Joseph.

Angela is distinguished from her companion by her penchant for inquiry (which is limited, superstition-ridden, and most often on the wrong track, but at least is persistent), while Lizzie is hard-headed and bossy. Both of them go off for a single drink and return staggering and falling, despite Angela's protests of self-discipline and Lizzie's drunken lectures to her on her lack of self-discipline. Lizzie Latterly is in some ways an interesting anticipation of Christy Kornavaun, being able to see in others the faults she is unable to see in herself. More than three decades after the creation of the Paycock and his butty, and of Sammy and Jerry (the drunks of 'A Pound on Demand'), O'Casey resharpened the old broad-comic techniques he had mastered at the beginning of his career to present a couple of old harpies who are very much paycocks in skirts.

It has been apparent that to O'Casey the hard life in Dublin works miracles to turn women into old shrews before they are chronologically old women, and in *Red Roses for Me* he develops the trinity of maiden, woman and crone as not only three individual females, but as a single progression toward the shrewish condition: 'All their faces are stiff and mask-like, holding tight an expression of dumb resignation; and are traversed with seams of poverty and a hard life. The face of Eeada is that of an old woman; that of Dympna, one coming up to middle age; and that of Finnoola, one of a young girl. Each shows the difference of age by more or less furrows, but each has the same expressionless stare out on life.' [**Roses, 136**.] The Old Harpies are a fixed condition of Dublin life, for whom any real spark of humour or gaiety, of life itself, is rare. Like most of O'Casey's people even they can on occasion be redeemable by an act of kindness or a bit of understanding, and even some of the worst of them; but the factors that militate against them are numerous and run deep in the main undercurrent of the society in which they live.

8

A Covey of Clerics

THERE must be many a cassock and clerical collar in the property room backstage at the Abbey Theatre, and the presence of a priest in an Irish play is almost as frequent as at an Irish wedding. Yet the first four plays of Sean O'Casey's, those dealing with tenement life in Dublin, are unusual for the absence of any such cleric.[1] The playwright's Protestant background may account for the omission of the Catholic priest, but this does not seem to be the only tangible explanation: in these plays designed for the prominently spotlighted Abbey stage there are so many controversies of various kinds (particularly the complex political ones) that O'Casey may well have had his hands full without attempting to introduce further entanglements. But the deletion was a temporary one, for once the first clergyman arrived, many others followed in close procession, totalling one bishop, one Protestant rector, and seven Catholic priests (with another off-stage pounding a drum). The first is the Bishop of *Within the Gates*, significantly the first play O'Casey wrote that was not intended specifically for the Abbey. Like most of the characters in that expressionistic play, the Bishop remains anonymous, although we learn from his sister that his Christian name is Gilbert, and we assume that he is a Roman rather than a high-church Anglican bishop, despite the London setting. O'Casey treats with some disdain the methods of the ageing Atheist, the Bishop's opposite number (who serves as surrogate father for Jannice), but he reserves his special scorn for the actual father, the Bishop. Much of the action of the play concerns the effect of the Bishop on Jannice, but the later portions focus greater attention on the plight of the Bishop himself, as O'Casey's scorn is modulated into concern. Pity is mixed with contempt in the presentation of the character, and this is visible in the initial introduction: 'The Bishop is a heavily built man of sixty or so. His head, his feet, and hands are large; his voice, once deep and sonorous, has become a little husky. The pretentious briskness of his movements is an attempt to hide from others the fact that he is beginning to fail. He is anxious to show to all he meets that he is an up-to-the-present-minute clergyman, and those who wear the stole are, on the whole, a lusty, natural, broad-minded, cheery crowd.' [Gates, 127.] This is hardly the description of a villain, although it is intended as a portrait of a definitely malignant force—at least to date.

The first scene of *Within the Gates* shows the Bishop to be an unsympathetic figure, pompous, patronising, hypocritical, and, most important, guilty of the cardinal sin of a lack of Christian kindness—yet it is his reversal in the last scene upon which the drama hinges. Haunted by a guilty past, the Bishop is brought face to face with that past: he learns that the young prostitute is his daughter and that her drunken shrew of a mother is the girl he seduced 'on a Sunday night, after the ora pro nobis people had pulled down their blinds and were slinking into sleep' [Gates, 165]. (The Bishop may have been able to withstand such confrontations with the past when he was in his prime, but his present failing condition makes him particularly vulnerable now.) His first efforts at rectifying his sins are futile, since he attempts, like King Claudius, to maintain his hold on his gains while repenting the means he used to attain them. He does not confess his guilt to Jannice, although he ironically calls her 'daughter' and 'my child'. He attempts to shunt her off into a convent and in this way shirk his real responsibilities towards her, but failing in this, he moves closer towards genuine repentance, even at the risk of 'becoming ridiculous to respectable and important opinion' [Gates, 205]—as his cold-hearted sister phrases it. Recognising that 'that has been my besetting sin all along' [Gates, 205], Gilbert acknowledges that 'by trying to save my honoured soul, I am losing it' [Gates, 206]. 'Go home, woman,' he says to his sister, 'and let me find a way to my girl and my God!' [Gates, 206.]

Although attempting to make the difficult change, the Bishop remains unregenerated when confronted by the old hag that is Jannice's mother, and he continues to deny that he is the Gilbert she recognises (three times he denies himself), and he shouts at her: 'If our politics were what they should be, you wouldn't be permitted to wander about interfering with people enjoying the innocent pleasures of the Park!' [Gates, 217.] Unable to be Christ, he is also unable to be wholly Christian. Jannice dies in his arms, making the sign of the cross, while the partially redeemed Bishop turns on his sister (a harder heart than his own) and orders her away: 'Go home, go home, for Christ's sake, woman, and ask God's mercy on us all!' [Gates, 231.] Beginning as a stock figure of the Religious Hypocrite, he seems to be making the obvious shift to the equally stereotypic Repentant Sinner, but is caught halfway on the nail of the cross he fashioned himself, emerging then as a balanced character trapped in the reality of a corrupt world.[2]

But balanced characters are rare in O'Casey's ultra-political *The Star Turns Red*. Concurring with Maxim Gorki that not only is art propaganda, but that life itself is propaganda, O'Casey created two symbolic priests in his drama of the ultimate clash between Communism and Fascism, the Purple Priest of the Rich personifying the most reactionary elements suggested by the Bishop, while the Brown Priest of the Poor represents those among the lower ranks of the clergy who really live Christ's concepts. In contrast to the Purple Priest's face 'fixed like a mask in lines of cold severity', the Brown Priest's 'face is gentle and kind, marred by a look of bewilderment' [Star, 270]. The former condones the flagellation of Julia for her defiance of the Leader of the Saffron Shirts, while the Brown Priest pleads for sparing her. He cannot, however, rise against the Purple Priest who is obviously his superior, and he is forced to second much of what the Purple Priest says. From the beginning he plays a secondary role, a half-willing sycophant to the dominant cleric. 'Did you notice that the Brown Priest kept his head down the whole of the time?' Caheer comments; 'He doesn't count,' [Star, 281] Brallain rejoinders. But the meek priest disobeys his superior by warning the Union leaders that Red

Jim's life is in danger, and is dismayed by the cynical coldness of their intention to betray their leader (the scene is strongly suggestive of Joyce's 'Ivy Day in the Committee Room'). 'I am almost persuaded that Red Jim is right when such as you go all against him!' [Star, 294] the bewildered priest says to them. When Red Jim arrives at the headquarters and tries to win the cleric to his cause, 'To be with us when the star turns red; to help us to carry the fiery cross. Join with us. March with us in the midst of the holy fire,' the Brown Priest refuses still, murmuring 'not yet,' [Star, 296] and leaves. But in the next scene, while the Purple Priest is praying that 'God grant the lash may teach the girl the danger of indecent dress and immodest manners' [Star, 319], his counterpart, who has constantly prayed for Julia's salvation, offers pie-in-the-sky in the form of 'an abundant and a golden life for all the workers' [Star, 321]. Yet by the end of *The Star* he has rejected his superior and joined the Communists, announcing in O'Caseyan terms that 'The star turned red is still the star/Of him who came as man's pure prince of peace.' [Star, 351.] His defection is even seconded by Kian, the Fascist brother of the slain Communist martyr, and the cry goes out to 'Pass out the Purple Priest of the politicians!' [Star, 353.]

By setting up the Purple/Brown priests as a contrasting pair, O'Casey avoided the one-sided position of the professional anti-clerical propagandist. Nor was this an isolated instance in which he professed his faith that elements among the ordained Catholic clergy might take their cue from Christian Communism rather than from Church support of the capitalist power structure (anticipating in the Brown Priests the 'worker priests' who emerged in post-war France): two decades later he returned to conflicting types of Roman clergymen, both in *The Bishop's Bonfire* and in *The Drums of Father Ned*. In the first there is the Very Reverend Timothy Canon Burren, parish priest of Ballyoonagh and very much a purple one, and simple Father Boheroe, an intelligent young curate with strong suggestions of the Brown Priest in his make-up. The former is in appearance a comic figure, although the dramatist is careful not to paint him in particularly unflattering colours, while the latter has

242

most of the virtues that O'Casey considers to be vital: 'he is in his early thirties, and of middle height. His clerical clothes are old and beginning to fade, with creases in coat, vest, and trousers; only the white collar is without one. His face is a rugged one, surmounted by a thoughtful, wrinkled brow; but his eyes are bright, searching at times, but often somewhat sad and thoughtful; though they are not incapable of a roguish twinkle or two when he sees or hears some foolish thing said or done by some foolish mortal.' [Bonfire, 23–4.] But most significant is O'Casey's designation of Father Boheroe as a 'man of the world as well as a man of God' [Bonfire, 24].

A third cleric, the title figure, is much discussed in *The Bishop's Bonfire*, although he never appears on stage.[3] He is a former Ballyoonagh farmer who has risen to important heights in the ecclesiastic world, though he is just plain Bill Mullarkey to the irreverent Codger. Feverish preparations to welcome him upon his return visit are central to the play: they include a bonfire composed of bad books and bad pictures, and the Canon (promoted to Monsignor during the course of the play) is instrumental in the driving of such wickedness from the community. Father Boheroe, on the other hand, is primarily concerned with sanctioning the coming-together of young lovers and with fighting for the Codger's rights to sing his joyous songs. 'You're clever, Father', says Monsignor Burren to the curate, '—and sincere, I hope—but your cleverness seems only to make persons more unhappy than they were. I'm afraid I cannot commend the way you try to lead my poor people towards illusions. Can't you understand that their dim eyes are able only for a little light?' [Bonfire, 79.] Monsignor Burren, despite the evident narrowness of such caveats to the full-lived priest, is a less than villainous man (O'Casey demonstrates his full power to expose the thoroughly vicious clergyman in the Purple Priest—and others), and may sincerely believe that the human mortal is too close to perdition ever to be allowed the sort of laxity that Father Boheroe would gladly grant. The attempted rebellions against his domination are unsuccessful in Ballyoonagh: purple dust stifles the town as the Monsignor triumphs through cajolery when threats prove ineffective. Boheroe, maintaining throughout that 'I shall never turn my back on a beautiful world, nor on the beautiful flesh of humanity, asparkle with vigour, intelligence, and health,' [**Bonfire**, 112] nonetheless admits his inability to offset the constricting effects of Church and state, the domains of the Monsignor and the Councillor. 'Don't be too hard on a poor priest unable to work a miracle!' [**Bonfire**, 114] he pleads, pathos replacing confidence in his last words to Foorawn, but his final statement of the play is still defiant: 'Oh, to hell with the Bishop's Bonfire!' [**Bonfire**, 114.]

The title priest of O'Casey's last full-length play, like his episcopal predecessor, never appears on stage during the course of *The Drums of Father Ned*, although he is presumably present throughout the action of the play in the town of Doonavale: instead his drum beats a continuous tattoo and his young followers voice his ideas—ideas similar to those of Father Boheroe and the Brown Priest. His reported personality is far livelier and more daring than either of his forerunners. Already a legend and a source of exasperation for his enemies, Father Ned encourages the youth of the town to sing and dance and live their lives to the fullest. He advocates the music of Schumann, Schubert, Bach and Mozart, much to the dismay of the parish priest, Father Fillifogue, a far more incompetent reactionary than Monsignor Burren. 'The wizard of the town', comments Fillifogue in anguished awe, '—here tomorrow; gone today!' [**Ned**, 55.] 'Your Father Ned's a menace to th' town an' th' whole counthryside,' [**Ned**, 32] insists the Mayor of Doonavale. But to the Mayor's son and the other young people Ned is the living resurrection—the resurrection of Doonavale and of Ireland, and they follow his drum into a political future in which they will overthrow the conservative Establishment. To them the answer to the constant question of the play, 'Where is Father Ned?' is: 'Here; but he might be anywhere, though some may think he's nowhere; again he may be everywhere; but he's always with th' dhrums.' [**Ned**, 55.]

In contrast to this cock-a-doodle-dandy cleric, the now-familiar Father Fillifogue is middle-aged, bald and humourless, his 'mouth seemingly forever compressed, his lips tight together in a mood of resigned annoyance with the world around him'. [Ned, 39]. He too rails against dancing, advocates burning books, and dates the downfall of contemporary morals with 'th' College lettin' th' students wear jeans' [Ned, 98]. He talks himself 'hoarse teachin' them th' right way to look at th' Pope's social teachin's' [Ned, 28] and thunders at the youth of Doonavale: 'I'll do th' thinking for yous; I'll say th' things that should be said; an' youse'll do th' things I'll tell youse to do.' [Ned, 96.] To O'Casey's delight they ignore the frantic priest's insistence upon their allegiance. Instead they follow the sound of Father Ned's revolutionary drum, despite the parish priest's censure, providing the playwright with the most optimistic ending since *The Star Turns Red.*

The range of negative qualities in Catholic clergymen moves for O'Casey between the ineffectual and limited on one hand and the vicious and dominating on the other. The best that he could say for such clerics is that they are ineptly out-of-date, as is the case with the Reverend George Canon Chreehewel, the parish priest of Clune na Geera. This bumbling priest puts in only a brief appearance in *Purple Dust*, the local church official coming to call on the British squires who are renovating the Tudor mansion. After the frightening portraits of the Bishop and the Purple Priest in the quasi-expressionistic dramas, Sean O'Casey turned back to his comic talents in dragging in Canon Chreehewel; but although primarily a comic figure, the Canon is soon obvious as the representative of middle-class hypocrisy who favours 'the slow movement of the past' over 'the reckless and Godless speed of the present' [Dust, 86]. He too campaigns against that primary source of all iniquity, the dancehall, as well as against the immodesty of abbreviated dresses (turning a blind eye to the excessively bare mistresses of the British squires, his gaze occupied by the cheque for twenty-five pounds donated by Poges). The Canon flatters Poges's preoccupation with restoring the past by resurrecting the mansion, hoping to enlist the Englishman's aid in ridding the community of dancehalls and O'Killigain. He is referring to the house when he says, 'It is almost a sacred thing to keep an old thing from dying,' [**Dust, 85**] but it is apparent that O'Casey is being ironic: the uselessness of the past in general and the superfluousness of the old priest in particular are implicated by the dramatist. Despite the diverse characterisations of such priests as the Purple one, Monsignor Burren, Father Fillifogue, and Canon Chreehewel, there is a basic common denominator: the cleric's stock-in-trade is hypocrisy, and even such relatively minor items as mores in dress become distinguishing characteristics of the narrow puritan.

There is little doubt that O'Casey interpreted Church domination in the new Irish state as an unhealthy indication of theocratic rule, and his later preoccupation with the countryside in lieu of the capital city gave him an opportunity to set his scene in the heartland of such rule. Particularly in the Clune na Geeras, Nyadnanaves, Ballyoonaghs, Doonavales, and Ballybeedhusts, the dust has settled thick with ecclesiastical purple, the Irish clergy having moved into dominant positions even beyond their previous powers. Canon Chreehewel is an insignificant beginning for O'Casey's series of Irish country priests, but most of his successors fulfil roles in the fantasy-comedies from *Cock-a-Doodle Dandy* to *The Drums of Father Ned* (until the vein gives out in 'Behind the Green Curtain', O'Casey transferring the function to a lay Catholic, the sinister Christy Kornavaun).

It is in *Cock-a-Doodle Dandy* that the author allows himself the full measure of his venom in depicting the extreme of the species in Father Domineer, who, by dint of murderous violence (if nothing else), qualifies for extremist honours. As parish priest of Nyadnanave and sole cock of that particular walk (there is no Father Boheroe to offset him and no Father Ned to drum him into insignificance), Domineer wields a mailed fist in stifling natural desires and civil liberties in the name of religion and Rome. The Julias of *The Star* and the Jannices of *Gates* are again the particular victims of the priest's bigotry and develop to even greater extents as O'Casey's singular heroines, Loreleen, Lorna, and Marion rebelling against the priest-fearing community and the teachings of the tyrannical Father Domineer in leaving Nyadnanave and Ireland. Domineer is the prototype of the humourless priest ('He is trying to smile now, but crack his mouth as he will, the tight, surly lines of his face refuse to furnish one' [**Cock, 155**]), echoing the bumbling Canon in deploring dancing and unilaterally legislating against salacious literature: 'How often have yous been warned that th' avowed enemies of Christianity are on th' march everywhere! An' I find yous dancin'! How often have yous been told that pagan poison is floodin' th' world, an' that Ireland is dhrinkin' in generous doses through films, plays, an' books! An' yet I come here to find yous dancin'! Dancin', an' with th' Kyleloch, Le Coq, Gallus, th' Cock rampant in th' disthrict, desthroyin' desire for prayer, desire for work, an' weakenin' th' authority of th' pastors an' masters of your souls! Th' empire of Satan's pushin' out its foundations everywhere, an' I find yous dancin', *ubique ululanti cockalorum ochone, ululo!*' [**Cock, 184.**]

But even the supernatural is against the puritanical priest, as the Cock—a free and boisterous spirit—mocks him at will. He attempts an exorcism of the Marthraun house, but emerges with a black eye and a burned foot, presumably successful in his struggle with the demon spirits. When the spirits strike again, the priest is carried off by the Demon Cock, while Marthraun, Mahan, and One-eyed Larry are knocked down. Father Domineer might have appeared as only an absurd figure, like the Canon of *Purple Dust*, or an inept failure like Father Fillifogue (Domineer's sponsoring of Julia's trip to Lourdes proves a waste of effort), except for the killing of Mahan's lorry driver at the end of the second scene. In a rage against the man because he is living with a woman in sin, he lashes out, knocking him down and killing him. Insisting that it was an accident, Father Domineer smooths the incident over by assuring the onlookers that he 'murmured an act of contrition into th' poor man's ear'. (Robin Adair rejoinders, 'It would have been far fitther, Father, if you'd murmured one into your own.' [**Cock, 189.**]) In the last scene, having to quit the parish because of the 'unhappy accident', he is determined to clean house before he goes, and undertakes his disastrous exorcism with bell, book, and candle. When his tussle with the free spirits results in his being badly battered about, he limits himself to persecuting the women instead, revealing again the sadistic core

247

in his campaign against lust and proving by negative example that his piety is inhumane and his morality a sham. His very name perverts *Dominus* into *domineering*.

The kind of Catholic priest portrayed in Domineer and his lesser incarnations is seldom seen on the Abbey stage; indeed, considering the dearth of the later O'Casey plays on that stage, is *never* seen. (Kindly and sympathetic clerics are far more standard, but not of the kind represented by Boheroe or the Brown Priest of the Poor.) It is a simple matter for O'Casey's detractors to charge that he is prejudiced against Catholics, and even that he gives Protestant clergymen preferential treatment: Reverend Clinton of *Red Roses for Me* is certainly one of O'Casey's favourite people. A champion of the poor and under-privileged, the Rector of St Burnupus is first seen when he comes to warn Ayamonn Breydon, his parishioner and friend, that the authorities intend to employ violence against the strikers. His image as an honest and heroic clergyman is sustained throughout the play and is accented immediately for the audience in his appearance: 'He is a handsome man of forty. His rather pale face wears a grave scholarly look, but there is kindness in his grey eyes, and humorous lines round his mouth.' [**Roses, 180.**] Moreover, his black clerical garb is relieved by a touch of bright colour, a green scarf, an important symbol for O'Casey of life, health, vitality.

In contrast to Reverend Clinton the bigoted vestrymen of St Burnupus are presented as proof that the Catholics hold no monopoly on narrowmindedness and hypocrisy: they rail against the altar flowers and act as strike-breakers, while the Rector remains firm and kind, although Mrs Breydon pleads with him to intercede and prevent Ayamonn from participating in the dangerous strike. 'I wish I could, dear friend,' [**Roses, 209**] he says, but he maintains that he has no right to interfere with Ayamonn's ideals. The saintly minister is human, however, losing his temper at the angry Inspector Finglas, also his parisioner,[4] who attempts to bully him into restraining Ayamonn: 'I have neither the authority nor the knowledge to deny it,' the reverend retorts, 'though I have more of both than you, sir!' [**Roses, 212.**]

Nor will he allow himself to be pressured into an anti-

Catholic position. When told by Foster and Dowzard that Ireland is on the verge of a 'hoppy Romish auto-dey-fey', Clinton replies with amusement, 'Well, let the Loyola boyos and King Bully fight it out between them.' [**Roses, 218.**] He invites Mrs Breydon and Sheila into the vestry for tea, brushing aside the Catholic girl's anxiety about entering the Protestant church by assuring her that 'there's no canonical law against taking tea made by a Protestant' [**Roses, 213**]. After the bloody battle between the strikers and Finglas's police, Ayamonn is carried in dead, and the minister has the body carried into the church, despite the protest of the select vestrymen. 'It is a small thing that you weary me, but you weary my God also,' he tells them. 'Stand aside, and go your way of smoky ignorance, leaving me to welcome him whose turbulence has sunken into a deep sleep, and who cometh now as the waters of Shiloah that go softly, and sing sadly of peace.' [**Roses, 223.**] Above the issues of the battle, Reverend Clinton embodies the virtues of dispassionate honesty and Christian warmth and sympathy in the face of hypocrisy, fear and hate. He is O'Casey's ideal clergyman, a figure apparently modelled from life, as the autobiographies indicate.

As David Krause notes, Reverend Clinton of St Burnupus is patterned after Rev. Edward Martin Griffin of St Barnabas,[5] who is introduced in the final pages of *Pictures in the Hallway*, when he arrives at his new parish and is immediately confronted by the Orange vestrymen. The volume is in fact dedicated 'TO THE MEMORY OF THE REV. E. M. GRIFFIN, B.D., M.A., ONE-TIME RECTOR OF ST BARNABAS, DUBLIN; a fine scholar; a man of many-branched kindness, whose sensitive hand was the first to give the clasp of friendship to the author'. It is essentially in the next volume, *Drums under the Windows*, that several small vignettes of the Rector appear: his solicitude for Sean's brother Tom marrying outside the faith, his ministering to the dying Tom and financing the funeral, his theological concern over the effects of Higher Criticism, and his support of Sean in having a debate over the question of the teaching of Irish in the new National University; and throughout there is the mutual regard and admiration that he and Sean had for each other.

In *Inishfallen* Reverend Griffin is seen one last time at the funeral of Sean's sister Ella, and on the last page of the volume the departing Sean Casside includes the minister in his final thoughts of Ireland, the legacy from his parents and from the Rector of St Barnabas. For all of the warm praise for Rector Griffin sprinkled throughout these three books, there is nonetheless that single statement of criticism (a hallmark of O'Casey's evaluations of those he loved: that single moment during which he catalogues the man's imperfections, as he had also done for his mother). In the 'House of the Living' chapter, concerned with Sean's intellectual maturation and the death of Ella, the moment of evaluation takes place, with no indication if this is a contemporary estimation or a later appraisal. He begins by assuming that the man he loves so much is a 'faultless man' but immediately corrects himself:

No, not faultless, for sometimes he showed he had a hasty temper, and he couldn't suffer fools gladly, both qualities endearing him all the more to Sean, who himself had a hasty temper and hated fools fiercely. He had, too, a puritanical detestation of even accidental indulgence in the claims of sex, other than those allowed by law and regulation of the Church, and a real sensitiveness that couldn't allow him long to look at the effects of poverty. He had told Sean, one time, that to do so would break him in pieces. He, too, had a curious childlike readiness to accept almost anything said by one who, he thought, loved and served the Church which, to him, sprang from the love and devotion of Saints Patrick, Columkille, Bridget, and Aidaun. Once in an argument around the causes of poverty, the Rector, laying an affectionate touch of his hand on Sean's arm, said, Remember, John, I have been young, and now am old; yet have I not seen the righteous forsaken, nor His seed begging bread. [Window, 140.]

It is in this summation of these human and fallible qualities of the admired man that the playwright hoarded the central elements for the creation of Reverend Clinton in *Red Roses*: his annoyance is seen in his contact with the foolish verger and his anger in his reactions to the vestrymen and the Inspector. And in Act Three, when Clinton and Finglas are

wandering through the slums of Dublin, the Rector is un-
nerved by the poverty-stricken surroundings: 'Let us go from
here. Things here frighten me, for they seem to look with
wonder on our ease and comfort.... Things here are of a
substance I dare not think about, much less see and handle.
Here, I can hardly bear to look upon the same thing twice.'
[Roses, 191.]

Reverend Griffin has his precursor in Harry Fletcher, the
rector who preceded him at St Barnabas. Whereas Griffin
had paid for the burial of poor Tom, it was Fletcher years
earlier who arrived as the new minister to find Tom seriously ill and the Casside family incapable of coping with him.
He immediately arranged for a hospital bed for Tom and
paid for the cab to take the sick man there. 'Tall, kind,
and handsome' [Hallway, 247], Fletcher is responsible for
Johnny's confirmation in the Church of Ireland, and is very
much the kind of enlightened man of the cloth that O'Casey
continued to admire. That such clergymen were few was
O'Casey's confirmed opinion throughout his career ('Nothing
seemed to be able to excite the clergy. They dreaded any
kind of a noise, and went about as if Jesus had never got out
of the manger. Not Mr Griffin, of course, or Harry Fletcher,
or his brother, Dudley. But the rest of them' [Window, 50]),
and the portrait of Harry Fletcher rivals that of E. M. Griffin
for its sympathy and admiration. Harry Fletcher too was
overly Romish for the Select Vestry of St Barnabas, with only
the poorer members of the congregation like Johnny Casside
siding with him. And in the end he was driven away: 'I
have to go. My bishop advised that it wasn't a good thing to
provoke contention among Christian people.' [Hallway,
298–9.] But Fletcher also has his foot of clay, his indifference
to the Irish language and his lack of involvement in the
plight of Ireland. Nonetheless, he represents for the young
O'Casey a type of real Christian that became a fixed point of
comparison thereafter for Sean O'Casey, the combined
prototype of Harry Fletcher and E. M. Griffin.

The counterpart of that prototype preceded them both, a
man of God whom O'Casey holds responsible for a basic
antipathy towards the Protestant Church that Fletcher and
Griffin only temporarily offset. This is the Reverend Mr

Hunter, the *bête noire* of Johnny Casside's childhood, who undertook to aggrandise Johnny's Protestant soul and claim it for salvation despite the torn and tattered appearance of the boy's exterior. 'The Protestant Kid Thinks of the Reformation' is O'Casey's title for the brief chapter of the first volume, in which he records the initial confrontation of the forlorn kid and his self-appointed spiritual pastor, 'a monster crow' [**Door, 135**] whose shadow falls upon the marbles that are Johnny's happy preoccupation when his eyes are too bad for school attendance. While Johnny views him as 'hunter the runter the rix stix stunter', the minister is quite intent on his mission on the boy's behalf, since he deems it 'necessary that he should be made into a firm protestant young man in this dark and sorrowful roman land' [**Door, 137**]. Hunter is the catalyst that propels the weak-eyed child into school and church, harrowing experiences for him because of his wretched condition as a poor boy among better dressed and better fed contemporaries, and a sickly child among those who quickly discern his vulnerability and make him a butt for their bullying. At school there is Slogan the schoolmaster and at Sunday School the hypocritical Miss Valentine, both of whom display contempt for his deficiencies.

The recurrence of the eye ailment spares Johnny from further torture, the surgeon Mr R. Joyce providing the letter of respite that keeps him out of the schoolroom; but T. R. S. Hunter[6] does not take secular authority as superior to his own, and Johnny goes back to the chamber of horrors because his compliant mother is unable to stand up to the minister. When Johnny rebels against Slogan's persecution by cracking open the schoolmaster's head and running home to hide, Hunter is once again at the Casside flat, commanding the boy's mother to hand over the miscreant—and this time Mrs Casside is magnificent in her refusal, finally separating the kid from his pastor. There is little nostalgia wasted on Hunter and his institutions when O'Casey reflects in tranquillity on the events of that childhood: 'The Reverend Hunter was born in protestant circumstances that make him a sky-pilot, and Johnny was born a protestant in circumstances that placed him in a position of being lugged along at the backside of this soft-hatted stiff-collared egg-headed oul' henchman of heaven, to be added to his swarm of urchins cowering and groping about in the rag-and-bone education provided by the church and state for the children of those who hadn't the wherewithal to do anything better.' [**Door, 146.**] At an early age Johnny Casside learned for himself that being a Protestant was not necessarily enough. With the full naïveté of a child he reports to a fellow-Protestant: 'I know a roman catholic woman ... when she meets me always asks me how is me eyes, and one day when it was rainin' she gave me a fistful of licorice balls.' [**Door, 172.**]

Not only did O'Casey champion those Protestant clerics who rebelled against the entrenched ignorance within the Church of Ireland, but expanded his range to include the Catholic priests who did the same within the Church of Rome. Such was the case with Dr O'Hickey and Dr McDonald, Irish priests who become almost legendary figures in the O'Casey pantheon of great fighters; in *Drums under the Windows* and right through the succeeding three volumes, O'Casey is unrelenting in wielding his cudgels for these rebels, whose cause he championed long after they had died fighting for it. *Drums* is dedicated to the former, and *Inishfallen* to the latter, and between the two dedicatory passages the gist of their story is told:

To

DR MICHAEL O'HICKEY

A Gael of Gaels, one-time Professor of Irish in Maynooth College. In a fight for Irish, he collided with arrogant Irish bishops, and was summarily dismissed without a chance of defending himself; taking the case to Rome, he was defeated there by the subtlety of the bishops, helped by a sly Roman Rota, ending his last proud years in poverty and loneliness.

Forgotten, unhonoured, unsung in Eire, here's a Gael left who continues to say Honour and Peace to your brave and honest soul, Michael O'Hickey, till a braver Ireland comes to lay a garland on your lonely grave.

To

WALTER MCDONALD, D.D.

Professor of theology in St Patrick's Roman Catholic
College, Maynooth, for forty years; a great man gone, and
almost forgotten; but not quite forgotten.[7]

The 'Lost Leader' chapter of *Drums* tells O'Hickey's story in
O'Casey's angriest epithets, a story in which the clergyman
fought alone for the cause of compulsory teaching of the
Irish language in the New University, against the solid
opposition of Irish bishops and the indifference and complicity of the Vatican, and frightened disregard from the
Gaelic League and Sinn Fein. The 'Silence' chapter of
Inishfallen records the McDonald story, not only of the
theologian's lonely voice in defence of O'Hickey, but of his
lifetime of dedication to a searingly intellectual Catholicism
expunged by a total darkness of ignorance that masqueraded
as official Catholic theology and learning. Parnell qualities
are endowed upon these two Roman clerics by their defender, who found in them aspects of himself as well: relentless opposition to ignorance, power structures, cowardice and
indifference, and the compact majority.

When O'Hickey and McDonald are the heroes, the villains
are Monsignor Mannix, President of Maynooth College, and
Cardinal Logue (usually renamed Cardinal Log by the word-
wit of Sean O'Casey). The latter appears and reappears often
as a Church hatchetman, first when he has W. P. O'Ryan's
liberal newspaper, *The Irish Peasant*, suppressed: what
O'Ryan wrote in his newspaper was 'condemned by the
Cardinal, though never read by him; for the Cardinal had
the power to see a hole through an iron pot; and so O'Ryan
was left alone to fight a host of snarling clergy who silenced
song and story, drove away the marching, kilted men, hunted
O'Ryan from the Boyne to the Liffey, then to the Dublin
Quay, and finally from the last spot where his clinging feet
still stood, away, away with you, from Ireland altogether,
away from her for ever and a day!' [**Window, 26.**] (O'Ryan
is of course another O'Casey hero, with the correct attributes
that the author was able to capsulate into a medallion: 'the
dark-eyed, black-haired W. P. O'Ryan, shy, sensitive, one

254

with the peasant, the worker, and the scholar' [**Window, 25**].
The Cardinal then turns from O'Ryan to Synge, from *The
Irish Peasant* to *Playboy of the Western World*: 'and didn't
the great Cardinal Logue condemn the thing without even
havin' to read it by a snap of his ecclesiastical finger an'
thumb that sounded in a catholic ear clear like a clap of
thundher?' [**Window, 185.**] From Logue to Log is an easy
transition for O'Casey, and from Log to Lug is another, and
the next issue in *Drums under the Windows* is his complicity
in the O'Hickey case. Not having read either O'Ryan's newspaper or Synge's play prepared Cardinal Logue admirably
in O'Casey's estimation to handle the O'Hickey matter without reading the Statutes under which the protest was dismissed; O'Casey summarises the Cardinal's career: 'This was
the enlightened boyo who put an end to W. P. O'Ryan's art
and industry community in the Boyne valley; this was he
who bawled shame towards Synge, and who condemned
Yeats's *Countess Cathleen*, without bothering his red-hatted
head to read the book of the play. The hetman of the Catholic Church in Ireland imposing his will on far better men
than himself. The Christian way of life!' [**Window, 197.**]
And, needless to add, there remained only Dr McDonald
for the Cardinal's next victim, but here O'Casey has his
chance to chortle with victorious glee. Angered by the politically volatile material in Dr McDonald's *Peace and War*, 'The
Cardinal threatened to make visitation of the College, and
punish severely all who had taught doctrine so much opposed
to Catholic Tradition. But changed things in Ireland made
the cautious, cunning, ignorant Cardinal stay where he was
in Arrah na Pogue Coelis, silent, sad, and anxious, for he
didn't know the hell what might happen next.' [**Inish, 364.**]
It reads like only a thin and Pyrrhic victory, but for the
champion of lost causes this moment of ecclesiastical atrophy
is worth exulting over.

In the last four volumes of the autobiographies there are
some three score names to reckon with, priests and canons
and monsignors and archbishops and cardinals enough to
stock a mock-Vatican of O'Casey's own construction. Many a
cleric is named in vain, such as the 'Reverend Father Francis
Joseph Ignatius Polycarp Dominicjerome Sebastian O'Cal-

laghan', who objects to Tennyson's *Voyage of Maeldune* sung in Gaelic as a slander to 'Ireland of the Virgins' [**Window**, 212]; other euphoniously named priests are Bishop O'Dawn O'Day, Father O'Franticain, and Dr Cockadoo, Lord Bishop of Blarney, as well as Father Clematis of the Cuneiform Order of Unimpassionate Canons Irregular and the Most Rev. Paschal Robinson, O.F.M. Archbishop McQuaid's 'declaration of excommunication on any catholic student who ventures to put his nose within the gates of Trinity College' [**Inish**, 327] earns no plaudits from O'Casey, and the archbishop finds himself catalogued among the pack who howl at Synge's *Playboy* as Mick McQuaid (just as the Codger knows that the Bishop was, is, and permanently will be nothing more than Bill Mullarky).

Of the great men of Church history, Cardinal Newman was only a 'non-commissioned officer' in 'La Grande Armée des Vatican' [**Inish**, 336]; nonetheless, Newman is cited as an honest intellect in the Church of Rome and, coupled with McDonald, as one of the 'many more eminent men who suffered and were abused for standing up to truth, giving her honour, and making this daughter of Time their dear sister' [**Crown**, 188]. By contrast Cardinal Spellman is recalled from a newspaper photograph, 'a grin on his face, standing before a kneeling Pole, surrounded by his wife and fifteen children, who had travelled to New York by air, though the journal said they were utterly penniless. It was said that the Cardinal had emptied his wallet of a wad of notes, and had given them all to the old Polish Ram; the journal adding that the Cardinal had entered New York without a penny. Left himself without a dime! Your need is greater than mine. And how! Now what sarcastic voice whispers that it wouldn't be long till the Cardinal's wallet would be as full as ever with the finest and fairest of dollar notes?' [**Sunset**, 34.] The sarcastic voice is heard often, with little sympathy for those high clerics imprisoned by iron curtains: in *Sunset and Evening Star* O'Casey quotes a report on 'the part Cardinal Stepinac took with Pavelic, the Fascist leader, in forcing them of the orthodox church over into the roman ditto' [**Sunset**, 300].

In his sixties Sean O'Casey recalled the events of his maturation as he was recording them with strong editorial comment in the autobiographies-in-progress. 'The hold of the faith had weakened well on Sean himself,' he remembers in *Drums under the Windows*. 'Though he hadn't said farewell, the anchor was getting weighed, and his ship of life was almost about to leave the harbour. He no longer thought that God's right hand, or His left one either, had handed the bible out of Heaven, all made up with chapter and verse and bound in a golden calf-skin.' [**Window**, 32.] The corpus of his life's work attests to his profound suspicion of the machinations of Heaven and the ministration of its representatives in the Christian Churches. As a lapsed Protestant he might be guilty (and has been accused) of prejudice in concentrating so often on the abuses of the Catholic clergy, but as an Irishman he might be understood to have focused on the Church so predominant in his native country. As an atheist he cites God with ease and invokes His works with wonder; nor is his atheism of the professional variety that he is patently critical of in his portrait of Ned the Hyde Park Atheist.

It is understandable that O'Casey's tendency towards severe criticism and even blasphemous mockery (that sarcastic voice) would discomfort those of his well-wishers who would prefer to nudge him at least part way back to orthodoxy: Brooks Atkinson introduces O'Casey by noting that 'although he described himself as a rationalist he was preoccupied with religion', nailing down this vague comment with the assertion that 'O'Casey was a believer; it is a temptation to misuse a religious term and call him an Old Believer.'[8] Dean Bernard of St Patrick's might wonder at the misuse by Atkinson of religious terms if he could have read O'Casey's version of the Dean's reaction to having a service in Irish on Saint Patrick's Day ('After the Dean had recovered out of a bud swoon by swallowing a big dollop of warmed whiskey, he asked, Is there anything else you'd like?' [**Window**, 216]). O'Casey's view of the Church he left and of the one he would not enter is available to Atkinson in *Inishfallen*: 'Rome, Maynooth; one sack, one sample. Intrigue, false pretences, expediency, concealment, silence. And, unfortunately, the Protestant Church in Ireland, and, indeed, many in the Anglican Church, too, are rallying to become

257

hardy non-commissioned officers in La Grande Armée des Vatican. . . . So it will be till honest and courageous men in the churches stand out for a proper conduct in God's service; or for no service at all.' [Inish, 335–6.] Aware of the scarcity of Fletchers and Griffins, O'Hickeys and McDonalds, and despondent at the dominance of Hunters and Bernards, Logues and Spellmans, O'Casey opted for no service at all.

9

A Cluster of Minor Characters

IN the closing minutes of *Hamlet*, after the last of the eight bodies has been removed from the stage (or buried at sea), it is apparent that Horatio and Fortinbras will not be able to carry on alone, and that the curtain will soon fall. Minor characters in plays most often fall into two groups: those who are dismally irrelevant (Tom Stoppard amused himself by toying with the insignificance, interchangeability, and super-fluousness of Rosencrantz and Guildenstern) and those who have been conscripted into service to perform a single piece of action or represent a fixed point of view. Chekhov was almost unique in understanding the essence of reality that could be achieved in the drama by allowing every minor figure to behave as if the action centred primarily upon him-self, and on occasion O'Casey allowed his Mrs Henderson or Brennan Moore that moment of egocentricity; but most often he acceded to the dictates of a structured drama that treated lesser lights as having little magnitude. In 'Time to Go' two cyclists, a Young Man and a Young Woman, stop for a meal at Michael Flagonson's tavern. They are on their way to the ruins of the Abbey of Ballyrellig, but it is soon apparent that the purpose they serve is to indicate that neither Flagonson nor the owner of the General Store, Bull Farrell, is at all aware of the existence of a nearby ruin of some beauty—and that they care nothing about it once they learn about it. Having performed so much yeoman service for the audience in revealing this aspect of Flagonson and Farrell, the cyclists are given a second function: Mrs Flagon-son overcharges them grossly for their meagre meal; the mercenary dishonesty of the Flagonsons now established, this will become the major theme of the play. Not permitted to tell us much about themselves, the cyclists are instrumental in revealing the essentials of the Flagonsons and Bull Farrell.

Such is the fate of flat characters: they are doomed to remaining only a facet of themselves like a moon perpetually in its last quarter. Yet when brought together from the O'Casey canon into groups displaying like characteristics, they too indicate broader patterns of group identities, paralleling the patterns apparent for their betters, the enviable rank of major figures. In the case of the walk-ons and extras, however, where character traits and family relationships are either indistinct or unimportant, they are more profitably collected in social categories, where more is determined by the group as a whole than from the individuality of the parts.

Autocrats

Rarely does O'Casey concern himself with a depiction of the rulers of society, although they are apparent in the negative, as their effects on the lives of the slum dwellers are exposed. More often they are represented by their emissaries, those members of officialdom who transmit authority directly. Inspector Finglas moves through the riverside slums of Dublin in epaulettes and braid, helmet and sword, contemptuous of the pitiful dregs of humanity lining the bridge parapets, describing them as 'flotsam and jetsam'. He reacts violently when one of the loungers accidentally spits on his polished boot: 'What th' hell are you after doing, you rotten lizard! Looka what you've done, you mangy rat!' [Roses, 190.] In *The Silver Tassie's* war scene a Visitor, 'dressed in a semi-civilian, semi-military manner' [Tassie, 40], passes through the wearied and dispirited soldiers, maintaining his official tone of missionary cheerfulness and lecturing the punished Barney (tied Christlike to a gunwheel) on the sacredness of private property and 'the uniform, the cause, boy, the corps' [Tassie, 41]. And through Hyde Park strolls the Bishop, announcing to the crippled chair attendants that 'God is in all, and God is all things' [Gates, 128], and representing ecclesiastical sanction of the status quo.

A comic transposition of the ambassador of the ruling establishment finding himself among his 'constituency' can be found in the plight of Lord Leslieson of Ottery St Oswald set down in the middle of the night in the Irish town of Kylenamoe. An emissary of the London Foreign Office on a political mission, carrying 'important despatches for the Prime Minister of England, the Earl of Epplepen, holidaying somewhere here in the Manor House of Killnalayne' [**Moon, 140**], Leslieson is an anachronism, in the wrong place at the wrong time. British rule long out of date, he finds himself the butt of Irish personality quirks, including touchiness about insults to Ireland (his references to Kylenamoe as a 'desolate district' [**Moon, 133**] are quickly taken up by the Irish as a vilification of the nation). Lord Leslieson begins as a solid-headed man of decisiveness, but is soon reduced to utter frustration by the quarrelsome Irish. A man for whom all directness is a straight line between two points, he attempts to remain in command, coherent and logical, but ends up sitting on a crate with his head in his hands, having despaired of ever getting his mission accomplished and at the mercy of Irish hospitality and generosity. But again he displays his class characteristics, offering to pay and even overpay for considerations that are not being offered for sale.

As a portrait of the Sassenach conqueror ruling the roost in Ireland, Leslieson is only a pathetic shadow, O'Casey having handled the British bulldog type satirically in *Purple Dust*: here Cyril Poges and Basil Stoke are also anachronistic, Ireland no longer being theirs, but the Tudor mansion that they have bought can still give them a small measure of autocracy. Unable to restore the past glories of English domination, they attempt to restore the house instead, seeing themselves as sober and serious men among the wild Irish children: 'All the Irish are the same,' Poges insists. 'Bit backward perhaps, like all primitive peoples, especially now, for they're missing the example and influence of the gentry; but delightful people all the same. They need control, though; oh yes, they need it badly.' [**Dust, 23.**] And so the Canon is paid off to keep the Irish in their place while allowing the masters of the mansion licence to behave as they wish. Their reverence for the past is nonetheless governed by their financial control of the present, and trunk calls to St Paul's for speculation on the market are insisted upon as necessary conveniences. The compact of the English squires and the

261

Irish priest fixes the centre of power in the community, as does the alliance between Councillor Reiligan and Canon Burren in *The Bishop's Bonfire*, where Reiligan has been made a Count of the Papal Court and the Canon promoted to Monsignor ('The Church an' State's gettin' together,' [**Bonfire**, 37] comments the Codger). Reiligan is 'the biggest money-man in the district, a loyal pillar of the clergy, and has a great power and influence in the affairs of the state—the local member of the Dail could never climb into a seat without the backing of Councillor Reiligan.' [**Bonfire**, 4.] The shift of power from British capital to Irish capital results in such portraits as that of Reiligan, Councillor Marthraun, Mayor Binnington and Deputy Mayor McGilligan, all businessmen with political enclaves of power; and in each case they have their Burrens, Domineers, Fillifogues—their purple priests.

The Star Turns Red is of course O'Casey's most humourlessly serious investigation of such power structures, where Lord Mayor, Purple Priest, and Saffron Shirt Leader constitute a united fasces of authority. The Mayor, invoking the spirit of the Christmas season, exults over their unified front and its presumed victory: 'Christ, the Prince of Peace, has conquered. The stay-in strike, arranged to begin tonight, is stopped before it started. The Bishops have spoken; the Saffron Shirts are marching; the Christian Front is holding a rally; the soldiers are under arms; the respectable workers have denounced the Reds; the Trades Congress have voted for peace, and are going to fling Red Jim from the Central Council. Christ, the King, has conquered.' [**Star**, 266–7.] The Mayor's list reads like a Who's Who of Rightwing Power, and each element presents itself in turn to accentuate the pattern formed. The Purple Priest of the Rich denounces the Red Star as 'the badge of the enemy, man's enemy, the Church's enemy, God's enemy' [**Star**, 271]. The Leader of the Saffron Shirts next attempts to have Jack remove his badge, insisting, 'We shall skim the scum from the State: the gaping mouth shall be shut tight; the feet that run in the way of riot shall be tied together; the violent shall be made meek; and the stubborn back shall be bent or broken' [**Star**, 275]; and in his wake he leaves Julia beaten and her father killed. The leaders of the General Workers' Union meet to find ways and means of taking power away from Red Jim, and the unholy alliance of these factions is cemented into a defence of capitalism and an attack on Communism. The battle of the emissaries of the Past against the delegates of the Future is fought in the final scene of the play, the soldiers and sailors joining the workers and the star turning red.

But this victory is won 'tomorrow, or the next day' and in the meanwhile the reality of a capitalist, parochial, and theocratic Ireland remains as a reality to be reckoned with—the scene and subject matter of most of the later O'Casey plays. In the rural settings the centre of power lies with such as Reiligan and Marthraun and Mahan, or (as in 'Time to Go') with the big farmer. Here there is a graded scale from Barney O'Hay, 'farmer owner of five acres', to Cousins, 'farmer owner of twenty acres', to Conroy, 'farmer owner of a hundred and fifty acres' [Time, 260]. Cousins is in the process of selling his cattle to Conroy, who beats him down by inches and ells to a price of his liking, apparently confident that he has the upper hand. When Kelly and the Widda Machree denounce the dishonesty of asking more than the item is worth or offering less, even O'Hay, the poorest of the farmers, defends a system that has victimised him, hoping to curry favour with the powerful Conroy. Conroy tries to bully the two idealists and calls in the Civic Guard to arrest such subversives as these that question the central principle of their economic system, and generally shows himself as unregenerate and unyielding, with a dogged strength and determination that keep him in power. The saintly pair elude their captors and magically illuminate the trees, but the miracle is short-lived: Conroy and Cousins go off to conclude their business deal, while Bull Farrell insists upon payment before allowing Barney O'Hay the phosphate he needs. The dejected poor farmer sums up the futility of his life: 'If I seen anything, an' if you seen anything, what was seen was only an halleelucination!' [Time, 292.]

The face of industrial capitalism is seen in the last plays of Sean O'Casey, particularly in *The Drums of Father Ned*, where the actual hold of the clergy can be observed as loosening, while power becomes centred exclusively in the secular hands of state officials representing moneyed interests. Father Fillifogue is already beset with Mr Murray's musical rebellion against his hymns and has been reduced to a flustered and blustering nonentity, while Alderman Binnington ('Mayor of Doonavale, a solicitor and owner of General Store') and Councillor McGilligan ('Deputy Mayor, a building contractor and builders' provider' [Ned, viii]) are concluding a business deal with Ulsterman Alec Skerighan, a deal involving timber from Communist countries. O'Casey's tongue-in-cheek has multiple effects here: business being business, even political enmity between North and South, Protestant and Catholic, is being swept aside; big business being big business, even the political campaign against Communism is swept under the rug in the name of profit. When the priest learns of the Russian timber on the wharf, he indignantly insists that it be burned ('Burn it as a reparation to God for landing atheistical timber on th' holy wharf of Doonavale' [Ned, 96]), but the businessmen are determined to make their profit, and the young rebels, Michael and Nora and Tom, argue for different reasons against the burning: 'It is the very wood we need to make fine sturdy window-frames an' fine doors for our homes; to put a sturdy an' sensible roof over our heads, and a safe an' pleasant floor undher our feet. What's more, Father Ned has said Take it, and be thankful.' [Ned, 97.] O'Casey is enjoying the disintegration of that unified fasces that seemed so strong in *The Star*, and is particularly delighted with the inner corruption by which the greedy businessmen turn against the demands of the clergy and indulge in trade with Communist nations for capitalist profits.

In 'Behind the Green Curtains' the playwright again plays havoc with stereotypes, offering a fairly sympathetic portrait of the factory owner Dennis Chatastray. Too weak to be the hero, he is nonetheless no greedy capitalist, allowing his Communist foreman free rein to run the operation with characteristic efficiency, and refusing to allow his skilled workers to be bullied out of his factory by the parochial committee steeled against their mixed marriage. An enlightened employer Chatastray knows that he is dependent upon the efficiency of his employees, and would conduct his business along logical and sensible lines if he were allowed. But the dark forces of ignorance and prejudice maintain an undercurrent of disruptive power that is as indifferent to the industrialist's concerns as it is to that of the workers, an indication that fascism is as antithetical to the capitalism that bred it as it is to socialism. Even the clergy as such are absent from 'Green Curtains', where power is vested in the hands of secular vigilantes like Christy Kornavaun and his masked fanatics. The journalist serves as mouthpiece and hatchetman for the clergy, using violence like that of the Saffron Shirts in the name of Catholicism. He is a self-righteous hypocrite more dangerous than the powers he serves, for it is apparent that control in the hands of the petty henchman may become an end in itself: that the dark forces unleashed by the righteous to protect its entrenched power may not be controllable at the end, and that power may pass from the conservative establishment to a violent and destructive fanatical fringe group. From *The Star Turns Red* to 'Behind the Green Curtains' O'Casey presents a spectrum of political danger with many variants, but with the one constant remaining the Communist ideals of Jack, Red Jim, and Martin Boeman.

Nor is the image of the autocrat limited in O'Casey's plays to political areas, but as always the concern in these plays comes back to the individual character, like the doctor who dictates as the medical officer of the Dispensary in 'Hall of Healing'. A petty tyrant in his own domain, he is the autocrat of the operating table, whose personal limitations result in his hardened attitude towards the pathetic lives of his patients. He is a Sunday drunkard whose Mondays are efforts to overcome the effects of his drinking, leaving him irritable and short-tempered with everyone. That it is taken out primarily on the sycophantic and tyrannical Alleluia mitigates the severity of audience reaction to the doctor and serves the cause of poetic justice. Nor is he without pathetic failings himself: he attempts to hide whatever feelings he has because he has despaired of being able to do anything for the sick and the dying, contrasting himself with his predecessor, who had attempted to break the routine of the prescribed 'bottles' but himself died of cancer. The doctor sees such a break from the established routine as inviting death, but remains—despite the pathos of his situations and the sympathy he tries to hide—guilty of ignoring the pleas of the dying who clamour for his attention. As petty autocrat he is as trapped by his own cynicism as the pathetic patients are by the system in which he flourishes.

Bureaucrats

Lord Leslieson carrying 'important despatches' more than meets his match in Irish contentiousness at the Kylenamoe railway station. He comes from an environment in which the red tape flows smoothly and endlessly (and although it may well end up where it began, accomplishing nothing, it at least gives the illusion of movement, like Zeno's arrow); now he finds himself in an environment in which the smallest deviation from routine results in complete confusion. Leslieson's approach is that of the urban bureaucrat, the cog in a well-oiled machine, but the Kylenamoe of Ireland is a rusty engine that cannot shift its gears too easily. And inevitably the ambassador is bogged down in the multifaceted disputes raging around him by porter, guard, engineer, residents, passers-by, and even the passengers. The most officious of the Irish contenders is a woman who emerges from the train to lodge her protest: in essence she is Lord Leslieson's counterpart, an urban Irish office-employee and pompously self-important. Her protest is lodged not in her own voice but in her capacity as the delegate of others ('Th' passengers have asked me to inquire into th' motionless condition of th' thrain for near a half hour o' time?' [**Moon, 148**]), and like all bureaucrats she cites higher authority for her demands: 'Th' one first-class passenger left in th' thrain's busy at a Report of this terrible wait in th' threat in the core of th' dead an' silent night.' [**Moon, 149.**] So that higher up in the chain of command that is office stratification someone even more important is writing a Report to someone even higher up.

Officiousness in manner is the diagnostic symptom of bureaucratic behaviour, and a belief in the orderly progress of things is characteristic of its attitude (if there is a railway station, there is a town; from railway station to manor house there is a road; a car hired at the railway station will take the emissary to the manor house). But bureaucracy is an urban phenomenon, and Lord Leslieson can no more get a car in the middle of the night in rural Ireland than Cyril Poges can get a trunk line call through to his broker in London after 10 p.m. They find themselves outside the Pale. It is also characteristic of the bureaucrat that he values his own significance in the petty-chain-of-being, and given a position of even the smallest authority he tends to become autocratic. Such is the case with air raid wardens, for example, as Special Constable Dillery and Constable Sillery in *Oak Leaves* descend upon the Hatherleigh household with angry demands, 'What d'ye mean in havin' that unobscured light there flashing about, an' th' blackout down?' [**Oak, 67**] and portentous warnings, 'She'll 'ave t' be taken seriously, if she happens again.' [**Oak, 68.**] But their measure of self-importance is soon reduced to nothing when the real authority arrives: Dame Hatherleigh berates the constables for flashing their torches in the house, treating them like disobedient children and letting them off with a scolding. 'Us follows you, ma'am, quick an' right,' [**Oak, 70**] they chorus together, and even the Special Constable's cap with a 'gigantic silver badge coruscating in front of it' [**Oak, 67**] becomes meaningless when confronting the aristocrat. (In 'Kylenamoe' the railway station official has a cap with a green band, while the train guard's cap has a silver one; the latter jealously guards the distinction between their stations, insisting, 'What he'd like is the silver band round his cap an' th' red one round mine.' [**Moon, 132.**])

Such petty symbols of status are points along the scale leading to the Lord Mayor's gold chain of office, while even mode of dress is sufficient to distinguish those with the rights of privilege. Charlie Bentham in *Juno* arrives with gloves and walking-stick and signs himself 'Charles Bentham, N.T.' [**Juno, 33**] but when the legacy fizzles out and Mary is pregnant, Mr Bentham (who 'made a banjax o' th' Will') escapes to England, leaving no forwarding address. His sense of responsibility ends with the collapsed fortune of the Boyle family, although he had been willing to undergo the indignity of contact with them and their neighbours as long as

Mary was potentially an heiress. Special pleading also characterises Peter Constant in *Oak Leaves* ('dressed in blue shirt, green tie, grey coat, and yellow trousers' [**Oak, 75**]); his position entitles him, he believes, to extraordinary considerations, and his money should be able to buy them for him and his family. He attempts to persuade Dame Hatherleigh to cable a friend in America, guaranteeing a place there for his wife (and he lets slip that he, too, intends leaving war-torn England). 'Our income would allow both of us to live there quite well; but this stupid Government won't let us take more than a miserable amount out of the country. I can lodge enough with you to assure your friend that he or she will suffer no financial loss.' [**Oak, 75.**] But Dame Hatherleigh is firm in her insistence that the Constants must stay and take their chances in England, and participate in the common struggle. Peter Constant, however, is indignant: 'I am a Liberal, and I wrote several letters to *The Times*. They'll know this, and if I'm still here, it means torture and the concentration camp for me!' [**Oak, 76.**] Bentham and Constant share a common sense of values in which responsibilities to them outweigh their responsibilities to others.

But Bentham and Constant apparently were born with the values of their class, while O'Casey also investigates a particular group that has bought into those values (and sold out their own in the process); his characterisation of corrupt Union officials is on a much larger scale than the vignettes of these two individuals. In *The Star* he depicts a handful of bureaucrats, five representatives of the workers who ally against the single figure of Red Jim. This excessive number indicates more than just a sketch of an isolated instance: it represents a group-identity, an underlying situation that is diagnostic, and most of Act Two concerns this quintet in contrast with Jim and his rather shaky lieutenant, Brannigan. Four of the five are on hand when the scene opens, being lectured by the Purple Priest, while Sheasker (Jim's self-appointed heir-apparent) looks down from his Caesar-like portrait. O'Casey's value judgments are immediately discernible from his introductory comments: the Secretary 'has a habit of sinking his head on his breast when he is nervous and undecided—which is often; and he is inclined to be cautious and evasive in his answers to questions'; Brallain is 'shifty and ambitious, with a foxy face'; Eglish is 'gathered in the shoulders . . . and likes to take things quietly'; and Caheer is 'thin and mean-looking, giving, sometimes, a little cough of hesitation before he speaks. He is keen, seeking authority rather than power, serving his own conceit.' [Star, 278.] But they have ample opportunity to show themselves as they are: Eglish and Caheer are weak and easily led, clutching at any opportunity that presents itself and self-deceived about easy victories; the Secretary realises the extent of their defection from Jim, and has definite regrets about their actions ('To give Red Jim his due,' he says, 'if it hadn't been for him the men would have had to creep back with their caps in their hands' [Star, 282]); Brallain assumes aspects of leadership, the brains behind the conspiracy, acknowledging his long-range plans: 'When Red Jim's down we can deal with Sheasker.' [Star, 283.]

The worst aspect of these conspirators is saved for Sheasker himself: his vanity and pomposity indicate the range of his totally bourgeois concepts, as he milks compliments for himself and the portrait from the sycophants. The Secretary attempts to be judiciously non-committal, but Eglish and Caheer drip flatteries, although both had castigated Sheasker before his arrival for his fawning on the clergy. Brallain remains aloof from the orgy of adulation, worried that the gift of a portrait from the Fireiron and Fendermakers' Union (along with other presents) might provide Jim with a weapon against the aggrandising conspirators. Again it is Brallain who has thought out the plans for the conspiracy, and while Caheer and Eglish delude themselves with hopes that Jim will capitulate easily, it is the Secretary who sees the situation clearly: 'He'll fight, I'm sure, he'll fight. That's all left for him to do. Take it from me, he won't swoon—he'll fight.' [Star, 285.] The five traitors are unable to stand up to Brannigan, much less to Jim, and fall apart when Jim arrives to resume command. In general Eglish, Caheer and the Secretary are only petty bureaucrats who take orders and carry them out; Brallain has illusions of actually taking command, but his attempts to stand up to Jim are only bravado, while Sheasker has thoroughly involved himself within the power

269

structure, destined to play Father Christmas at the Lord Mayor's celebration. All that stands in the way of these five assuming their newly chosen roles in the established order is Red Jim, O'Casey's most idealised hero, a hero for the future only.

Petit Bourgeoisie

Only a small segment of the O'Casey parade of characters is significantly lower middle-class, and only a handful at most are actually tradesmen. The early one-act 'Nannie's Night Out' takes place in Polly Pender's shop, the Laburnum Dairy, 'a small dairy and provision shop in a working-class district' [**Nannie, 303**], and although Nannie's escapade dominates the action of the play, of central importance is the character of the fifty-year-old widow, Polly Pender. Both Nannie and Mrs Pender have that quality of strength that O'Casey admired; Nannie's burns itself out in self-destruction, and it is the shopkeeper who emerges as a forerunner of Juno and Mrs Breydon. O'Casey describes her as 'a tall, straight, briskly moving woman, of about fifty; age hasn't yet taken all the friskiness of youth out of her. She is a widow, living alone—all her children being either married or dead—working from morning till night, the shop brings her in just enough to keep her going.' [**Nannie, 304.**] And after an eventful day of being hit between the eyes by a bad egg returned by an irate customer, cheated of a doll by a small girl, and almost robbed by a young thug, Polly Pender puts out the light and closes up for the night, deciding to remain alone rather than marry one of the three old codgers. Polly is hardly a portrait of a successful tradesman whose attitudes are shaped by his concern with his trade. Nor is 'Needle' Nugent a better example of the artisan class. Having made a suit for Captain Boyle, the tailor learns from the solicitor that Boyle will not be getting any of the inheritance. He apprehends Boyle in bed and walks off with the suit he made, impervious to the paycock's attempts to talk him into making a coat for him as well.

It is in 'Time to Go' that O'Casey concentrates on a dissection of the merchant who buys cheap and sells dear, and both to excess. The central concern in the one-act play is

with mercantile Ireland, where the norm is cheat-thy-neigh-
bour so that even the cheated acquiesce in an all-pervasive
code of behaviour. The big farmer gets the best of the bargain, while the smaller one takes the most that he can from
the one-sided arrangement, and the owner of the very small
farm can only plead helplessly for credit. Those who innocently cycle into the trap are forced to pay excessively for
their meagre repast. Michael Flagonson, the tavern owner, is
not only persistent in his dishonest business dealing but
actually contemptuous of those who do not cheat. Bull
Farrell, the crooked storekeeper, is full of bravado about
standing up to the clergy by refusing to buy them off with
donations to their charity; he browbeats Flagonson about
this, only to have the tables turned on him when the naïve
O'Hay reports that Farrell's anonymous gift to Canon
Whizzer has been broadcast by the clergyman despite the
storekeeper's 'modesty'. But the most pernicious of all is Mrs
Flagonson, the jingler of the coins, who cheats the cyclists
and bullies her husband into fully condoning her practices:
her finger pokes Flagonson into whatever action she wants
performed.

Into this environment come Kelly and the Widda, each
of whom has accepted the doctrine of selling dear and buying cheap, but each of whom has now felt pangs of conscience for their deal over the cow sold by the Widda to
Kelly. It is only when she feels guilty for having asked too
much and he for having paid too little that the spell is
broken; together they form a rebellious force that challenges
the accepted system and results in Flagonson calling in the
police to arrest the subversives. With their new insights the
two rebels also seem to have developed supernatural powers
of flying by nets flung at them by the manipulators of a dishonest society, Kelly predicting that 'Soon yous'll all be
no more than are those two barren, deadened trees. Then
when yous are silent stiffs, others will count your coins.'
[Time, 289.]

Not all the counters of coins are as nefarious and mean-
spirited as the denizens of that Irish country town in 'Time
to Go'; for some it is only a venial sin, like the miser-who-is-
not-quite-a-miser, Brennan Moore of *Red Roses*, one of the

271

three landlords in the O'Casey canon. Constantly concerned about the safety of his shekels in the Bank of Ireland, and continually supplementing his rents by street-singing for pennies, he nonetheless spends his own money in having the madonna repainted for his benighted Catholic tenants, enjoying both his act of generosity and his sport at their expense when they worry about the statue's disappearance. He is a lovable old man, loved by O'Casey himself, and the nickname of Brennan o' the Moors is both parallel and parody: he may not be a dashing highwayman with a Robin Hood bent, but he is his own minstrel and takes from his own money to give to the poor. The landlord of *The Shadow of a Gunman* is a Mr Mulligan who comes to collect back rent due from Seumas Shields, but gets only an argument for his pains from the disdainful Seumas, who insists, 'You'll get your rent when you learn to keep your rent-book in a proper way.' [Shadow, 101.] Mulligan serves his eviction notice, having objected to Shields writing letters to the newspapers complaining about the property, and to his having allowed lodgers into his rooms, although Mulligan is careful not to offend so dangerous a lodger as the gunman ('not that I'm sayin' anythin' again' you, sir' [Shadow, 103]).

But whereas Moore and Mulligan are essentially concerned about their rents, Miss Mossie in 'Bedtime Story' is mostly preoccupied with respectability: O'Casey classifies her as 'a very respectable lodging-house keeper' [Bedtime, 226], and John Jo Mulligan is in a panic lest she awaken and find Angela Nightingale in his rooms. She is a fearful guardian of her property, puritanical and proper, yet there is a strong indication that she is sexually repressed, having once entered Mulligan's room while walking in her sleep and attempted to seduce him. That at least is Mulligan's version of it, while Miss Mossie only acknowledges to have been sleep-walking. In weighing the personalities of the three landlords it can only be asserted that O'Casey enjoys himself at the expense of all three: none is a particularly characteristic totem of the mercenary and corrupt system that the dramatist is often dissecting; that role is reserved for such entrepreneurs as Flagonson, Farrell, Conroy, Reiligan, Marthraun, Binnington and McGilligan—and the clergyman they kowtow to.

O'Casey reserved his special venom for the employers of young Johnny Casside in *Pictures in the Hallway*. Seven chapters are devoted to Johnny's humiliating experiences as an employee of Hymdin, Leadem & Company,[1] where he is initiated into manhood and browbeaten by the flunkeys of the bosses, seduces his fellow-employee Alice, polishes his technique in stealing from the firm, encounters the dregs of frightened humanity selling their souls in order to keep their jobs, as well as sensitive ones like himself trapped permanently in the snares of necessity, and rises to heights of personal pride in getting himself sacked for refusing to allow himself to be fined for insubordination. The characterisations of the employers, Mr Anthony Dovergull and his brother Mr Hewson, are etched with an acid borrowed from Dickens, to which O'Casey adds his own spittle. A later job at Jason and Company gets Johnny Casside no closer to a permanent position with security, as again he defies the mores of the downtrodden petty bourgeoisie by refusing to be infinitely grateful for the scraps thrown to him. Because he will not remove his hat before the cashier when collecting his wages, Johnny is again cashiered. The schoolboy who cracked his schoolmaster's skull in retaliation for corporal punishment has come no closer as an adolescent to bowing before authority. 'You go back to where you came from, said Johnny vehemently, thrusting an arm through the little window and pointing a finger at Jason; go back and count your gains behind the back o' Jesus; but before you go, tell this bald-headed boyo to hand over all that's comin' to me, quick!' [**Hallway, 281.**]

Assorted Proletarians

A large majority of O'Casey's characters come from the working class, and many of them have already been inspected on the basis of their personalities and functions as major figures in the plays. Given his political directions it follows that O'Casey would have been particularly partial to the proletarians whose cause he championed and among whom he himself swung a pick and an axe. In an age in which leftwing writers glorified the archetypal worker as a paragon of sound mind in a sound body, contrasting in health

273

with the diseased bourgeoisie and the decadent aristocracy, O'Casey was remarkably free from such stereotypes, despite the strongly propagandist portraits of Red Jim and Drishogue, Jack and O'Killigain. That giant in overalls drawn by Hugo Gellert and William Gropper was accepted by O'Casey as an ideal, a rare individual who had risen above the contemporary muck in which an overwhelming majority were unfortunately mired; it is interesting that such ideal proletarians were acknowledged for leadership qualities both by their fellow-workers and by their employers, the bosses often relying heavily upon them. The loss of his best lorry-driver chagrins Sailor Mahan; Reiligan wants to keep his Manus Moanroe; and even Poges recognises the importance of Jack O'Killigain. Long before the American Left despaired of a vast working-class vote for a Henry Wallace (and later feared that that same vote might actually go to George), when Labour Party victories in England produced Ramsay MacDonalds instead of Lenins (in forty-five years of an independent Ireland no Labour Party ever received as much as ten per cent of the seats in the Dail), O'Casey was carefully weighing the difference between the ideal and the attainable.

When four workingmen are portrayed, as in *Purple Dust*, one is a foreman (a Gellert giant), the second is a loyal follower with an interesting mind of his own, while the two others are dolts, comic figures who accept the status quo and bicker among themselves about how to shove a desk in through a narrow doorway—and even O'Dempsey is party to that demeaning argument. (A fifth old codger, sent by the parish priest to work in the manor house, is absurdly breaking holes in the ceiling in a hunt for the spot from which to suspend the light fixture.) Two others in the play are domestics, the middle-aged butler and the young maid, and so much imbued with the ethos of their masters as to render them inert as members of the proletariat: they follow their bosses into destruction, unable to free themselves from slavish dependence upon the ruling élite. Their condition is analogous to that of Barney O'Hay, that pitiful owner of a mere five acres, the rural proletarian of whom the urban Left have long despaired: the compliance of the peasant with his miserable way of life leaves him unable to rebel against the storekeepers' victimisation and the big farmer's aggrandisement.

Nor does O'Casey have any qualms about employing his 'lumpen' proletarians for comic purposes, whether they are the drunken Paycock and his Joxer butty, or the two working-class drunks of 'A Pound on Demand', where Jerry and Sammy fall all over each other in the Post Office attempting to convince the clerk that Sammy has a legitimate right to receive a pound from his savings account despite his inability to write his name legibly. The foibles of the individuals may well be taken as the limitations of their class, but it is as comic individuals that the playwright focuses on them. Sammy Adams is too drunk to be able to understand the situation and continues to repeat the same obvious mistakes: his argumentativeness prevents him from limiting his aggressiveness to self-supporting aspects of the quarrel; instead he defeats his own purposes. Jerry, the soberer of the two, is 'patiently' manipulating him in the demand for the money, often revealing his ulterior motive as a sponger. He has no compunction about getting his butty into trouble, using him without qualms, while Sammy assumes that he has every reason to share Jerry's eagerness for the money. He is not only frustrating his own efforts to get his own money for drink (the first level of humour in the skit), but also frustrating the soberer man's greed by his self-defeating quarrelsomeness (the second level).

Uneducated and often literal-minded, many of O'Casey's worker-types live exceedingly limited lives and project unfortunately limited points of view. Like Mark and Michael, the Home Guard in *Oak Leaves*, they are often no better than they can be expected to be, their attention controlled by their immediate needs and concerns. They do their job, gripe a bit, ask for their tea, but except for their own small corner they have no larger view of what is going on. Even revolutionary workers, those under the influence of Red Jim, are not immune to relapses into defeated attitudes and compliance: the two workers at the Lord Mayor's house in *The Star* are full of miltant talk, sitting down on the job and telling the Mayor that 'it's

time the workers began putting their bums into soft places'
[**Star, 331**]. In much of their conversation the effect of Jim's
indoctrination seems adequate, but there is a querulous edge
to some of their statements that anticipates a possibility of
backsliding, and although they stand their ground before
the Mayor himself, they are quick to give in to the Lady
Mayoress and quick to accuse each other of having lapsed.
'I can never understand why some workers are ready to fall
on their knees the minute a well-dressed cow flits in front
of them,' [**Star, 335**] says the 2nd Workman, a criticism that
is inadvertently a diagnosis of his own condition. And even
more serious is the quick collapse of their assurance of
victory when Joybell breaks the news that the police have
marched on Union headquarters to arrest Jim: 'The people
have failed again. The workers must sleep again; must sing
sad and slow, and sleep again.' [**Star, 336.**] But with the
sound of the bugle for the workers to assemble, they break
out of their despair and go off to join the ranks.

The pattern developed in the last act of *The Star Turns
Red* of rise-fall-rise (the two workers having attained a
plateau of assurance undergo a decline and a resurgence)
is reversed in O'Casey's treatment of the two Rough
Fellows in *Cock-a-Doodle Dandy*. At first these 'peasants
working on the bog' [**Cock, 119**] are images of that healthy
and self-assured worker glorified in Marxist hagiography:
O'Casey designates the first as a 'young, rough-looking
Fellow, well-set and strong' and dresses him in 'dark-brown
corduroy trousers, belted at waist, grey shirt, and scarf of
bright green, with yellow dots' [**Cock, 129**] (his companion
wears 'light-brown corduroy trousers, check shirt, and has
a scarf of light yellow, with green stripes, round his neck'
[**Cock, 130**]). The colourful costuming bodes well for them,
as do two of their initial attitudes, an appreciative eye for
the beauty of Loreleen (with voices of poetic blarney not
unlike that of O'Killigain) and their assertive demands for
higher wages from Marthraun and Mahan. They modulate
from love-song to shouts of defiance, from 'Arra, what
winsome wind blew such a flower into this dread, dhried-up
desert?' [**Cock, 130**] (to Loreleen) to 'You give a guaranteed

week, or th' men come off your bog!' [Cock, 131] (to their bosses).

But Loreleen warns them that she is not for decent men, and it is their 'decentness' which undermines them as potential heroes of the O'Caseyan mould; they are immediately terrified when their desert-flower is presumably transformed into a 'fancy-bred fowl', capitulating into God-fearing subservients: 'th' Missioner said last night that young men should think of good-lookin' things in skirts only in th' presence of, an' undher th' guidance of, old and pious people.' [Cock, 132.] Their potential disintegrates at this point, and they are next seen as stretcher-bearers carrying Julia to the train bound for Lourdes. In their final appearance they have obviously come full circle from their first appreciation of the earthy beauty of Marthraun's daughter. This time they are dragging her forward to be punished, having caught her in a car with Sailor Mahan, and have stolen the money Mahan intended for Loreleen. Whatever diamond was imbedded in their roughness seems permanently crumbled, the jeweller's hand being Father Domineer's and their setting the bogs of Nyadnanave.

Working-class solidarity is often shaky and proletariat ethics often shoved under the carpet (the Rough Fellows who were demanding an extra shilling in the wages of all the workers—Ayamonn's symbolic shilling—wind up stealing Mahan's money for themselves alone), and it is difficult for O'Casey's proletarians to decide between the speeches of their militant leaders and the pressures of their bourgeois society. When Russian timber is reputed to be unloaded in the harbour of Doonavale, the local workers are unsure of their own reaction, but combine antipathy for their bosses with adherence to the voice of their religion: they are intent at first on destroying the shipment. 'What's this whisper about Red timber on th' wharf of Doonavale?' asks the Man of the Musket; 'Communist timber,' echoes the Man of the Pike; 'Atheist timber,' [Ned, 95] adds the Girl at the Door. It is apparent that Nora McGilligan's purpose in leading the others to this confrontation is merely gay maliciousness, for she is the first to insist that the wood not be burned. When Father Fillifogue, torn between defending the Mayor and Deputy Mayor from the mob and insisting on the burning of the timber, actually gives the order, the Man of the Pike is hesitant: 'I dunno, Father, about burnin' it. We handled it outa th' ship, an' nothin' has happened to us.' [Ned, 96.] Nora and Michael then take over the leadership of the 'mob', dissuading them from following Fillifogue and leading them in the direction of Father Ned's drum and the meeting hall, where they will be elected in their fathers' places. 'Folly th' crowd,' says the Man of the Pike, 'an' youse won't lose your way, for people are on their way from th' Glen of the Light, from th' Meadow of Knowledge, an' from th' Gap of Courage; all assemblin' on th' fringe of th' town to march to th' Hill of th' Three Shouts.' [Ned, 101.] If these workers ever wavered, they quickly return to the fold, led by Nora and Michael and Tom, and by the drum of Father Ned. Though Oscar McGunty, also a Doonavale worker, came rushing in to tell Father Fillifogue that the door of the presbytery had been painted a flaming red, he now blows the trumpet to herald the meeting.

Brannigan in *The Star* embodies another weak spot in the health of the working class: although a forceful militant who is eminently successful in bringing Sheasker and his bunch to their knees, he goes off and gets roaring drunk on the money he has taken from them. Jim is furious when Brannigan is reported to have run amok 'in a pub down the street, driving everyone out and drinking their beer!' [Star, 300]—and Brannigan is brought before Jim under guard. 'When you're sober, Brannigan,' Jim tells him, 'you're the Union's finest member; when you're drunk, you're a swine!' [Star, 303.] And Jim undertakes Brannigan's resurrection: whereas all the pledges signed for the Church have been meaningless in keeping Brannigan sober, Jim's demand is sufficient to transform him into a trusted lieutenant. The terminology that Red Jim uses in describing the change in his aide is consciously Biblical: 'My comrade was dead, and is alive again; he was lost, and is found!' [Star, 304]—illustrating O'Casey's insistence that the salvation of the workers as a class is definitely dependent upon a kind of miraculous transformation. The early plays concentrated heavily on their limitations, and this concentration continued on into even the most politically optimistic plays. O'Casey's optimism when displayed cannot actually be equated with naïveté (as various critics maintain when juggling with the discomfiting issue of the dramatist's politics): it depends upon the realisation of several necessary conditions, including the education and re-moralisation of the proletariat, before the star can possibly appear, much less actually turn red.

The Down-and-Out

There is of course an area of the problem that is for O'Casey quite hopeless: those for whom miracles will never be forthcoming. Artistotle disqualified in advance those who are incurably sick or insane from candidacy as tragic heroes; O'Casey seconded the elimination despite the thrust of his humanitarian feelings. The road to Lourdes is a dead end for Julia, with only bravery in the face of death left for her as any sort of alternative to actual despair. She is unfortunately one of the Doomed, a classification that first presents itself with the entrapment of Harry Heegan in a wheelchair and then becomes a dominant motif in *Within the Gates*. But O'Casey is careful to differentiate between the inevitable death of Jannice (who is killed by her illness while she is living life fully) and the really doomed, the Down-and-Out who surrender to death by not living. Godfrey and Herbert, the younger and older chair attendants, are of the latter group, each with a crippled leg and wondering 'Wot'll we do when we file to be able to walk!' [Gates, 120.] Their situation would normally elicit sympathy if it were not for their crippled attitudes: they are depressed by the singing of the Chorus and actively hate the Dreamer for his intimate relationship with life: 'I 'ates that poet chap; I 'ates 'im! 'Ate 'is liveliness. Fair cheek 'ee 'as.' [Gates, 120.] The Dreamer, in consequence, wastes little sympathy on them. 'Here, you two derelict worshippers of fine raiment— when are you going to die!' [Gates, 120] he asks, asserting that 'No one has a right to life who doesn't fight to make it greater.' [Gates, 121.] The battle between them continues throughout the play, as does the parade of the Down-and-

279

Out: 'Suddenly, in the near distance, is heard the roll of a muffled drum, and the mournful chant of the Down-and-Out. The scene seems to grow dark and the air chilly. The two Attendants stiffen, and lines of fright chase away the lines of joy from their faces. The Young Woman, frightened too, turns pale, half rises from her seat, and stares into the distance.' [Gates, 158.] Jannice is also susceptible to the call of the hopeless and it is with great effort that she resists their hypnotic chant.

The battle develops for Jannice's soul: the Bishop, her father, sees the way of the Down-and-Out as the way of salvation and urges her and the chair attendants to join the mournful parade of chanters; the Dreamer and the Atheist argue against the death-grip of the doomed marchers, urging Jannice to stay with life to the end. To the Bishop the Down-and-Out are 'God's own aristocracy, the poor in spirit! Their slogan, Welcome be the Will of God; their life of meek obedience and resignation in that state of poverty unto which it has pleased God to call them, a testimony that God's in His heaven, all's well with the world.' [Gates, 196.] Herbert and Godfrey agree to be saved, but the Bishop now ignores them, his concern being exclusively with his daughter: 'They came close, my child, they came close. They will get you some day, if you do not let me save you now.' [Gates, 197.] The Down-and-Out are a rather ambiguous lot: the Bishop urges Jannice to join them, but immediately afterwards he tries to get her to let him save her instead, in order to avoid her being claimed by them. But there is no ambiguity in the resistance of both the Dreamer and the Atheist to the call of the doomed, and Jannice withstands their call unto the end.

Like *Within the Gates*, 'Hall of Healing' revolves around a situation of despair, but such opponents of despair as the Dreamer and the Atheist are absent in this short play. Instead there is a feeling of completed doom, a hell scene that may be echoed in the title: the doctor who had sympathetically cared for the miserable is now dead himself (God abstracted out of a hopeless world) and the incumbent doctor is resigned to a helpless futility. Alleluia guards the door, but the poor clamour to be allowed in out of the cold.

The contrasts in attitudes among the dispensary patients run the gamut: Red Muffler tries to break through the bureaucracy and indifference to get immediate help for his sick daughter, while Black Muffler is thoroughly conditioned to the routine of the hall of healing, accepting it without a fight. Green Muffler is a novice in the clinic, not having learned the complex mechanical routine of its functioning. He undergoes his initiation: having been told to bring three empty bottles for his medicines, he is astonished to be given pills instead (even the habitual state is not reliable), and denounces the system in his exit speech: 'God forbid I'd ever come here again; but if I have to, I warn that certain person not to mention bottles to me; for if that certain person does, he'll be a sufferin' soul in Purgatory himself, without a one to help him out!' [Hall, 268.] And Red Muffler's wife, Grey Shawl, arrives at the end to announce the death of their child. Red Muffler excoriates the doctor who would not heed his pleading: 'The pair of yous can go home now, an' snore away some other buddin' life! Yous are afraid to fight these things. That's what's th' matter—we're all afraid to fight!' [Hall, 272]— which brings him close to the attitudes of the Dreamer and the Atheist.

Jannice, the Young Woman of *Within the Gates*, has her counterpart in Jenny Sullivan, the Young Woman of 'Hall of Healing'. She too is moribund, but she has not yet learned the extent of her illness; she is timid and understates its seriousness (in contrast to Jentree's overstress of his), preferring to bide her time waiting, allowing other patients to see the doctor ahead of her. She fears the truth about her illness and is brought face-to-face with it when the doctor sends her to the Consumption Dispensary: 'Looka what I've got; looka what he's given me! . . . A note to the Consumption Dispensary o' Charles Street. I'm done for now. I feel faint. I'll lose me job an' all, now. It's me death warrant!' [Hall, 265.] Jenny does not possess Jannice's capacity to die dancing, but she is the sort of person O'Casey is most sympathetic with: she has every reason to live (she is young and beautiful), but she is doomed, and all that is left to her is the Old Woman's kindness in comforting her and seeing her home. Mollser Gogan in *The Plough* and Mollser Conroy in the short story 'A Fall in a Gentle Wind' round out a trio of young female consumptives in the O'Casey canon, the first Mollser carried off in her coffin in the last act, while the second is carried off in an ambulance to the Hospice for the Dying at the end of the story. In *Inishfallen* O'Casey remembers the occupants of his building: 'The young girl below was coughing again. He could see in his mind's eye the bed in which she lay, a heap of clothing, confused with the restless tossing and turning of one in an advanced state of consumption.' [Inish, 156–7.]

The sick and the crippled are the obviously doomed, but so are the hopelessly poor. In *Red Roses* the three vendors, old Eeada, middle-aged Dympna and young Finnoola, have only their religion for hope, their dependence on the statue of Our Lady of Eblana's Poor. 'Each has the same expressionless stare out on life' [Roses, 136], and dressed in black they hawk their wares along the riverside under Dublin's leaden sky, bemoaning their conditions and despondent of any future. To them Dublin is a 'graveyard where th' dead are all above th' ground' [Roses, 186]. Ayamonn's fantasy of a resurrected Dublin, a queen of a city, awakens the three women momentarily, and in that fantasy Finnoola dances with Ayamonn. But the dream ends and reality returns: 'I was lost in a storm of joy, an' many colours, with gay clothes adornin' me,' Dympna reports; 'Dhreamin' I musta been,' adds Finnoola, 'when I heard strange words in a city nearly smothered be stars, with God guidin' us along th' banks of a purple river, all of us clad in fresh garments, fit to make Osheen mad to sing a song of the revelry dancin' in an' out of God's own vision.' [Roses, 203.] But the recurrence of drab reality does not totally destroy the efficacy of the dream, for that dream was a glimpse into a possible future rather than into an impossible paradise. Unlike the Down-and-Out there is a choice for the riff-raff of the Dublin riverside street: they swell the ranks of Ayamonn's Union and join the strike, the wounded Finnoola coming to the church to report the death of Ayamonn Breydon.

Some of the author's greatest sympathy and finest talent

are expended on the downtrodden wife in the story 'The Star-Jazzer', a victim of the tenements who for one glorious moment (like Finnoola) abandons the world of ugliness that is her permanent existence for a mad and wonderful dance alone under the stars at midnight. A household drudge, she has spent the full eighteen hours of her usual Tuesday at washing the clothes, repeatedly trudging up and down ten flights of stairs to fill her bucket at the pump in the back yard; her epiphanic moment is a wild dream of escape, religious ecstasy and autoeroticism, but it returns her to the necessity of mounting the stairs in the dark, more exhausted than ever. Her youth is a dead past ('She should make her mind resolute to burn that photograph. . . . It was merely a sigh for a lost slim figure, pretty face, and a curly mass of brown hair. If she went to a dance there wouldn't be many boys nosing around her now. . . . Eight years of it had skimmed the cream out of her life . . . It was only alone now and in the dark that she could dance before the stars' [Jazzer, 284]); the present intrudes immediately in the demanding body of her husband once she gets into the family bed: 'it wasn't fair for him to bully her into his embraces when she was so tired, tired, tired.' [Jazzer, 285-6.] With six children in eight years of marriage, a full day of washing the family clothes, and a moment of star-jazzing in the dark of the night, she is too tired to resist the inevitable defeat.

The Military

Attitudes towards soldiers are usually mixed, but one distinction that is always an important one is between *ours* and *theirs*, and in the case of Ireland under the Union Jack this dichotomy had even greater significance. British conscription of Irishmen to fight for the Crown was as prevalent as American use of Negro 'volunteers' to fight for Mister Charlie: economic deprivation makes the security of an Army career attractive and even imperative, for the underprivileged. *I Knock at the Door* records the enthusiasm with which Johnny's brothers, Tom and Michael, followed the haunting sound of Benson's drum into Her Majesty's armed forces, escaping the drab prospects of job-hunting in Dublin (and the complete degradation of Benson and both brothers seems to follow logically from either their Army experiences or their inability to adjust to demobilisation). While Irish soldiers fought for Britain in the trenches in France, British soldiers were being killed by Irish insurgents in Dublin during Easter week of 1916: the confused reaction to this paradox is seen in Bessie Burgess's hysteria, on one hand denouncing Captain Brennan, 'th' professor of chicken-butcherin' there, finds he's up against somethin' a little tougher even than his own chickens, an' that's sayin' a lot!' [**Plough, 233**] while on the other championing the Dublin Fusiliers on their way to the trenches where her son is fighting: 'There's th' men marchin' out into th' dhread dimness o' danger, while th' lice is crawlin' about feedin' on th' fatness o' the land!' [**Plough, 191.**] And *The Silver Tassie* portrays those sons of Bessie Burgess before, during, and after the conflicts of the Great War, the survivors and the maimed.

The concentration on political inter-involvement does not carry over from *The Plough* to *The Tassie*, where O'Casey's preoccupation is with the soldier as human being rather than as Irishman or West Briton. None of the Dubliners fighting in France is particularly concerned with the war against Germany or the British cause: they are involved with the War and with life-and-death, and with the human problems of being a soldier. As the trio prepares to return to the battlefield, Harry Heegan, drunk with the glory of the football victory and the adulation of Jessie Taite, considers extending his leave without permission, but Barney Bagnal is the soul of reality: 'No, no, napoo desertin' on Active Service. Deprivation of pay an' the rest of your time in the front trenches. No, no. We must go back!' And Teddy Foran, having wrecked his flat in a tantrum because of his wife's presumed infidelity, sounds the note of bitterness: 'A party for them while we muck off to the trenches!' [**Tassie, 31.**] The war scene itself is diagnostic: the nameless and almost faceless group of soldiers complain about their lot, are visited by a civilian intent on improving morale, receive packages from home containing prayer books and a ball to play with, and prepare to go back into battle. Harry himself is never seen, but the

4th Soldier is designated as being 'very like Teddy' [**Tassie, 37**], while Barney the compliant civilian is in the stocks for having stolen a chicken. The second half of the play deals with the crippled footballer, the blinded wife-beater, and the fortunate chicken-thief, with arms and legs and eyes intact, and the prize of Jessie Taite to reward him for having survived unharmed. Yeats's criticism that O'Casey had not participated in the Great War and therefore did not know it at first hand is irrelevant: *The Tassie* is about War and the Human Animal, a universalised condition at the centre of which the dramatist has isolated Three Soldiers for careful scrutiny.

By contrast the Irish warriors in *The Plough* are civilians playing at soldiers, but playing seriously because of their convictions. Nonetheless, Jack Clitheroe might have remained on the sidelines had his rank of Commandant not been forthcoming (or had Nora been successful in keeping news of it from him). A bricklayer by profession, and newly married to a clinging wife, Jack saw in even the pathetically unprofessional Citizen Army a touch of romantic glory ('he bought a Sam Browne belt, an' was always puttin' it on an' standin' at th' door showing it off, till th' man came an' put out th' street lamps on him,' [**Plough, 166**] gossips Mrs Gogan). Insufficient motivation does not alter the fact of Commandant Clitheroe's death, nor does the patriotism of Lieutenant Langon prevent his lamenting, 'Everyone else escapin', an' me gettin' me belly ripped asundher!' [**Plough, 234**.] The Irish Volunteer officer dies in the arms of the Citizen Army captain, while the denizens of Dublin's slums unite to appropriate those basic necessities and frivolous luxuries of life that had always been denied them. And acts of heroism are not limited to the combatants, Fluther and Bessie contributing the same kinds of self-sacrifice demanded of the military.

But Captain Brennan, in uniform and under arms to free Ireland from British rule, reacts violently to the actions of self-interest displayed by the populace: 'Irish be damned! Attackin' an' mobbin' th' men that are riskin' their lives for them. If these slum lice gather at our heels again, plug one o' them, or I'll soon shock them with a shot or two

meself!' [**Plough,** 232.] If there is anything equivocal in
O'Casey's handling of the looters in the play, there certainly is not in a recording of the events of Easter Week in the
autobiographies: 'Sean watched their wonderful activity,
and couldn't desecrate their disorder with dishonour. All
these are they who go to Mass every Sunday and holy day
of obligation; whose noses are ground down by the clergy
on the grindstone of eternal destiny; who go in mortal fear
of the threat of a priest, he thought; but now he was glad
to see they hadn't lost their taste for things material. In spite
of the clergy's fifing and drumming about venial and mortal
sin, they were stretching out their hands for food, for
raiment, for colour, and for life.' [**Window,** 412.]

Attitudes towards the British troops in Ireland during
the Easter Rising and the subsequent Troubles appear in
the plays and the autobiographies, where regular Army
troops, Auxiliaries, and Black and Tans play their parts.
'If it's the Tommies,' moans Seumas, 'it won't be so bad,
but if it's the Tans, we're goin' to have a terrible time.'
[**Shadow,** 146.] In this case it is the Tans, and Grigson has
a terrible time, and Minnie is arrested and shot; in *The
Plough* it is the Army, the Wiltshires, who come to take
away the body of dead Mollser, Corporal Stoddart asking,
'Was she plugged!' [**Plough,** 249] and sounding disappointed when he hears that it was only consumption. Sergeant
Tinley expresses his annoyance at the guerrilla tactics of
the insurgents: 'That's not playing the goime: why down't
they come into the owpen and foight fair!' [**Plough,** 255.]
The final moments of the play show the Corporal and the
Sergeant having tea in the emptied flat, and singing 'Keep
the Home Fires Burning'. Tommies during Easter Week,
the Tans during the Troubles: the pattern for the two plays
parallels the pattern in the autobiographies. It is a British
soldier who marches Sean home from arrest in the granary,
only to find that there is no food in the flat. Sean indicates
that 'a huckster's round the corner, but I've no money to
pay for it.' ''E'll give it, 'e'll 'ave to; you come with me,
said the Tommy; Gawd blimey, a man 'as to eat!' [**Window,**
422.] But in *Inishfallen*, in the 'Raid' chapter, the sound of
broken door-glass is an ominous one for Sean: 'Which were

they—the Tommies or the Tans? Tans, thought Sean, for the Tommies would not shout so soullessly, nor smash the glass panels so suddenly; they would hammer on the door with a rifle-butt, and wait for it to be opened. No; these were the Tans.' [Inish, 61.]

O'Casey's system of analysis becomes a sophisticated one after numerous experiences in embattled Ireland, and he muses over the distinctions between the regular Army men, the professional Auxies, and the hired thugs that were the Tans: 'he guessed that a part of them were the Auxies, the classic members of sibilant and sinister raiders. The Tans alone would make more noise, slamming themselves into a room, shouting to shake off the fear that slashed many of their faces. The Auxies were too proud to show a sign of it. The Tommies would be warm, always hesitant at knocking a woman's room about; they would even be jocular in their funny English way, encouraging the women and even the children to grumble at being taken away from their proper sleep.' [Inish, 63.] These hairline distinctions are soon supported by the events of the raid, when Sean finds himself caught between the humiliating demand of a Tans officer to shout to Hell with Ireland, and a military officer who saves him by ordering him out into the street.

The Black and Tan style of victimisation is recast years later for the Prerumble to *The Drums of Father Ned*, when Binnington and McGilligan are the butt of their taunts during a raid. Four Tans and an Officer have great sport at their expense, attempting to force the two sworn enemies into shaking hands. These Tans are as vicious as any portrayed by O'Casey, the Officer giving the command to his men to fire at the Sinn Fein: 'I'll court-martial any man who hits arm or leg of these Sinn Fein murderers. Hit head, hit belly, and hit heart!' [Ned, 11.] Yet there is a mitigating element in this later portrayal, not that O'Casey has mellowed in his attitude towards them, but that his focus is on the Binnington-McGilligan feud. Both Irishmen are somewhat commendable in their bravery, preferring death to shaking hands with each other, but they are also symptomatic of what is wrong with Irish bravery: their kind has flourished under the new nation. The Officer of

287

11

the Tans is shrewd in letting them live when his men are eager to kill them: 'No, you fool! Can't you see that these two rats will do more harm to Ireland living than they'll ever do to Ireland dead?' [Ned, 10.] He is assuming that the British will retain control of the country and that the Binningtons and McGilligans will prevent the Irish from ever uniting into a successfully rebellious force. O'Casey, commenting on the new Ireland, sees these two as diagnostic of the corruption and hatred that rules the new nation.

The Literati

Mirror in My House, the cumulative title for Sean O'Casey's six volumes of self-examination, serves as a mammoth Portrait of the Artist, both self-consciously and with an attempt at objectivity in its casting of the artist as Johnny/Sean Casside. In the plays, however, there is little projection of O'Casey himself as a character, as a personality translated into fictional situations, but on several occasions the playwright offers a commentary on the literary scene in Ireland. This commentary is prevalent in the auto-biographies, where O'Casey as critic spares no one in his incisive investigation. Respect for Joyce and Shaw, fondness for Lady Gregory, admiration tempered by a critical glance for Yeats,[2] and scorn for many another of the ranking dignitaries can be found in the last four books, with AE ('Dublin's Glittering Guy'), George Orwell, Noel Coward, and James Agate suffering multiple bruises and lacerations. An overall dramatic recasting of the characters of the literary scene did not come until late in O'Casey's career, in 'Behind the Green Curtains', the one play in which the literary establishment is the primary centre of interest. Whether the view here reflects O'Casey's recollection of Dublin literati during the 1920s or is actually a hypothesising of Irish intellectuals of the 1950s based on O'Casey's attempts to keep abreast of changes in Ireland, is not specifically discernible from the play itself: it is probably an amalgam of both. It may also represent a cumulative process of the entire age captured in a single series of events.

The Lionel Robartes whose death touches off the contretemps in the play owes a great deal to the figure of William

Butler Yeats, and O'Casey is careful to sign Yeats's name to the dead man in several ways (the Robartes name; the invocation of Yeats in the scene—'If only we had Yeats with us now!' [**Curtains, 18**]; and Robartes's Protestant background). Robartes is described by Chatastray as one 'who was always ready to help young actor and writer; a famous playwright, a doctor of literature; a distinguished lecturer' [**Curtains, 17–18**]. When Whycherly McGerra, the dramatist, sneers at the mention of Yeats's name ('Makes me mad to see people fancyin' thundher an' lightning in Ireland's sky when th' name of Yeats is mentioned' [**Curtains, 19**]), there are indications of the extent to which the play is a *drame à clef*, especially in the light of a telling passage in *Inishfallen*: 'Some in Dublin hated Yeats, official catholics feared him, and a group of younger writers disliked his booming opinions on literature and insubstantial things without any local habitation or name. A number of these last, headed by F. J. [*sic*] Higgins, the poet, Liam O'Flaherty and Brinsley MacNamara, the novelists, and Cecil Salkeld, the young painter, had started a Radical Club to nourish the thoughts and ambitions of the young writers, in opposition to the elderly and wild speculation of Yeats and the adulatory group that trailed longingly after him. Some of these wanted to hook in Sean so that his newer influence might be useful in putting Yeats in his improper place.' [**Inish, 169.**] For the record it should be noted that the 'Curtains' group consists of an Abbey actor, a dramatist, a poet, a gossip writer and a patron of the arts.

The quintet in 'Curtains' is not unlike the quintet of Union misleaders in *The Star*: two of the group are minor nonentities, almost indistinguishable from each other (McGeera and actor Bunny Conneen are sycophantic spongers, intellectually dishonest and usually conforming, despite their occasional inclinations to kick against the pricks). Jack McGeelish, the gossipist, is the most reprehensible of the five: he lacks all pretension to being a serious artist of any kind, and is the most pernicious backbiter; on the other hand, Leslie Horawn, the poet and member of the Irish Academy, seems somewhat better than the other three: although much like the others most of the time, he is most often the instigator of a movement to rebel and is least given to personal infighting—but in the last analysis, he too conforms. Chatastray, of course, is intended to stand apart from the minor four, and has the opportunity of being the central male figure of the play. It is on his decision that the action hinges: had he chosen to follow his convictions, he would have emerged as the hero, winning Reena and proving himself, thus relegating Boeman to the position of the author's spokesman and a catalytic agent of the action.

Chatastray is a factory owner and art patron; he distinguishes himself in his moments of resolution, refusing to fire Boeman, and refusing to prevent the intermarriage that threatens to ruin his business. He has definite doubts about the Church and its politics, and makes an effort to resist, denouncing the sham artists as frauds; but at the crucial moment he finds himself too tied to his established world to be able to shatter the status quo. He gives up Reena and the terrors of having to think for himself, which would mean ostracism and physical danger, for acquiescence and conformity. O'Casey's satiric technique in *The Star*, the off-centre kind of names he gives his villains (Caheer, Eglish, Sheasker, Brallain) is duplicated here in McGeera, Horawn, McGeelish, Conneen, and Chatastray.

The Sean O'Casey as budding writer, immersed in many of the arts and awakening to the world of vital culture, is mirrored in the autobiographic Casside and the quasi-autobiographic Ayamonn Breydon. Lesser portraits of that artist can be found in the Dreamer, a passionate believer in the efficacy of story and song, and beginning to find himself publishing his efforts, and in Donal Davoren, the poet manqué, whose self-entrapment in the image of Shelley dooms any legitimate involvement with poetry. Davoren is a poseur and, as Krause notes, 'actually a "shadow" of a poet, a "shadow" of a gunman—a shadow-man who doesn't know who he is.'[3] Donal's labelling of himself, in a desperate moment of self-criticism, as a poet and a poltroon, indicates only a partial acknowledgment of his sham: he has not associated his defection as a responsible human being (allowing Minnie to bear his burden) with his effete playing of the role of a poet. His inability to participate actively in the reality of life around him limits his potential as an artist. The Dreamer's position is much superior, but he himself is not the centre of the action of *Within the Gates*, where the tragic heroine takes precedence over the chronicler of tragic events. Only Ayamonn lives his life and his art fully, and is the artist rewarded by an active role in the reality of existence. Conversely, a special scorn is reserved for the scribblers of the Press who pervert their function, the Christy Kornavaun of 'Curtains' and, comically, the two journalists of 'Figuro'—one of whom is blind, while the other is deaf. The headnote to 'Curtains' contains O'Casey's statement of belief in the legitimacy of the Fourth Estate when its practices are honest: 'As if journalists weren't writers, too! They are the most influential of all, for these are they who speak, not only to some of the people all the time, or all the people some of the time, but to all the people all the time. Therefore are they very dangerous if so be they refuse to walk, not within the light—for few of us do or can—but within the shadow of truth, courage, and sincerity.' [**Curtains, 1.**]

Rogues' Gallery
Special notice should be given a mysterious trio called Kelly, Burke, and Shea in the course of Sean O'Casey's autobiographies. They take on a life of their own, despite the little information given about them or even the suggestion that they are always the *same* Kelly, Burke, and Shea throughout, for at times O'Casey refers to them in the plural as well. What they stand for soon becomes apparent: they are those faceless and soulless who are outside the Pale, the deformers of life both for themselves and for anyone on whom they can exert their influence.

They make their first appearance innocently enough when Johnny is visiting Kilmainham Jail and wishes he were back on his own street instead, away from this 'Royal Risidence'; the three at this point are the children he plays with: 'he wished he was well away out of it all; at play with Kelly or Burke or Shea; or tryin' to say something nice to Jennie Clitheroe.' [**Hallway, 45.**] In their next

291

incarnation, early in *Drums*, they are credited with complicity in the writing of an epic book on Home Rule, 'compiled from the original sources by the sage himself, deep in a corner under a secret rowan-tree, in the dim cloisters of the old Abbey of St Fownes, the Soggart Aroon acting as secretary, assisted by Kelly and Burke and Shea all in their jackets green, with the Bard of Armagh stringing the harp to *He's the Man You Don't See Every Day* to give their minds a lift.' [**Window,** 14–15.] It is apparent here that Kelly-Burke-Shea are Irish to a fault, and they soon show up in the crowd at the *Playboy* rioting, in a delightfully Joycean catalogue that O'Casey often indulged in: 'Shoved hither and thither he was by Shamus O'Brien, Kelly and Burke and Shea, Clare's dragoons, Lesbia with her beaming eye, the Exile of Erin, the Lily of Killarney, Slattery's mounted fut, Father O'Flynn, the Rose of Tralee,' [**Window,** 172] and so on. And towards the end of *Drums* the trio is representative of those Irish soldiers who went to fight in France for God, Asquith, and King George V: 'the swinging columns of Kellys, Burkes, and Sheas tramped to the quays, and, singing, went forth to battle for England, little nations, and homes unfit for humans to live in.' [**Window,** 400.]

And in describing the Civil War period in *Inishfallen* O'Casey sums up the situation in his succinct statement that 'The Kelleys, the Burkes, and the Sheas were at one anothers' throats.' [**Inish,** 114.] Their final form is the sinister one, the point at which O'Casey sees them archetypally as The Enemy, the worst of the 'Micks', the narrowminded and the vicious. *Sunset and Evening Star* opens with a warning letter from Irish-Americans who have seen *Juno* in New York and are offended by the maligning of the Irish and by the foul language: the letter is signed by Kelly, Burke, and Shea, and O'Casey comments, 'Sign your name, Kelly, sign your name, Burke, sign your name, Shea—this'll put the wind up him! O advocates of heaven. Their letter was a *cry di curé.* Comrades of the great war against profunity! Oh, sweet and salient natures! A chosen three, who carry great green banners in St Patrick's Day Purrade, and are blessed by father Spiellman as they go bye byes.' [**Sunset,** 2.] The development of the three from innocent playmates to the sworn enemy reflects many another such transition in O'Casey's attitudes toward the characters who peopled his world and were transmuted to his stage. He saw the best in even the worst of them, but remained worldly enough to recognise the dangers in their fanatical allegiance to their faiths, in their refusal to think for themselves, in their hatred of what they did not understand, and in their worship of Death and negation of Life.

Notes

PREFACE (pp. vii–x)

  1. David Krause, *A Self-Portrait of the Artist as a Man: Sean O'Casey's Letters* (Dublin: The Dolmen Press, 1968), p. 10.

  2. Krause, *Sean O'Casey: The Man and His Work* (New York: Macmillan, 1960), p. 30.

  3. Saros Cowasjee, *Sean O'Casey: The Man Behind the Plays* (London: Oliver and Boyd, 1963).

1. THE WORLD SCENE (pp. 1–9)

  1. This is the sort of contention that is best supported by internal evidence (the later plays themselves and the autobiographies), but an external piece of evidence need not be overlooked: even so hostile a critic of O'Casey's self-exile as Gabriel Fallon comments regarding the year 1961 that O'Casey was 'a regular reader of the *Irish Times*' (*Sean O'Casey, The Man I Knew*, Boston: Little Brown and Co., 1965, p. 195). Fallon, however, would never agree that O'Casey kept in sufficient contact with his Irish material: 'James Joyce succeeded in bringing his Dublin away with him; O'Casey regrettably left his behind' (ibid., p. 116).

  2. See *The Green Crow*, pp. 194–5, and *Rose and Crown*, p. 160.

  3. An important supplement exists in O'Casey's strong background in Irish lore and legend, a rural introduction to Ireland available to even the most urban of Dubliners during his developing years. The 1922 story 'The Corncrake' is an instance in which O'Casey used folk material for his first efforts, and the one-act play 'The End of the Beginning' he reminds us in his autobiography 'is almost all founded on a folk-tale well known over a great part of Europe. All O'Casey's children have read it under the name of *Gone is Gone*' (*Sunset*, p. 318).

2. A PRIDE OF PAYCOCKS (pp. 10–65)

1. 'The Corncrake' (1922) antedates the published plays and contains early hints of the type. As David Krause comments, 'It is an amusing story about some practical jokers who make fools of two "arguefying" old codgers, a pair of bull-necked clowns who are roughly-sketched portraits of the kind of comic characters he was to create in his plays' (*Sean O'Casey*, p. 35). The comic pair, Ginger Gilligan and Lanky Lonergan, have no particular characteristics of their own in this short yarn except that they argue with each other constantly and over any issue. The 'mischievous gossoons', Shawn Beg and Sheumas Ruadh, have leprechaunish qualities that the playwright employed at various times in the plays.

2. In *Drums under the Windows* O'Casey describes his experience in St Vincent's Hospital, where he apparently encountered the prototype for Sylvester Heegan and conceived of the situation on which *The Tassie* was based. As the author tells it, during prayers 'Sean recognised the voice of the leader as that of Den Daffy, in for urethral stricture, due for an operation soon, and dreading it: a big, burly, bald-headed docker, own brother to Sylvester Daffy ... [and] own brother, too, to Cock Daffy, one of the best football backs Dublin had ever known' (*Drums*, p. 375). Add the Great War and O'Casey's play begins to take shape.

3. Robert Hogan's explanation is decidedly different: 'The act has occasionally been criticised because Simon and Sylvester's appearance in the hospital is both unexplained and improbable. It seems a mistake to criticise a nonrealistic play on realistic grounds, however, and about as valid as criticising *Alice in Wonderland* for containing improbabilities' (*The Experiments of Sean O'Casey*, New York: St Martin's Press, 1960, pp. 67–8).

4. '—nothin' but thrash, too. There's one I was lookin' at dh'other day: three stories, The Doll's House, Ghosts, an' The Wild Duck—buks only fit for chiselurs!' (*Juno*, p. 23). There is a fine coincidence in O'Casey's choice of Ibsen here, since James Joyce in his *Stephen Hero* manuscript (not published until 1944 and in no way available to O'Casey in 1924) has Simon Daedalus attempt to read his son's favourite playwright, Henrik Ibsen (the famed Henry Gibson of Joyce's university days): 'Mr Daedalus, anyhow, suspected that *A Doll's House* would be a triviality in the manner of *Little Lord Fauntleroy* and, as he had never been even unofficially a member of that international society which collects and examines psychical phenomena, he decided that *Ghosts* would probably be some uninteresting story about a haunted house. He chose the *League of Youth* in which he hoped

to find the reminiscences of like-minded roysterers and, after reading through two acts of provincial intrigue, abandoned the enterprise as tedious' (*Stephen Hero*, London: Jonathan Cape, 1960, pp. 92–3. U.S. ed. Norfolk, Connecticut: New Directions, 1963, p. 88.) What a paycock we have in Simon!

5. O'Casey calls the play *The Hawk's Well* (*Inishfallen*, pp. 372–3).

6. Drink is the curse, cure, plague and panacea of the Irish working class, and always good on stage for a comic situation. Fluther's attempts at teetotaling in the first act are soon derided by his enthusiasm in the pub scene and his even greater enthusiasm for 'liberating' a jug of whiskey in the third act. But he is never quite the total drunk that Boyle is at the end of *Juno*, nor as drunk as Boyle's double in 'A Pound on Demand', Sammy Adams. Without the Boyle family situation as serious backdrop for his drunker self-destruction, Sammy's dilemma is exclusively comic, but paycock characteristics are significantly revealed. His butty Jerry is obsessively concerned with Sammy succeeding in his withdrawal of a pound from postal savings: the less-drunk Jerry acts the role of the solicitous friend, standing up for Sammy's rights and attempting to keep Sammy standing up long enough to sign for the money. But it is obvious that Sammy's pound if procured will provide for Jerry's drinks as well, and Jerry like Joxer is transparent as a fair-weather sponge.

7. Joxer Daly is introduced by Boyle as 'Past Chief Ranger of the Dear Little Shamrock Branch of the Irish National Foresters' (*Juno*, p. 49).

8. Mrs Gogan calls herself Maggie in Act One, Cissie and Jinnie in Act Two, and Jennie in Act Three (*Plough*, pp. 163, 202, 204, 228); Fluther addresses her as Jinnie (p. 204). O'Casey quotes her as saying, 'Ne'er a one o' Jennie Gogan's kids was born outside of th' bordhers of the Ten Commandments' (*Inishfallen*, p. 387), but the text actually reads: 'any kid, livin' or dead, that Jinnie Gogan's had since, was got between th' bordhers of th' Ten Commandments!' (*Plough*, p. 204).

9. She too is overendowed with first names: she begins as 'comely Bessie Ballynoy' and then refers to herself twice as Nellie (*Inishfallen*, pp. 60, 67, 71).

10. Anthony Butler does not cast so sanguine an eye upon such petty thievery: he suspects a serious psychological malady is involved in O'Casey's early tendency toward light-fingeredness, invoking the psychiatrist Flugel on the subject: 'Flugel

pointed out that paranoia often leads to crime, and the pilfering fits into the picture in this way' ('The Early Background', *The World of Sean O'Casey*, ed. Sean McCann, London: Four Square Books, 1966, p. 29).

11. It should come as no surprise that the critic who took O'Casey to task was James Agate. In *Sunset and Evening Star* O'Casey indicates that 'Agate had been invited to see the play and give his views on it in the coming issue of the *Sunday Times*. Agate came, watched the rehearsal through, and, on the following Sunday, denounced the play as a worthless one; more, that it was an attack on England when England was helpless and unable to reply!' (p. 162).

12. Except from the kindest member of the audience, O'Casey himself. Many years later he comments on Poges and Stoke: 'The characters are foolish, inept, pompous; but they are comic, at times pathetic, and all through likeable, if not exactly lovable. But Time and Change do not care a damn for these lovable things, neither can the playwright care either. All that they are, and all they represent, must go' ('Purple Dust in Their Eyes', *Under a Colored Cap*; New York: St Martin's Press, 1963, p. 264).

13. An examiner of O'Casey's methods of characterisation must rely heavily upon those airtight nutshells of character-depiction so often presented by the playwright as initial introductions to his people. David Krause observes that 'something should be said about his expansive stage directions. He probably picked up the habit from his early reading of Shaw's plays. One could argue that, in the strict sense, the kind of subjective comments both of these playwrights make on their characters in the stage directions properly belong to the novel rather than the drama. The playwright can only use dialogue to introduce the reflections and judgments that the novelist develops through indirect discourse, But apparently O'Casey was not one to be intimidated by such strict logic, and like Shaw he assumed that genius can make its own rules' (*Sean O'Casey*, p. 252).

14. Although the manservant Barney announces the Canon as 'Creehewel' (*Dust*, p. 85), the spelling is 'Chreehewel' both in the list of 'Characters in the Play' (p. 2) and when the First Workman refers to him (p. 9).

15. The wording of Juno's prayer is exactly that of Mrs Tancred, except that 'Sacret Heart o' Jesus' is substituted for 'Sacret Heart of the Crucified Jesus'.

16. In *I Knock at the Door* the prototype of Alleluia-Aloysius is given the name Francis.

297

17. That this is at all in Aloysius's favour can be evidenced from the 'Pain Parades Again' chapter of *I Knock at the Door*, where Mrs Casside, upon return from the eye clinic, sings 'The Rose of Tralee', accompanied by Johnny.

18. O'Casey's tendency to endow factory foremen with far more positive characteristics than these is an important one: in most cases the foreman is a proletarian leader, a man of political consciousness and a highly valued worker who has earned his position, respected by both his employer and those who work at his command. This phenomenon will be discussed in Chapter 4.

19. O'Casey reports that 'On August 5, 1953 . . . Radio Eireann announced that a new Dispensary was about to be built, at a cost of something over a thousand pounds, in Killashandra, Co. Cavan, to replace a shack that had existed there as a dispensary for near on a hundred years. And what kind of a Dispensary, these days, can be built for the price mentioned? Are they building there a small cabin of clay and wattles made?' (*Sunset*, p. 317).

20. Marthraun's top-hat occasion with 'His Brightness' has its parallel in an incident O'Casey records with a 'man who owns a doctorate in a university' who accosts O'Casey for instructions on the proper placement of his top-hat during a reception for 'His Excellency', Timothy Healy (*Inishfallen*, pp. 208–11). O'Casey's attitude is the same towards the University man and 'His Excellency' as it is toward Marthraun and 'His Brightness'.

21. Volume IV of *Collected Plays* does not include the 'Morality' label on the title page of *Within the Gates*, but it is retained in *Selected Plays of Sean O'Casey* (New York: George Braziller, 1954), p. 373.

22. There is no first name of McGilligan in the listing of the characters of the play, but his wife twice addresses him as Mick; the London edition of the play has as its subtitle 'A Mickrocosm of Ireland', O'Casey apparently engaging the term Mick as a label for his Irish paycocks.

23. Young Michael Binnington is no Mick, having been named for Michael Collins. O'Casey is at his subtlest in establishing this correspondence: a picture of Collins hangs in the Binnington living room, and young Binnington's age suggests that he was born in the mid-1920s.

3. A VENERATION OF MOTHERS (pp. 66–93)

1. O'Casey's method of dating is rather cavalier: he was born 30 March, 1880.

2. *The Backward Look: A Survey of Irish Literature*, London: Macmillan 1967, p. 216 (U.S. ed. *A Short History of Irish Literature: A Backward Look*, New York: Capricorn Books 1968, p. 216).

3. O'Casey did not begin work on *Red Roses* and on the autobiographies until after the Spanish Civil War had begun (he uses it as a point of reference in *Purple Dust*, as will be noted in Chapter 4). There is some evidence that the three colours were a later emendation dating from a realised parallel with the colours of the Spanish loyalist cause, for in *I Knock at the Door* the first mention of the mother's plants is of 'two geraniums, one white, the other red, and the purple-cloaked fuchsia blossoming blithely amid the wrack of the common things around them' (*Knock*, p. 232). But two volumes later the autobiographer changes his flower arrangement to red, gold, and purple, although the actual order varies (see *Drums*, pp. 309, 311, 312, 319, 322, 325).

4. Playwright Denis Johnston is convicted of this shortcoming when he visits O'Casey in Devon in *Sunset and Evening Star* (pp. 96–8).

5. O'Casey used the same effect again in 'The Moon Shines on Kylenamoe,' where Martha echoes her husband's last words—for strictly comic purposes in this case.

6. The printed edition of the play unfortunately gives this speech to Mrs Binnington, but it is obvious that this is an error, and that only Nora's mother, Mrs McGilligan, can be the speaker.

4. THE HERO AS HERO (pp. 94–144)

1. R. M. Fox identifies the source character: 'One man I knew was Captain Seumas McGowan of the Irish Citizen Army who appears in the play as Maguire, the rebel with the bag of bombs, who goes "catching butterflies at Knocksedan" ' ('Civil War and Peace', *The World of Sean O'Casey*, p. 48). John Keohane reports a visit to O'Casey in 1964: 'When he learned I lived in Sligo he had another talking point. Seumas McGowan, a Sligoman, he said was one of his best friends during the "troubled times", but "I suppose the poor fellow is dead and gone" ' (ibid., p. 178).

2. As had O'Casey himself. This, and several other characteristics that will be mentioned later, indicate an odd degree of autobiographic coincidence in the portrayal of Seumas Shields. But as we have seen in Chapter 2, O'Casey is in many ways sympathetic with Seumas and uses him at times as a spokesman.

3. In *Inishfallen* O'Casey parallels the historic events of *The*

Gunman in a chapter titled 'The Raid', where he postulates the figure of the Cuckold as Hero in juxtaposition to the Lover as Coward. Sean is visited in his tenement room by a neighbour, Mrs Ballynoy, after a raid; her husband is presumably 'on a country job', and she seeks refuge in Sean's bed. But before she can actually execute her seduction of the timorous Casside, the Tans return and find Charlie Ballynoy and his arsenal in the carpentry shed, and the unsuspected gunman is dragged away shouting like Minnie, 'Up th' Republic!' (p. 78).

4. A partial explanation for the absence of the traditional young male hero from the early O'Casey plays may be gleaned from the personalities of O'Casey's brothers, the Tom, Michael and Archie of the early autobiographies. Each in his own way is decidedly disappointing; each falls victim to the degrading influences his environment exacts, a condition analogous to that described by Joyce in *A Portrait of the Artist as a Young Man* (1916): 'When the soul of a man is born in this country there are nets flung at it to hold it back from flight' (London: Heinemann, 1964, p. 188. U.S. ed. New York: Viking Press, 1964, p. 203). In emulation of the father whose personal superiority he very much believed in, Sean flew by those nets—but was the only one of the siblings to do so successfully.

5. An important predecessor to Manus Moanroe is 'Father' Keegan, the spoiled priest of George Bernard Shaw's *John Bull's Other Island,* a play much admired by O'Casey.

6. At the beginning of the play Ayamonn is rehearsing the murder of King Henry VI by Gloster, the infamous Shakespeare villain who in the next drama, *Richard III,* went on to woo and win the widow of another of his victims. Inspector Finglas attempts to duplicate Richard's wooing but without success. O'Casey's use of Shakespeare in *Red Roses* (symbol of the House of Lancaster in the War of the Roses) may have some significance: for all his villainy, Richard was a man of action, a dynamic leader. In Act Two of *Red Roses* Ayamonn is reading *Hamlet:* the inactive hero muses over his potential course of action and suggests that the introspective Ayamonn might also prove to be 'pigeon-livered, an' lack gall/To make oppression bitther' (*Roses,* p. 163). That the playwright is putting Shakespeare to work for him is further substantiated by the changes wrought on the rehearsal scene from its depiction in the second volume of the autobiography to *Red Roses for Me:* in the former Johnny Casside plays Henry to his brother's Richard, but in the play Ayamonn has the role of the man of action (see 'Shakespeare Taps at the Window,' *Pictures in the Hallway,* p. 22).

7. Edgar's attitude is echoed by John Osborne's Jimmy Porter: 'There aren't any good, brave causes left. If the big bang does come, and we all get killed off, it won't be in aid of the old-fashioned, grand design. It'll just be for the Brave New-nothing-very-much-thank-you' (*Look Back in Anger* [1956]: London: Faber and Faber, 1962, pp. 84–5).

8. O'Casey, who often duplicates material in both a play and the autobiographies, re-uses the argument between Michael and the elder Irishmen in the 'Wild Life in New Amsterdam' chapter of *Rose and Crown*. A comparison of a segment from each will indicate the parallel usage:

—Oh, said Sean, trying to shuttle the argument off, the wide-open spaces are needed when a row starts between Wittenberg and Knox on the one hand, and Maynooth and the Vatican on the other. In these disputes, we are like frightened birds jostling each other in the dark. (*Crown*, p. 239.)

. . .

Michael. A fella would want to be within the wide-open spaces when a row starts between Wittenberg and Knox, on the one hand, and Bellarmine and Maynooth, on th' other. In these desperate disputes we are but frightened birds jostling together in the dark. (*Ned*, pp. 90–91.)

9. Often paying great homage to James Joyce, O'Casey not only praises and defends him against his detractors, but has allowed many bits and pieces of Joyce's art to fuse into his own. Michael is of course quoting Stephen Dedalus's epic blasphemy as delivered to Mr Deasy in the second chapter of *Ulysses* (1922): '—That is God.... A shout in the street' (London: Bodley Head, 1958, pp. 31–2. U.S. ed. New York: Random House, 1961, p. 34). Not all of O'Casey's admirers have been overjoyed at the Joycean influence; Robert Hogan comments that 'Fortunately his [O'Casey's] language has been tempered by Shakespeare and the Elizabethan playwrights, and by Milton and the King James Bible. Unfortunately it has been tempered by Shelley and Joyce' (*Experiments*, pp. 145–6).

10. The conflict was presented overtly in the early, rejected play *The Crimson in the Tri-Colour*. Krause comments that 'In this play he had dramatised one of his most urgent concerns, the antagonism between Labour and Sinn Fein—Democracy vs. Nationalism. He tried to show that the future of Ireland had to be built upon the principles of 1913 as well as 1916, Larkin's working class General Strike as well as Connolly's middle class Rising' (*Self-Portrait*, p. 13).

5. THE HEROINE AS HERO (pp. 145–89)

1. Julia, the young girl in *The Star Turns Red* whose instincts lead her to prefer the dance hall to the union hall, is O'Casey's youngest heroine at nineteen. Both girls in *The Drums of Father Ned* are 'nineteen or twenty'. Monica (*Oak Leaves and Lavender*) is twenty, as is Marion, the maid in *Cock-a-Doodle Dandy* ('twenty or so'), although O'Casey is not specific about Loreleen, the young daughter, and Lorna, the young second wife. Avril (*Purple Dust*) is 'twenty-one or so', while Mary Boyle (*Juno and the Paycock*), Nora Clitheroe (*The Plough and the Stars*), and Jessie Taite and Susie Monican (*The Silver Tassie*) are all twenty-two ('or so'). The heroines of *The Shadow of a Gunman* and *Red Roses for Me*, Minnie and Sheila, are twenty-three; Jennie (*Oak Leaves*) is twenty-four; and Keelin (*The Bishop's Bonfire*) twenty-five. Angela Nightengale, the gay lass of 'Bedtime Story', has seen a bit of the world and is designated as 'a girl of twenty-five to twenty-seven'; Reena Kilternan ('Behind the Green Curtains') is twenty-six. Two of O'Casey's maturer heroines are the Widda Machree in 'Time to Go' ('a young woman of thirty') and Souhaun in *Purple Dust* (thirty-three).

2. The source figure for Sheila has been identified and interviewed by Sean McCann, who relates an incident from O'Casey's courtship of the elusive Maire: it involves a police inspector who visited Maire's father on occasion and thus became an object of O'Casey's jealous suspicions. 'O'Casey was not convinced that the visits were as innocent as Maire made out. He believed that the policeman was there courting Maire. Eventually he used this as part of "Red Roses for Me". "O'Casey saw himself as the dead hero Ayamonn, Maire as Sheelagh, the girl who put a bunch of red roses on his coffin as she stood outside the church with a policeman by her side" ' ('The Girl He Left Behind', *The World of Sean O'Casey*, pp. 35–6).

3. 'John Millington Synge', *Blasts and Benedictions* (ed. Ronald Ayling, New York: St Martin's Press, 1967, p. 37).

4. Although curly-headed Jennie does not always have the same eye colour: 'Shy, grey-eyed Jennie Clitheroe, with her curly head' (*Knock*, p. 133) has 'deep brown eyes' by the time Johnny kisses her (*Knock*, p. 293).

5. The Alice of the 'Alice, Where Art Thou?' chapter changes from Alice Boyd (*Pictures*, p. 153) to Alice Norris by the end of the chapter (*Pictures*, p. 174).

6. Sean McCann's capsule summary of the Maire-Nora Creena correlation reads: 'He dedicated a play to her, he devoted a whole chapter of *Inishfallen Fare Thee Well* to her. He wrote a

multitude of letters and poems to her. And yet this woman has remained mysteriously in the background of the O'Casey story, known only by the fictitious name of Nora Creena' ('The Girl He Left Behind', *The World of Sean O'Casey*, p. 30). McCann's title of course is an echo of O'Casey's chapter title in *Inishfallen*, 'The Girl He Left Behind Him'.

7. Robert Hogan, in publishing the play in *Feathers from the Green Crow*, comments on the parallel with Millie and credits Ronald Ayling with the parallel to Jannice. Hogan also adds that Nannie 'must surely take her place next to Juno Boyle and the Bessie Burgess of O'Casey's most brilliant early plays' (p. 302).

6. ARGUFIERS AND LEPRECHAUNS (pp. 190–218)

1. *Blasts and Benedictions*, p. 18.

2. In the 'Pax' fantasy of *Inishfallen* the Ulsterman sings a version penned by O'Casey himself which concludes: 'Lero, lero, do an' dero,/Tae hull with th' Pope's devalerian chum!/Call all the kind neighbours an' arrm them with sabers,/Says Wullie boy Scutt an' Dickie McCrum!' (p. 87).

3. In *Inishfallen* he appears as Roary O'Bawlochonoe (p. 83).

4. *A Short History of Irish Literature*, p. 219. If O'Connor is accurate, it is another case of double jeopardy, since AE receives a rough going-over on his own as the figure in the 'Dublin's Glittering Guy' chapter of *Inishfallen*.

5. Variant spellings (Sleehaun, Sleehawn) appear at times in the text, but the name itself is used infrequently, the character most often referred to and addressed as Codger.

7. SENIOR CITIZENS (pp. 219–38)

1. The Old Woman has unconsciously picked up the name John from the Young Woman's song, and echoes another song, 'Oh no, John, no John, no.' 'Go your way' is a translation of the Irish song, 'Shoos Aroon'.

2. The Irish comic genius is served well by the interaction between simple people and complex mechanisms. O'Casey's dialogue between Mrs Watchit and Feelim on reading the electricity meter has its parallel in Flann O'Brien's *At Swim-Two-Birds*, where the reading of a gas meter is the source of a comic dissertation.

8. A COVEY OF CLERICS (pp. 239–58)

1. In one of the unproduced plays written prior to his first Abbey production, a play titled *The Harvest Festival*, there is an important inclusion: as Krause notes, the play 'dealt with a

series of conflicts between some labourers and the Church . . . Lady Gregory praising several scenes and particularly the characterisation of a Clergyman' (*Sean O'Casey*, p. 34). Gabriel Fallon recalls an incident from the days when O'Casey was working on *Juno*: 'he read me a scene which took place between a character called The Covey and a priest, a Catholic missioner. It was a very funny scene but it never appeared in the play' ('The Man in the Plays', *The World of Sean O'Casey*, p. 202).

2. In *The Flying Wasp* ('The Cutting of an Agate') O'Casey answers the charge that Gilbert is monolithically villainous: 'The Bishop was never contemplated by me as either oily or as a scoundrel. He is good-natured, well-intentioned, religious, and sincere; but he is timid, mistaking good-nature for the fire of the Holy Ghost, and life has passed him by' (London: Macmillan, 1937; pp. 48–9).

3. Neither does Father Farrell in *Juno*: his messenger, Jerry Devine, brings news of a job for Captain Boyle (and is treated like the messenger in *Anthony and Cleopatra* for his efforts).

4. During the description of the 1913 Dublin labour dispute in *Drums under the Windows* O'Casey details Sean's narrow escape from two drunken constables: 'a helmeted inspector had stepped out from a group standing at the Pillar, and had said sharply to the drunken ruffians, Let him go, let him go; and Sean had recognised the voice of Inspector Willoughby who long ago had headed a summons against him for allowing the Pipers' Band to play past a protestant church while service was going on—the very church where his father and mother had married, and all of them had been baptised' (p. 331).

5. *Sean O'Casey*, p. 21. In his only full use of the name, Krause lists the middle name as Martin, while O'Casey's only use of the full name has him as Edward Morgan Griffin (*Pictures*, p. 352). Anthony Butler also opts for Morgan ('The Early Background,' *The World of Sean O'Casey*, p. 21).

6. Anthony Butler catalogues the pieces that went into O'Casey's mosaics of Hunter and Slogan: 'At that time the Rector and incumbent of St Mary's was the Rev. James Hunter Monahan, D.D., who was also Precentor of Christ Church Cathedral. . . . The schoolmaster of St Mary's National School was a Mr James Logan, and both he and the Rev. Monahan were to appear in the Autobiographies; one as the Rev. T. R. S. Hunter and the other as Mr Slogan. Elsewhere in this book the late Dean Emerson draws attention to the fact that the initials 'T. R. S.' were those of the curate, so that the Rev. T. R. S. Hunter might be intended as a composite picture' ('The Early

Background', *The World of Sean O'Casey*, p. 19). Rev. N. D. Emerson adds that the description of the clergyman's appearance fits the curate, not the Rector' ('Notes on a Sermon', *The World of Sean O'Casey*, p. 159).

7. The dedication to *The Drums of Father Ned* ('The Memory be Green') is also to Dr McDonald, as well as to four other Irish and Irish-American Catholic clerics who displayed the defiant bravery that O'Casey advocated: 'Each in his time was a Drummer for Father Ned, and the echoes of their drumming sound in Ireland still' (page v). The last of the group, a Father Michael O'Flanagan, condoned and abetted the stealing of turf by his freezing parishioners and was relieved of his parish by his Bishop; his story is told in the dedicatory headnote and in *Inishfallen*, pp. 154–5.

8. Brooks Atkinson, *The Sean O'Casey Reader* (New York: St Martin Press, 1968, xi).

9. A CLUSTER OF MINOR CHARACTERS (pp. 259–305)

1. Butler notes that 'the company he calls Hymdin, Leadem & Co. in *Pictures in the Hallway* was in fact Leedom, Hampton & Co. of 50 Henry Street (valuation £210), a firm which dealt in china, delph and hardware' ('Early Background', *The World of Sean O'Casey*, p. 24). He also identifies Jason and Company as Easons, while Catherine Rynne quotes an O'Casey letter that says, 'When I worked in Easons, I had to be in at 4.15 every morning, ending at six' ('O'Casey in His Letters', ibid., p. 250).

2. It has been suggested to me that Sleehaun in *Bonfire* is O'Casey's caricature of G.B.S. and Shanaar in *Cock* his caricature of W.B.Y.

3. Krause, *Sean O'Casey*, p. 66.

Selected Bibliography

I Primary

Collected Plays Vol. 1, London: Macmillan, 1949: *Juno and the Paycock, The Shadow of a Gunman, The Plough and the Stars*, 'The End of the Beginning', 'A Pound on Demand'.

Collected Plays Vol. 2, London: Macmillan, 1949: *The Silver Tassie, Within the Gates, The Star Turns Red*.

Collected Plays Vol. 3, London: Macmillan, 1951: *Purple Dust, Red Roses for Me*, 'Hall of Healing'.

Collected Plays Vol. 4, London: Macmillan, 1951: *Oak Leaves and Lavender, Cock-a-Doodle Dandy*, 'Bedtime Story', 'Time to Go'.

The Bishop's Bonfire, New York: Macmillan, 1955.

The Drums of Father Ned, New York: St Martin's Press, 1960.

Behind the Green Curtains, 'Figuro in the Night', 'The Moon Shines on Kylenamoe', London: Macmillan, 1961.

I Knock at the Door, New York: Macmillan, 1939.

Pictures in the Hallway, New York: Macmillan, 1942.

Drums under the Windows, New York: Macmillan, 1945.

Inishfallen, Fare Thee Well, New York: Macmillan, 1954.

Rose and Crown, New York: Macmillan, 1952.

Sunset and Evening Star, New York: Macmillan, 1949.

Mirror in My House (collection of the six autobiographies listed immediately above), New York: Macmillan, 1956.

Windfalls, London: Macmillan, 1934.

The Flying Wasp, London: Macmillan, 1937.

The Green Crow, New York: George Braziller, 1956.

Feathers from the Green Crow, ed. Robert Hogan, Columbia: University of Missouri Press, 1962.

Under a Colored Cap, New York: St Martin's Press, 1963.

Blasts and Benedictions, New York: St Martin's Press, 1967.

The Sean O'Casey Reader, New York: St Martin's Press, 1969.

II Bibliographical

Mikhail, E. H., *Sean O'Casey: A Bibliography of Criticism*, London: Macmillan, 1972.

III Secondary

Books and Pamphlets

Armstrong, William A., *Sean O'Casey* (Writers and their Work No. 198), London: Longmans, Green & Co., 1967.

Ayling, Ronald (ed.), *Sean O'Casey* (Modern Judgements), London: Macmillan, 1969.

Benstock, Bernard, *Sean O'Casey* (Irish Writers Series), Lewisburg Pa.: Bucknell University Press, 1970.

Benstock, Bernard, (guest editor), *James Joyce Quarterly* 8 (O'Casey issue; Fall 1970).

Cowasjee, Saros, *Sean O'Casey: The Man Behind the Plays*, London: Oliver and Boyd, 1963.

Cowasjee, Saros, *O'Casey*, London: Oliver and Boyd, 1966.

Fallon, Gabriel, *Sean O'Casey: The Man I Knew*, London: Routledge and Kegan Paul, 1965.

Goldstone, Herbert, *In Search of Community: The Achievement of Sean O'Casey*, Cork: Mercier, 1972.

Hogan, Robert, *The Experiments of Sean O'Casey*, New York: St Martin's Press, 1960.

Kilroy, Thomas (ed.), *Sean O'Casey: A Collection of Critical Essays* (Twentieth Century Views), Englewood Cliffs N.J.: Prentice-Hall, 1975.

Koslow, Jules, *The Green and the Red: Sean O'Casey, the Man and His Plays*, New York: Golden Griffin Books, 1950.

Krause, David, *Sean O'Casey: The Man and His Work*, New York: Macmillan, 1960.

Krause, David, *A Self-Portrait of the Artist as a Man: Sean O'Casey's Letters*, Dublin: Dolmen Press, 1968.

Margulies, Martin B., *The Early Life of Sean O'Casey*, Dublin: Dolmen Press, 1970.

McCann, Sean (ed.), *The World of Sean O'Casey*, London: New English Library, 1966.

O'Casey, Eileen, *Sean*, London: Macmillan, 1971.

O'Casey, Sean, *The Sting and the Twinkle: Conversations with Sean O'Casey*, edited by E. K. Mikhail and John O'Riordan, New York: Barnes and Noble/London: Macmillan, 1974.

Malone, Maureen, *The Plays of Sean O'Casey*, Carbondale Ill.: Southern Illinois University Press, 1969.

Substantial Articles in English in Scholarly Journals

Armstrong, William A., 'History, Autobiography, and *The Shadow of a Gunman*', *Modern Drama* 2 (Feb. 1960), 417–24.

Armstrong, William A., 'The Sources and Themes of *The Plough and the Stars*', *Modern Drama* 4 (Dec. 1961), 234–42.

Ayling, Ronald, 'Feathers Finely Aflutther', *Modern Drama* 7 (Sep. 1964), 135–47.

Ayling, Ronald, 'Sean O'Casey: Fact and Fancy', *Massachusetts Review* 7 (Summer 1966), 603–12.

Ayling, Ronald, 'Popular Tradition and Individual Talent in Sean O'Casey's Dublin Trilogy', *Journal of Modern Literature* 2 (Nov. 1972), 491–504.

Ayling, Ronald, 'Sean O'Casey and the Abbey Theatre Company', *Irish University Review* 3 (Spring 1973), 5–16.

Benstock, Bernard, 'A Covey of Clerics in Joyce and O'Casey', *James Joyce Quarterly* 2 (Fall 1964), 18–32.

Blitch, Alice Fox, 'O'Casey's Shakespeare', *Modern Drama* 15 (Dec. 1972), 283–90.

Bromage, Mary C., 'The Yeats-O'Casey Quarrel', *Michigan Quarterly Review* 64 (Winter 1958), 135–44.

Colum, Padraic, 'Sean O'Casey', *Theatre Arts Monthly* 9 (June 1925), 397–404.

Colum, Padraic, 'The Narative Writings of Sean O'Casey', *Irish Writing* 6 (Nov. 1948), 60–69.

Cowasjee, Saros, 'The Juxtaposition of Comedy and Tragedy in the Plays of Sean O'Casey', *Wascana Review* 2 (1966), 75–89.

Daniel, Walter C., 'Patterns of Greek Comedy in O'Casey's *Purple Dust*', *Bulletin of the New York Public Library* 66 (Nov. 1962), 603–12.

DeBaun, Vincent, 'Sean O'Casey and the Road to Expressionism', *Modern Drama* 4 (Dec. 1961), 254–9.

Edwards, A. C., 'The Lady Gregory Letters to Sean O'Casey', *Modern Drama* 8 (May 1965), 95–111.

Esslinger, Pat M., 'Sean O'Casey and the Lockout of 1913: *Materia Poetica* of the Two Red Plays', *Modern Drama* 6 (May 1963), 53–63.

Esslinger, Pat M., 'The Irish Alienation of O'Casey', *Eire-Ireland* 1 (Spring 1965–66), 18–25.

Fitzgerald, John J., 'Sean O'Casey's Dramatic Slums', *Descant* 10 (Fall 1965), 26–34.

Hogan, Robert, 'O'Casey's Dramatic Apprenticeship', *Modern Drama* 4 (Dec. 1961), 243–53.

Howard, Milton, 'Orwell or O'Casey?', *Masses and Mainstream* 8 (Jan. 1955), 20–26.

Krause, David, 'The Playwright's Not for Burning', *Virginia Quarterly Review* 34 (Winter 1958), 60–76.

Krause, David, 'The Rageous Ossean: Patron-Hero of Synge and O'Casey', *Modern Drama* 4 (Dec. 1961), 268–91.

Krause, David, 'O'Casey and Yeats and the Druid', *Modern Drama* 11 (Dec. 1968), 252–62.

McHugh, Roger, 'The Legacy of Sean O'Casey', *Texas Quarterly* 8 (Spring 1965), 123–37.

McLaughlin, John J., 'Political Allegory in O'Casey's *Purple Dust*', *Modern Drama* 13 (May 1970), 47–53.

Mercier, Vivian, 'O'Casey Alive', *Hudson Review* 13 (Winter 1960–61), 631–6.

O'Riordan, John, 'Sean O'Casey: Colourful Quixote of the Drama', *Library Review* 22 (Spring 1970), 235–42.

Parker, R. B., 'Bernard Shaw and Sean O'Casey', *Queen's Quarterly* 73 (Spring 1966), 13–34.

Pixley, Edward E., '*The Plough and the Stars*—The Destructive Consequences of Human Folly', *Educational Theatre Journal* 22 (Mar. 1961), 75–82.

Reid, Alec, 'The Legend of the Green Crow: Observations on Recent Work by and about Sean O'Casey', *Drama Survey* 3 (May 1963), 155–64.

Ritchie, Harry M., 'The Influence of Melodrama on the Early Plays of Sean O'Casey', *Modern Drama* 5 (Sep. 1962), 164–73.

Rollins, Ronald G., 'Sean O'Casey's Mental Pilgrimage', *Arizona Quarterly* 17 (Winter 1971), 293–302.

Rollins, Ronald G., 'Sean O'Casey's *The Star Turns Red*: A Political Prophecy', *Mississippi Quarterly* 16 (1963), 67–75.

Rollins, Ronald G., 'Form and Content in Sean O'Casey's Dublin Trilogy', *Modern Drama* 8 (Feb. 1966), 419–25.

Rollins, Ronald G., 'O'Casey and Synge: The Irish Hero as Playboy and Gunman', *Arizona Quarterly* 22 (Autumn 1966), 216–22.

Rollins, Ronald G., 'Shaw and O'Casey: John Bull and His Other Island', *Shaw Review* 10 (Oct. 1967), 60–69.

Smith, Bobby L., 'Satire in O'Casey's *Cock-a-Doodle Dandy*', *Renascence* 19 (Winter 1967), 64–73.

Smith, Bobby L., 'Satire in *The Plough and the Stars*: A Tragedy in Four Acts', *Forum* 10 (1969), 3–11.

Smith, Bobby L., 'From Athlete to Statue: Satire in Sean O'Casey's *The Silver Tassie*', *Arizona Quarterly* 27 (Winter 1971), 347–61.

Snoddy, Oliver, 'Sean O'Casey as Troublemaker', *Eire-Ireland* 1 (Winter 1966), 23–38.

Templeton, Joan, 'Sean O'Casey and Expressionism', *Modern Drama* 14 (May 1971), 47–62.

Todd, R. Mary, 'The Two Published Versions of Sean O'Casey's *Within the Gates*', *Modern Drama* 10 (Feb. 1968), 346–55.

Index

Abbey Theatre, 2, 11, 25-6, 35, 82, 186, 201, 239, 248, 289, 303
Adair, Robin, 54-5, 111-14, 124, 130, 174-6, 210-11, 217, 221, 247
Adams, Sammy, 237, 275, 296
Agate, James, 288, 296-7
Alice (*Figuro*), 111, 181, 183, 210, 225, 227; (*Hallway*), xi, 181, 273, 302; ('I Wanna Woman'), 185, 188, 189
Aloysius, 51-2, 227-8, 265, 280-81, 297
Anti-clericalism, 28, 75-6, 77, 242, 253-6
Aristocracy, 11, 26-7, 29, 37, 40, 43, 58, 81, 83-4, 126, 260-61, 264, 267, 274
Aristophanes, 225
Aristotle, 279
Atheism, 27, 30, 47, 70-71, 109, 119, 128, 142, 168-9, 179, 195-7, 277
Atkinson, Brooks, 257, 305
Atrophy, 8, 10, 53, 55, 58, 65, 74, 93, 103-4, 111, 113, 114, 122, 124, 131, 142, 144, 146, 149-50, 155, 162-4, 170, 173-5, 182, 183, 204, 210-13, 218, 224, 225, 228, 255, 271, 274, 276, 279, 290, 293, 300
Auden-Isherwood, 41
Autobiographies, 304; *see also* individual titles
Auxies, 2, 54, 208, 228-30, 286-7; *see also* Black and Tans, Tommies, Troubles
Avreen, Jack, 184-5
Avril, 36-9, 41, 128-31, 170-74, 180, 212-13, 245, 301
Ayling, Ronald, x, 302

Ballad Singer, 225
Ballanoy, Charlie, 299; Mrs, xi, 32, 296, 299
Ballybeedhust, 8, 179, 246

Ballyoonagh, 8, 58, 104, 217, 243, 246
Ballyrellig, 259
Barman (*Plough*), 31
Barney (*Dust*), 39, 170, 274, 297
Basawn, Dan, 135-6, 197-8, 215
Battles, Daisy, 32, 148, 149, 155, 181, 183, 189, 200
'Bedtime Story', xii, 4, 23, 155, 183-4, 272, 302, 306
'Behind the Green Curtains', xii, 8, 133, 135-7, 152, 178-80, 197-8, 204, 237, 246, 264-5, 288-91, 302, 306
Bella *see* Casside, Ella
Bellman, 111-12
Benson, 78, 165-6, 283-4
Bentham, Charles, 16, 20, 34, 35, 46, 96, 140, 164, 212, 235, 267, 268
Bernard, Dean, 258
Berrill, Darry, 42-3, 189; Mrs, 189
Bill (*Roses*), 121
Binnington, Alderman, 61-5, 92-3, 134-5, 178, 192, 222, 224, 244, 262, 264, 272, 278, 287-8, 300-301; Mrs Elena, xi, 62-3, 65, 91-3, 135, 178, 192, 199; Michael, 63-5, 92-3, 133-5, 177-8, 244, 264, 278, 298, 300-301; Binningtons, 140, 178
Birdlike Lad, 111, 135, 210-11, 227
Bishop's Bonfire, The, xi, xii, 8, 58-61, 103-8, 151-7, 162-4, 178, 183, 205-6, 213-14, 217-18, 242-4, 262, 302, 306
Black and Tans, 2, 24-5, 62, 147-8, 207, 223, 286-8, 299; *see also* Auxies, Tommies, Troubles
Black Muffler, 281
Blasts and Benedictions, 190, 303, 306
Blind Man, 291
Boeman, Martin, 135-7, 178-80, 197-8, 264-5, 290
Boheroe, Father, 60-61, 105-7, 154, 155, 163, 218, 242-4, 246, 248

Bourgeoisie, 10-12, 22, 33, 34, 54, 64, 71, 79, 86, 90, 92-3, 104, 138-41, 159-60, 164, 169, 181-2, 184, 212, 245, 262-4, 267-74

Boyle, Capt. Jack, 10-16, 18-21, 23, 26, 28, 29, 31, 34, 35, 37, 38, 40, 42-4, 46, 47, 51, 53-4, 57, 66, 69, 83, 90, 140, 164, 231, 237, 270, 275, 296, 304; Johnny, 16, 18, 38, 46, 70, 82, 96, 98, 103, 141, 149, 230, 231; Juno, 10-12, 14, 16, 34, 38, 50, 53, 66, 67, 69-70, 75, 82-3, 89, 90, 91, 93, 106, 119, 146, 164, 230-31, 233, 270, 297, 303; Mary, 11, 12, 16, 18, 38, 46, 53, 66, 67, 69-70, 82, 89, 91, 97, 140-41, 144, 164, 169, 218, 233, 267-8; 301; Boyles, 2, 13, 67, 141, 231, 267

Brallain, 116-18, 138, 241, 268-70, 290

Brannigan, 117-18, 268-9, 278

Brennan, Capt., 32, 97-8, 114, 160-62, 284-5

Breydon, Ayamonn, 67-73, 75, 115, 118-24, 130, 132, 141, 148-9, 167, 168, 180, 193, 197, 216, 248-9, 277, 282, 290-91, 300, 302; Mrs, 67-73, 79, 80, 83, 88, 91, 93, 115, 119, 121, 123, 167, 168, 230, 248-9, 270

Brown, Priest, 91, 115, 117, 241-2, 244, 248

Burren, Canon, 58, 59, 103-110, 132, 163, 217, 218, 242-4, 246, 262

Burgess, Bessie, 28, 29, 31-2, 34, 62, 85-90, 93, 97-8, 103, 143-4, 146, 160-61, 187, 198, 200-201, 230-33, 284, 285, 303; her son, 86-7, 89, 284

Burke, 291-3

Businessman ('Kathleen'), 162, 198

Butler, Anthony, 296, 304, 305

Caheer, 116-118, 138, 241, 268-70, 290

Carey, Eileen, 81, 183

Carranaun, 60-61, 104, 205-6

Carrigeen, Angela, 237

Casside, Archie, 300; Ella, x, 78, 165-6, 187, 215, 250; Johnny/Sean, 32, 33, 42, 72, 74-6, 78, 80-82, 88, 119, 143, 148, 155, 156, 165-6, 181-3, 187-9, 193-4, 199-203, 249-53, 257, 273, 283, 286-91, 297, 299, 300, 301, 302, 304; 1st Johnny, 199; Michael, 78, 165, 283-4, 300; Mr, 74, 78, 165, 300, 304; Mrs Susan, 33, 52, 66-7, 69, 71-82, 93, 156, 165-6, 199-200, 230, 250, 252,

297, 299, 304; Tom, 78, 165, 249, 251, 283-4, 300; Cassides, 251

Catholicism, 24-5, 47, 50, 59, 61, 66, 68-9, 88, 94, 104, 113, 114, 122, 124, 131, 134-6, 156, 167, 168, 182, 185, 190-95, 197, 198, 204, 205, 232, 239, 245, 246, 248-9, 253-8, 264-5, 271, 290, 301, 303; see also Religiosity, Protestantism

Chatastray, Denis, 8, 136-7, 179-80, 197, 264-5, 289-90.

Chekhov, Anton, 259

Chesterton, G.K., 25

Chreehewel, Canon, 39-40, 128, 245-7, 261, 297

Clematis, Father, 256

Clinton, Rev., 115, 123, 124, 193, 248-51

Clitheroe, Jack, 29, 31, 47, 87, 97-8, 114, 160-62, 232, 235, 285; Nora, 29-32, 47, 86-9, 97-8, 143-4, 146, 159-65, 169, 182, 230, 232-3, 235, 285, 302; Clitheroes, 27, 30, 125, 159

Clitheroe, Jenny, 181-2, 291, 302

Clooncoohy, Daniel, 59-61, 104-6, 154, 163-4, 206

Cloyne, 39, 130, 170-74, 274

Clune na Geera, 8, 41, 53, 213, 245-6

Cock-a-Doodle Dandy, xii, 2, 6, 8, 47, 53-58, 91, 111-14, 124, 135, 150, 173-8, 210-11, 213-15, 219-21, 246-8, 276-7, 301, 306; see also Demon Cock.

Collected Plays, xii, 294; see also individual titles

Collins, Michael, 298

Comic, 12, 14, 15, 17, 22, 24, 26, 35, 39, 42, 46, 51, 141, 155, 162, 170, 177, 193, 208-10, 213, 225, 226, 228, 230, 233-4, 237, 242, 245, 246, 260, 261, 274, 275, 291, 294, 303

Commedia dell' Arte, 225

Communism, 47, 50, 64, 90, 115, 124-125, 133, 136-7, 141, 167-9, 197, 202, 204, 223-4, 234, 241-2, 262-5, 277, 295, 297; see also Socialism, Political Perspectives

Conneen, Bunny, 179, 289-90

Connolly, James, 137-8, 143, 301

Conroy ('Time'), 54-5, 263, 271, 272

Conroy, Cornelius, 226, 299; Martha, 226, 299

Conroy, Mollser, 282

Constant, Peter, 234, 268

'Corncrake, The', xii, 294

Cornelius, 39, 213, 274

Coulter, Jim, 197

Cousins, 263, 271
Covey, 27, 30-31, 42, 47, 88, 97, 141-4, 155, 160, 188, 221, 224, 232, 235, 303
Coward, Noel, 288
Cowasjee, Saros, xi, 294
Craftsmanship, 29-30, 45, 51, 69-71, 132-3, 264, 297
Creena, Nora, 182-3, 302
Crimson in the Tri-Colour, The, 301
Crosby, Bing, 2, 113

Daffy (Cock, Dan, Sylvester), 295
Daly, Joxer, 10, 12-16, 19, 29, 31, 37, 38, 43, 53, 54, 57, 237, 275, 296
Davoran, Donal, 19-25, 28, 37, 39, 62, 94-6, 103, 110-11, 207-8, 228-29, 235, 272, 290-92
Deaf Man, 291
Demon Cock, 111-13, 135, 174-6, 210, 214-15, 246
Derrill, Barry, 42-3
de Valera, Eamonn, 50, 53
Devanny, Jimmy, 228
Devine, Jerry, 16, 34, 96, 97, 140-41, 164, 235, 304
Devon, 1, 3, 8, 42, 299
Dickens, Charles, 273
Dillery, 267
Doctor ('Hall'), 51-2, 265, 280-81
Domineer, Father, 54, 56-8, 64, 111-12, 114, 132, 175-76, 211, 219, 246-8, 262, 277
Donaldson, Frank, 193-4
Doonavale, 8, 62-4, 135, 177, 192, 216, 244-6, 264, 277-8
Doosard, Edward, 193-4
Dostoevsky, Feodor, 184-5
Dovergull (Anthony and Hewson), 273
Down-and-Out, 70, 83, 108, 150-51, 214, 235, 279-83
Dowzard, 193-4, 202, 248-50
Dreamer, 108-11, 114, 120, 130, 143-4, 150-51, 189, 197, 279-81, 290-91
Drums of Father Ned, The, xi, xii, 2, 8, 61-5, 90-93, 132-5, 140, 152, 177-8, 191-3, 216-17, 222, 242, 244-6, 263-4, 277-8, 286, 300-301, 304, 306
Drums under the Windows, xii, 3, 73-4, 78, 80, 119, 143, 165-6, 187-8, 201-2, 249-50, 253-7, 286, 292, 295, 299, 304, 306
Dryden, John, 97
Dublin, 1-5, 7, 8, 26, 30, 33, 42, 52, 53, 66, 120, 122, 148, 186, 187, 195, 198, 199, 210, 216, 223, 225, 229, 238, 249, 251, 254, 282-5, 289, 294, 303, 304
Dunphy, 128, 181
Dympna, 70, 121, 216, 238, 282

Eeada, 70, 121, 216, 238, 282
Egan, Tom, 143
Eglish, 116-18, 138, 168-70, 290
Emerson, Rev. N. D., 304
'End of the Beginning, The', xii, 8, 42-3, 45, 189, 294, 306
England (Great Britain), 1, 4, 6-7, 22, 35, 43-4, 48-50, 58, 124, 125, 141, 179-80, 200, 206, 234, 261, 267, 268, 274, 283, 292, 297
Evangelists (*Gates*), 108
Evans, Feemy, 25
Exile (Banishment, Emigration), 1, 2, 81, 104, 113, 137, 141, 174-6, 179-80, 217, 218, 221
Expressionism, 5, 17, 89, 121-2, 149, 166-7, 239, 245

'Fall in a Gentle Wind, A', xii, 282
Fallon, Gabriel, 294, 303
Fantasy (Non-Realism, Supernatural), 57-8, 90, 91, 111-13, 121-22, 135, 140, 162, 174-7, 193, 209-20, 227, 246-7, 263, 271, 282, 283
Farmer ('Kathleen'), 162
Farrell, Bull, 259-60, 253, 271, 272
Farrell, Father, 28, 53, 304
Feathers from the Green Crow, xi, xii, 302, 306
Felicity, 204
Feydeau, Georges, 26
Figure (*Dust*), 212-13
Figuro, 210
'Figuro in the Night', xi, 8, 65, 111, 135, 181, 210, 221-3, 225-7, 291, 306
Fillifogue, Father, 63, 94, 177-8, 216-17, 244-7, 262, 264, 277-8
Finglas, Tom, 68, 122, 169, 194, 248-51, 260, 300, 302
Finnoola, 70, 121-2, 238, 282, 283
First Workman (*Dust*), 39, 41-2, 51, 53, 60, 127-9, 211, 274, 297; (*Star*), 276
Fitzgerald, Barry, 25-6
Flagonson, Mr, 259-60, 271, 272; Mrs, 259-60, 271
Fletcher, Dudley, 252; Harry, 251, 258
Flying Wasp, The, 303-4, 306
Flynn, Uncle Peter, 30-32, 42, 61, 88, 97, 141-2, 221, 232, 235
Foreman (*Oak*), 44, 48, 49, 151-2

312

Foran, Teddy, 18, 101-2, 186, 284-5; Mrs, 18, 185-6, 284
Foster, 193-4, 202, 248-50
Fox, R. M., 299
Francis, 297
Free Stater ('Kathleen'), 162, 198

Gallogher, James, 2, 95, 215, 228-9
Galvin, Patrick, 33
Gardener, 108-10, 150, 196, 235
Garnett (Edward and David), xi
Gellert, Hugo, 274
Gilbert (Bishop), 108-10, 150-51, 196, 234-5, 237, 239, 241, 245, 260, 303-4; his sister, 233-7, 240-41, 280
Gilligan, Ginger, 294-5
Giraudoux, Jean, 225
Girl (Oak), 210
Girl at the Door (Ned), 277
Glazier, John, 193-4
Godfrey, xi, 108, 195-6, 235, 260, 279-80
Gogan, Mollser, 88-9, 98, 150, 161, 204, 233, 282, 286; Mrs, xi, 30-34, 62, 88-9, 97, 159, 161, 230-33, 285, 296; unnamed baby, 88, 190, 221
Good, Fluther, 25-33, 42-5, 47, 51, 88, 97, 142-4, 160, 188-9, 224, 233, 285, 296
Gorki, Maxim, 241
Gray, Thomas, 35-6
Green Crow, The, xi, xii, 294, 306
Green Muffler, 281
Gregory, Lady Augusta, 81-4, 201, 288, 303; Robert, 82
Grey Shawl, 281
Griffin, Rev. E. M., 249-51, 258, 304
Griffith, Arthur, 143
Grigson, Adolphus, 24-5, 33, 207-8, 228-9; Mrs, 24-5, 95, 208, 228-30, 233
Gropper, William, 274
'Gulls and Bobbin Testers', xii

Halibut, Daniel, 23
'Hall of Healing, The', xii, 4, 51-2, 150, 207, 227-8, 265, 280-81, 306
Harvest Festival, The, 303
Hatherleigh, Dame, 44-6, 48, 83-5, 207, 267, 268; Edgar, 44, 46-9, 83-4, 124-7, 134, 151-2; her husband, 46, 48, 83-4, 151, 234; Hatherleighs, 7, 44, 204
Healy, Timothy, 298
Heegan, Harry, 16-18, 85-6, 89, 89-104, 107, 108, 129, 140, 157-9, 279, 284-5; Mrs, 16-18, 85-6, 89, 90,

100, 230; Sylvester, 15-19, 23, 37, 45, 100, 257, 295; Heegans, 157, 295
Hemingway, Ernest, 101
Henchy, Mr, 74
Henderson, Julia, 95, 215, 228-30, 233, 259
Herbert, xi, 108, 196, 235, 260, 279-80
Higgins, F. R., 289
Higgins, Hughie, 213-14
Hogan, Robert, 295, 301, 302-3
Horawn, Leslie, 289-90
Horniman, Annie, 82
Housman, A. E., 98
Hunter, Rev. T. R. S., 76-7, 251-3, 258, 304
Hyde Park, 4, 35, 109, 257, 260

Ibsen, Henrik, 20, 295
I Knock at the Door, xii, 4, 33, 52, 72, 76-8, 80, 156, 165, 198-200, 251-3, 283-4, 297-9, 301, 306
Industrialisation, 6-8, 84-5, 132
Inishfallen, Fare Thee Well, x, xi, xii, 25, 26, 32, 74-75, 78, 82-4, 138-9, 166, 182, 249-50, 254-7, 282, 286-7, 289, 292, 295, 296, 298, 299, 302, 303, 306
Ireland, 1, 4, 7-8, 10, 15, 19, 22, 28, 34, 35, 43, 44, 48, 50, 52-3, 81, 92, 103-5, 125, 127, 128, 133, 137, 138, 141, 162, 175-7, 179-80, 183, 188, 196, 200-202, 204, 209, 222, 239, 244, 246, 247, 249-51, 253, 254, 261, 263, 266-7, 271, 274, 283, 285-9, 294, 298, 305
'Irish in the Schools', xii
Isabella see Casside, Ella
'I Wanna Woman', xii, 4, 184-5

Jack (Cock), 114, 132, 247, 274; (Star), 89-91, 114-19, 124, 128, 129, 134, 167, 180, 262, 265, 274
Jannice, 108-10, 120, 130, 149-51, 154, 159, 166, 185-9, 196, 235-7, 239-41, 246, 279-81, 291, 302
Jason, 273, 305
Jayes, Jen, 203
Jennie (Oak), 44, 47, 49, 125-6, 151-3, 302
Jentree, 207, 281
Jerry (Pound), 237, 275, 296
Jester, Sir Jake, 117
Jimmy ('Figuro'), 111, 210, 225, 227; ('Kathleen'), 139-40, 162, 198
'Job, The', xii
Jock, 100-101

313

Joey ('Kathleen'), 198
Johnny ('Figuro'), 181; ('Kathleen'), 198
Johnston, Denis, 299
Joy, 49, 152-3, 203-4
Joybell, 90, 117, 167, 191, 205, 276
Joyce, James, 10, 77, 134, 158, 242, 288, 292, 294, 295, 300, 301
Joyce, R., 76, 252
Julia (Cock), 55, 88, 111, 113, 150, 204, 211, 221, 247, 277, 279; (Star), 90-91, 115, 118, 124, 129, 166-8, 170, 180, 191, 241-2, 246, 262, 301
Juno and the Paycock, xii, 2, 4, 10-16, 34, 50, 53-4, 67, 75, 82, 83, 89, 96, 140-41, 144, 149, 164, 230-31, 237, 267, 295-7, 301-2, 303, 304, 306

'Kathleen Listens In', xii, 6, 42, 89-90, 139-40, 162, 198, 221-2
Kelly/Kelley, 291-3; ('Time'), 111, 117, 263, 271
Keohane, John, 299
Kian, 89-91, 115-116, 118, 168, 242
Killsallighan, Tom, 133-4, 177-8, 264, 278
Kilternan, Reena, 136-7, 178-80, 290, 302
Kiss Me Kate, 2
Kornavaun, Christy, 136, 197-8, 202, 205, 237, 246, 265, 291
Krause, David, x, 141, 249, 290, 294, 297, 301, 303, 304, 305
Kylenamoe, 8, 261, 266

Lad ('Hall'), 52
Langon, Lieut., 285
Lanigan, Alice, 189
Larkin, James, xi, 116, 135, 137-8, 301
Larry, One-eyed, 111-13, 214-15, 247
Latterly, Lizzie, 237
Lenin, V. I., 274
Leslieson, Lord, 208-9, 226, 260-61, 266-7
Life Force, 28, 47, 50, 81, 83, 92, 102, 105-6, 108-10, 117-18, 122, 124-5, 134, 139, 143-4, 147, 151-3, 155, 157-8, 180, 183-4, 186, 204, 210-11, 217, 243-4, 247, 248, 279, 286
Linanawn, Mave, 180-81
Lockout of 1913, 3, 116, 137, 301, 304
Logan, James, 304
Logue, Cardinal, 254-5, 258
London, 1-4, 35, 40, 42, 175-6, 184-5, 195, 239, 261, 267

Lonergan, Lanky, 294-5
Lord Mayor, 91, 116, 191, 223-4, 262, 267, 270, 275-6; Lady Mayoress, 276,
Lynch, Judge, 193

MacDonald, Ramsay, 274
Machree, Widda, 111, 176-7, 263, 271, 302
MacNamara, Brinsley, 289
Madigan, Maisie, 230-31
Maguire, 19, 94-6, 98, 228-9, 299
Mahan, Sailor, 53-8, 63, 64, 111-13, 132, 174, 176, 214, 247, 263, 274, 276-7
Maire, 302
Malamud, Bernard, 137
Man in the Kilts, 198, 222
Man in the Trilby Hat, 196
Mann, Thomas, 84
Manning, Mrs, 82
Mannix, Monsignor, 254
Man of the Musket, 277
Man of the Pike, 277-8
Man with the Big Drum, 198
Man with the Stick, 196, 207
Marion, 54-8, 61, 111-14, 130, 173-6, 211, 219-20, 301
Mark, 375
Marthraun, Loreleen, 53-8, 61, 111-14, 173-5, 211, 214, 220-21, 246, 276-7, 301; Lorna, 53-6, 58, 61, 111-13, 173-75, 211, 246, 301; Michael, 8, 53-8, 60, 62-4, 111-14, 124, 174-6, 211, 214, 219-21, 247, 262-3, 272, 276-7, 298; Marthrauns, 247
Martyn, Edward, 82
Mary (Oak), 45
Maxwell, Surgeon, 101, 157-8
McCann, Sean, 302
McDonald, Michael, 253-6, 258, 304
McGeelish, Jack, 289-90
McGeera, Whycherly, 289-90
McGilligan, Councillor, 62-5, 92-3, 133-5, 177, 192-3, 222, 224, 262, 264, 272, 278, 287-8, 298, 300-301; Mrs Meeda, xi, 63, 65, 91-3, 135, 192, 198, 299; Nora, 63-5, 92-3, 134-5, 177-8, 264, 277-8, 299, 301; McGilligans, 178
McGowan, Seumas, 299
McGunty, Oscar, 192, 278
McQuaid, Michael, 256
Melbayle, Noneen, 136-7, 178-9, 197
Menken, H. L., 205
Michael (Oak), 203, 234, 275; (Star), 90-91, 115, 117-18, 167, 262

314

Middleton, Georgie, 199; Mr, 198-9
Mild Millie, 187-8, 215, 302
Mirror in My House, 288, 306; *see also* individual titles
Misogyny, 24, 25, 55, 95, 219-20, 246-7
Moanroe, Manus, 59-61, 103, 107, 108, 127, 130, 132, 254, 255, 257, 163, 205, 218, 274, 300
Molière, 225
Monahan, Rev. James Hunter, 304
Monican, Susie, 18, 99-101, 156-9, 185, 191, 302
Moon Shines on Kylenamoe, The, xii, 128, 180-81, 208-9, 226, 260-61, 266-7, 299, 306
Moore, Brennan, 121, 123, 194-5, 215-16, 259, 271-2
Moore, Mr, 83, 84
Moorneen, Sheila, 67-8, 71, 115, 120-24, 130, 132, 148, 166-8, 180, 182, 216, 249, 302
Mossie, Miss, 23, 272
Most Respectable Man, 91
Mulehawn, Michael, 208-9, 267
Mullarky, Bishop, 163, 214, 218, 243-4, 256; Farmer, 59, 106, 163
Mullcanny, xi, 70-72, 119, 121, 168-9, 195, 196
Mullen, Michael, x
Mulligan, John Jo, 23, 155, 183-5, 272
Mulligan, Mr, 19-20, 190, 228, 272
Murphy, Michael, 222-3
Murray, Mr, 216-17, 264

Names, discrepancies, xi, 182, 296-8, 302-5; peculiarities, 290; charactonyms, 35, 156
Nannie, 186-7, 222, 270, 303
'Nannie's Night Out', xii, 4, 186-7, 221, 222, 224-5, 270
Nautical Motif, 13-16, 44-5, 53-4
Ned (Atheist), 108-9, 143-4, 150-51, 195-6, 235-6, 239, 257, 280, 281
Ned, Father, 61, 64, 93, 133, 178, 244, 246, 264, 278, 304
Newman, John Henry, 256
New York, 1, 193
Nightingale, Angela, 23, 183-4, 272, 302
Norton, Simon, 15-17, 19, 45, 100, 157, 295
Nugent, Needle, 53, 230, 270
Nyadnanave, 8, 111, 114, 174-5, 219, 221, 246, 277

Oak Leaves and Lavender, xii, 6, 43-52, 83-5, 103, 115, 124-7, 132, 151-3, 202-4, 206-7, 210, 227, 233-4, 267, 268, 275, 301, 302, 306
O'Balacaun, Roory, 121, 195, 198-200, 303
O'Brien, Flann, 303
O'Brien, William, 138-9
O'Callaghan, Father, 255-6
O'Casey, Sean, biographical data, 1, 66-7, 298, 302, 303; psychology, 81; *see also* Casside, Sean
O'Cockadoo, Dr, 256
O'Connor, Frank, 67, 212, 298, 303
O'Day, Bishop, 256
O'Dempsey, Philib, 39, 41-2, 65, 128-31, 170-72, 211-12, 272
O'Farrell, Ayamonn, 198-202, 211
O'Flaherty, Liam, xi, 289
O'Flanagan, Father Michael, 305
O'Franticain, Father, 256
O'Hay, Barney, 263, 271, 274-5
O'Hickey, Walter (D.D.), 253-5, 258
O Houlihan, Kathleen, 89-90, 140, 162, 163; Miceawl, 198; Sheela, 89-90, 162; O Houlihans, 6, 140, 198, 222
O'Hurrie, Andy, 209
O'Killigain, Jack, 39-41, 127-34, 141, 170-72, 180, 211-13, 245, 274, 276
Old Age, 31, 57, 80, 181, 187, 216, 217, 219-38
Old Man ('Figuro'), 181, 225-6; (*Star*), 90-91, 115, 167, 191, 223-4, 226
Old Woman ('Figuro'), 181, 225-7, 303; (*Gates*), 108, 144, 235-7, 240-41; ('Hall'), 51, 227-8, 281; (*Oak*), 49, 227; (*Star*), 89-91, 115, 167, 224, 226
O'Morrigun, Drishogue, 44, 47-50, 83, 84, 103, 114, 124-6, 129, 134, 151-3, 180, 202, 206, 244, 274
O'Murachadha, 201-2
One-Eye, 215
O'Neill, Eugene, 145, 206
Orwell, George, 288
O'Ryan, W. P., 254-5
Osborne, John, 300
O'Shea, Katherine, 188
Oul Joe, 225
Owens, Tommy, 95, 228

Parnell, Charles Stewart, 1, 116, 198-200, 202, 237, 254
Pearse, Patrick, xi
Pender, Polly, 187, 222, 225, 270

Penrhyn, Abraham, 48, 203, 206-7, 227; Monica, 45-50, 83, 115, 124-7, 129, 134, 151-3, 180, 206-7, 218, 301

Pictures in the Hallway, xi, xii, 3, 32, 69, 78-9, 119, 148-9, 165, 181, 193-4, 199-200, 211, 215, 240, 251, 273, 291, 300, 304, 305, 306

Plough and the Stars, The, x, xi xii, 2, 4, 25-34, 44, 51, 85-9, 96-8, 126, 141-4, 146, 149, 150, 155, 159-62, 188, 221, 230-33, 282, 284-6, 296, 302, 306

Pobjoy, Ernest, 49, 203-4, 207, 234

Poges, Cyril, 7, 34-43, 54, 58, 65, 131-2, 170-72, 211, 213, 245, 261, 267, 274, 297

Policeman (*Gates*), 235

Political Perspectives, 7, 22, 47-8, 65, 67-8, 79, 84, 90-91, 114-27, 129, 131, 134, 135, 140, 151, 162, 167-8, 191, 198-204, 211, 222, 223, 234, 239, 241-2, 244-5, 250-51, 255, 262-5, 267, 273, 279, 284, 297

Porter (*Cock*), 8, 53, 111-12, 213-14; (*Door*), 52

Postmaster (*Dust*), 39, 170, 213

'Pound on Demand, A', xii, 4, 43, 237, 275, 296, 306

Powell, Minnie, 21-5, 85-96, 103, 130, 146-9, 151, 228-30, 233, 286, 290, 299, 302

Proletariat, 8, 12, 16-17, 21, 24, 25, 33, 53, 55, 99, 104, 126, 138-40, 142-3, 164, 165, 171, 186, 211, 226, 241, 254, 262-5, 270, 273-9, 295, 297, 303

Protestantism, 24-5, 61, 67, 69, 74, 88, 134-6, 156, 178, 179, 190-95, 197, 204, 205, 216, 232, 239, 248-53, 257, 264, 301, 304; *see also* Catholicism

Proudhon, Pierre Joseph, 33

Puritanism, 23, 27, 32, 44, 48, 54-6, 61, 90, 97, 101, 113, 114, 136, 147, 148, 154, 155, 157, 163, 167, 168, 176-8, 181, 184-6, 188, 201, 205-7, 219, 225-6, 229, 232, 233, 243, 245-8, 254, 264, 272, 277; *see also* Religiosity, Sexuality

Purple Dust, xii, 7, 8, 34-43, 51, 60, 61, 65, 127-32, 134, 152, 170-74, 177, 211-13, 223, 245-7, 261, 274, 297, 298, 301-2

Purple Priest, 116-18, 168, 223, 241-3, 245-6, 262, 268

R. A. F., 83, 103-4

Rankin, Richard, 59-61, 155, 163, 167, 205-6, 214

Red Jim, xi, 115-18, 124, 128, 135, 138, 168, 191, 241-2, 262-3, 265, 268-70, 274-6, 278

Redmond, Rosie, 27, 32, 97, 142, 188-9, 224

Red Muffler, 51, 227, 281

Red Roses for Me, xi, xii, 3, 67-73, 75, 80, 83, 115, 118-24, 132, 148-9, 166-9, 183, 193-5, 197, 200, 215-16, 238, 248-51, 260, 271-2, 282, 298, 300, 302, 306

Reiligan, Councillor, 58-62, 103, 105, 132, 134, 163, 217, 244, 262-3, 272, 274; Foorawn, 59-61, 104-8, 130, 151, 153-6, 158, 159, 162-4; Keelin, 59-61, 104-7, 153-5, 162-4, 167, 170, 205, 218, 302; Michael, 59, 105-7, 134; Reiligans, 63, 214

Religiosity, 11, 15, 20, 21, 26-8, 31, 47, 48, 52-6, 59, 61, 62, 64, 68, 75-7, 83, 87, 91, 96, 101, 106, 108, 112, 113, 121, 124, 135, 136, 150-51, 154-7, 176, 185, 188, 190-95, 197-8, 205, 208, 214, 219, 221, 225, 228, 235-7, 239-58, 260, 262, 263, 269, 271, 277, 278, 280, 282, 284, 286, 292-3

Republican ('Kathleen'), 162, 198

Robartes, Lionel, 288-9

Robinson, Rev. Paschal, 256

Romance, 22-4, 49, 68, 95, 97, 104-7, 109-11, 114, 120, 125-31, 133, 136-7, 139, 146-7, 151-3, 155, 163, 166, 169, 170, 174, 175, 177-82, 189, 224-5, 228, 245, 276

Rose and Crown, xii, 25, 113, 134, 193, 256, 294, 300-301, 306

Rough Fellows, 111, 174, 176, 219, 276-7

Ruskin, John, 200

Russell, George, 212, 288, 303

Rynne, Catherine, 305

Saffron Shirt Leader, 116, 167, 241, 262

St Barnabas, 249-51

St Burnupus, 3, 193, 248-9

St Mary, parish of, 1

St Marychurch, 1

Salkeld, Cecil, 289

Salvation Army Officer, 108-10, 150

Sammy (*Roses*), 190, 215

Samuel, 250

'Seamless Coat of Kathleen, The', xii

Sean O'Casey Reader, The, 305, 306

Second Workman (*Dust*), 39, 41-2, 51, 53, 60, 128-9, 211, 274; (*Star*), 276
Secretary (*Star*), 116-17, 138, 140, 268-70
Selected Plays of Sean O'Casey, 298
Sergeant (*Bonfire*), 111-12, 214
Sexuality, 32, 44, 56-8, 61, 65, 101, 107, 109, 110, 114, 125, 131, 134, 139, 142, 148, 151, 152, 154-7, 159, 163, 167, 170, 173, 174, 178, 181-7, 189, 205, 210, 219, 223-5, 227, 272, 273; see also Romance, Puritanism
Shadow of a Gunman, The, x, xii, 2, 19-25, 32, 33, 94-96, 146-9, 190, 207-8, 228-30, 272, 286, 290-91, 299, 302, 306
Shakespeare, William, 20, 44, 71, 107, 120, 124, 166, 190, 240, 259, 300, 301, 304
Shanaar, 57, 111-12, 219-21, 305
Shaw, G. B., 3, 9, 12, 182, 288, 297, 200, 205
Shawn Beg, 295
Shea, 291-3
Sheasker, 116-17, 138, 191, 268-70, 278, 290
Shelley, Percy Bysshe, 20, 21, 23, 124, 290, 301
Sheumas Ruadh, 295
Shields, Seumas, x, 19-27, 30, 37, 42, 47, 51, 54, 62, 94-6, 146, 190, 207-8, 228, 272, 286, 299
Shillayley, Bernadette, 63, 92-3, 133-4, 140, 177-8, 184, 301
Sillery, 267
Silver Tassie, The, xii, 2-5, 15-19, 35, 45, 83, 85, 89, 98-104, 108-10, 114, 121, 156-9, 185-6, 191, 260, 284-5, 295, 302, 306
Sinn Fein, 2, 87, 254, 287, 301
Skerrigan, Alec, 62, 64, 178, 190-93, 205, 264, 300-301
Sleehaun, Michael, 59-61, 106, 107, 154, 155, 163, 205, 217-221, 224, 226, 243, 256, 262, 303, 305
Slogan, Mr, 77, 252, 273, 304
Socialism, 16, 33, 79, 96-7, 137, 140-43, 188; see also Communism, Political Perspectives
Sophocles, 145
Souhaun, 36-41, 65, 130-31, 170-74, 245, 302
Spanish Civil War, 3, 73, 125, 127, 180, 298
Spellman, Cardinal, 256, 258, 292
Staff Wallah, 35

Stage Directions/Descriptions, 6-7, 28, 37, 40-42, 44, 49, 53, 57, 65, 80, 81, 84, 85, 91-2, 99, 109, 112, 127, 130, 134, 136, 142, 146, 149, 152-4, 158, 159, 163, 164, 166-7, 170, 171, 173, 182, 186, 187, 194, 203-6, 210-17, 219, 221, 229-32, 234, 236, 238, 240-42, 244, 246-8, 250-55, 269-70, 276, 282, 297
Stage Irishism, 26, 33-4
'Star-Jazzer, The', xii, 283
Star Turns Red, The, ix, xii, 3, 5-6, 89-91, 114-19, 128, 134, 135, 138, 140, 166-8, 191, 222-4, 226, 241-2, 245, 246, 262-3, 265, 268-70, 275-6, 278-90, 301, 306
Stephens, James, 95
Stepinac, Cardinal, 256
Stern, Creeda, 203
Stoddard, Cpl., 142-3, 286
Stoke, Basil, 7, 34-43, 128, 130, 131, 170-73, 212, 245, 261, 297
Stoppard, Tom, 259
Sullivan, Jenny, 150, 228, 281-2
Sunset and Evening Star, xii, 1, 25, 33, 52, 105, 202-3, 256, 292, 294, 296-9, 306
Symbolism, 6, 69-75, 79, 81, 109, 147-9, 153, 154, 156, 248, 276, 278, 298-9
Synge, J. M., 180, 201, 254, 256, 292, 302

Taite, Jessie, 18, 85-6, 89, 99-102, 129, 157-9, 185, 235, 284-5, 302
Tancred, Mrs, 50, 70, 82-4, 230, 297; Robbie, 82, 96
Taylor, Pvt., 98
Tennyson, Alfred Lord, 256
Textual Problems, xi
Thornton, Tomaus, 198
Timahoe, Sally, 197
'Time to Go', xii, 8, 54-55, 88, 111, 176, 259-60, 263, 270-71, 302, 306,
Tinley, Sgt., 286
Toller, Ernst, 101
Tom (*Oak*), 45
Tomasheen, Sean, 208-9, 215, 267
Tommies, 33, 85, 87, 142-3, 187, 283-7; see also War, Auxies, Black and Tans
Trade Unionism, 11, 12, 56, 64, 67, 70, 73, 113-23, 137-42, 168-9, 192, 193, 221, 223, 248-9, 262, 268, 276-7, 282, 301, 304
Tragedy, 12, 17, 29, 60, 98, 103, 145, 149, 150, 153, 166, 230, 231, 279, 291

Tragi-comedy, 25, 103, 230; *see also* Comic, Tragedy
Troubles (Easter Rising/Civil War), 1, 2, 22, 32-3, 44, 61, 64, 82, 87, 94-8, 137-8, 141-3, 147-8, 159-62, 187, 207-8, 222-3, 228-30, 232, 284-8, 292, 299, 301
Tutting, Deeda, 47-9, 124, 202, 204, 244
Tynam, Mr, 222-3

Under a Colored Cap, 297, 306
U.S.S.R., 47, 49, 105, 124, 133, 140, 202-3, 264, 277

Valentine, Miss, 156, 252
Visitor (*Tassie*), 35, 160, 284

Wagner, Richard, 110
War, Boer, 148, 200-201; World War One, 2, 4-5, 16-18, 35, 83, 85-8, 98-103, 157, 223, 260, 284-5, 292, 295; World War Two, 6, 34, 43-4, 46, 48-50, 83, 103-4, 114-15, 124-7, 151-2, 202-4, 227, 234, 267, 268
Warrington, Donah, 203

Watchit, Mrs, 45-6, 203, 233-4, 303
Wesker, Arnold, 146
White, Johnny, 225
Whizzer, Canon, 271
Wilde, Oscar, 10
Willoughby Inspector, 304
Windfalls, 306
Within the Gates, xi, xii, 3, 5, 35, 43, 47, 58, 83, 108, 120, 143-4, 149-51, 187, 195-7, 207, 233-7, 239-41, 246, 260, 279-81, 290-91, 298, 306
Woman (*Window*), 201
Woman Passenger ('Moon'), 209, 266
Wordsworth, William, 131

Yeats, W. B., 2-3, 10, 12, 26-30, 82, 201, 254, 285, 288-9, 295, 298, 305
Younger Girl ('Curtains'), 197
Young Man ('Time'), 259-60
Young Son of Time (*Oak*), 210, 217
Young Woman ('Time'), 259-60
Youth, 23, 31, 35, 61, 64, 134, 145-6, 154, 166-7, 177, 210, 217, 224, 244-5, 281, 301-2